UNIVERSITY
OF
OXFORD

School of
Management Studies

Companies Without Borders

This collection presents a selection of key articles on transnational corporations which had previously appeared in UNCTAD–DTCI's journal *Transnational Corporations*. As well as looking closely at the current global context and developments in current international business theory, articles cover:

- the changing relationship between transnational corporations and governments;
- foreign direct investment and international migration;
- the promotion of transnational investment;
- foreign direct investment and economic development;
- trade and foreign direct investment policies;
- the North American Free Trade Agreement and foreign direct investment;
- East-Asian investment and trade.

Making available state-of-the-art research from leading thinkers in international business this collection will be invaluable for students and researchers of the subject.

Contributors: Manuel R. Agosin, Geoffrey Bannister, John H. Dunning, Persephone Economou, Michael Gestrin, John M. Kline, Carl H. McMillan, Padma Mallampally, Charles-Albert Michalet, Maurice Odle, Sylvia Ostry, Terutomo Ozawa, Francisco J. Prieto, Carlos A. Primo Braga, Alan M. Rugman, Karl P. Sauvant, John M. Stopford and Raymond Vernon.

Transnational Corporations is a refereed journal published three times a year by the UNCTAD Division on Transnational Corporations and Investment. In the past, the Programme on Transnational Corporations was carried out by the United Nations Centre on Transnational Corporations (1975–1992) and by the Transnational Corporations and Management Division of the United Nations Department of Economic and Social Development (1992–1993). The basic objective of this journal is to publish articles that provide insights into the economic, legal, social and cultural impacts of transnational corporations in an increasingly global economy and the policy implications that arise therefrom. It focuses especially on political–economy issues related to transnational corporations. In addition to articles, *Transnational Corporations* features book reviews. The journal welcomes contributions from the academic community, policy makers and staff members of research institutions and international organizations. Manuscripts can be submitted to the editor, Karl P. Sauvant, or to the associate editors, Fiorina Mugione and Persephone Economou.

Companies Without Borders

Transnational Corporations in the 1990s

Published by International Thomson Business Press on behalf of UNCTAD, Division on Transnational Corporations and Investment

INTERNATIONAL THOMSON BUSINESS PRESS
I(T)P   An International Thomson Publishing Company

London • Bonn • Boston • Johannesburg • Madrid • Melbourne • Mexico City • New York • Paris
Singapore • Tokyo • Toronto • Albany, NY • Belmont, CA • Cincinnati. OH • Detroit, MI

Companies Without Borders

Copyright © 1996 UNCTAD, Division on Transnational Corporations and Investment

First published 1996 by International Thomson Business Press

I⊕P *A division of International Thomson Publishing Inc.*
The ITP logo is a trademark under licence

British Library Cataloguing-in-Publication Data
A catalogue record for this book is available from the British Library

First edition 1996

Typeset in Times by J&L Composition Ltd, Filey, North Yorkshire
Printed in Great Britain by T. J. Press Ltd., Padstow, Cornwall

ISBN 0–415–12526–X

International Thomson
Berkshire House
168–173 High Holborn
London WC1V 7AA
UK

International Thomson
20 Park Plaza
14th Floor
Boston MA 02116
USA

Contents

Figures

Tables

Contributors

Manuel R. Agosin, Professor, Department of Economics, University of Chile, Santiago, Chile.

Geoffrey Bannister, Professor, Anderson School of Management, The University of Mexico, Albuquerque, New Mexico, United States of America.

John H. Dunning, State of New Jersey Professor on International Business, Rutgers University, Newark, New Jersey, United States, and Emeritus Research Professor of International Business, University of Reading, Reading, United Kingdom.

Persephone Economou, Transnational Corporations Affairs Officer, Division on Transnational Corporations and Investment, UNCTAD, and Consultant, The World Bank, Washington, DC.

Michael Gestrin, Associate Transnational Corporations Affairs Officer, Division on Transnational Corporations and Investment, UNCTAD, Geneva, Switzerland.

John M. Kline, Deputy Director, Karl F. Landegger Program in International Business Diplomacy, School of Foreign Service, Georgetown University, Washington, DC, United States.

Carl H. McMillan, Professor at the Department of Economics, Carleton University, Ottawa, Canada.

Padma Mallampally, Transnational Corporations Affairs Officer, Division on Transnational Corporations and Investment, UNCTAD.

Charles-Albert Michalet, Professor, University of Paris Naterre, Paris, France, and Consultant, Foreign Investment Advisory Service, The World Bank, Washington, DC, United States.

Maurice Odle, Chief, Advisory Services for Investment and Technology, Division on Transnational Corporations and Investment, UNCTAD, Geneva, Switzerland.

Sylvia Ostry, Chairperson, Centre for International Studies, University of Toronto, Toronto, Canada.

Terutomo Ozawa, Professor of Economics, Colorado State University, Fort Collins, Colorado, United States.

Francisco J. Prieto, Professor, Instituto de Estudios Internacionales, University of Chile, Chile.

Carlos A. Primo Braga, Economist, International Trade Division, International Economics Department, The World Bank.

Alan M. Rugman, Professor of International Business, University of Toronto, Ontario, Canada.

Karl P. Sauvant, Chief, Research and Policy Analysis Branch, Division on Transnational Corporations and Investment, UNCTAD, Geneva, Switzerland.

John M. Stopford, Professor, London Business School, United Kingdom, and Stockholm School of Economics, Stockholm, Sweden.

Raymond Vernon, Clarence Dillon Professor of International Affairs Emeritus at the John F. Kennedy School of Government at Harvard University, United States.

Note

The UNCTAD Division on Transnational Corporations and Investment serves as the focal point within the United Nations Secretariat for all matters related to transnational corporations. In the past, the Programme on Transnational Corporations was carried out by the United Nations Centre on Transnational Corporations (1975–1992) and the Transnational Corporations and Management Division of the United Nations Department of Economic and Social Development (1992–1993). In 1993, the Programme was transferred to the United Nations Conference on Trade and Development. The objectives of the work programme include to further the understanding of the nature of transnational corporations and of their economic, legal, political and social effects on home and host countries and in international relations, particularly between developed and developing countries; to secure effective international arrangements aimed at enhancing the contribution of transnational corporations to national development and world economic growth; and to strengthen the negotiating capacity of host countries, in particular developing countries, in their dealings with transnational corporations.

The term 'country' as used in this publication also refers, as appropriate, to territories or areas; the designations employed and the presentation of the material do not imply the expression of any opinion whatsoever on the part of the Secretariat of the United Nations concerning the legal status of any country, territory, city or area or of its authorities, or concerning the delimitation of its frontiers or boundaries. In addition, the designations of country groups are intended solely for statistical or analytical convenience and do not necessarily express a judgement about the stage of development reached by a particular country or area in the development process.

Mention of any firm name, experience or policies does not imply the endorsement of the United Nations.

The following symbols have been used in the tables:

- Two dots (..) indicate that data are not available or are not separately reported. Rows in tables have been omitted in those cases where no data are available for any of the elements in the row.
- A dash (–) indicates that the item is equal to zero or its value is negligible.
- A blank in a table indicates that the item is not applicable.
- A slash (/) between dates representing years, e.g. 1988/89, indicates a financial year.
- Use of a dash (–) between dates representing years, e.g. 1985–1989, signifies the full period involved, including the beginning and end years.

In addition

- Reference to 'dollars' ($) means United States dollars, unless otherwise indicated.
- Annual rates of growth or change, unless otherwise stated, refer to annual compound rates.
- Details and percentages in tables do not necessarily add to totals because of rounding.
- The material contained in this study may be freely quoted with appropriate acknowledgement.

The views expressed here are those of the authors and do not necessarily represent those of the United Nations.

Preface

In today's world economy, the market system is widely accepted as the principal mechanism governing economic transactions. This requires paying closer attention to the actors interacting in that system and the implications of their actions. Increasingly, those actors are privately owned firms, a great number of which are transnational corporations. Over the past twenty years, considerable progress has been made in understanding the behaviour of these corporations and its implications for economic development. Today's world economy, however, raises new challenges and opportunities for both governments and transnational corporations and provides a new background against which the contribution of these corporations to economic development can be maximized.

To shed new light on these developments, the Division on Transnational Corporations and Investment of the United Nations Conference on Trade and Development – the focal point within the United Nations system for all matters related to foreign direct investment and transnational corporations – has brought together in this publication, entitled *Companies Without Borders: Transnational Corporations in the 1990s*, a collection of articles previously published in *Transnational Corporations*, the refereed, triennial journal of the Division. In addition to those articles published in a celebrational issue of that journal on the occasion of the twentieth anniversary of the then Commission on Transnational Corporations, the book contains other notable contributions already published in *Transnational Corporations*.

The chapters of Part I highlight the changes in the international economic system and the role of transnational corporations as lead actors in that transformation. Against this background, the chapters of Part II focus on the role of transnational corporations in salient features of today's world economy – privatization, regional integration, migration and the transition from a centrally planned to a market-based economic system. With the recognition of the positive contribution of transnational corporations for growth and development, the chapters in Part III look at the redefined role of governments in aiding the conduct of international business transactions by private firms and the issues arising from a growing policy interdependence.

The volume was prepared by Karl P. Sauvant, Persephone Economou and Fiorina Mugione.

Rubens Ricupero
Secretary-General
United Nations Conference on Trade and Development
Geneva, November 1995

Part I

1 Transnational corporations and the changing international economic system*

Charles-Albert Michalet

This article attempts to answer an important question: given the growing role of transnational corporations and transnational banks during the past three decades, is it possible to say that the very nature of the international economic system has changed? An epistemological approach has been chosen to point out that the traditional Ricardian trade theory is no longer a relevant paradigm for the new world economy. The first part contrasts the basic assumptions of the traditional trade model with the new features of the world economy. The second part relates current economic policy dilemmas to the inadequacies of the traditional model as a framework for Government intervention.

This article deals with an ambitious question: given the growing role played by transnational corporations (TNCs), including transnational banks, the emerging process of integrated international production and the increasing importance of off-shore finance, is it possible to demonstrate that, as a result of these developments, the very nature of the international economic system has changed? To put it differently, is it still relevant to apply the classical analytical framework suggested by David Ricardo at the beginning of the last century to the new world economy? Does it make sense to keep the same paradigm for economic policy decisions and negotiations at the national and multilateral levels despite the changing behavioural patterns of firms and States?

For most observers and decision makers, especially for managers of large firms, such a question might appear naïve. For them, it is obvious that the world economy is totally different today from what it was thirty years ago. For those who are involved in inter-

* Reprinted from *Transnational Corporations*, vol. 3, no. 1 (February 1994), pp. 9–21.

national business, it is a daily experience that the rules of the game are no longer the same. Nevertheless, all empirical evidence that can be brought to support this viewpoint is unable to demonstrate that the very nature of the international economy has changed. The empirical argument is unconvincing because disproving the novelty of the changes in the world economy is always possible – especially for historians. Historians are eager to point out that some types of TNCs and foreign direct investment (FDI) existed already during the last century and even earlier. For the French historian Fernand Braudel (1986), the world economy emerged, along with capitalism, during the sixteenth century, before the formation of nation-States.

It is possible to argue against such historians by emphasizing the growing economic weight and role of TNCs over the past three decades and by underlining the novelty of their organization and management techniques. However, from the viewpoint of the initial question of whether the international economic system has changed as a result, it is still the case that quantitative arguments cannot be used to give a convincing answer. An alternative approach is therefore needed. One such approach is the epistemological approach, inspired by Okun's theory of paradigms, according to which the empirical evidence is never immediately grasped by observers, but is deciphered through the use of paradigms. Those paradigms are supposed to be relevant for as long as they enjoy the consensus of the scientific community. In the case of international economics, the dominant paradigm is the theory of trade rooted in Ricardo's theory of comparative advantage proposed in the early nineteenth century. Obviously, since the publication of the *Economic Principles* in 1817, the Ricardian model has become more sophisticated through the contributions of many scholars. Nevertheless, the basic assumptions remain the same, including an international division of labour that is exclusively based on trade among nation-States. It is noteworthy that most research on TNC structures and strategies has been conducted by academics specializing in business management and not international economics. Therefore, a gap still exists between those who are interested in international business and those who are interested in international trade. Unfortunately, policy makers in Governments and international organizations dealing with issues in international economics often refer to – explicitly or implicitly – the orthodox Ricardian paradigm. As a result, they are unable to cope with the new features of the world economy. Because the old paradigm only focuses on trade among nations, TNC activities are outside its universe and cannot be understood. Nevertheless, following the growing importance of TNCs in the restructuring of the world economy, as well as their increasing impact on national economies, it is becoming more and more difficult to ignore them. Consequently, in the past few years, an increasing number of publications, irrespective of their nature, are devoting whole chapters or sections to TNCs and FDI. Unfortunately, TNCs and FDI are not yet integrated in a unified concept of the world economy. They are treated as addenda to the traditional analysis of an international economy that advocates the absence of interventions. The agenda of the Uruguay Round negotiations provides an illustration of the pregnancy of the old paradigm.

The initial question regarding the changing nature of the international economic system must therefore be formulated in a different way: if the old Ricardian paradigm is no longer relevant to the new characteristics of today's world economy, does that mean that the very nature of the international economy has changed? The first part of this article is devoted to contrasting the assumptions of the old paradigm with the basic features of today's world economy. The aim of that exercise is not to criticize the Ricardian paradigm, including all its refinements as developed by Ricardo's followers. The objective of that part is to emphasize the structural limitations of the dominant paradigm to take into account fully the nature of today's world economy and to advocate the need for a radical change. The second part of the article explores the need for a new paradigm. Today, most Governments are facing several economic policy dilemmas. To a large extent, the current confusion reflects the inadequacy of the traditional paradigm as a framework for economic policy at the macroeconomic and microeconomic levels. Monetary and fiscal policies, foreign-exchange policy, trade policy, labour policy and industrial policy are deeply affected by the new rules of the game in today's world economy. However, owing to the pregnancy of the Ricardian paradigm, Government decisions are not able to deal with the crucial changes that are transforming the world economy. Therefore, the impact of Government actions is far from what has been expected, and both liberal and Keynesian advocates of economic reforms are in disarray.

Such a disarray mirrors the lack of a new intellectual framework to deal with the new challenges of the emerging world economy. It is beyond the scope of this article to offer an alternative model. The enduring economic crisis in Europe and the success stories in Asia might also be helpful in accelerating a process by which the research community realizes that it is time to elaborate a new conceptual approach for today's world economy.

THE INADEQUACIES OF INTERNATIONAL TRADE THEORY

One way to demonstrate that the international economy has changed is to show that the old Ricardian paradigm is no longer relevant for the new world economy. That demonstration will be conducted in two steps. First, the basic assumptions of the old paradigm will be described briefly and, second, those assumptions will be challenged against the rules of the game of the new world economy.

The basic assumptions of the old paradigm

In the *Economic Principles*, Ricardo laid down the analytical framework for an international optimal allocation of resources among nations based on the principle of comparative advantage (in contrast to Adam Smith's absolute advantage) under a free-trade regime. The sophistication brought later to the original 'two countries – two goods' model by prominent economists occurred within the Ricardian paradigm. For example, Heckscher, Ohlin, Samuelson and others developed a neo-classical framework for the Ricardian concepts. The same applies to those economists who have introduced new variables, such as technology (W. Leontief and R. Vernon) and, more recently, oligopoly theory and economies of scale (P. Krugman and the advocates of the so-called 'strategic trade policy'). Even these modifications of the classical paradigm do not cope effectively with the new features of the world economy. In essence, they do not radically challenge the three basic assumptions of the classical trade theory, namely:

- The old paradigm is uni-dimensional. The benefits of free trade and the subsequent optimal allocation of resources are exclusively related to the exchange of goods and services among nation-States based on the principle of comparative advantage. Capital flows, technology transfer and labour migration are excluded from the model.
- Comparative advantage is determined by the factor endowments of nation-States. These endowments – labour, capital, land and technology – must be subject to constant returns to scale; otherwise, it would be impossible to define an optimal division of labour among nations. It must be stressed that comparative advantage is determined *ex ante*, that is before the opening of an economy to trade, according to the static comparative approach. Factor immobility within the borders of a nation-State is the most crucial assumption

of the model. As has been demonstrated by R. Mundell, relaxing the factor immobility assumption does not preclude the hypothetical existence of an international optimal allocation of resources. But, then, this result will be reached through the movement of capital and, as a consequence, goods are no longer traded among countries. In other words, trade theory cannot survive if the factor immobility assumption is dropped.

- Nation-States are the only actors in the international economy. Country borders determine the characteristics of the 'black boxes' inside which factors of production are combined in perfectly competitive markets. As a result of this approach, firms are not taken into account. Trade is reduced to a relationship among nation-States. Data provided in the balance-of-payments accounts are the only relevant source of information to assess the external economic situation of a country.

The rules of the game in today's world economy

The new rules of the game in the world economy are in contradiction with the basic assumptions of the Ricardian paradigm. The world economy today is a multidimensional system within which factors of production move according to decisions that are made by transnational agents operating in oligopolistic markets.

To understand the dynamics of the new world economy, it is necessary to consider together trade flows, capital movements, inward and outward FDI, technology flows and labour movements. Such an approach implies not only that exports and imports of goods and services are no longer the exclusive forms of economic transactions among nation-States, but also that the various dimensions of the world economy are tightly interconnected. Therefore, it is no longer feasible to develop separate analytical frameworks for trade, financial markets, international monetary movements and migration as if these belonged to distinct fields that are subject to separate theories. Neither can the workings of the world economy be understood by simply adding up distinct pieces of knowledge. The very nature of the new world economy is the existence of close interactions between FDI, trade, technology transfer, finance and labour movements. Exports that flow from country A to country B induce new opportunities and constraints for FDI. These investments are financed from local and international sources. Technology transfer and the presence of expatriates with experience in a company's activities can improve an affiliate's performance. Foreign affiliates generate import and export flows that can benefit country A and country B. In the new world economy, trade has become a part of a package that includes also capital, technology and human resources. Competitive performance is more and more dependent on countries' and firms' ability to combine various fields of expertise. World-wide economic integration is no longer built solely on more intense trade flows among countries; it is now the result of a multidimensional and complex set of interrelations. A new way of comparing the level of economic development among countries is by observing the pre-dominant forms of their integration into the world economy. The most developed countries are connected to other countries through both inward and outward flows of trade, FDI, technology and capital. Less developed countries are connected mainly only through trade. For those countries, FDI, technology and capital flows play only a minor role – especially outward FDI, technology transfer and capital lending – when compared with exports of raw materials. For these countries, the old paradigm is still largely relevant. But this is no longer true in the case of the newly industrializing economies and, *a fortiori*, in the case of the developed countries.

In contradiction with the old paradigm, factors of production are increasingly crossing national borders. In most cases, FDI implies an outflow of capital from home to host countries. As far as labour movement is concerned, managers, engineers and technicians often become expatriate workers in foreign affiliates. Technology, a component of all FDI projects, also flows to host countries. Finally, the process of delocation, that is the closing of productive facilities in the home countries and the establishment of new productive units abroad, may be thought of as moving a piece of land from one country to the other. Therefore, with factor endowments continuously changing, it is no longer possible to define a nation-State's comparative advantage. In fact – and depending on the level of development of a host country – FDI is becoming a crucial determinant of a country's pattern of specialization. However, in the new world economy, comparative advantages are defined *ex post* instead of *ex ante* (as in the traditional paradigm).

Furthermore, and in contradiction with the old paradigm, nation-States are no longer the only players in the world economy. Decisions regarding the location of new activities, or the relocation of existing ones, are taken by TNCs. Increasingly, the funding of economic activities in developed, as well as in developing, countries is made by transnational banks operating from off-shore financial centres that are outside the jurisdiction of central banks. A significant share of international trade – about one-third – consists of intra-firm flows. Prices of goods and services that are channelled from one foreign affiliate to the other are not determined by the market as in the traditional paradigm. *Ex post* specialization in production is the result of TNCs' decisions to locate some of their activities abroad. Such decisions are made after comparing the benefits offered by alternative locations. Finally, TNCs themselves select the location best suited to enhancing their own competitiveness, as has been described by John H. Dunning in the eclectic paradigm (Dunning, 1988). In the new world economy, gains from competitiveness benefit TNCs; and this is a substitute for the old paradigm's welfare gains generated by free trade and assumed to benefit equally nation-States. The world market does not resemble the perfect market laid down in textbooks of international trade. Oligopolistic competition is the rule of the game and economists are aware that an oligopolistic market does not produce the conditions for an optimal allocation of resources.

Finally, because of the strategies and structures of the new world economy's main actors, the TNCs, the borders of national economies have become blurred. The historical coincidence between a State and a nation is put into question, and with that the traditional basis for political sovereignty. This is why economic policy is becoming more complex and the outcome of Governments' economic measures is often uncertain. This situation is one of the major implications resulting from the nature of the emerging world economy.

ECONOMIC POLICY DILEMMAS

In today's world economy, there are many instances in which domestic economic policies appear to be working badly. The impact of monetary and fiscal policies on growth, investment, employment, trade and capital movements is often uncertain. Industrial policy has lost a good deal of its *raison d'être*, following the growing difficulty in answering the question 'who is us?' The bottom line of economic policy dilemmas is found in the widening dichotomy that exists between the globalization process and the national interest.

Uncertainties of macroeconomic policy

Monetary and fiscal policies, the two traditional main instruments of economic policy, have become less effective under the rules of the game that characterize the new world economy. With capital mobility, the targets of monetary and fiscal policies can no longer be reached with certainty. In certain cases, changes in interest rates or taxation may trigger unexpected and counterproductive effects. Governments are no longer in a position to use monetary and fiscal measures without considering their domestic impact from a world-wide perspective. The power of transnational banks, when confronted with policies of central banks, does not need to be proved: the restructuring of the European Monetary System in August 1993 is one illustration of the weakness of these public institutions in resisting pressures from transnational banks. The effect of changes in interest rates on firms' investments are dubious. By borrowing abroad (e.g. in the Euromarket), TNCs are able to avoid paying higher interest rates for financing domestic investments. Although lower interest rates may have a positive impact on firms' domestic investments, the money borrowed may be used to finance FDI as well. Similar uncertainties regarding the effectiveness of Government policy may be observed in the case of fiscal policy. With capital mobility, the taxation of profits from financial investments cannot be significantly different among countries; national tax rates have to be adjusted to the lower existing rate if capital flight is to be avoided.

Trade policy is confronted with similar dilemmas. Notwithstanding the rules of the General Agreement on Tariffs and Trade, countries cannot use tariff or non-tariff barriers against foreign imports to improve their current account without taking into consideration the fact that protectionist measures could also hurt their export-oriented national firms that have located abroad part of their manufacturing activities so as to become more competitive in the world market. On the other hand, the growing liberalization of trade favours outside sourcing and, as a consequence, the subsequent import of components by national firms from their affiliates abroad. Exchange-rate intervention may also have counterproductive results. An undervaluation of the national currency does not guarantee an automatic improvement of the current account, at least in the short term. Once again, the import content of the exported goods reduces the positive impact of a depreciation on exports. At the same time, a depreciated domestic currency may deter local firms from investing abroad and, as a result of missing an acquisition opportunity, or because they have failed to be a first mover, national firms can lose world market shares.

Industrial policy at bay

The rationale for industrial policy is to strengthen national firms. From the adoption of an import-substitution model to the provisions of support for 'national champions', the objective of industrial policy – irrespective of a country's level of development – is to help local firms in the public or private sectors to compete against imported products or acquire the size that will enable them to enter – or to stay in – the selective 'club' of world leaders in some industries.

Because of this national – sometimes even nationalistic – approach, Governments have been suspicious of foreign investors crossing borders and developing business in the host country and eventually competing with local firms for domestic market share. Therefore, most investment codes and national regulations used to discriminate against foreign companies. Although the restrictions imposed on foreign investors have, traditionally, been more constraining in developing than in developed countries, some concerns about FDI were held in common. By limiting foreign participation in the ownership of local firms, imposing local-content requirements and import-compensation ratios and making technology transfer a prerequisite for FDI approval, Governments aimed at pursuing two objectives: to protect national firms against the powerful competition from TNCs and to use FDI as a tool for the industrial development of their countries. Foreign firms were welcomed as long as it could be demonstrated that they would be able to help the Government in reaching the medium- and long-term objectives of its national plans. In some industries, FDI was prohibited for non-economic reasons. This was the case for industries that were considered as having strategic importance for the national sovereignty of the country (defence-related industries, communications, transportation, steel, electricity, water, gas), as well as in the production of commodities for export that were crucial for strengthening the domestic currency.

Since the mid-1980s, Governments' attitudes towards TNCs have changed drastically. Instead of being suspicious of TNCs, Governments now welcome them. In most countries, previous investment codes have been liberalized, incentives have multiplied and administrative procedures have been simplified. At the same time, an increasing number of countries are establishing investment promotion agencies to attract and service potential investors, to improve the country's image abroad and to implement promotion strategies. The promotion of a country's attractiveness to foreign investors is now a key priority (Wells and Wint, 1992). Because it is difficult to be attractive and, at the same time, keep a constraining set of trade-related investment measures, countries are abolishing these measures, are substituting them with incentives, or tie them to each other. Investors have to commit themselves to export part of their output, create employment, or locate their facilities in depressed regions within a host country in order to benefit from those incentives. But there is no obligation to submit applications, and investment projects increasingly do not need official authorization. Ultimately, the on-going liberalization of FDI laws will put an end to the discrimination against foreign investors.

Global strategy versus national interest

The uncertainty and confusion that are plaguing macroeconomic as well as industrial policies are, to a large extent, the result of the transformation of the world economy. Macroeconomic theory, which is used as a framework for Government intervention, refers to national aggregates based on national-accounting techniques that ignore the rules of the game of the new world economy. Industrial-policy objectives are determined by a nationalistic approach that no longer corresponds to the strategy and structures of TNCs, whatever their country of origin. The old paradigm impedes Governments from realizing that the political frontiers of a country no longer coincide with the economic borders. As was discussed in the previous section, the widening dichotomy between a nation and a State is not only the result of a greater openness of the economy – with openness defined in terms of trade flows – but also, and above all, the result of the multidimensional nature of its integration into the world economy. This has an important implication: TNCs are the most significant economic players in the world economy, although this is not yet recognized by the existing official economic data, national administrations and international institutions.

Moreover, TNC strategies and structures have been evolving in the past three decades, with significant implications for host and home countries (UN-DTCI, 1993). Since the 1980s, an increasing number of TNCs have followed global strategies and have adopted global structures. Gradually, more and more TNCs are moving away from multinational strategies and structures. A global approach means, first of all, that investment decision-making is less local market-oriented than in the case of a multinational strategy; TNCs' main target is expanding world market shares. Second, foreign affiliates located in different countries tend to be specialized, and flows among them are internalized to reduce transaction costs. The implications of the global strategies and structures of TNCs explain most of the paradoxical results that presently confront those host and home-country Governments that uphold the traditional policies. An illustration of these results may be found in the cases of trade and industrial policies.

With TNCs following global strategies and structures, any effort to assess a country's competitiveness on the basis of its current account is misleading. Following a global approach, TNCs are locating their activities according to the comparative advantages of potential host countries. These companies manufacture and market their products in a number of countries. As a consequence, imports of home countries consist, in part, of inputs produced abroad by the affiliates of the home country's TNCs. At the same time, an increasing share of the turnover of those TNCs is generated by their foreign affiliates selling in the markets of host countries, or exporting to third countries, including the home country. Finally, to evaluate the competitiveness of a national economy on the basis of the performance of its trade balance is becoming irrelevant. In today's world economy, the competitiveness of a country has to be measured by the world market shares of the companies located in its territory. According to that approach, market shares include exports from a country and sales abroad of the foreign affiliates of TNCs based in that country. If country X has a negative current-account balance in the automotive industry or in chemicals, for instance, this does not mean that the competitiveness of that country in those industries is weak, because, at the same time, companies originating from country X and operating in those industries may have increased their world market shares and improved their cash flows. Under these circumstances, is it still relevant to refer to the national origin of a company? The promotion of FDI is a good case for pointing out the ambiguities of the question raised by Robert Reich (1991): 'who is us?'

In a paradoxical way, it is not certain that the liberalization of FDI laws will be the crucial factor for attracting inward investment. During the 1960s and 1970s – and despite restrictions on TNC activities imposed by developing countries – the share of FDI directed to those countries was higher than in the 1980s, and was more evenly distributed among them. Transnational corporations following a multinational strategy – as opposed to a global strategy – adapted to the restrictions imposed by host countries so long as access to local markets was guaranteed and protected from external competition. For TNCs adopting a multinational strategy, the international competitiveness of their foreign affiliates was of secondary importance as long as their output was sold in the protected local market. Any additional costs induced by trade-related investment measures would be passed on to the local consumers. With a global strategy, the logic is totally different: outward FDI, the delocation of manufacturing or services activities, mergers and acquisitions are all aimed at strengthening a firm's competitiveness in the world market. Therefore, local constraints, such as 'red tape', complex regulations, etc., are no longer acceptable to TNCs, because they increase transaction costs and, thus, affect their international competitiveness. A global firm is not ready to spend a lot of time negotiating with a host-country Government; instead, it looks for another, more convenient location. Today, countries are no longer in a position to screen and control potential investors as was the case in the past decades; on the contrary, companies select countries on the basis of their location-specific comparative advantages. But those comparative advantages are not to be confused with those in the Ricardian paradigm. Comparative advantages are evaluated by TNCs according to their likely contribution to the strengthening of their own international competitiveness.

In a multidimensional world economy, not only are the *ex ante* static comparative advantages of the old paradigm irrelevant, but also the comparative advantages that make a territory attractive are no longer the result of natural endowments. Increasingly, comparative advantages are created. Comparative advantages are built up, first, by the activities of foreign affiliates and their linkages with local firms and, second, by the governmental measures aimed at improving a country's investment climate. To use Michael Porter's 'diamond' (Porter, 1990), a country with a large diamond will be at the same time attractive to both foreign and national investors, notwithstanding the fact that foreign and local firms are not necessarily investing in that country for the same reasons. From the point of view of employment and value added, the best situation can be reached when the delocating operations of the home-based TNCs are compensated by new activities developed by foreign-based TNCs. As a result, the traditional foundation of industrial policy – to support national companies – is no longer relevant: what is good for General Motors in France is as good for the French economy as what is good for Renault.

However, when defining their FDI promotion policies, Governments have to be very attentive to changes in TNC corporate strategies. For instance, in the past, global strategies and internalization processes were supposed to go together. In the future, with the spread of 'network', 'virtual' or 'hollow' firms that are becoming a substitute for tightly controlled networks of specialized affiliates linked through ownership, as opposed to a set of agreements among independent partners, things might be different (Michalet, 1991). As a consequence, measures for strengthening local production units that are efficient and able to comply with the network's specifications might become as important for attracting TNCs as FDI promotion.

The basic lesson is that the world economy is in a constant process of transformation. The 1980s have been characterized by two main factors. First, the tremendous attraction to FDI exercised by Europe and the United States through, mainly, mergers and acquisitions. Second, the growing number of TNCs from a growing number of home countries has resulted in intense competition among these companies, compounded by stagnant growth in the Triad countries, especially in Europe and the United States. The 1990s might see a revival of FDI in Latin America, as well as the continuing attraction of the South and South-East Asian countries, with India becoming a new 'country–continent' target, after China. But whatever future trends may be, the dynamism of the world economy has been pushed and will continue to be pushed by TNCs and their activities.

CONCLUDING REMARKS

Transnational corporations are the main agents of the transformation of the world economy. In the above sections, it has been pointed out that dramatic change has not been integrated into mainstream economic theory, which continues to stick to the old Ricardian paradigm. With the declining role of the nation-State, TNCs are playing an increasingly crucial role in the functioning of the world economy. The new concept of governance (Dunning, 1992) requires therefore that Governments satisfy, to the extent possible, TNC demands for trained human resources, good communications and transportation networks, transparent and stable laws and regulations, social order and political stability. An enabling environment is one in which firms' transaction costs are reduced as much as possible; that is, market forces are not constrained or distorted. Finally, that logic would require that the regulation of the world economy would need to be left to world market forces. From that viewpoint, there is obviously a need neither for State intervention, nor for an international framework for TNC activities.

Unfortunately, the world market does not look like the one

described in a macroeconomic textbook. There is no doubt that competition exists, but it is not the type that is supposed to lead to an optimal allocation of resources. The world market is an oligopolistic market. To protect themselves against the inherent uncertainties of oligopolistic competition, firms play several alternative games. One is the competitiveness game: to be a leader in the world market, or to be the best in a niche and then eliminate competitors (at least, most of them). Another game is buying competitors through cross-border mergers and acquisitions. A third game is forming strategic alliances with competitors with the objective of reinforcing the capabilities of the firms in the alliance, especially in financing research and development and in controlling access to markets through technological norms and distribution networks. The first two oligopolistic games are conducive to increasing industrial concentration. The third game may eventually be used as a tool for developing cartels. In the face of those corporate strategies, the optimistic view is to trust TNC rationality in being able to generate alternative forms of efficient organization that are substitutes for a perfect market. It would be the triumph of hierarchies against markets. In contrast, the pessimistic view is to compare oligopolistic competition with economic warfare. Advocates of that approach will put pressure on Governments to obtain support for national companies in their struggle against foreign ones. In both cases, the ideal world of free trade depicted by the old international trade paradigm seems to be far removed from the realities of today's world economy.

REFERENCES

Braudel, Fernand (1986). *Perspective of the World* (New York: Harper and Row).

Dunning, John H. (1988). *Explaining International Production* (London: Unwin Hyman).

——— (1992). 'The global economy, domestic governance, strategies and transnational corporations: interactions and policy implications', *Transnational Corporations*, 2, 1 (December), pp. 7–45.

Michalet, Charles A. (1991). 'Strategic partnership and the internationalization process', in Lynn K. Mytelka, ed., *Strategic Partnerships and the World Economy* (London: Pinter Publishers), pp. 37–50.

Porter, Michael (1990). *The Competitive Advantage of Nations* (New York: The Free Press).

Reich, Robert (1991). *The Work of Nations* (New York: Simon & Schuster).

UNCTAD, Division on Transnational Corporations and Investment (1993). *World Investment Report 1993: Transnational Corporations and Inte-*

grated International Production (New York: United Nations), United Nations publication, Sales No. E.93.II.A.14.

Wells, Louis T. and G. Alwin Wint (1992). 'Marketing a country', *Foreign Investment Advisory Service Occasional Paper 1* (Washington, DC: International Finance Corporation).

2 Transnational corporations
Where are they coming from, where are they headed?*

*Raymond Vernon***

Transnational corporations[1] now dominate international flows of goods and services. The identity of the headquarters country once was a significant factor helping to explain the international behaviour of such enterprises; but transnational corporations from different countries are rapidly losing their distinctive national patterns of behaviour. In some product markets, scale and transaction-cost factors help to explain the behaviour of these firms. But in markets with high entry barriers and few participants, the rivalries among the participants are so critical that firm behaviour can best be explained as a struggle to weaken known adversaries or to counter their aggressive moves.

Four decades ago, the transnational corporation (TNC) was widely regarded as a peculiarly United States form of business organization, a manifestation of the existence of a pax Americana. Today, every industrialized country provides a base for a considerable number of TNCs which, collectively, are becoming the dominant form of organization responsible for the international exchange of goods and services. Indeed, by the end of the 1980s, even the larger firms in some of the rapidly industrializing countries of Asia and Latin America had joined the trend (Fujita, 1990; Lall, 1991; TCMD, 1992).

For scholars who want to understand the factors affecting international trade in goods and services, these changes are of consummate importance. In the past, whenever the international behaviour of TNCs appeared at odds with a world regulated by comparative advantage and capital market theory, the deviation could be treated as idiosyncratic, the basis for a footnote in passing. But today, with

* Reprinted from *Transnational Corporations*, vol. 1, no. 2 (August 1992), pp. 7–35.

TNCs dominating the international traffic in goods and services, the question of what determines their behaviour takes on considerable significance.

One cannot pretend to be providing a definitive answer to this central question in the pages that follow; that is a labour that will take many minds over an extended period of time. But this article has two goals that contribute to that central task. The first is to persuade the reader that explanations of the behaviour of TNCs which draw on the national origins of the enterprises as a major explanatory variable are rapidly losing their value, to be replaced by an increased emphasis on the characteristics of the product markets in which the enterprises participate. And the second is to plant a few ideas regarding the motivations and responses of TNCs that must figure in any rounded explanation of the behaviour of these enterprises in the various product markets they face.

UNITED STATES FIRMS ASCENDANT

The sudden growth of United States-based transnational networks after the Second World War was in fact some time in the making. Many decades earlier, the first signs that large enterprises might find themselves pushed to develop a transnational structure were already beginning to appear. Setting the stage for the development of these transnational networks were the dramatic improvements in the technologies of transportation and communication, coupled with the vastly increased opportunities for scale economies in industrial production. Operating with high fixed costs and low variable costs, a new crop of industrial firms felt especially vulnerable to the risks of price competition. And, by the beginning of the twentieth century, these risks were beginning to be realized; the country's industrial leaders, including firms in machinery, metalworking and chemicals, were coming into bruising contact not only with rivals from the United States but also with some from Europe.

Facing what they perceived to be dangerous and destructive competition, the leaders in many United States industries went on the defensive. By the beginning of the century, many of the new industries of the country had organized themselves in restrictive market-sharing arrangements and were reaching out to their European competitors to join agreements that were global in scope.

From the first, however, it was apparent that these restrictive arrangements were fragile responses to the threat of competition, especially for firms based in the United States (Hexner, 1945;

Stocking and Watkins, 1946, 1948). The diversity and scope of the United States economy, coupled with a hostile legal environment, made it difficult for United States leaders to stifle the appearance of new firms inside the country; and those same factors put a brake on the leaders from engaging in overt collusion with European rivals. At times, it is true, global market-sharing agreements nevertheless persisted, especially when patents and trade marks provided a fig leaf for the participants; but, by and large, the role of United States firms in these restrictive arrangements was cautious and restrained.

While participating in the international division of markets in a number of products before the Second World War, many large firms also established the first of their foreign affiliates during that period. Commonly, however, large firms used those affiliates to implement their restrictive agreements with other firms, as in the case of the Du Pont–ICI affiliates located in Latin America. Often, too, firms established such affiliates as cautionary moves against the possibility that other firms with which they were in competition might be in a position to cut them off from raw materials in times of shortage, or from markets in times of glut. United States firms that were engaged in extracting and processing raw materials, for instance, typically developed vertically integrated structures that covered the chain from well-head or mine shaft to the final distribution of processed products; and because other leading firms shared the same fear, partnerships among rivals commonly appeared at various points in these vertical chains, in the form of jointly owned oilfields, mines and processing facilities. Meanwhile, other United States firms, such as General Motors, Ford and General Electric, established affiliates in Europe to serve as bridgeheads in the event of an outbreak of warfare among industry leaders; and such bridgeheads, consistent with their function, were usually allowed to operate with considerable independence and autonomy (Chandler, 1990, pp. 38–45, 205–233; Wilkins and Hill, 1964, pp. 360–379; Jones, 1993; Wilkins, 1970, pp. 93–96).

After the Second World War, there was a decade or two in which the defensive responses of United States-based firms to their perceived risks in world markets were a little less in evidence. The reasons were too obvious to require much comment. The proverbial 'animal spirits' of United States business were already at an elevated level, as a result of the technological lead and financial advantages that they enjoyed over their European rivals. Dramatic advances in communication and transportation were enlarging the stage on which those spirits could be released. The real cost of those services was rapidly declining; and with the introduction of containerized freight, airborne deliveries and the telex, the range of those services was widening. These improvements expanded the business horizons of United States-based firms, allowing them to incorporate more distant locations in the marketing of their products and the sourcing of their needed inputs.

The first reaction of most United States firms to their expanding product markets was to meet those demands by increasing their exports from the home base. But, as numerous case studies attest, the establishment of local producing affiliates soon followed. Almost all of the first manufacturing affiliates established in foreign countries after the Second World War were dedicated to serving the local markets in which they were located.[2] And as a consequence, during the 1960s, about four-fifths of the sales of such affiliates were directed to such markets (Lipsey and Kravis, 1982, p. 3).

The motives of firms for serving local markets through foreign producing affiliates rather than through exports were usually complex. In some cases, for instance, the establishment of a foreign producing affiliate was simply perceived as a more efficient means of serving the foreign market, a consequence of the fact that sales in the market had achieved a level sufficient to exploit the existing economies of scale in production. But other factors were contributing to the scope and timing of these decisions as well. There were indications, for instance, that the decisions taken to establish affiliates abroad, whether for the marketing of products or for the production of required materials and components, were often reactive measures, stimulated by some perceived threat and intended as a hedge against the threat. Once a United States firm lost its unique technological or marketing lead, as seemed inevitable in most products over the course of time. Governments might be tempted to restrict imports in order to encourage domestic production. In that case, the foreign affiliate served to protect existing market access.

But even without the threat of action by Governments, United States-based firms frequently faced threats posed by rivals in the product markets in which they operated. And some rich anecdotal evidence strongly suggests that foreign affiliates were often being created as a hedge against such threats. That hypothesis may help to explain why, in the first few decades after the Second World War, United States-based firms were engaged in follow-the-leader behaviour in the establishment of foreign affiliates; once a United States-based firm in an oligopolistically structured industry set up an affiliate in a given country, the propensity of other United States-based firms in the oligopoly to establish affiliates in the same country was visibly heightened (Knickerbocker, 1973, pp. 22–27; Yu and Ito, 1988).

Such a pattern, of course, does not conclusively demonstrate that the follower is responding defensively to the behaviour of the leader. Alternative hypotheses also need to be entertained such as the possibility that both follower and leader are responding to a common outside stimulus, or that the follower was responding in the belief that the leader had done a rational analysis equally applicable to both their situations. However, various individual cases strongly suggest that such follow-the-leader behaviour can, in many cases, be attributed to the follower's desire to hedge a threat posed by the leader. Although the follower may be unsure whether the leader has properly analysed the costs and benefits of its move in establishing a foreign affiliate, the follower is understandably fearful of allowing a rival to enjoy the benefits of undisturbed exploitation of its foreign opportunities. As long as the number of rival producers in the market is small, therefore, following the leader often seems to entail smaller downside risks than failing to follow. If the leader was right in making its move, failing to follow would give the leader an unrivalled opportunity to increase its competitive strength, whether by increasing its marketing opportunities or by reducing its production costs; and if the leader was wrong, the follower's risks from committing the same error would be limited by the leader's having shared in it.

If the hedging of a threat was sometimes necessary for the growth of United States-based TNCs, however, it was certainly not sufficient for such growth. Still to be explained was why in so many cases United States-based firms chose to establish producing affiliates rather than to exploit their strengths through licensing or other contractual arrangements with local firms. In some cases, the high transaction costs associated with searching out and dealing with local firms may provide an adequate explanation. But here, too, a heavy weight can be put on explanations that see the establishment of a foreign affiliate in part as a hedge against various risks. Whenever licensing agreements are negotiated, both parties face the uncertainties generated by asymmetrical information; the licensee is uncertain of the value of the information he or she is to receive, while the licensor is uncertain of the use to which the licensee proposes to put the information. Moreover, enforcing the provisions of any licensing agreement carries both parties into areas of major uncertainty, based partly on the difficulties of monitoring the agreement and partly on the difficulties of enforcing its provisions.

In any event, the late 1960s registered a high-water mark in the spread of the transnational networks of United States-based industrial enterprises, as the number of foreign affiliates that were added annually to such networks reached an all-time high (UNCTC, 1978, p. 223). For at least a decade thereafter, the number of foreign affiliates added annually to the transnational networks of United States-based industrial enterprises was much reduced. Without firm-by-firm data of the kind that has been compiled by the Harvard Multinational Enterprise Project for the period up to 1975, it is hard to know more precisely what was going on at the firm level during the succeeding years. But the rate of growth of those networks appeared to pick up again in the latter 1980s.

The high rate of growth since that time, however, appears to be based on somewhat different factors from those that prevailed in earlier decades. From anecdotal evidence, it appears that United States-based firms continue to use their transnational networks to transfer newly generated products and processes from the United States to other countries. But with the United States lead greatly diminished in the generation of new products and processes, it is doubtful that the transmission of new products and processes from United States parents to foreign affiliates plays as important a role in the business of United States-based enterprises as it did some decades ago. Indeed, by the 1990s, the ostensible purpose of some United States-based firms in establishing foreign affiliates in Japan was to acquire new skills for their transnational networks, not to diffuse them, in the hope that their Japanese experience would strengthen their competitive capabilities in markets all over the world.[3] With Japanese and European firms acquiring affiliates in the United States at the same time for the same purpose, it was apparent that the distinctive characteristics of United States-based transnational networks were beginning to fade.

Another factor that was beginning to change the behaviour of United States-based enterprises was the increasing familiarity of their managers with the problems of operating in foreign environments. At least until the 1970s, in their decisions on when and where to establish affiliates abroad, United States-based firms had been giving a heavy preference to the familiar. Careful analyses of the geographical sequence by which United States-based firms established manufacturing facilities abroad demonstrated that historically there had been a heavy preference for setting up the first foreign production unit in Canada, with the United Kingdom taking second place and Mexico third.[4] By the 1960s, United States-based firms were bypassing Canada for Europe and Latin America as the first point of foreign manufacture; and by the 1970s, although Europe and Latin America continued to provide the principal first-production sites, Asian sites were beginning to turn up with increasing frequency (Vernon and Davidson, 1979, pp. 52, 134–135).[5]

The role played by experience during these early postwar decades could be seen even more directly by trends in the reaction times of United States-based firms in setting up foreign production facilities. Where new products were involved, United States-based firms characteristically set up their first production sites within the United States. But eventually they set up production sites abroad as well; and in measure as these firms gained experience with producing in a given country, the time interval involved in setting up production facilities in the country for new products showed a marked decline. Moreover, to the extent that the number of foreign production sites for any product increased, the time interval in setting up another facility in a foreign country also declined. By the 1970s, therefore, United States-based firms were beginning to show less hesitation in setting up production affiliates abroad for their new products, and were scanning a rapidly widening circle of countries for their production sites.

The pattern towards which United States-owned transnational networks seem to be moving, therefore, is one in which the parent firm in the United States is prepared to survey different geographical locations on their respective merits, with a much reduced presumption in favour of a United States location. Instead, when assigning tasks to the various units of their transnational networks, United States business managers are increasingly likely to discount the distinction between home-based and foreign facilities, except as governmental restraints compel them to recognize that factor. This does not mean that the role played by geography is altogether obliterated. United States-based firms, for instance, continue to rely on Latin America more than on Asia to provide their low-cost labour needs, while the reverse is true for Japanese firms.[6] But the sense of uncertainty associated with producing outside the home economy has substantially declined, and the preference for nearby production locations such as those in Latin America over more remote locations such as those in Asia has declined as well.

For enterprises operating in oligopolistic markets, however, a major source of uncertainty remains. Even when such enterprises are fully familiar with the foreign environments in which they are obliged to operate, they are still exposed to the predatory and pre-emptive tactics of their rivals in the oligopoly. The reasoning that led

the international oil and minerals firms to develop vertically integrated structures before the Second World War, therefore, can be
glimpsed in more recent decades in the behaviour of United States-
based firms operating in oligopolistic markets. For instance, United
States-based oil companies, having been separated from some of their
captive crude oil supplies by the nationalizations of the 1970s, remain
unwilling to rely upon the open market for the bulk of such supplies
despite the existence of a large public market for the product. Facing
the latent threat posed by the vertical integration of the Saudi Arabian
and Venezuelan state-owned oil companies, United States-based
firms are repairing and strengthening their upstream links.[7]

Such cautionary behaviour, moreover, is not confined to the raw
materials industries. Similar behaviour is apparent among United
States firms in the electronics industry. Under pressure to reduce
the costs of labour-intensive components, firms such as IBM and
Texas Instruments have chosen to manufacture a considerable part
of their needs within their own transnational networks rather than rely
upon independent suppliers; and a major factor in that decision,
according to many observers, has been the fear that predatory rivals
might withhold the most advanced versions of those components
from competitors while incorporating them in their own products
(United States Congress, Office of Technology Assessment, 1991,
pp. 97–100; Schwartz, 1992, especially p. 149; Teece, 1987).

For some United States-based enterprises, it has been only a small
step from using their foreign affiliates as feeders for manufacturing
facilities in the United States to using those facilities to fill requirements arising anywhere in the network. And by the 1980s, it had
become apparent that this process was well advanced (Lipsey, 1987,
pp. 39–42). Of course, in practically every transnational network, the
parent unit in the United States typically continued to occupy a
unique position. Characteristically, the parent firm's United States
sales still accounted for the bulk of the network's sales; its United
States facilities were responsible for the most important research-and-
development work in the network; and its United States offices still
coordinated some of the network's functions that might benefit from a
centralized approach, such as the finance function. But the direction
was clear: although the centralized functions of the network would
presumably remain in the United States indefinitely, the historical and
institutional forces that resisted the geographical diffusion of other
functions to locations outside the United States were growing weaker.

A more novel trend, however, has been the growing propensity of
United States-based firms to enter into alliances of one kind or

another with transnational networks based in other countries – typically, in other highly industrialized countries. Such alliances, for instance, sometimes take the form of a joint venture established to perform a specified function, or of an exchange of licences in a specified field. At times, the arrangements link suppliers to their customers; but at other times, the parties involved in such limited linkages appear to be direct rivals. A considerable literature is already developing regarding the operation of these alliances (Contractor and Lorange, 1988; Gomes-Casseres, 1989; Lewis, 1990; Lynch, 1989; Parkhe, 1991). Although the definitions of such alliances are muddy and the data far from complete, they seem to be concentrated in industries in which barriers to entry are high and technological change is rapid and costly.

Part of the motivation for these alliances is apparent: an effort of each of the participating firms to reduce the risks associated with lumpy commitments to new research-and-development projects and to ensure that they are abreast of their competitors in their research resources. The alliances, therefore, are not much different in function from the jointly owned mines and oilfields that rival refiners and marketers shared in decades gone by, such as ARAMCO in Saudi Arabia, Southern Peru Copper in Peru and HALCO in Guinea. Moreover, with common interests linking rivals to their suppliers and to one another in these new alliances, the likelihood that any one of the rivals might steal a technological lead on the others is obviously reduced. Like the partners in the raw material affiliates, therefore, there may well be a sense among some of the partners in the new alliances that their ties with rivals and suppliers could be used to reduce the harshness of future competition among them.

There is one respect, however, in which many of the new alliances differ from those in the raw material industries. In industries with rapidly changing technologies and swiftly changing markets, the interests of the participants in any given alliance are likely to be relatively unstable; such firms will be constantly withdrawing and regrouping in order to satisfy their rapidly shifting strategic needs. Nevertheless, the possibility that these arrangements will serve at times to take the edge off the competition in some product markets remains very real.

Yet, for all the evidence that defensive motivations have been dominating the behaviour of United States-based enterprises, there are various signs that the animal spirits of some United States managers can still be roused. One sign of such spirits has been the global spread of United States-based firms in various service industries, including fast foods, advertising services and management consulting. Some of these service-oriented firms have developed transnational networks simply by following their transnational clients abroad in an effort to maintain an existing relationship. But others, relying on a technological or managerial capability that their foreign rivals had not yet matched, have bravely set out to master new environments without any apparent defensive motivation. Such initiatives, it appears, depend on the extent to which enterprises feel protected by some unique firm capability, such as a technological or managerial lead, or a patent or trade mark.[8] But whether or not such situations are common in the future, defensive responses can be counted on to compel many large firms in the United States to maintain and extend their transnational networks.

EMERGENCE OF THE EUROPEANS

European industrialists often enjoy a reputation for sophistication and urbanity that equips them specially for the role of global entrepreneurs. But their performance as a group after the Second World War presents a very mixed picture.

In the decades just prior to the Second World War, the principal strategy of the leading European firms had been to protect their home markets from competition, not to seek out new foreign markets. When they established affiliates in foreign countries, their disposition had been to concentrate on countries to which their home Governments had close political ties (Franko, 1976, p. 81). And their typical reaction to the threat of international competition in those decades had been to develop market-sharing arrangements along national lines.

In the immediate postwar period, European firms continued to cling to their home markets. Absorbed in the rebuilding of their home economies and saddled with the need to catch up technologically, they had little slack to devote to the establishment of new foreign facilities. True, enterprises headquartered in some of the smaller countries that possessed a technological edge, such as the pharmaceutical companies of Switzerland and The Netherlands, as well as the machinery firms of Sweden, often felt compelled to set up affiliates outside their home countries in order to exploit their technological lead and to finance their ongoing innovational efforts; and the affiliates they set up in foreign countries typically operated with greater autonomy in foreign locations than some of their United States rivals. Moreover, manufacturing firms headquartered in the larger European

countries were not altogether averse to establishing producing affiliates in areas over which their home Governments still exercised
strong political or economic influence. Between 1945 and 1965, for
instance, firms headquartered in the United Kingdom established
about 400 manufacturing affiliates in Australia, Canada and New
Zealand (Harvard Multinational Enterprise Project data banks).

The disposition of European firms to identify closely with their
home Governments has some of its roots in history. Until recently,
many were family-owned enterprises, with a long history of dominance in some given city or region. Some were so-called national
champions, accustomed to especially favourable treatment by their
Governments in the provision of capital and the purchase of output
(Michalet, 1974). The idea of maintaining close ties to their home
Governments when operating abroad, therefore, represented an easy
extension of their relationships at home.

After 1960, the emergence of a common market on the European
continent began to affect the strategies of European firms. At first,
however, these developments did little to encourage European firms
to set up affiliates in other countries within the area. For one thing,
the promise of a duty-free market among members of the European
Community actually served to eliminate one of the motivations for
creating such affiliates, namely the threat that frontiers might be
closed to foreign goods. And with land distances relatively small
and national markets relatively limited in size, the economic reasons
for establishing such affiliates often did not appear compelling.

On the other hand, by the 1960s, United States-based companies
were beginning to set up their affiliates in Europe in large numbers.
Data from the Harvard Multinational Enterprise Project show that,
whereas in the fifteen years between 1945 and 1959 United States
parents had established some 300 manufacturing affiliates in Europe,
between 1960 and 1975 United States parents established nearly
2,000 manufacturing affiliates in Europe. Typically, the first landing
of the United States invaders was in the United Kingdom, despite that
country's delay in entering the European Community; but the United
States-based firms were not long in establishing affiliates on the
continent as well.

One might have expected the appearance of those affiliates to
stimulate moves to renew the restrictive market-sharing agreements
of the prewar period; but the environment following the end of the
Second World War was much less conducive to such agreements. For
one thing, rapidly expanding markets and swiftly changing technologies generated an environment that made agreements difficult. In

addition, although the enforcement of the United States antitrust laws had grown lax in the postwar period, the European Community itself had adopted (and was occasionally enforcing) some exemplary measures aimed at preventing enterprises from dividing up the European market (Goyder, 1988, especially pp. 71–133).

Eventually, however, most large European firms were led through the same defensive cycle that some United States-based firms had already experienced. Having re-established export markets for their manufactured goods in many areas, including the Middle East and Latin America, they faced the same kind of threat that had moved their United States counterparts to set up producing affiliates abroad, namely the fear of losing a market through import restrictions. By 1970, manufacturing firms based in Europe were adding affiliates to their transnational networks in numbers over twice as high as those recorded by their United States-based counterparts (Harvard Multinational Enterprise Project data bank).

Moved largely by defensive considerations, European firms were adding rapidly to their holdings in the United States. There, they showed a strong preference for investing in existing firms rather than launching wholly new undertakings, and a strong disposition to team up with a United States firm in the process.[9] Such entries, some European managers supposed, would give them exposure to the latest industrial technologies and marketing strategies, thus strengthening their ability to resist the onslaught by United States firms in their home markets and in third countries.

By the end of the 1960s, however, the Europeans had begun to have less reason to fear the dominance of United States-based firms. By that time, the differences in technological achievement between United States firms and European firms had obviously shrunk. And access to capital no longer favoured United States firms. Not surprisingly, then, some of the motivations that lay behind the expansion of the European networks grew more akin to those of networks headquartered in the United States; that is, largely defensive moves aimed at protecting a foreign market from import restrictions or copycat responses to the initiatives of rivals in setting up an affiliate abroad (Flowers, 1976).[10] In an apparent response to such stimuli, the number of European-owned affiliates appearing in various parts of the world rapidly increased (Harvard Multinational Enterprise Project data bank).

These new transborder relations, one should note, have not wholly obliterated the distinctive national traits that have characterized European firms. German enterprises, for instance, continue to huddle in the shelter of their big banks, French companies in the protective cover of their national ministries. Moreover, despite the existence of the European Community, European firms continue to owe their existence to their respective national enabling statutes, which reflect wide differences in philosophical values and political balance. The United Kingdom, for instance, cannot agree with its continental partners on such fundamental issues as the responsibilities of the corporation to its labour force; whereas corporate managers in the United Kingdom are typically seen as the agents for their stockholders, continental Governments generally take the view that labour has a quasi-proprietary stake in the enterprise that employs it, which managers are obliged to recognize. Differences such as these have served to block projects for the creation of a European company under the European Community's aegis.

Nevertheless, cross-border mergers are growing in number in Europe. In 1987, among the large industrial enterprises based in the European Community, only seventy-five cases were recorded in which a firm based in one country gained control of a firm based in another European Community country; but by 1990 the number had risen to 257 (European Commission, 1991, p. 228). Indeed, in this universe of large industrial firms, the number of such transborder acquisitions in 1990 for the first time exceeded the number of such acquisitions involving firms in a single member country.

In part, the trend towards cross-border mergers is a consequence of the many liberalizing measures that the member countries of the European Community have taken with regard to capital flows. In addition, however, there appears to be a visible weakening of the family conglomerate, a distinctly national form of big business. In Italy, for instance, where that kind of structure has been particularly prominent in the private sector, the country's leading family conglomerates have fallen on especially hard times.[11]

The disposition of many firms to cling to the shreds of their national identity will lead many of them to hesitate over transborder mergers and consolidations in which they are not the surviving entity; or, when they finally succumb to the pressures for merger, to insist on retaining a minority interest in the affiliate that has joined the network of the foreign-based firm. That same disposition suggests why European firms appear to give a heavier preference to consortia and alliances as a way of combining their strengths with a foreign firm than United States-based competitors would do. But, because such arrangements are likely to be fragile over time, transborder mergers may be the preferred vehicle in spite of the obstacles. Such mergers may still generate resistance and hostility in some countries.[12] But a few decades from now, the national differences in Europe's business communities are likely to prove no more important than the differences between Texas-based enterprises and Massachusetts-based enterprises in the United States.

In explaining the growth of the networks of firms based in Europe, then, we return to some of the same themes that were stressed in the case of United States-based firms. When summarizing the factors that have pushed United States-based enterprises to develop and expand their transnational networks in the past decades, the stress was on the continuous improvements in the technology of communication and transportation as the powerful exogenous factor; the decisions of the United States-based firms to expand their enterprises were seen in large part as a response aimed at reducing the uncertainties and countering the threats that accompanied such developments. One feels sure that these generalizations will carry the observer a considerable distance in understanding the behaviour of European-based firms as well.[13] Over time, the differences that heretofore have distinguished United States-based from Europe-based transnational networks are likely to diminish, as the conditions of their founding and early growth begin to lose their original importance.

LATECOMER JAPAN

The factors behind the growth of TNCs based in Japan, a phenomenon of the past two or three decades, will bring us back to the same emphasis on defensive motivations, including the need of Japanese enterprises to protect their interests against the hostile acts of foreign Governments and business competitors, and the desire to build up their competitive strengths by exposing themselves to the most challenging technological and marketing environments. Indeed, the defensive motivations that commonly lie behind the creation and spread of TNCs are likely to act even more powerfully on Japanese than on their United States-based and Europe-based competitors. To see why, it helps to review briefly the evolution of Japan's industrial structure (see, for example, Wilkins, 1990).

From the earliest years of the Meiji restoration in the last decades of the nineteenth century, the industrial structure of Japan exhibited some distinctive national characteristics. Half a dozen conglomerate organizations dominated the core of Japan's modern economy, each with its own captive bank, trading company and portfolio of manufacturing and service enterprises. The conglomerate structure, well developed before the Second World War, was only modified a little by Japan's loss of its foreign territories and by the ensuing occupation. Japanese firms lost their investments in those territories; but these investments had largely been controlled by the so-called new *zaibatsu*, companies that depended for their existence on Japan's foreign conquests and that had very little stake in the home economy itself. In Japan proper, the holding companies that sat at the apex of each conglomerate were liquidated during the occupation. But the member firms of each conglomerate maintained their old ties by cross-holdings of stock and by shared memories of past loyalties. And in the 1960s and 1970s, as foreign enterprises began to show some interest in acquiring control over Japanese firms, member firms within each conglomerate systematically built up their cross-holdings even further as a means of repelling foreign companies (Ito, 1992, p. 191).

From the early emergence of these conglomerate organizations, a fierce rivalry existed among them – but a rivalry based much more on comparative rates of growth and market shares than on nominal profits. Within each conglomerate, the financing of the contest was left to the conglomerate's captive bank rather than to public capital markets. But the general scope and direction of the lending by these banks to their affiliates were largely determined by continuous consultation with key government agencies, including especially the Ministry of Finance, the Bank of Japan, and the Ministry of International Trade and Industry.

By the 1980s, however, it was becoming apparent that major changes were taking place in the conglomerate structures. Perhaps the most obvious change was the dramatic shift in the financing practices of the industrial firms. As the rate of growth of the Japanese economy slowed down a little in the 1980s and as the need to finance capacity expansion grew less urgent, Japanese firms found that internally generated cash was going a much longer way towards meeting their capital needs. At the same time, under pressure from foreign sources and from Japan's own financial intermediaries, the Ministry of Finance was gradually relaxing its tight controls over the development of internal capital markets, thereby providing Japanese companies for the first time with a real option for raising their capital needs through the sale of stocks and bonds in public markets. Concurrently, Japanese firms were being granted permission to raise capital in foreign currencies, by selling their securities abroad or borrowing from foreign banks. Japanese banks, trading houses and other service facilities, therefore, were strongly represented in the outflow from Japan of direct investment to major foreign markets.[14] And because Japanese manufacturing firms were always a little uncomfortable when dealing with foreigners as service suppliers, the existence of those service facilities in foreign markets eased the way for the manufacturers to establish their affiliates outside Japan (Gittelman and Dunning, 1992).

In accounting for the changes in the character of the transnational networks based in Japan, however, one must place particular emphasis on the increasing technological capabilities of these enterprises. In the very first stages of the development of transnational networks by Japan-based firms in the 1960s and 1970s, some scholars entertained the hypothesis that these firms would develop a pattern of foreign direct investment quite different from that pioneered by United States-based and Europe-based firms (Kojima, 1978, pp. 85–87). At that stage, Japan's penetration of foreign markets for manufactured goods had been most in evidence in South and South-East Asia, and had been concentrated heavily in relatively simple items such as batteries, radios, noodles and other consumer goods, items in which Japan's comparative advantage was already fading. Given the unsophisticated nature of the products and the lack of a need for after-sales services, Japanese producers usually used their affiliated trading companies as their agents in foreign markets. Indeed, in many cases, the Japanese producers were not large enough even to consider marketing their own products abroad, and so had no choice but to rely on trading companies.

In these cases, therefore, when the risk that the Government might impose restrictions became palpable, it was the trading company that typically took the lead in establishing a local production facility, often through a three-way partnership that combined the trading company with a local distributor and with the erstwhile Japanese exporter (Yoshino, 1976, pp. 95–126). From this early pattern, it appeared that the Japan-based TNCs might root themselves much more deeply in their foreign markets than the United States-based and Europe-based companies, with results that might prove more benign from the viewpoint of the host country.

By the 1980s, however, the patterns of foreign direct investment by Japanese firms were converging towards the norms recorded by their United States and European rivals (Encarnation, 1992, pp. 9–35). As with United States-based and Europe-based firms, the object of Japanese firms in establishing a producing affiliate abroad was commonly to protect a market in a relatively differentiated product that originally had been developed through exports from Japan.

Compared with United States-based or Europe-based firms, however, the stake of Japanese firms in the export markets of other industrialized countries soon grew very large.[15] The spectacular growth of Japanese exports to the markets of such countries exposed Japanese firms once more to threats of restrictive action on a major scale. At this advanced stage, however, the markets to be protected were considerably different in character from those that the first generation of Japan-based TNCs had developed. One difference was in the identity of the markets under siege, now located mainly in the United States and Europe. Another was the nature of the products involved; these were relatively sophisticated products, such as automobiles, video cameras and computer-controlled machine tools. And a third was the channels of distribution involved: sophisticated products such as these were usually marketed through channels under the direct control of the manufacturers rather than through trading companies.

The networks that Japan-based firms created in response to the new threats came closer to emulating those of the United States-based and Europe-based firms with transnational networks. Moreover, like those of their European rivals, many of the foreign acquisitions by Japan-based firms were explained by a desire to acquire advanced technological skills; this motive was especially apparent in the acquisition of various medium-sized high-technology firms in the United States (Kester, 1991; Kogut and Chang, 1991).

Although the transnational networks that Japan-based firms produced in this second generation bore much greater resemblance to the networks of their counterparts from other developed countries, some characteristic differences remained. One such characteristic was the high propensity of Japan-based TNCs to control their producing affiliates tightly from Japan. Symptomatic of that fact was the near-universal use of Japanese personnel to head their foreign affiliates.[16] A striking illustration of the same desire for control was the limited leeway allowed to affiliates in the acquisition of capital equipment; Australian affiliates of Japanese firms, for example, possessed far less leeway in the selection of new machinery than did the affiliates of United States-based or Europe-based firms (Kreinin, 1988). Some signs existed in the 1990s that a few Japanese firms were breaking away from their traditional controls and were giving their foreign affiliates greater leeway, but they were still the exception.[17]

The early reluctance of Japan-based firms to develop a transnational network and the tendency of the foreign affiliates of such firms to rely upon their established sources in Japan have been attributed to a number of different factors. They have been variously explained as a consequence of the relative inexperience of Japanese firms with the novel problems of producing abroad, as a result of the heavy reliance on the consensual process in firm decision-making, or as a consequence of the extensive use of just-in-time producing processes, which demand the closest coordination between the firms and their suppliers (Kester, 1991, p. 109). Introducing strangers into the system, according to the argument, entails major modifications in firm practices that cannot be achieved overnight.

Nevertheless, by the end of the 1980s, Japan-based firms were expanding their transnational networks at an unprecedented rate. What is more, their manufacturing affiliates in the United States and Europe were drawing a considerable fraction of their inputs from sources located in the host country (Gittelman and Dunning, 1992). Moreover, it appeared that some of the very factors that had slowed the growth of Japan-based transnational networks in the past could be expected to reinforce the expansion rather than to slow it down. For example, the desire of Japanese firms to rely on Japanese sources means that the foreign affiliates of major Japanese firms are pulling large numbers of satellite suppliers with them into foreign locations; and, while this has not been an unknown phenomenon in the establishment of the networks of firms based in the United States, it appears to be an especially powerful force in the case of Japan-based firms (Wilkins, 1990, pp. 612–616).[18] Moreover, if one pair of authoritative observers is to be believed, Japanese firms already are being drawn into Europe by the conviction that they must assimilate some distinctive regional character if they are to be successful in major industries, such as automobiles and electronic equipment (Gittelman and Dunning, 1992). Finally, given the intense rivalry of Japanese firms, with its stress on market share, it is not unreasonable to expect a pattern of copycat follow-the-leader behaviour even stronger than that observed with respect to firms based in other countries.

Whether the Government of Japan will seek at some point to restrain the overseas movement of its firms through administrative guidance is unclear; but even if it makes such an attempt, there is no certainty that the attempt would prove effective. The growing financial independence of Japanese firms means that the Ministry of Finance and MITI have lost one of their principal sources of coercion. The commitment by Japanese firms of a large proportion of their assets to foreign locations means that they will be exposed to stimuli not strikingly different from those affecting their United States and

European rivals. Developments such as these promise to contribute to the convergence of Japan-based transnational corporations towards the norms typical of transnational corporations based in other countries (Lipsey, 1991, p. 87).

PATTERNS OF THE FUTURE

In the future, as in the past, some powerful exogenous factors will influence the spread of transnational corporations, including changes in the technologies of transportation, communication and production. But it is not easy to project the consequences of such changes. For instance, if just-in-time manufacturing takes on added strength, the clustering tendency of related enterprises should grow stronger. But if flexible manufacturing processes gain in strength, smaller and more self-contained plants could dominate, reducing the tendency towards clusters (Auty, 1992; Dunning 1992, especially pp. 158–162). Despite uncertainties of this sort, however, it can be anticipated that transnational networks and transborder alliances, already a major factor in international economic flows, will grow in importance.

The response of Governments

How Governments will respond to that situation is a little uncertain. Although globalization and convergence may prove to be major trends defining the behaviour of transnational corporations in the future, it is implausible to assume that Governments will stand aside, allowing such behaviour to develop as it may. With jobs, taxes, payment balances and technological achievement seemingly at stake, Governments are bound to act in an effort to defend national interests and respond to national pressures. Their efforts, involving carrots in some cases and sticks in others, will continue to pose threats and offer opportunities to the transnational corporations.

Some of these governmental responses will take the form of restrictions, unilaterally adopted, aimed at holding inbound and outbound foreign direct investment in check, But from all the signs, political leaders in the major developed countries seem aware that national autarky is not an available option, unless a country is prepared to absorb some overwhelming costs. That recognition explains why so many countries now eye the possibility of developing regional blocs – areas large enough to satisfy the modern requirements of scale and scope, and small enough to promise member countries that they will exert some influence in shaping their joint economic policies.

There is a surface plausibility to the idea that such blocs may figure importantly in the future, a plausibility reflected in the pre-eminence of Japanese interests in South and South-East Asia, European interests in Africa, Eastern Europe and the Middle East, and United States interests in Latin America. But it is easy to misinterpret the significance of those concentrations. It may be, as already suggested, that these concentrations reflect little more than the myopic learning process of business managers, and that increasing experience will push them towards scanning over a wider geographical range.

In any case, when seen through the eyes of the managers of transnational corporations based in the industrialized areas, their principal stake by far lies in other industrialized areas, not in the hinterlands of their respective 'regions'. That has been the case for decades, and it has shown no signs of changing in recent years. To be sure, such enterprises will not hesitate to use the influence of their respective Governments to promote their interests in these regions. But from the viewpoint of the firms, such efforts will be a sideshow compared with their respective stakes in other industrialized economies.

At the same time, the influence that individual Governments are in a position to exert over their respective transnational corporations appears to be rapidly on the decline. Although Governments have been known to remain blind to the obvious for remarkably prolonged periods of time, that ineluctable fact should eventually lead them to limit their unilateral efforts at control. Where control of some sort still seems necessary or desirable, the option remaining will be to pursue mutually agreed measures with other countries. In the decades ahead, the United States, Europe and Japan are sure to find themselves addressing the feasibility and desirability of international agreements that define more fully the rights and obligations of transnational corporations. Although most other countries may be slower to address the issue, a few, such as Singapore and Mexico, along with the non-European members of OECD, are likely to be involved as well. Already some of the elements of an international system are in place with respect to a few functional fields, such as the levying of corporate income taxes. It does not stretch the imagination very much to picture international agreements on such subjects as the competition of Governments for foreign direct investment, the threats to market competition posed by restrictive business practices and mergers, the rights and obligations of transnational corporations in national political processes and other issues relating to such enterprises.

The development of theory

In the past, as transnational networks appeared and grew, some researchers concerned with understanding the causes of their behaviour found it useful, even indispensable, to distinguish such enterprises according to their national base. If strong tendencies towards national convergence persist, distinctions based on the national origin of the network are likely to lose their analytic and descriptive value, and distinctions on other dimensions are likely to grow in importance. Even more than in the past, distinctions based on the characteristics of the product market and the production process are likely to prove particularly fruitful.

As observed earlier, many transnational corporations created global networks in response to perceived threats, operating under circumstances in which ignorance and uncertainty were endemic. For the most part, these enterprises operated in product markets with significant barriers to entry, including static and dynamic scale economies, patents and trade marks. With the passage of time, however, a considerable proportion of these enterprises overcame their sense of acute uncertainty in foreign markets, especially as the products and their related technologies grew more stable and standardized.

These tendencies often reduced barriers to entry, increased the number of participants, and elevated the role of price competition. In the production and sale of metals and petroleum, for instance, the number of sellers on world markets inexorably increased and the role of competitive pricing grew. In big-ticket consumer electronics, despite the persistent efforts of sellers to differentiate their products, an intensification of competitive pricing among sellers also has become commonplace. In such cases, there is considerable utility in models that cast the participants as fully informed actors operating in a market in which their choices are known, under conditions in which some scale economies exist (Helpman and Krugman, 1985, pp. 225–259; Grossman and Helpman, 1991, pp. 197–200). There is no reason why models that are based on these assumptions should not generate useful first approximations to the behaviour of transnational corporations in a considerable number of industries.

Other models may also have something to contribute, such as those that view transnational networks as the consequence of decisions by firms to internalize certain types of transactions. The international market for the sale of technology and management skills, for instance, is a grossly inefficient market from the viewpoint of both buyer and seller (Teece, 1986; Galbraith and Kay, 1986). Internalization can be viewed as a response to those inefficiencies, in a setting in which the enterprises are otherwise fully aware of the set of choices they confront and of the facts bearing on those choices (Casson, 1987, pp. 1–49; Williamson, 1971).

Models based on the internalization hypothesis therefore fit comfortably into the structure of the models described earlier, based essentially on a neoclassical framework driven by costs and prices. But they have tended to crowd out the analysis of other motivations that seem at least as important in explaining the behaviour of the managers of such enterprises. For instance, various measures taken by a firm to create a transnational network may be driven by another motive, namely a desire to avoid being exposed to the predatory behaviour of rivals, including the risk that such rivals might cut off needed supplies or deny access to a distribution system during some future contingency.

That possibility pushes the modeller in a very different direction in attempting to explain the behaviour of TNCs. Such enterprises continue to figure prominently in many product markets that have not yet attained a stable middle age. In such markets, the number of producers is often sharply limited, products and related services are often highly differentiated, technologies are in flux and price differences are not the critical factor in competition. Moreover, externalities of various kinds commonly play a dominant role in locational decisions, as when enterprises try to draw on various national environments to produce the stimuli they think will improve their competitive strengths. Firms engaged in producing microprocessors, aircraft engines and wonder drugs, for instance, are strongly influenced by one or another of these factors.

Needless to say, where the number of rivals in a market is low, that fact fundamentally conditions the strategies of the participants. Some of them may long for the security of a market-sharing arrangement, and may even take some tentative steps in that direction, such as entering into partnerships with some of their rivals. But developing an effective market-sharing arrangement is usually difficult and dangerous.

In any event, when a limited number of participants are involved in a product market, theorists must entertain the possibility that the firms engaged in such markets see any given transaction as only one move in a campaign stretching across time. In each transaction, the principal objective of the firm is to strengthen its position in relation to its rivals or to neutralize the efforts of its rivals to steal a march; and with that objective paramount, 'share of market' becomes a critical measure of success. In such circumstances, invading a rival's principal market may prove a useful defensive strategy, aimed at reducing the rival's propensity for warfare elsewhere. And, given the imperfect knowledge under which each firm is assumed to operate, a policy of following a rival into new areas of supply and new markets may be seen as a prudent response to the rival's initiatives.[19]

Of course, models built on such behavioural assumptions, by shedding many of the assumptions underlying the neoclassical model, relinquish the support provided by a comprehensive body of well-explored theory. Instead, the analyst is thrown into a world of uncertain outcomes, explored so far largely by game theorists, specialists in signalling theory and others outside the neoclassical mainstream. It is hardly surprising, therefore, that most of the scholars who have sought to model the behaviour of the TNC have avoided the implications of high uncertainty and limited numbers, and have preferred to concentrate on hypotheses that require less radical departures from neoclassical assumptions.

Nevertheless, any serious effort to project the behaviour of TNCs in the future will have to recognize that, in many major product and service markets, the players will see themselves as engaged in a campaign against specific adversaries in a global market, with individual decisions being shaped in light of that perception. At different times and places, there will be efforts to call a truce, efforts to weaken specific adversaries and efforts to counter the aggressive behaviour of others; and the behaviour that emerges will not be easily explained in terms of models that satisfy neoclassical conditions. Therein lies a major challenge for those who are attempting to cast light on the behaviour of TNCs through the systematic modelling of their behaviour.

NOTES

** This article was prepared with the generous support of the National Bureau of Economic Research and the Center on Business and Government of the Kennedy School at Harvard University. It will also be published, in slightly altered form, in Kenneth Froot, ed., *Foreign Direct Investment Today* (Chicago, University of Chicago Press, 1993). I am indebted to Ernest Chung and Subramanian Rangan for their research support in the preparation of this article, as well as to

Richard Caves and Lawrence H. Wortzel for their incisive comments on an earlier draft.

1 Out of deference to the usage preferred by the editors, the term 'transnational corporation' and the acronym 'TNC' are used here to denote a network of related enterprises, composed of a parent in one country and subsidiaries or affiliates in other countries.

2 Even as late as 1975, about two-thirds of the manufacturing subsidiaries of United States-based firms were engaged almost exclusively in serving the local markets in which they were located (Curhan *et al.*, 1977, p. 393).

3 'American business starts a counterattack in Japan', *New York Times*, 24 February 1992, p. 1. A survey conducted by MITI in January 1990 reports that 38 per cent of the foreign direct investors in Japan responding to the survey listed 'engineering skill is high' as a reason for their investment, while 18 per cent listed 'collection of technical information and market information'. Reproduced in *Nippon 1991: Business Facts and Figures* (New York, JETRO, 1992, p. 109).

4 The generalizations are based on an unpublished study of the manufacturing subsidiaries of 180 United States-based TNCs as of 1964. The 180 firms, whose transnational networks are covered in the computerized files of the Harvard Multinational Enterprise Project, comprised all large United States-based firms with substantial foreign manufacturing facilities (Vaupel, 1971).

5 The study is based on the same TNCs as those in Vaupel (1971). Conclusions in the two paragraphs following are based on data in the same study.

6 United Nations data affirm the preference of United States-based and Japan-based firms for direct investment in nearby locations during the years 1971 to 1986, as well as the tendency of these geographical preferences to decline over time (UNCTC, 1988, table A.5. pp. 518–520).

7 'Why kings of crude want to be pump boys' provides an account of the downstream movements of the various state-owned oil companies, and new upstream ties forged by Gulf Oil, Sun Oil, Citgo and Texaco (*Business Week*, 21 March 1988, pp. 110–112).

8 The reader will recognize this theme as a major element in John H. Dunning's 'eclectic theory'. For his view of United States foreign-direct-investment trends in relation to the theory, see Dunning (1985, pp. 66–70).

9 'In the period from 1960 to 1970, about 80 per cent of the manufacturing affiliates established by European parents in the United States were through acquisition of or mergers with United States firms; the comparable figure for manufacturing affiliates of United States parents in Europe for the same period was 67 per cent (Harvard Multinational Enterprise Project data bank).

10 The assumption that the spread of European networks is to be attributed in part to follow-the-leader behaviour, at least until the 1970s, is fortified by some unpublished studies undertaken by Fred Knickerbocker (1973), whose analysis of the behaviour of United States-based manufacturing affiliates is cited elsewhere in this article.

11 See 'Leaders that have lost their way', *Financial Times*, 21 January 1992, p. 18, for an account of the troubles of the Agnelli and Pirelli family conglomerates.

12 For a rich account of such hostilities in France's reactions to the Agnelli family's efforts to acquire control over Perrier, see 'Dynastic hopes fall flat in France', *Financial Times*, 25 March 1992, p. 14.

13 A study of European banking confirms the existence of each of the major tendencies identified above; see Campayne (1992).

14 In the 1980s, the relative importance of services in the outflow of foreign direct investment from Japan was substantially higher than that from the United States, the United Kingdom, Germany or France (UNCTC, 1991, p. 16, table 6).

15 Data on the identities of the world's leading TNCs in the latter 1980s, with partial statistics on their respective stakes in foreign markets gleaned primarily from annual reports, appear in UNCTC (1988).

16 For instance, a study of the United States affiliates of Japanese electronic firms reports that only 2 per cent of Japanese electronics firms in the United States had United States chief executive officers (United States Congress, Office of Technology Assessment, 1991, p. 99).

17 'Japan's less-than-invincible computer makers', *The Economist*, 11 January 1992, pp. 59–60.

18 See also 'Benefits beyond the automotive sector', *Financial Times*, 18 February 1992, p. 28, for an account of Nissan's impact in north-east England. A hint of the strong tendency of Japanese firms to buy from enterprises with which they have close links appears also in Gittelman and Dunning (1992).

19 Bower (1992) omits any reference to such possibilities. See also Graham and Krugman (1989), where such possibilities are not presented in the 'theory' section of the report but in an annex entitled 'Industrial-Organization Explanations of Foreign Direct Investment'.

REFERENCES

Auty, Richard M. (1992). *Changing Competitiveness of Newly Industrialized Countries in Heavy and Chemical Industry: Effects of the Product Cycle and Technological Change.* Amsterdam: University of Amsterdam.

Bower, Anthony G. (1992). Predicting locational decisions of multinational corporations. N-3440-CUSTR. Santa Monica, California: RAND.

Business Week (1988). Why kings of crude want to be pump boys. 21 March, pp. 110–112.

Campayne, Paul (1992). Cross investment in the EC banking sector. In *Multinational Investment in Modern Europe: Strategic interaction in the integrated community*, J. Cantwell, ed., London: Edward Elgar, pp. 298–328.

Casson, Mark (1987). *The Firm and the Market: Studies on Multinational Enterprise and the Scope of the Firm.* Cambridge, Massachusetts: The MIT Press.

Chandler, Alfred D. (1990). *Scale and Scope: The Dynamics of Industrial Capitalism.* Cambridge: The Belknap Press.

Contractor, F. J. and Peter Lorange, eds (1988). *Cooperative Strategies in International Business.* Lexington, Massachusetts: Lexington Books.

Curhan, Joan P., William H. Davidson and Rajan Suri (1977). *Tracing the Multinationals: A Sourcebook on US-based Enterprise.* Cambridge, Massachusetts: Ballinger Publishing.

Dunning, John H., ed. (1985). *Multinational Enterprises, Economic Structure and International Competitiveness.* New York: John Wiley.

Dunning, John H. (1992). The competitive advantage of countries and the activities of transnational corporations. *Transnational Corporations*, 1, 1 (February), pp. 135–168.

The Economist (1992). Japan's less-than-invincible computer makers. 11 January, pp. 59–60.

Economou, Persphone (1990). Enterprises from Eastern Europe and the USSR. *The CTC Reporter*, 30 (Autumn), pp. 46–47.

Encarnation, Dennis J. (1992). *Rivals Beyond Trade: America versus Japan in Global Competition*, Ithaca, New York: Cornell University Press.

European Commission (1991). *20th Report on Competition Policy.* Brussels, Belgium.

Flowers, E. B. (1976). Oligopolistic reactions in European and Canadian direct investment in the United States. *Journal of International Business Studies*, 7, 2 (Fall–Winter), pp. 43–55.

Franko, Lawrence G. (1976). *The European Multinationals.* New York: Harper and Row.

Fujita, Masataka (1990). TNCs from developing countries. *The CTC Reporter*, 30 (Autumn), pp. 42–45.

Galbraith, Craig S. and Neil M. Kay (1986). Towards a theory of multinational enterprise. *Journal of Economic Behavior and Organization*, 7 (March), pp. 3–19.

Gittelman, Michelle and John H. Dunning (1992). Japanese multinationals in Europe and the United States: some comparisons and contrasts. In *Multinationals in the New Europe and Global Trade*, Michael W. Klein and Paul J. J. Welfens, eds, Berlin: Springer-Verlag, pp. 237–268.

Gomes-Casseres, Benjamin (1989). Joint ventures in the face of global competition. *Sloan Management Review*, 30, 3 (Spring), pp. 17–26.

Goyder, D. G. (1988). *EEC Competition Law.* New York: Clarendon Press.

Graham, Edward M. and Paul R. Krugman (1989). *Foreign Direct Investment in the United States.* Washington, DC: Institute for International Economics.

Grossman, Gene and Elhanan Helpman (1991). *Innovation and Growth in the Global Economy.* Cambridge, Massachusetts: The MIT Press.

Helpman, Elhanan and Paul R. Krugman (1985). *Market Structure and Foreign Trade.* Cambridge, Massachusetts: The MIT Press.

Hexner, Ervin P. (1945). *International Cartels.* Chapel Hill, North Carolina: University of North Carolina Press.

Ito, Takatoshi (1992). *The Japanese Economy.* Cambridge, Massachusetts: The MIT Press.

Jones, G., ed. (1993). *United Nations Library on Transnational Corporations: A Historical Perspective.* London: Routledge.

Kester, W. C. (1991). *Japanese Takeovers: The Global Quest for Corporate Control.* Boston, Massachusetts: Harvard Business School Press.

Knickerbocker, Frederick T. (1973). *Oligopolistic Reaction and Multinational Enterprise.* Boston, Massachusetts: Division of Research, Graduate School of Business Administration, Harvard University.

Kogut, Bruce and Sea Gin Chang (1991). Technological capabilities and Japanese foreign direct investment in the United States. *The Review of Economics and Statistics*, 73, 3 (August), pp. 401–413.

Kojima, Kiyoshi (1978). *Direct Foreign Investment: A Japanese Model of Multinational Business Operations.* London: Croom Helm.

Kreinin, Mordechai E. (1988). How closed is Japan's market? Additional evidence. *The World Economy*, 11, 4 (December), pp. 529–542.

Lall, Sanjaya (1991). Direct investment in South-East Asia by the NIEs: trends and prospects. *Banca Nazionale del Lavore Quarterly Review*, 179 (December), pp. 463–480.

Lewis, Jordan D. (1990). *Partnerships for Profit: Structuring and Managing Strategic Alliances.* New York: The Free Press.

Lipsey, Robert E. (1987). Changing patterns of international investment in and by the United States. Working Paper No. 2240. Cambridge, Massachusetts: National Bureau of Economic Research.

——— (1991). Foreign direct investment in the United States and U.S. trade. *The Annals of the American Academy of Political and Social Science,* 516 (June), pp. 76–90.

——— and Irving B. Kravis (1982). U.S.-owned affiliates and host-country exports. Working Paper No. 1037. Cambridge, Massachusetts: National Bureau of Economic Research.

Lynch, Robert Porter (1989). *The Practical Guide to Joint Ventures and Corporate Alliances.* New York: John Wiley.

Michalet, Charles-Albert (1974). France. In *Big Business and the State*, Raymond Vernon, ed., Cambridge, Massachusetts: Harvard University Press.

Parkhe, Arvinde (1991). Interfirm diversity, organizational learning, and longevity in global strategic alliances. *Journal of International Business Studies*, 22, 4, pp. 579–601.

Schwartz, Jacob T. (1992). America's economic-technological agenda for the 1990s. *Daedalus*, 121, 1 (Winter), pp. 139–165.

Stocking, George W. and Myron W. Watkins (1946). *Cartels in Action: Case Studies in International Business Diplomacy.* New York: 20th Century Fund.

——— (1948). *Cartels or Competition?* New York: 20th Century Fund.

Teece, David J. (1986). Transaction cost economics and the multinational enterprise. *Journal of Economic Behavior and Organization*, 7, 1 (March), pp. 21–45.

——— (1987). Capturing value from technological innovation: integration, strategic partnering and licensing decisions. In *Technology and Global Industry: Companies and Nations in the World Economy*, Bruce R. Guile and Harvey Brooks, eds, Washington, DC: National Academy Press, pp. 65–95.

Transnational Corporations and Management Division, United Nations Department of Economic and Social Development (1992). *World Investment Report 1992: Transnational Corporations as Engines of Growth.* Sales No. E.92.II.A.19.

United Nations Centre on Transnational Corporations (1978). *Transnational Corporations in World Development: A Re-examination.* Sales No. E.78.II.A.5.

———— (1988). *Transnational Corporations in World Development: Trends and Prospects.* Sales No. E.88.II.A.7.

———— (1991). *World Investment Report 1991: The Triad in Foreign Direct Investment.* Sales No. E.91.II.A.12.

United States Congress, Office of Technology Assessment (1991). *Competing Economies: America, Europe and the Pacific Rim.* OTA-ITE-498. Washington, DC: Government Printing Office.

Vaupel, James W. (1971). Study of manufacturing subsidiaries of 180 US-based multinational enterprises as of 1964. Paper presented at June conference, Turin, Italy.

Vernon, Raymond and W. H. Davidson (1979). *Foreign Production of Technology-Intensive Products by U.S.-Based Multinational Enterprises.* Report to the National Science Foundation, No. PB 80 148638.

Wilkins, Mira (1970). *The Emergence of Multinational Enterprise.* Cambridge, Massachusetts: Harvard University Press.

———— (1990). Japanese multinationals in the United States: continuity and change, 1879–1990. *Business History Review*, 64 (Winter), pp. 585–629.

———— and Frank Ernest Hill (1964). *American Business Abroad: Ford on Six Continents.* Detroit, Michigan: Wayne State University Press.

Williamson, Oliver E. (1971). The vertical integration of production: market failure considerations. *American Economic Review*, 61 (May), pp. 112–123.

Yoshino, Michael Y. (1976). *Japan's Multinational Enterprises.* Cambridge, Massachusetts: Harvard University Press.

Yu, C. J. and K. Ito (1988). Oligopolistic reaction and foreign direct investment. *Journal of International Business Studies*, 19, 3 (Fall), pp. 449–460.

3 Foreign direct investment and economic development*

Terutomo Ozawa

Although transnational corporations play the crucial role as transplanters of technology, skills and access to the world market, how they facilitate structural upgrading and economic growth in developing countries has not been adequately conceptualized in terms of a theory of economic development. This article develops a dynamic paradigm of TNC-assisted development by recognizing five key structural characteristics of the global economy as underlying determinants. The phenomena of trade augmentation through foreign direct investment, increasing factor incongruity, and localized (but increasingly transnationalized) learning and technological accumulation are identified as three principles that govern the process of rapid growth in the labour-driven stage of economic development and, eventually, the emergence of TNCs from the developing countries themselves also plays a role in this process.

The theory of foreign direct investment (FDI) has so far been built most extensively around industrial organization economics, the theory of the firm and economics of internalization, with a particular focus on either market structure or the firm as a unit of analysis. Surprisingly, it has not been conceptualized in terms of a theory of economic development (how FDI facilitates structural upgrading and economic growth), despite the crucial role TNCs play as generators and transplanters of technology, skills and linkages to the world market.[1] As John Dunning (1988a, p. 21) phrased it, 'One of the lacunae in the literature on international business is a dynamic approach to its role in economic development'; there is little systematic exposition of 'the impact of (TNC) activity on dynamic comparative advantage'.

* Reprinted from *Transnational Corporations*, vol. 1, no. 1 (February 1992), pp. 27–54.

Many developing countries, especially the Asian newly industrializing countries and the emerging newly industrializing countries (Indonesia, Malaysia and Thailand), and more recently some Latin American countries (especially Brazil, Chile and Mexico), are successfully developing by opening up their economies under outward-oriented policies, albeit in varying degrees. Although outward orientation alone is not a sufficient condition for rapid growth, it does create a climate favourable for the transfer by TNCs – and the absorption by local enterprises – of modern managerial, production and marketing technologies which are the *sine qua non* of industrial modernization. Undoubtedly, TNCs are the prime mover behind the industrial dynamism of those rapidly developing countries. Indeed, they are now increasingly counted upon to duplicate their role as development agents elsewhere in the world, especially in Eastern Europe, which is turning outward by adopting pro-market policies. Moreover, TNCs now originate not only from the advanced countries but also more and more from rapidly growing developing countries, notably the newly industrializing countries (NICs), and those TNCs, especially in manufacturing, are more active in other developing countries than in the advanced countries.

There is thus a definite need to incorporate the recognized developmental functions of TNCs into a theory of open-economy development so as to explain, in one integrated theoretical paradigm, what type of investment activities of TNCs can facilitate a process of industrial upgrading and growth in a developing host country and in what ways; and how the developing country itself, once it gathers momentum for industrialization, is, in turn, induced to create its own TNCs in the wake of such TNC-facilitated economic transformation. The aim of the present article is to move in that direction by integrating the relevant ideas and analytical models into a synthesized framework so as to delineate the causal relationship between the operations and economic development of TNCs, particularly in the early critical stages of transformation in a labour-surplus developing country.

STRUCTURAL CHARACTERISTICS OF THE WORLD ECONOMY

Theories of international economic activities are built on some perceived realities of the world economy. Some basic structural characteristics (SC) need to be analysed for the purpose of constructing a dynamic theory of TNC-facilitated structural upgrading. Five of them are described below:

- SC No. 1 *Inter-economy divergences in supply and demand conditions*

  The individual economies are divergent in their factor endowment and level of technological competence on the supply side, and in consumers' needs and tastes on the demand side.

- SC No. 2 *Firms as creators and traders of intangible assets*

  Individual firms are the major generators, procurers and disseminators of technology, skills and marketing channels.

- SC No. 3 *A hierarchy of economies*

  There is a hierarchy (and sub-hierarchy) of economies, globally as well as regionally, with respect to economic development; 'leader' economies serve as growth centres for a cohort of 'follower' economies. In other words, the individual economies in the world are at various stages of industrial upgrading and per capita income (that is, at different stages of dynamic comparative advantage in terms of levels of technological competence and factor proportions).

- SC No. 4 *Natural (stage-compatible) sequencing of structural upgrading and development*

  The currently advanced economies gradually went through multiple phases of industrial upgrading, each phase compatible with its corresponding factor endowment (capital–labour ratio) and technological capacity, albeit over a long period of time by today's standards. This evolutionary path fits the notion of an optimal sequencing of development starting from the initial stage of labour-intensive, low-skill manufacturing (or from the initial stage of natural resource extraction) and moving on to the subsequent stage of relatively physical capital-intensive industrial activities and finally to the more advanced stage of human capital-intensive growth. When that sequencing is allowed to develop, evolutionary forces are set in motion to improve steadily the country's industrial structure, step by step, in the most orderly manner.

- SC No. 5 *A strong trend away from inward-looking and towards outward-looking orientation in trade and investment policy, but simultaneously an increasing recognition that Government, though it should deregulate and privatize economic activities so as to unleash the vitality of the private sector, can play a positive role in augmenting the market system*

There are basically two types of trade and investment regimes: an outward-looking, export-oriented (OL–EO) type, and inward-looking, import-substituting (IL–IS) type. But their features are often combined to produce a hybrid regime, though it still can be identified as either more strongly or weakly characterized by one approach. It is now widely recognized that OL–EO is more effective than IL–IS in achieving a faster growth and structural upgrading in the developing countries. Many of the developing countries, once enamoured of IL–IS under economic nationalism, are switching to OL–EO. This new *zeitgeist* is a powerful force for rapid changes in international economic relations. At the same time, the crucial role that Governments can play in supporting the competitive market to assist the development of export industries and structural upgrading is increasingly recognized.

CONVENTIONAL THEORIES OF INTERNATIONAL BUSINESS AND STRUCTURAL CHARACTERISTICS

From time immemorial, different regions have been exchanging goods with each other, enriching themselves in the process. The predominant basis for trade has been interregional divergences in supplies of primary factors, technological and climatic conditions and patterns of demand (SC No. 1). It was indeed against the supply side of this structural feature alone that first Adam Smith and then David Ricardo set out to theorize the phenomenon of trade and its benefits. Smith introduced the doctrine of absolute advantage, which is built on the economies of scale realizable from an extended market through exports, while Ricardo constructed the doctrine of comparative advantage, which is enhanced by specialization-induced allocative efficiency. The Heckscher–Ohlin theory, too, was founded on the *uneven* distribution of factors of production among countries. All of those trade theories assume the international immobility of factors (hence, the permanence of SC No. 1), partly because of the informational and socio-psychological costs of transactions involved in transferring them[2] and, perhaps more importantly, for the sake of analysing trade alone.

The conventional trade theories thus capture international exchanges of commodities basically as *arbitrage* operations that exploit and profit from any differentials in price and availability of commodities between different locations, the differentials being determined by productivity and factor endowments. Moreover, all of those conventional trade theories treat firms as if they were non-existent because of the usual assumption of perfect competition; hence no firm-specific advantage is permissible. What matters is the country-specific features that bring about discrepancies in pre-trade commodity prices among countries. That is to say, those conventional theories are constructed against the background of SC No. 1 alone.

The theory of FDI as it has derived from Stephen Hymer's seminal work (1976) explicitly recognizes and, indeed, places in the spotlight the existence of firm-specific assets (SC No. 2). In other words, FDI draws on the role of firms as creators and exploiters of intangible corporate assets. Hence it is no longer logical to assume perfect competition. FDI is viewed to take place only in imperfect markets. It is, moreover, the firm, not the country, that is the *real actor* motivated to trade intangible assets across national borders.

But the basis for FDI resides not only at the level of individual firms, but also at the level of regions or countries; that is, SC No. 2 should be related back to SC No. 1. Paul Krugman (1990, p. 83), for example, relates firm-level variables to country-level variables:

> multinational enterprise occurs whenever there exist related activities for which the following is true: There are *simultaneously transaction cost incentives to integrate these activities within a single firm and factor cost or other incentives to separate the activities geographically.*
>
> Suppose, for example, there is a two-stage product process consisting of a capital-intensive upstream activity and a labour-intensive downstream activity and that (for any of the usual causes) there are compelling reasons to combine these activities inside vertically integrated firms. Suppose further that countries are sufficiently different in factor endowments that, unless these activities are geographically separated, there will be unequal factor prices. Then the result will clearly be the emergence of firms that extend across national boundaries. (Emphasis added.)

As is well known, this way of explaining the emergence of TNCs has long been stated in Dunning's eclectic paradigm (1981b, 1988b), in which the necessary triumvirate conditions for international production are specified: (a) the firm must possess some ownership-specific advantages; (b) to exploit those advantages, internalization (local production under equity ownership) is more beneficial to the firm than arm's-length transactions (exporting and licensing, for example); and (c) overseas locational factors are more favourable than domestic ones. Dunning was among the first who started to combine SC No. 2 and SC No. 1 in theorizing the direct investment of TNCs.

Raymond Vernon's product-life-cycle theory of trade and investment (1966) explicitly brings in SC No. 3, namely a hierarchy of economies, as an additional factor. New products are initially introduced in a high-income country, notably in the United States during the 1950s and 1960s, but will eventually spread to the world, first to other advanced countries, but later to the developing countries, in a trickle-down fashion as the products mature and become technologically standardized. It is a dynamic model of changing comparative advantage and technology transfers. Yet how the transfer of standardized production affects the economic development and structure of the developing host countries is outside the explanatory property of the model. It is a model constructed from the perspective of an innovating advanced country.

TOWARDS A DYNAMIC PARADIGM OF DEVELOPMENT FACILITATED BY TNCs

Any developing country, if it is serious about raising its standard of living, must open its economy so as to avail itself of opportunities to trade, interact with and learn from the already advanced. In fact, ever since the industrial revolution in England, industrialization in the rest of the world, wherever successful, has been a 'derived' phenomenon. Continental Europe succeeded by following the United Kingdom's footsteps through commercial contracts and conscious efforts for learning and emulation (Landes, 1969). So did the United States: 'America started off as a copier' (Thurow, 1985).[3] Likewise, Japan's economic miracles in both the pre- and post-Second World War periods have been based on that mechanism of learning and emulation.

A process of learning and emulation necessarily means the existence of a hierarchy of economies in terms of stages of economic development and national wealth (SC No. 3), *a structure that creates opportunities for the less developed to emulate the advanced – and for the advanced to transfer their knowledge and skills down the hierarchy.* The advanced countries are the rich reservoirs of industrial technology, information and experiences which the followers can tap. They also provide the promising export markets from which the less developed can earn precious hard currencies. As Adam Smith observed (1776/1908, p. 378), 'A nation that would enrich itself by foreign trade is certainly most likely to do so when its neighbours are all *rich and industrious*' (emphasis added). Nowadays, those trading and learning opportunities are all the more enhanced, because the advanced countries themselves take the initiative to make use of hierarchical relations by way of the activities of their TNCs and their official economic and technical assistance.

But to exploit those *hierarchical externalities* fully (positive externalities emanating from SC No. 3), a developing country must *align its pattern of comparative advantage and its stage of development with advanced countries*. That is to say, a stages-compatible order of sequencing structural upgrading (SC No. 4) needs to be achieved. For the sequence of development should not be jumbled as is the case with the IL–IS approach; the process needs to be organized step by step, and stage by stage, in an evolutionary fashion along the lines demonstrated in the past by the currently advanced countries. This means that, when a country is still scarce in human and physical capital but abundant in labour (unskilled and semi-skilled), any attempt to build a capital-intensive, skill-requiring industry is ineffective and unachievable. Such a country must first focus on introducing labour-intensive industries to employ its most abundant factor. After all, economic development is characterized by the steady accumulation of physical and human capital, which produces the sequential pattern of dynamic comparative advantage in any market-based, growing economy. Such a path assures *compatibility* between the factor intensities and technological requirements of the economic activities pursued at a particular stage and the domestic availability of appropriate factors and technological capacity.

Indeed, it was Adam Smith (1776/1908) who emphasized the importance of 'a natural order of things' in the developmental sequence of an economy (the 'natural progress of opulence'). He envisaged intersectoral complementarities (first, between 'town' and 'country', between agriculture and manufacturing, and then, later, between manufacturing and foreign trade) and the accumulation of capital and the development of political/technological/organizational capacities ('order and good government' and the natural progression of manufactures from the 'necessities' to the 'conveniences' and to the 'elegancies of life') (pp. 290–314).

In that regard, the 'stages theory of competitive development' recently introduced by Michael Porter (1990) deserves special attention. He maintains that, 'despite the diversity of most economies, we can identify a predominant or emergent pattern in the nature of competitive advantage in a nation's firms at a particular time' (p. 545) by way of four distinct stages: (i) factor-driven, (ii) investment-driven, (iii) innovation-driven, and (iv) wealth-driven. But (Porter, 1990, p. 546) 'the first three stages involve successive upgrading of a nation's competitive advantages and will normally be associated with progressively rising economic prosperity', while 'the fourth stage is one of drift and ultimately decline'.

The factor-driven stage (akin to Smith's agriculture-first phase) is characterized either by natural-resource-based activities (primary extraction) or by labour-intensive manufacturing. The investment-driven stage, on the other hand, is associated with the manufacturing of intermediate and capital goods (heavy and chemical industrialization) and infrastructural building (housing, transportation, communications and public works construction). The innovation-driven stage arrives when a country is human-capital abundant and active in research and development (R&D). Most developing countries are in the factor-driven stage, and some are already well on their way to the investment-driven stage.

It is important to keep in mind that *a particular stage of competitive development is associated with a particular pattern of export competitiveness*. The factor-driven stage is related to factor-based trade advantages (in either primary goods or labour-intensive goods), the investment-driven stage to scale-based advantages (in large-scale, capital-intensive goods), and the innovation-driven stage to R&D-based advantages (in high-tech manufactures). Thus economic growth and transformation is accompanied by the changing patterns of dynamic comparative advantage.

Interestingly enough, moreover, *the pattern (nature and direction) of FDI, both inward and outward, changes* pari passu *with the structural transformation of the economy*. For example, the beginning of the factor-driven stage attracts resource-seeking or labour-seeking inward FDI. The transition from the labour-driven to the investment-driven stage generates outward investments towards lower-wage countries in labour-intensive manufacturing (and in resource extraction abroad, particularly if the economy happens to be natural-resource scarce) and attracts inward investments in capital and intermediate goods industries. Similarly, the transition from the investment-driven to the innovation-driven stage brings about *simultaneously* inward investments in technology-intensive industries and outward investments in intermediate goods industries. This orderly flow of investment tends to occur as long as the country pursues an unjumbled 'progress of opulence'.

As shown in Figure 3.1, those stages can be distinguished in terms of the changing endowment proportions of three major factors used in

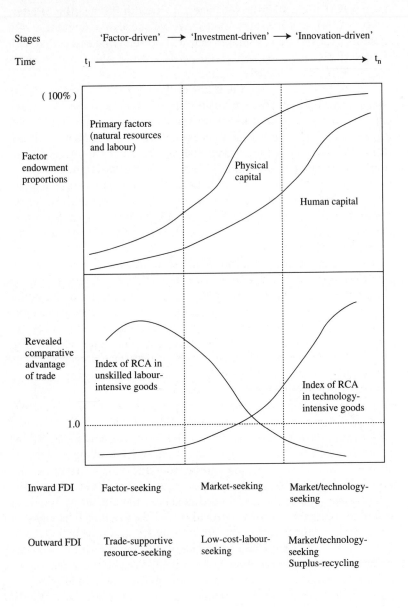

Figure 3.1 Stages of development, changing factor proportions and dynamic comparative advantage

a nation's overall industrial activity: resources (both natural and labour), physical capital and human capital. In other words, the nation grows by upgrading its structure as its factor and technological endowments change with the accumulation of physical and human capital (relative to resources): *the higher the per capita gross national product (GNP), the larger the per capita stock of physical and human capital relative to that of resources and the larger the per capita stock of human capital relative to that of physical capital.* The economy continuously evolves to develop new comparative advantages by shifting from technologically less sophisticated, low-productivity products to more sophisticated, higher-productivity industrial activities (analogous to Smith's sequence of 'necessities–conveniences–elegancies'). For example, this changing pattern of dynamic comparative advantage may be measured in terms of an index of the revealed comparative advantage in unskilled labour-intensive goods and an index of the revealed comparative advantage in physical/human capital-intensive goods as schematically illustrated in the figure. At the same time, different stages-based patterns of FDI, both inward and outward, appear over a certain span of time, a span determined by how rapidly a given economy industrializes, as outlined.

Indeed, the stages-based evolutionary progression of FDI has been most clearly demonstrated by Japan's rapid post-war structural transformation and its concomitant FDI. As elaborated elsewhere (Ozawa, 1991a, 1991b, 1991c), Japan's industrial structure has so far metamorphosed in three continuous stages, accompanied by different stages-specific patterns of FDI – and is currently undergoing the latest, fourth, stage:

Phase I: Expansion of labour-intensive manufacturing in textiles, sundries and other low-wage goods (what may be called 'Heckscher–Ohlin industries') (1950 to the mid-1960s).

Accompanied by selective imports of capital goods (embodied technology) and purchase of licensing agreements (disembodied technology), and followed by the 'elementary (low-wage labour-seeking)' type of FDI in standardized, labour-intensive industries in the neighbouring Asian countries (starting in the late 1950s, but notably after the mid-1960s and growing strongly, especially after the revaluations of the yen in the early 1970s).

Phase II: Scale-economies-based modernization of heavy and

chemical industries, such as steel, shipbuilding, petrochemicals and synthetic fibres ('non-differentiated
Smithian industries') (the late 1950s to the early 1970s).

Accompanied by the incessant adoption and adaptation of advanced Western technology, mostly through
licensing but also via joint ventures (inward FDI) in
petrochemicals, machinery and chemicals, and the 'resource-seeking' (later followed by the 'house-cleaning')
type of outward FDI in resource-extractive and processing industries (most actively throughout the 1960s and
1970s).

Phase III: Assembly-based mass production of consumer durables,
such as automobiles and electric/electronics goods ('differentiated industries') (the late 1960s to the present).

Continuous adaptation of, and improvement on,
imported technology and stepped-up domestic R&D,
and accompanied by the 'export-substituting-cum-sur-
plus-recycling' type of outward FDI in overseas assembly operations in automobiles, electronics and related
parts and components, as well as banking and finance
(especially after the Plaza Accord of 1985), most
actively in the United States and Europe.

Phase IV: Mechatronics-based flexible manufacturing, small-lot,
multi-variety production, along with innovations in
HDTV, new materials, fine chemicals, advanced micro-
chips and opto-electronics ('Schumpeterian industries')
(the early 1980s onwards).

Hosting inward FDI in chemicals, pharmaceuticals and
machinery, and generating the 'triadization' type of outward FDI in which Japanese TNCs are establishing the
intraregional clusters of integrated operations and strategic alliances in the Americas, Europe and the Pacific
Rim.

The Japanese experience thus delineates the *close interrelatedness*
between structural upgrading, dynamic comparative advantage and
FDI, along the paths of its physical/human-capital-intensive factor
endowment and technological progress. Because of the rapidity of
Japan's economic transformation, its structural progression (from
the 'H–O industries' to the 'non-differentiated Smithian industries', to the 'differentiated Smithian industries', and finally to the
'Schumpeterian industries') actually retraces, in a highly time-com-

pressed fashion, the evolutionary changes previously experienced by the advanced Western countries over a much longer span of time. And international business is *the main cause* of this structural growth acceleration.

Indeed, there have been a number of empirical studies made on the relationship between a nation's changing pattern of comparative advantage in manufactured goods and the accumulation of physical and human capital.

Bela Balassa's study (1979/1989, p. 26), for example, concluded that:

> The empirical estimates show that inter-country differences in the structure of exports are in a large part explained by differences in physical and human capital endowments. The results lend support to the 'stages' approach to comparative advantage, according to which the structure of exports changes with the accumulation of physical and human capital. The approach is also supported by inter-temporal comparison for Japan, which indicates that Japanese exports have become increasingly physical capital and human-capital-intensive over time.

He then extracted (p. 26) some important policy implications:

> To begin with, [those findings] warn against distorting the system of incentives in favour of products in which the country has a comparative disadvantage. The large differences shown among product categories in terms of their capital intensity point to the fact that there is a substantial penalty for such distortions in the form of the misallocation of product factors. This will be the case in particular when the system of incentives is biased in favour of import substitution in capital-intensive products and against exports in labour-intensive products.

These types of distortions are naturally reduced when a developing country pursues an OL–EO strategy of development rather than an IL–IS one (SC No. 5). And it has been empirically and amply proved, and now accepted as an axiom, that the OL–EO approach is far superior to its IL–IS counterpart in growth performance and industrial upgrading in the developing countries, for the former allows efficacious market-guided evolutionary forces to operate at maximum efficiency.

In short, those structural characteristics of the global economy (SC Nos 3, 4 and 5) that have not been explicitly reckoned with as determinants in the conventional theories of FDI constitute a new global environment highly conducive to an expansion of trade, FDI, knowledge transfer and economic growth, a climate significantly favourable for TNCs. Those characteristics have to be brought into analysis as explanatory factors in an effort to construct a theory of FDI in the field of economic development.

COMPARATIVE-ADVANTAGE-AUGMENTING TYPE OF FOREIGN DIRECT INVESTMENT

Throughout the present article, the term FDI is used in a very broad sense: it is meant to describe the transfer of *development ingredients* of all sorts by TNCs (that is, intangible corporate assets, finance and links with global markets) in *both* the traditional form of investment (whole or majority equity ownership) and 'new' forms (minority ownership and a variety of non-equity contractual arrangements, such as licensing, managerial contracts and turnkey operations (Oman, 1984).

What is crucial for outward-looking, export-based development is that FDI needs to be approached in such a manner that the developing countries' existing or potential comparative advantage can be fostered and fully maximized, that is in a comparative-advantage-augmenting fashion. Here, the notion of pro-trade FDI (and that of anti-trade FDI) introduced by Kojima (1975) is quite relevant. Kojima's macro-economic theory of FDI (Kojima, 1975; Kojima and Ozawa, 1984) is built on two key propositions. One is the Ricardian doctrine of comparative advantage, the other his own proposition as a supplement:

Proposition I: Countries gain from trade and maximize economic welfare when they export comparatively advantaged goods and import comparatively disadvantaged goods.

Proposition II: Countries gain *even more* from an expanded basis for trade when intangible assets are transplanted from the home countries' comparatively disadvantaged industries on to the host countries' comparatively advantaged ones (both current and potential).

The second proposition indicates a mutually beneficial type of FDI that parallels the mutually gainful type of trade posited in the first proposition. Ricardo built his trade model on the assumed immobility of factors (hence the persistence of SC No. 1). Furthermore, he thought that, even if factor movement occurred, it would be of the anti-trade type – and for that matter, indeed, of the hollowing-out type (Ricardo, 1817/1888, p. 77):

> It would undoubtedly be advantageous to the capitalists of England, and to the consumers in both countries, that under [the circumstances of higher labour and productivity in Portugal in absolute terms] the wine and the cloth should *both* be made in Portugal, and therefore that the capital and labour of England employed in making cloth should be removed to Portugal for that purpose. (Emphasis added.)

Thus, once factor mobility is admitted, Portugal alone ends up producing *both* goods; hence there would be no basis for trade. The end result is that Portugal flourishes, whereas England is hollowed out and languishes. Surprisingly enough, however, it did not occur to Ricardo that if, *instead of* moving to Portugal 'the capital and labour of England employed in making cloth', Portugal's secret (technology) of higher productivity in cloth is transferred to England through FDI, not only is England saved from hollowing out, but also both nations can prosper *even more*, since England's comparative advantage in cloth is now *enhanced* by such technology transfers. More surprisingly, Ricardo resorted to the doctrine of absolute advantage when it came to factor movement.

Kojima's distinction between pro-trade FDI and anti-trade FDI is criticized as 'normative' (Gray, 1985), but it can be converted into 'positive' analysis when it is combined with the structural characteristics of Nos 3, 4 and 5, since the comparative-advantage-oriented policy of market-friendly OL–EO economies is such that pro-trade FDI rather than anti-trade FDI will be automatically attracted to such a regime. The IL–IS regimes set up in labour-surplus, capital-scarce developing countries are the ones that attract anti-trade FDI into their highly protected, stage-incompatible, import-substituting industries. The phenomenon of a comparative-advantage expansion made possible by FDI in the OL–EO regimes will hereafter be identified as trade augmentation through FDI.

OUTWARD ORIENTATION AND SUPERGROWTH IN THE INITIALLY LABOUR-SURPLUS DEVELOPING COUNTRIES

The income growth effect envisaged in the static Ricardian model of trade (which allows no transfer of factors and no structural change) can be summarized as follows:

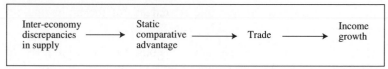

According to Ricardo, as gains from trade are realized through specialization and reallocation of resources into comparatively advantaged industries (that is, attainment of allocative efficiency), national income rises, but no outward shift of the country's production possibility curve occurs because there is *neither* factor growth *nor* technological progress. The whole purpose of the Ricardian model is to show the basis for, the direction of, and gains from, trade and nothing more.

Yet this *static* model can be transformed into a *dynamic* structural upgrading model once the role of TNCs as a facilitator of industrial transformation and the additional set of structural characteristics are explicitly brought into analysis as causative factors.

Economic development under OL–EO policy is a function of dynamic comparative advantage, but here the magnitude of comparative advantage is not only determined by SC No. 1 alone, but also enhanced – and upgraded – by the confluence of SC Nos 2, 3, 4 and 5. This is *a dynamic paradigm of FDI-facilitated development* (hereafter called the dynamic paradigm) which depicts the *magnified* power of trade as an engine for growth. The power of trade is magnified because (i) a strong outward orientation reduces market distortions and encourages competition; (ii) the basis for trade is expanded by comparative-advantage-augmenting (CAA) FDI (inward as well as outward), and hence a greater expansion of trade; and (iii) self-propelling market forces are set in motion to upgrade the country's industrial composition towards higher value-added sectors in an 'unjumbled' manner, given a market-friendly environment (including incentives and supportive infrastructure) by the Government. The net result is a supergrowth of OL–EO economies accompanied by rapid structural upgrading, the type of 'economic miracles' exhibited by the Asian newly industrialized countries (NICs). A high correlation between outward orientation and supergrowth has been empirically confirmed in many situations (Balassa, 1989; World Bank, 1991). But the causative links between those two phenomena are still left unexplained. One possible growth mechanism is suggested for this black box:

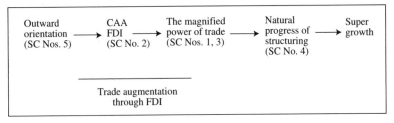

More specifically, how this scenario unfolds itself over a time period, say from t_1 to t_5, can be explained in terms of the dynamic paradigm. Consider a typical developing country that is initially plagued with high unemployment and low income (Figure 3.2).

(t_1) A labour-abundant developing country (with high unemployment and underemployment) adopts an outward-looking, export-focused path of development (SC No. 5), thereby reducing market distortions and setting free the market forces for stage-compatible economic activities. A market-friendly economic system thus emerges with a strong outward orientation towards trade and investment interactions with advanced countries. The country thus stands to benefit from the *hierarchical externalities* (SC No. 3).

(t_2) This initial condition attracts inward FDI in standardized labour-intensive manufacturing activities, that is in a comparative-advantage-augmenting fashion (in a direction conducive to trade augmentation through FDI). At the start, the developing host country usually supplies labour from its unemployed (mostly urban) and underemployed (mostly rural) labour pool at low wage rates (a process well postulated by Arthur Lewis (1954) in his model of unlimited labour supply). TNCs, often in joint ventures with local interests, are able to develop export-oriented manufacturing without generating upward pressure on local wages, although they usually pay a real wage rate higher than the local average, especially in fringe benefits (for example, lunches, basic health care and training). Low wages are the basis for price competitiveness. Exports are mostly of the intra-firm type, either purchased as intermediate goods by the investing TNCs or marketed through the distribution channels of TNCs (on the theoretical level, that phase of export growth corresponds to the Smithian 'vent-for-surplus' phenomenon (Myint, 1958).

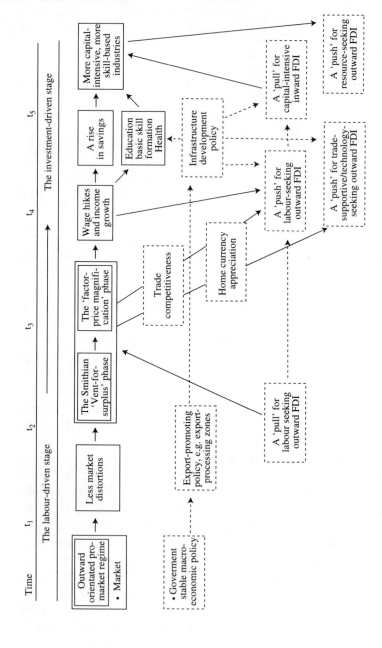

Figure 3.2 Outward orientation, FDI-magnified trade competitiveness and structural upgrading in a developing country

(t_3) But the more labour-seeking FDI flows in, the sooner the disappearance of unemployment, if not underemployment. Upward pressures on wages appear, and local wages begin to rise (that is, the Lewisian phase of unlimited labour supply ends along with the Smithian 'vent-for-surplus' phenomenon, and the 'factor-price-magnification' effect (Stolper and Samuelson, 1941) now takes over, as long as labour utilization continues to be pursued under OL–EO policy).

(t_4) The rising wages and the increasing availability of jobs, though still in low-productivity (hence low-wage by international standards) sectors, will result in a rapid rise in national income and an expansion of domestic markets. Wage rates are still low, but all family members (not only the traditional breadwinner, the father, but also the mother and their adolescent children) who seek employment can find jobs; hence a rise in family income.[4]

Given the appropriate incentives (for example, attractive interest rates on deposits, tax exemptions and hard-currency-denominated deposits), this increased household income can generate domestic savings.[5] Employment also leads to basic skill formation via training and a stronger desire to upgrade skills, a higher motivation for learning. The country's factor endowment begins to change from low-skilled labour abundance to a relatively more capital abundance and a greater skill accumulation.

As a consequence, a *factor incongruity* emerges soon between the hitherto promoted export industries (whose competitiveness depends on a high input ratio of low-wage, unskilled labour to capital) and the country's changing factor endowment (which now becomes less and less unskilled-labour abundant). This is an ineluctable outcome of the labour-driven process of development and may be called *the principle of increasing factor incongruity*. Those grassroots developments (improved job opportunities, rising wages, increased household savings and the desire to seek education and upgrade one's skills) are crucial in shifting the country's factor endowment towards more human- and physical-capital abundance, endogenously paving the way to the next phase of investment-driven industrialization.

As wages rise, the country's comparative advantage in labour-intensive industries naturally wanes. Given the macroeconomic stability that ensures a competitive exchange rate for the country's currency at the start of economic development, the more successful labour-intensive exports are (that is, the greater the improvement in the country's balance-of-payments conditions), the greater the chances that the currency will begin to appreciate. Higher wages and the appreciated currency thus render low-productivity, labour-intensive industries less competitive, compelling domestic industry to move into higher value-added, more capital-intensive sectors. At that point, in order to protect their hard-won export markets, local entrepreneurs, as well as TNCs, begin to transplant their existing operations to other developing countries where they can still find a supply of low-wage labour. Of course, those local firms that succeed in moving upmarket (via an introduction of labour-saving measures and new higher value-added varieties, or moving into a more capital-intensive industry) may remain at home.

This is an interesting – and seemingly paradoxical – turn of events: *a once highly labour abundant (hence low-wage) developing country itself has metamorphosed, over a relatively short span of time, into an active foreign investor, seeking lower-wage labour in other developing countries.*[6] Its firms now possess their own advantages and experiences freshly gained over the period of from t_1 to t_4 (SC No. 2), mostly through the 'apprenticeship' of firms to foreign technical assistance (Amsden, 1989, p. 20). The Japanese, back in the 1950s, 1960s, and 1970s, and more recently the Asian NICs have amply demonstrated the capability of followers to come up with their situation-specific improvements on imported technology as well as their own innovations. This may be called *localized learning and technological accumulation* (Lall, 1983; Stiglitz, 1987; Cantwell and Tolentino, 1990) and has been emphasized by Cantwell and Tolentino (1990) as the key determinant of FDI from developing countries. That becomes even more relevant in the later stages of development that are increasingly characterized by a growing abundance of human capital.

What is more, the momentum of learning in both production and marketing skills continues and even takes the form of technology-seeking, information-gathering and trade-supportive outward investment in advanced countries. Thus 'localized learning' now actually turns to more and more 'internationalized learning'.

Increasing factor incongruity is also observed as primary resource-seeking outward investment and is induced in search of secure supplies of natural resources abroad. In particular, as a natural-resource-indigent 'Ricardian' economy experiences rapid industrialization, it inevitably becomes more and more dependent on overseas resources (Ozawa, 1987). This incongruity between the resource requirements of the economy and its own endowments (and hence the rising vulnerability of dependence on imported industrial resources) can only be dealt with by means of FDI in resource-extractive industries abroad so as to secure long-term supply bases. All this outward FDI is fully compatible with and supportive of the evolving pattern of comparative advantage, enhancing the basis for trade (that is, trade augmentation through FDI is in operation).

(t_5) By now, the country is on the threshold of the investment-driven stage in which more physical-capital and more skill-intensive industries are to be built; it may not be long before the country is classified as a newly industrialized country. To build higher value-added, more scale-dependent industries, the role of the Government becomes even more crucial in providing physical infrastructural facilities, education, public health, R&D incentives and other 'public goods'. As compared with the labour-driven stage, which can be left largely to the dictates of the market with the minimum selective involvement of Government, the development of more advanced industries entails an appropriate management of external-ities (market imperfections), since education and training (which are the causes of positive externalities) are now the key industrial inputs, along with the mimimum scale of operation required by indivisible capital investments and the accompanying economies of scale. The Government is thus called upon to provide the stage-appropriate institutions and infrastructural investments to sup-port dynamic comparative advantage (Ozawa, 1987; Dunning, 1988a, 1991; World Bank, 1991).

Although the above scenario is presented in a highly stylized fashion, it nevertheless fits very nicely with the recent experience of Asian newly industrialized countries, which have been skilfully taking advantage of *both* inward and outward FDI as catalysts of industrial transformation. In fact, they are already in the midst of investment-driven industrialization or even at the beginning of innovation-driven growth in some sectors.

In this stages-theoretic framework of analysis, it is often said that Asian NICs are following the footsteps of Japan, and that emerging NICs (Indonesia, Malaysia, the Philippines and Thailand) are, in turn, duplicating the experiences of NICs and that others (Bangladesh, China, India, Pakistan and Sri Lanka) are about to repeat the same labour-driven episode. That sequential pattern of development in the Asian-Pacific region is often referred to as 'a wild-geese flying formation' (after the phrase introduced by Kaname Akamatsu in 1935[7]). But Japan itself has been closely emulating the West in its effort to catch up and take over – and has very quickly succeeded in going through the first three stages described by Porter, thereby emerging as a high advanced economy. Japan's rapid industrial transformation in the period following the Second World War discussed earlier illustrates the efficacy of a stages-based 'progress of opulence' and may serve as an important paradigm for developing countries.

The wild-geese flying formation or a stage-based development can alleviate the 'fallacy of composition' problem of OL–EO industrialization: if the developing countries adopt the OL–EO approach all at once, will there be enough export markets? As Bela Balassa (1989, p. 28) succinctly phrased it:

> The stages approach to comparative advantage . . . permits one to dispel certain misapprehensions as regards the foreign demand constraint for manufactured exports under which developing countries are said to operate. With countries progressing on the comparative advantage scale, their exports can supplant the exports of countries that graduate to a high level.'

TNCs are no doubt the facilitators of that type of *market recycling* as they are able to shift manufacturing activities from one location to another, in a fashion compatible with the prevailing factor and technological endowments of the economies of host countries, within a hierarchy of economies (SC No. 3).

CONCLUSIONS

Although the functions of TNCs as providers of technology, management expertise, finance and links with the world market have often been mentioned, the role of their FDI in industrial upgrading and growth has not been incorporated into a theory of outward-oriented economic development. The dynamic paradigm presented here recognizes five crucial structural characteristics of the world economy as explanatory factors. Those structural features fall under the rubric of the environment–system–policy frame of analysis proposed by John Dunning (1988a). Hence, the dynamic paradigm may be construed as one detailed structural model of this genre.

Focusing on the case of a representative developing country, that is an initially labour-surplus economy, the dynamic paradigm traces out the *intertemporal* sequence of interactions between FDI (first inward and, later, outward) and structural transformation, a sequence that results in an evanescent pattern of comparative advantage during the course of labour-driven industrialization. That is the stage from which the Asian NICs have just graduated, and which many other developing countries are expected to go through in their early phase of development.

The operational mechanism of the dynamic paradigm so far rests on three basic principles: those of trade augmentation through FDI (according to Kojima, 1975), of increasing factor incongruity and of localized (but increasingly transnationalized, at least in part) learning and technological accumulation (according to Cantwell and Tolentino, 1990). Some more conceptual work is needed to explore the investment-driven and the innovation-driven stages in order to complete the stages theory of TNC-facilitated growth in its entirety. No doubt the demand-side factors play a greater and greater role as development proceeds to later stages. This evolutionary aspect of demand needs to be explicitly conceptualized. Perhaps what may be tentatively called the principle of catch-up in income and increasing diversity in tastes is a relevant consideration. In that regard, the Japanese experience, which encompasses all the developmental stages from the factor driven to the innovation driven in a highly condensed time-capsule, may serve as an important guidepost. Yet such a comprehensive analysis requires far more space than is available in the present article. Only the first dimension has been elaborated, which is none the less the most relevant to the role of TNCs as 'jump-starters' for economic development.

NOTES

1 There are several important works that touch on some key developmental aspects of FDI by treating it either as an agent of economic growth or as a function of such growth (Dunning, 1981a, 1988a; Dunning and Cantwell, 1990; Tolentino, 1993; Cantwell and Tolentino, 1990; Kojima, 1975; Kojima and Ozawa, 1985; Ozawa, 1979, 1991a, 1991b, 1991c). But those works are still tangential to the dynamic (intertemporal) process of structural transformation in developing host countries and do not yet constitute a well-structured *sui generis* theory of TNC-facilitated economic development.

2 For example, Smith (1776/1908, p. 291) observed: '[the fortune] of the trader who is obliged frequently to commit it, not only to the winds and the waves, but to the more uncertain elements of human folly and injustice, by giving great credits in distant countries to men, with whose character and situation he can seldom be thoroughly acquainted.' Ricardo (1817/1888, p. 77) also stated: 'Experience . . . shows that the fancied or real insecurity of capital, when not under the immediate control of its owner, together with the natural disinclination which every man has to quit the country of his birth and connections, and intrust himself, with all his habits fixed, to a strange government and new laws, check the emigration of capital.'

3 Thurow (1985, p. 1) continues: 'New England's textile mills hired

craftsmen (we would now call them engineers) who had worked in, or toured, the British textile mills and had memorized or written down enough of what they had seen to copy those mills in the New World. American history school books remember this copying as a good example of Yankee ingenuity. British history school books see it in another light: as theft. America stole British technology.'

4 The rapid build-up of the garment industry in Bangladesh provides an interesting example: 'Women who never worked before are earning between $40 and $55 a month – far above the projected 1991 national per capita income of $202 a year. Many of these women's husbands, meanwhile, can get work only as day labourers or rickshaw drivers, earning around $1 a day.' *The Wall Street Journal*, 6 August 1991, p. A8.

5 Balassa (1989) points out a strong correlation between export growth and domestic savings. What is argued in this article suggests one causal link.

6 For recent stories on TNCs from developing countries, see, for example, Fujita (1990), Cantwell and Tolentino (1990), and Tolentino (1993).

7 See Akamatsu (1961). The interaction between TNCs and the flying-geese formation is explored in Ozawa (1990).

REFERENCES

Akamatsu, Kaname (1961). A theory of unbalanced growth in the world economy. *Weltwirtschaftliches Archiv*, 86, pp. 196–217.

Amsden, Alice H. (1989). *Asia's Next Giant: South Korea and Late Industrialization*. Oxford: Oxford University Press.

Balassa, Bela (1979/1989). The changing pattern of comparative advantage in manufactured goods. *Review of Economics and Statistics*, 61 (May), pp. 259–266. As reproduced in *Comparative Advantage, Trade Policy and Economic Development*. New York: New York University Press.

——— (1989). *New Directions in the World Economy*. New York: New York University Press.

Cantwell, John A. (1989). *Technological Innovation and Multinational Corporations*. Oxford: Basil Blackwell.

——— and Paz Estrella E. Tolentino (1990). *Technological Accumulation and Third World Multinationals*. Discussion Paper No. 139, Department of Economics, University of Reading, Series B, III.

Dunning, John H. (1981a). Explaining the international direct investment position of countries: Toward a dynamic or developmental approach. *Weltwirtschaftliches Archiv*, 11, pp. 30–64.

——— (1981b). *International Production and the Multinational Enterprise*. London: George Allen & Unwin.

——— (1988a). *Multinationals, Technology and Competitiveness*. London: Unwin Hyman.

——— (1988b). *Explaining International Production*. London: Unwin Hyman.

——— (1991). Governments–markets–firms: towards a new balance? *The CTC Reporter*, 31 (Spring), pp. 2–7.

——— and John A. Cantwell (1990). The changing role of multinational enterprises in the international creation, transfer and diffusion of technology. In *Technology Diffusion and Economic Growth: International and National Policy Perspectives*, F. Arcangeli, P. A. David and G. Dosi, eds, Oxford: Oxford University Press.

Fujita, Masataka (1990). TNCs from developing countries. *The CTC Reporter*, 30 (Autumn), pp. 42–45.

Gray, Peter H. (1985). Multinational corporations and global welfare: an extension of Kojima and Ozawa. *Hitotsubashi Journal of Economics*, 26 (December), pp. 125–133.

Hymer, Stephen (1976). *The International Operations of National Firms.* Cambrdige, Massachusetts: The MIT Press.

Kojima, Kiyoshi (1975). International trade and foreign investment: substitutes or complements. *Hitotsubashi Journal of Economics*, 16 (June), pp. 1–12.

———— and Terutomo Ozawa (1984). Micro- and macro-economic models of direct foreign investment: toward a synthesis. *Hitotsubashi Journal of Economics*, 25 (June), pp. 1–20.

———— (1985). Toward a theory of industrial restructuring and dynamic comparative advantage. *Hitotsubashi Journal of Economics*, 26 (December), pp. 135–145.

Krugman, Paul (1990). *Rethinking International Trade*, Cambridge, Massachusetts: The MIT Press.

Lall, Sanjaya (1983). Multinationals from India. In *The New Multinationals*, Sanjaya Lall, ed., Chichester: John Wiley & Sons, pp. 21–87.

Landes, David S. (1969). *The Unbound Prometheus.* Cambridge: Cambridge University Press.

Lewis, W. Arthur (1954). Economic development with unlimited supplies of labour. *The Manchester School of Economic and Social Studies*, 12 (May), pp. 139–191.

Myint, Hla (1958). The 'classical theory' of international trade and the underdeveloped countries. *Economic Journal*, 68 (June), pp. 317–337.

Oman, Charles (1984). *New Forms of International Investment in Developing Countries.* Paris: OECD.

Ozawa, Terutomo (1979). *Multinationalism, Japanese Style: Political Economy of Outward Dependency.* Princeton, NJ: Princeton University Press.

———— (1982). A newer type of foreign investment in third world resource development. *Rivista Internazionale di Scienze Economiche e Commerciali*, 29 (December), pp. 1133–1151.

———— (1987). Can the market alone manage structural upgrading? A challenge posed by interdependence. In *Structural Change, Economic Interdependence and World Development*, 1, J. H. Dunning and M. Usui, eds, Basingstoke, United Kingdom: Macmillan, pp. 45–61.

———— (1990). Multinational corporations and the 'flying-geese' paradigm of economic development in the Asian Pacific region, paper presented at the 20th Anniversary World Conference on Multinational Enterprises and 21st Century Scenarios, Tokyo (July).

———— (1991a). Japanese multinationals and 1992. In *Multinationals and Europe 1992*, B. Burgenmeier and J. L. Mucchielli, eds, London: Routledge, pp. 135–154.

———— (1991b). The dynamics of Pacific Rim industrialization: how Mexico can join the Asian flock of 'flying geese'. In *Mexico's External Relations* in the 1990s, Riordan Roett, ed., Boulder and London: Rienner, pp. 129–154.

—————— (1991c). Japan in a new phase of multinationalism and industrial upgrading: functional integration of trade, growth and FDI, *Journal of World Trade*, 25 (February), pp. 43–60.

Porter, Michael (1990). *The Competitive Advantage of Nations*. New York: Free Press.

Ricardo, David (1817/1888). *Principles of Political Economy and Taxation*. In *The Works of David Ricardo*, J. R. McCulloch, ed., London: John Murray, pp. 1–584.

Smith, Adam (1776/1908). *An Inquiry into the Nature and Causes of the Wealth of Nations*. London: Routledge; New York: E. P. Dutton.

Stiglitz, J. E. (1987). Learning to learn, localised learning and technological progress. In *Economic Policy and Technological Performance*, P. Dasgupta and P. Stoneman, eds, Cambridge: Cambridge University Press, pp. 125–153.

Stolper, W. F. and P. A. Samuelson (1941). Protection and real wages. *Review of Economic Studies*, 9 (November), pp. 58–73.

Thurow, Lester C. (1985). *The Management Challenge: Japanese Views*. Cambridge, Massachusetts: The MIT Press.

Tolentino, Paz Estrella E. (1993). *Technological Innovation and Third World Multinationals*. London: Routledge.

Vernon, Raymond (1966). International investment and international trade in the product cycle. *Quarterly Journal of Economics*, 80 (May), pp. 190–207.

World Bank (1991). *World Development Report*. Washington, DC: World Bank Publications.

Part II

4 Re-evaluating the benefits of foreign direct investment*

John H. Dunning

During the past twenty years, both the country- and firm-specific factors influencing foreign direct investment have changed significantly. For their part, countries adopted a much more welcoming stance towards inbound investment and increasingly see it as a means of upgrading the competitiveness of their indigenous resources and capabilities. Corporations, on the other hand, are increasingly taking a more systemic approach to their global activities and are pursuing more integrated production and marketing strategies. Both these developments are affecting the balance of the costs and benefits of foreign direct investment to host countries, and also the appropriate actions that Governments should take to ensure that it advances their long-term economic objectives. In considering some of these issues, this article identifies the ways in which different kinds of activities may affect domestic competitiveness, and stresses the need for Governments to reorient their macro-organizational policies so that they may best gain from being linked to the globalizing economy of the 1990s.

INTRODUCTION

Thirty-six years ago, the first comprehensive analysis of the consequences of inbound foreign direct investment (FDI) for a host country was published (Dunning, 1958). The subject of study was the United Kingdom; since that date, similar investigations have been undertaken – with varying degrees of sophistication – for almost every country in the world.[1] Hundreds of books, theses and Government reports, and thousands of papers in academic and professional journals have been written on the topic,[2] and scarcely a day goes by

* Reprinted from *Transnational Corporations*, vol. 3, no. 1 (February 1994), pp. 23–51.

without some newspaper or magazine article lauding or denigrating the globalization of business activity.

Why, then, is it needed to revisit the subject? Has not everything worthwhile already been said or written about the role of transnational corporations (TNCs) in economic development? Quite apart from its spectacular growth over the past decade,[3] two sets of reasons for the current resurgence of interest could be offered. Each reflects the changes in attitudes towards the costs and benefits of FDI that have occurred over the past twenty years; the first is by *countries* and the second by *firms* – particularly by TNCs.[4]

THE CHANGING ATTITUDES OF COUNTRIES

In the early 1990s, most Governments acclaimed FDI as 'good news', after a period of being highly critical – if not downright hostile – to these investments in the 1970s and early 1980s. There are a number of possible explanations for this change of heart, some of which are set out in Figure 4.1.

- Renewed faith of most countries in the workings of the market economy, as demonstrated, for example, by the wholesale privatization of State-owned assets and the deregulation and liberalization of markets over the past eight to ten years. While these events are being most vividly played out in Central and Eastern Europe and in China, the need to remove structural market distortions has also been aknowledged in many other parts of the world – notably in the European Union, India, Mexico and Viet Nam.
- The increasing globalization of economic activity and the integration of international production and cross-border markets by TNCs (UNCTAD, DTCI, 1993).
- The key ingredients of contemporary economic growth – created assets, such as technology, intellectual capital, learning experience and organizational competence – are not only becoming more mobile across national boundaries, but also increasingly housed in TNC systems.[5]
- A growing number of economies – especially in East Asia – are now approaching the 'take off' stage in their economic development; as a result, competition for the world's scarce resources of capital, technology and organizational skills is becoming increasingly intensive.
- The economic structures of the major industrialized nations are converging, with the implication that competition between firms

- **From a country's perspective**
  - Renaissance of the market system.
  - Globalization of economic activity.
  - Enhanced mobility of wealth-creating assets.
  - Increasing number of countries approaching the 'take-off' stage in development.
  - Convergence of economic structures among developed countries and some newly industrializing economies.
  - Changing criteria by which Governments evaluate FDI.
  - Better appreciation by Governments of the costs and benefits of FDI.

- **From a firm's perspective**
  - Increasing need to exploit global markets (e.g. to cover escalating research-and-development costs).
  - Competitive pressures to procure inputs (raw materials, components, etc.) from the cheapest possible sources.
  - Regional integration has prompted more efficiency-seeking investment.
  - Growing ease of trans-border communications and reduced transport costs.
  - Heightened oligopolistic competition among leading firms.
  - Opening up new territorial opportunities for FDI.
  - Need to tap into foreign sources of technology and organizational capabilities and exploit economies of agglomeration.
  - New incentives to conclude alliances with foreign firms.
  - Changes in significance of particular locational costs and benefits.
  - Need to better balance the advantages of globalization with those of localization.

Figure 4.1 The changing world of foreign direct investment

from those nations is becoming both more intra-industry and more intensive.

- The criterion for judging the success of FDI by host Governments has changed over the years in a way which has made for a less confrontational and a more cooperative stance between host countries and foreign investors. More particularly, the emphasis in evaluating inbound TNCs over the past two decades has switched from the direct contribution of foreign affiliates to economic development to their wider impact on the upgrading of the competitiveness of host countries' indigenous capabilities and the promotion of their dynamic comparative advantage.
- Finally, the learning experience of countries about what TNCs can or cannot do for host countries has enabled their Governments to

understand better how to assess their impact and to take action to ensure that TNCs promote more efficiently host countries' economic and social goals.

The world economy in the mid-1990s is, indeed, a very different place from that of even a decade ago; and the changes that have occurred have had implications both for the responses of individual nation-States to FDI, as well as for the very character of FDI itself.

THE CHANGING BEHAVIOUR OF FIRMS

The events outlined above have also affected the attitudes, organizational structures and behaviour of business corporations. For example, these corporations have found it increasingly necessary to capture new markets to finance the escalating costs of research and development and marketing activities, both of which are considered essential for preserving or advancing the competitiveness of firms.[6] Cross-border strategic alliances and networks have been pursued for similar reasons, as well as to encapsulate the time it takes to innovate and learn about new products, processes and management cultures. Firms have been no less pressured to reduce costs and improve the quality of raw materials and components. As a growing number of countries are building their own arsenals of skilled labour and technological capacity, foreign investors are finding it more and more desirable to diversify geographically their information-gathering and learning capabilities. Competition in internationally oriented industries is becoming increasingly oligopolistic, while – as it is later described in more detail – the nature of the competitive advantages of firms and the factors influencing their locational choices have become very different in the early 1990s from those of only a decade or so ago.

Finally, in the more complex global environment of the 1990s, TNCs are being forced to pay more attention to achieving the right balance between the forces making for the global integration of their activities and those requiring them to be more oriented and sensitive to localized supply capabilities and consumer tastes and needs – what Akio Norita of Sony has referred to as 'glocalization'. For, alongside the acknowledged benefits of globalization, there is a growing awareness, particularly among the citizens of smaller countries, of the need to preserve – and, indeed, promote as a comparative advantage – their distinctive cultures, institutional structures, life styles, working relationships and consumption preferences. Many TNCs ignore such country-specific differences – that many observers, for instance J. Naisbitt (1994), believe will become important in the future – at their peril.[7]

At one time, firms used to engage in international transactions primarily through arm's-length exporting and importing. Today, the main vehicle is FDI and cooperative alliances. Initially, these latter forms of cross-border commerce were driven by trade; today, they largely determine trade. Outside the primary sector, upwards of two-thirds of the world's exports of goods and services are accounted for by TNCs; and 30–40 per cent of these take place within these same institutions (60–70 per cent in the case of intangible assets, such as technology and organizational skills) (Dunning, 1993a; UNCTAD, DTCI, 1993).

In the 1990s, TNCs are the main producers and organizers of the knowledge-based assets that are now primarily responsible for advancing global economic prosperity; they are also the principal cross-border disseminators of the fruits of these assets. It is true that the ambience of innovatory activities, the availability of risk capital and the educational infrastructure is strongly influenced by the actions of Governments. It is true, too, that a myriad of small firms and individual entrepreneurs are significant seed-beds of new ideas and inventions. However, economic progress is being shaped increasingly by the way in which new knowledge and organizational techniques are systematized and disseminated. Sometimes, the market system is able to perform satisfactorily this task by itself. However, because many emerging innovations are both generic and multi-purpose and have to be coordinated with other assets to be fully productive, firms frequently find it beneficial to supplement or supplant external markets by their own governance systems. Sometimes, too, the efficient production and use of created assets requires firms to cooperate and even to be located in close proximity to each other.[8]

To some extent, this has always been the case. One of the earliest definitions of a business enterprise was that it was a coordinated unit of decision taking;[9] today, a firm is better described as a coordinator of a network of interrelated value-added activities (Dunning, 1993b). In the past, the boundaries of the firm were firmly determined by its ownership. Now, *de facto*, they are much fuzzier, as their capability to control the allocation of resources may be exercised through a variety of cooperative arrangements or networking agreements.[10] The more activities a firm pursues, the more it engages in coalitions with other firms and the more countries it produces in, or trades with. In that event, its competitiveness is likely to be determined by its ability to integrate these activities systematically.

The systemic view of TNCs implies very different governance structures than those implemented by traditional foreign investors. Rather than acting as an owner of a number of fairly autonomous, or 'stand-alone', foreign affiliates, each of which is expected to earn the maximum economic rent on the resources invested in it, the systemic TNC aims at managing its portfolio of spatially diffused human and physical assets – including those owned by other firms over which it has some property rights – as a holistic production, financial and marketing system. Of course, there are costs of coordinating intra- and inter-firm cross-border activities, and these will ultimately determine the extent of a firm's territorial expansion. But recent advances in international transport and telecommunication technologies have pushed out these limits. In the cases in which corporations have shed some of their foreign assets, this has been mainly done to reduce the scope or diversity of their activities, rather than the geography of their international transactions.

A final feature of the FDI in the 1980s and 1990s, which accords with the systemic view of TNC activity, is that, probably, as much as 90 per cent of that activity is currently undertaken by established TNCs; that is, it is *sequential* rather than *initial* investment. This is not to deny that new TNCs are emerging all the time – probably at a rate of 4,000 to 5,000 a year,[11] and increasingly, from developing countries, notably China; but, as yet, the total foreign capital stake of these companies is quite small. Research has established that sequential FDI – which, as far as a particular country is concerned, might be a first-time investment – is not only likely to be more geared to the interests of the investing company's value activities, but is also likely to generate its own unique costs and benefits, that is over and above those generated by the initial investment (Kogut, 1983; Buckley and Casson, 1985). These essentially arise from the consequences of transnationality *per se*. They include gains such as those arising from the diversification of exchange risk and economic uncertainty, the spreading of environmental volatility and the opportunity to exploit better the economies of geographical scope and specialization. They also include the costs of coordinating the activities and markets of foreign affiliates in widely different business cultures and political regimes (Kogut and Kulatihala, 1988) and those associated with the setting-up and sustaining of cross-border networks of intra- and inter-firm relationships.

TYPES OF FOREIGN DIRECT INVESTMENT AND COUNTRIES

Global economic events of the past decade or so, particularly those driven by technological advances, regional integration and the realignment of economic systems and policies, have altered fundamentally the perception of Governments of host countries of how FDI can contribute towards their economic and social goals. These same events have also caused a reappraisal by firms of *why* and *how* – and, indeed, *where* – they need to engage in international transactions. It is for these reasons that the current generation of scholars – not to mention Governments and firms – continues to want to know more about the benefits (and costs) of FDI. To what extent and in what way is the global economy causing these to change? What may national and regional administrations do to ensure that inward TNC activity contributes the maximum benefits to their economic and social needs and aspirations?[12]

With these introductory remarks in mind, I will make two very simple statements, which are as timely today as they were twenty years ago and which policy makers concerned with assessing the benefits of FDI would do well to constantly bear in mind:

- History and geography matter. Policy makers should seek to learn from their successes and failures of the past and from those of other countries; but they should not be slaves to those successes and failures. In light of the perceived contribution of FDI to economic development, they should devise and implement the macro-organizational strategies most suited to their own unique situations and needs.
- Policy makers should be cautious about expecting easy generalizations about the consequences of FDI. Not only will its effects vary according to the kind of FDI undertaken, but these effects will also depend on the economic and other objectives set by Governments, the economic policies pursued by them and the alternatives to FDI open to them.

In order to focus better the remainder of this article, it is assumed that the principal criterion by which national administrations evaluate inbound FDI in the 1990s is by *its perceived contribution to the improvement of the competitiveness or the productivity of the resources and asset-creating capabilities located within their areas of jurisdiction.*[13] This, indeed, is probably the single most important medium- to long-term economic objective of the great majority of nations, particularly of those that are most dependent on foreign sources of supply and foreign markets for their prosperity.

How, then, might competitiveness of a country be advanced? Figure 4.2 identifies five main ways:

- By a country's firms producing more efficiently whatever they are currently producing, for example by reducing organizational costs and/or raising labour or capital productivity.
- By the innovation of new, or improvements in the quality of existing, products, production processes and organization structures.
- By a reallocation of resources and capabilities to produce goods and services that are in better accord with the country's comparative dynamic advantage.
- By capturing new foreign markets – provided this is cost effective.
- By reducing the costs, or speeding up the process, of structural adjustment to changes in global demand and supply conditions.

The potential contribution of inbound FDI to each of these ways or vectors of upgrading competitiveness is fairly self-evident. It may provide resources or capabilities otherwise unattainable, or only

---

- Increase efficiency of its existing asset development through more effective deployment through more effective quality-control procedures; by networking with other firms; more cost-effective sourcing; reducing lead times (and by raising labour and capital productivity).
- Innovate new products, processes and organizational structures (e.g. by improving national innovatory systems, exploiting better the economies of the spatial clustering of related activities and ensuring that risk capital is available for start-up firms.
- Improve the allocation of its resources and capabilities (e.g. from less to more productive activities and towards those in which perceived dynamic comparative advantage is increasing.
- Capture new markets (e.g. by improving knowledge about foreign markets and about customer needs and by better marketing and distribution techniques.
- Reduce the costs and/or increase the speed of structural adjustment (e.g. by encouraging flexible labour markets; enhancing the quality of retraining programmes; minimizing bureaucratic inefficiencies; appreciating fiscal and other incentives for industrial restructuring; and by a greater willingness to accept and adjust to change).

Figure 4.2 Five ways for a host country to upgrade its competitiveness and comparative advantage

attainable at a higher cost. It may steer economic activity towards the production of goods and services deemed most appropriate by domestic and international markets. It may boost research and development and introduce new organizational techniques. It may accelerate the learning process of indigenous firms. It may stimulate the efficiency of suppliers and competitors, raise quality standards, introduce new working practices and open up new and cheaper sources of procurement. It may provide additional markets. It may better enable a host country to tap into, or monitor, the competitive advantages of other nations. It may inject new management talent and entrepreneurial initiatives and work cultures. It may encourage the formation of cross-border cooperative alliances, technological systems and inter-firm networking. It may foster the geographical clustering of related activities that generate their own agglomerative economies. In short, it may interact with the *existing* competitive advantages of host nations and affect their *future* competitive advantages in a variety of ways.

Some of these ways are summarized in a schema set out in Figure 4.3. This figure is an adaptation and extension of Michael Porter's 'diamond' of competitive advantage (Porter, 1990).[14] It suggests that inbound FDI may affect not only the four facets of the diamond, but also the actions of host Governments and the mentality of competitiveness of the constituents in the host country. This may be done, for example, by injecting more market-oriented beliefs and practices, by encouraging more harmonious labour relations and by raising the quality standards expected by consumers.

It is worth noting that the significance of the individual attributes of the diamond of competitive advantage may vary not only between countries, but also within a particular country over time. Thus, for example, the relative importance of the production and efficient deployment of created assets and the means by which these are transmitted over space have increased as the world economy has become more globalized. Similarly, there are suggestions that the way in which complementary activities are organized along the value-added chain and the agglomerative economies to be derived from a spatial clustering of these and other related activities are becoming more significant. By contrast, the optimum number of domestic firms competing in their home market is probably falling, as the geographical focus of competition becomes more regional or global; at the same time, the domestic availability of natural resources is generally becoming a less critical competitive advantage than it used to be.

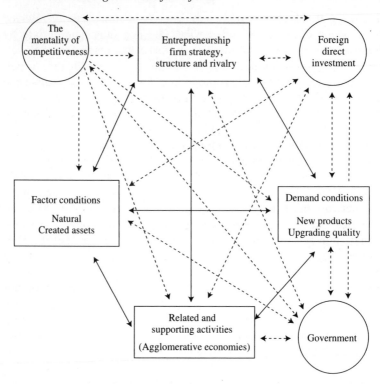

Figure 4.3 The diamond of competitive advantage
Source: Porter (1990) as modified by the author.

I would be the first to accept that most of the competitive advantages just described are also available to domestic firms; but it is my contention that the unique attributes of FDI – and especially those that arise from the transnationality of the investing firms – offer financial, production, marketing and organizational benefits over and above those that indigenous firms may possess or can acquire.

At the same time, there are costs to a host country of inbound TNC activity. These may be divided into two groups. The first comprises various payments (e.g. profits, interest, dividends, royalties, management fees) that have to be made to attract or maintain foreign investors. These vary along a continuum. At the one extreme, there are payments below which a non-resident firm is unwilling to invest; at the other, there are payments above which a country is not prepared to accept the investment. The payments actually made depend on the bargaining skills and negotiating power of the TNCs and Governments of the host countries. These, in turn, depend on the price that a host country would have to pay to acquire the benefits of FDI in alternative ways and the options open to the investing companies to locate their activities in other countries. In the 1960s and 1970s, the main anxiety of host Governments was that the monopoly power of TNCs would enable those companies to extract unacceptably high shares of the value added to their affiliates. Today, a greater concern is that, without the inbound investment, host countries may be deprived of the advantages of being part of an integrated international production and marketing system (UNCTAD, DTCI, 1993).

The second type of cost associated with FDI arises when the behaviour of the investing firms, typically geared to advance their global objectives, is perceived to produce unwelcome consequences for the host country. These include the restrictions that a parent company may impose on the sourcing of raw materials and components of its affiliates and the markets these affiliates may serve. The affiliates may also be limited in the range of products they produce, the production processes they employ, the amount and kind of research and development they undertake and the pattern of their networking with indigenous firms. Through transfer-pricing manipulation, it is also possible that income earned in the host country be syphoned off to the home (or some tax haven) country.

SOME DETERMINANTS OF THE NET BENEFITS OF FOREIGN DIRECT INVESTMENT

What determines the net benefits of inbound FDI? What can Governments do to ensure that such investment best contributes to the upgrading of their indigenous resources and capabilities? The short – but hardly satisfactory – answer is that it all depends on the kind of FDI, the conditions that prompted it, the existing competitive advantages of the host country and the economic policies pursued by host and other Governments. But, unfortunately, economists can go a little further than that by identifying the situations in which a specific host country is likely to gain the most from FDI and, in sub-optimal situations, what that country might do to increase the gain. In particular, the benefits to be reaped from FDI critically depend on the type and age of the investment, the economic characteristics of the host country and the macroeconomic and organizational strategies pursued by host Governments.

Table 4.1 The main types of foreign direct investment

1. *(Natural) resource-seeking*
   - Physical resources
   - Human resources

2. *Market-seeking*
   - Domestic markets
   - Adjacent (e.g. regional) markets

⎫ Mainly motives for initial foreign direct investment

3. *Efficiency-seeking*
   Rationalization of production to exploit economies of specialization and scope
   - Across value chains
     (i.e. product specialization)
   - Along value chains
     (i.e. process specialization)

4. *Strategic (created) asset-seeking*
   To advance regional or global strategy
   To link into foreign networks of created assets
   - Technology
   - Organizational capabilities
   - Markets

⎫ Mainly motives for sequential foreign direct investment

Types of foreign direct investment

Table 4.1 sets out the main types of FDI, the classification being based on the *raison d'être* for the investment. The first two, viz. *resource-seeking* and *market-seeking* investment, represent the main motives for an initial foreign entry by a firm – be it in the primary, secondary or tertiary sectors. The latter two embrace the main modes of expansion by established foreign investors. These sequential investments are frequently aimed at increasing the efficiency of regional or global TNC activities by integrating assets, production and markets; these are called *efficiency-seeking* investments. However, sequential and, occasionally, first-time investments are increasingly taking the form of *strategic asset-seeking* investments, the main purpose of which is to acquire resources and capabilities that an investing firm believes will sustain or advance its core competences in regional or global markets. These assets may range from innovatory capability and organizational structures to accessing foreign distribution channels and a better appreciation of the needs of consumers in unfamiliar markets.[15] Strategic asset-seeking investment is frequently the most expeditious way of acquiring these kinds of competitive advantages (Wendt, 1993).

In the 1960s and 1970s, most FDI was of the first or second type, although regional integration in Europe and Latin America was beginning to lead to some efficiency-seeking (or rationalized) FDI, particularly by large United States TNCs in industries like automobiles, consumer electronics and office equipment. There was also a small amount of strategic asset-seeking investment usually by United States firms that had not been among the first of their industry to invest in Europe, but, encouraged by the prospects of market growth, were seeking a speedy means of catching up with their rivals.

In the 1980s and early 1990s, FDI has been increasingly of the third and fourth type. Exceptions include first-time investments by TNCs from developing countries and a new generation of investments by TNCs from developed countries. But, upwards of 75 per cent of all intra-Triad TNC activity since the mid-1980s has been by established European, United States or Japanese TNC companies that, from the start of their internationalizing programmes, have sought to coordinate the deployment of their domestic and foreign assets. These firms have viewed each of their foreign affiliates and, frequently, their associated suppliers and industrial customers, not as self-contained entities, but as part of a regional or global network of activities.

While FDI in developing countries, accounting for about one-third of all new FDI during the period 1988–1992 (UNCTAD, DTCI, 1994a), remains primarily of a market- or resource-seeking kind, this, too, is changing. Increasingly, the liberalization of markets and regional integration in Asia and Latin America is enabling foreign investors to view their production and sourcing portfolios from a regional, rather than a national, perspective. The sub-region comprising the Eastern coastline of China, Hong Kong, Taiwan Province of China and Viet Nam is a case in point. More and more, too, many developing countries are being drawn into the hinterland of globalizing firms from developed countries as, in their bid to remain competitive, these firms are continually seeking new markets and cheaper, better quality and more stable sources of supply.

However, unlike the 1960s and 1970s, most investments now taking place in developing countries and economies in transition by TNCs from developed countries are not autonomous; rather, they are part of an integrated international production system (UNCTAD, DTCI, 1993). This means that the decisions of TNCs of what to produce in a particular country, where to source their inputs and who to sell their output to, are based not only on the locational attractions of that country *vis-à-vis* other countries, but also on what is perceived to best advance the global interests of TNCs, rather than the interests of one of their foreign affiliates, or group of affiliates. *Inter alia* (and I shall return to this point later), this requires that Governments of host countries, in the formulation and implementation of their domestic macroeconomic strategies – and especially those that affect the decisions of foreign investors – be cognizant of the strategies of Governments of other countries whose firms are competing for the same resources and markets (Dunning, 1992).

In Table 4.2, the attributes of each type of inbound FDI that are most likely to enhance the competitive advantages of recipient countries are identified. In practice, the precise contribution of each type of investment will be both activity and firm specific. It is also likely to vary according to the age of the investment; generally speaking, the local value added of a foreign affiliate is positively correlated with its age – and, perhaps most important of all, it will depend on the organizational strategies and economic policies adopted by host Governments. Some of these strategies and policies are examined later in this article, but, in compiling Table 4.2, it is assumed that these are broadly consistent with the dictates of the international market-place and that they are primarily directed towards enhancing the dynamic competitive and comparative advantages of the resources and capabilities within their jurisdiction.

The conclusions of the tables summarizing the research findings of scholars[16] and the experience of national authorities are self-evident. Each type of FDI has its own particular contribution to make to the five ways of upgrading competitiveness identified in Figure 4.2 and the four facets of Porter's diamond illustrated in Figure 4.3. For example, through the transfer of resources and capabilities, and transactions with domestic firms, both market- and resource-seeking TNCs have the potential to raise the productivity of indigenous resources and capabilities, improve quality standards and stimulate economic growth. In the right circumstances, efficiency-seeking FDI can assist host countries to restructure their economic activities more in line with their dynamic comparative advantages; reduce the costs of structural adjustment; and foster more demanding purchasing standards by firms and consumers. Strategic asset-seeking investment may help integrate the competitive advantages of the acquired firm with those of the acquiring firm and increase competition between domestic firms. However, this type of FDI, unlike the

Table 4.2 Some likely contributions of different types of foreign direct investment to the upgrading of competitiveness of host countries

---

1. *Natural resource-seeking*
   (a) Provides complementary assets (technology, management and organizational competence).
   (b) Provides access to foreign markets.
   (c) May or may not lead to local spin-off effects on industrial customers, e.g. secondary processing activities.
   (d) Raises standards of product quality.
   (e) May or may not foster clusters of resource-based related activities.

2. *Market-seeking*
   (a) As 1(a) above.
   (b) Fosters backward supply linkages and clusters of specialized labour markets and agglomerative economies.
   (c) As 1(d) above; also raises domestic consumer expectations of indigenous competitors.
   (d) Stimulates local entrepreneurship and domestic rivalry.

3. *Efficiency-seeking*
   (a) Improves international division of labour and cross-border networking; entices comparative advantages of host countries.
   (b) Provides access to foreign markets and/or sources of supply.
   (c) As 2(b) above.
   (d) As 1(d) and 2(e) above.
   (e) Aids structural adjustment.

4. *Strategic asset-seeking*
   (a) Provides new finance capital and complementary assets.
   (b) As 1(b) above.
   (c) As 2(d) above.
   (d) As 3(a) above.

---

other types, may be undertaken with the specific purpose of transferring the assets acquired from the host to the home country, and this may work to the disadvantage of the competitiveness of the former country.[17]

The contribution of each type of FDI also varies according to the part (or parts) of the value chain in which it is undertaken. Investment in each part may be motivated differently. For example, some kinds of foreign-owned research-and-development activities are truncated replicas of those of the parent companies; some are akin to efficiency-seeking foreign production; and some are designed to gain an insight into the innovatory activities of the host country and, where permitted, to participate in foreign research consortia.[18] The latter motive explains the presence of foreign TNCs in regional clusters of research and development in the United States, the European Union and Japan. However, in general, inbound FDI – providing it helps advance the dynamic comparative advantage of host countries – is likely to have the most beneficial effect when it is directed to those parts of the value chain in which the potential for upgrading productivity is the greatest.

Spatial and country influences

What, then, are the important factors determining the location of TNC activity in the 1990s? How do they differ from those of twenty years ago? What determines the kind of competitive advantages offered by countries seeking to attract FDI? What should be the attitude and policies of national Governments towards FDI in the 1990s in light of globalization? And how do these attitudes and policies differ from those displayed in the 1960s and 1970s?

In answer to the first question, Table 4.3 sets out a selection of some generic spatial characteristics that scholarly research has shown to affect the geography of TNC activity. These characteristics – each of which embraces a number of specific cost- or revenue-determining variables – have a different impact on each type of FDI described earlier.[19] They are also likely to vary according to the industry,[20] asset portfolios and strategies pursued by the investing firms.[21] And their significance as inbound FDI determinants will also depend on the attributes of particular host countries, such as size, stage of economic development, industrial structure, degree of economic interdependence with the rest of the world and physical and psychic distances from the main investing countries.

Most of the spatial characteristics, as well as the industry, firm- and country-specific contextual variables that influence them, are well known both to scholars and business enterprises alike. Yet, in the past, the expectations of Governments – and particularly Governments of low-income countries – have been shattered because they have not taken into account sufficiently the unique characteristics of their resources and organizational capabilities. The benefits of inward FDI for Nigeria or Taiwan Province of China are unlikely to be the same as those for India; those now experienced by Chile and Viet Nam are quite different from those of ten to fifteen years ago; those currently gained in Malaysia and Botswana from efficiency-seeking FDI are scarcely comparable with each other; and those that result from market- and resource-seeking FDI are likely to be highly

Table 4.3 Some country-specific attributes affecting foreign direct investment

---

1. *Those which chiefly impact on direct production costs and benefits*
   - Spatial distribution of natural resources, created assets and markets.
   - Input prices, quality and productivity (e.g. labour, energy, materials, components, semi-finished goods).
   - Investment incentives and disincentives (including performance requirements etc.).
   - Comparative economies of centralization versus decentralization of different segments of value chain, viz. production and marketing.

2. *Market-seeking*
   - Cross-border transport and communication costs.
   - Artificial barriers (e.g. import controls) to trade in goods and services.
   - Societal and infrastructural provisions (commercial, legal, educational, transport and communication).
   - Differences in cross-country political ideologies, language, culture, business, customs and the ethos of competitiveness.
   - Economic system and policies of host Governments. The organizational and institutional framework for resource allocation.
   - The opportunities to exploit the agglomerative economies of industrial districts.

Source: Adapted from table 4.1 in Dunning (1993a).

dependent on the development and macro-organizational policies of host Governments relative to those implemented by other Governments competing for the same type of FDI.

With respect to the second question, the significance of the spatially related variables set out in Table 4.3 has changed considerably over the past two decades. As their share of total production costs declined, so did the drawing power of natural resources and unskilled labour, while that of created assets and the opportunities of networking with local firms rose.[22] As the unique competitive advantages of TNCs became both more mobile and systemic, these firms have increasingly chosen to locate their value-added activities in countries that can offer the most cost-effective complementary assets and the quality of infrastructural support that an integrated international production or marketing strategy requires. In this connection, intending investors usually place their need for state-of-the-art facilities for the cross-border transmission of information, technology and finance at the top of their locational priorities. An effective and trustworthy legal framework – particularly in its ability to enforce property rights and resolve contractual disputes – comes a close second. At higher levels of economic development, the quality of a country's educational and technological infrastructure becomes more critical.

More generally, as the organizational and transaction costs of economic activity have become relatively more important – and there is some evidence (Stiglitz, 1989; Wallis and North, 1986) that these are also positively related to the complexity of a nation's industrial structure – countries that can offer a business environment that is conducive to minimizing these costs are, *ceteris paribus*, likely to gain an increasing share of inbound investment. Recently, two surveys were conducted, one on the determinants of Japanese FDI in the United Kingdom's manufacturing sector, and the other on the location of international offices (Dunning, 1991). In both surveys, transaction- and coordinating-cost variables (such as those related to inter-personal relations, information asymmetries, language and culture, searching for and dealing with sub-contractors, learning about the quality of communications and adapting to local business practices and customer needs and bureaucratic controls) were ranked considerably higher as investment determinants than were traditional production-cost-related variables.

Host Government policies

Elsewhere (including in this journal), I have written extensively on the ways in which the actions of Governments affect – for good or bad – the location and structure of TNC activities (Dunning, 1991, 1992, 1993b, 1994). In this article, I focus on the main changes in host Government organizational strategies over the past two decades that have affected the most the level and distribution of FDI.

Foremost among these changes has been a softening in the attitudes towards FDI. This has resulted in a widespread liberalization of policies that previously constrained these investments. In addition, as has already been mentioned, the criterion by which most countries evaluate inbound TNC activity has shifted from its direct contribution to local value added to its longer-term consequences for the competitiveness of indigenous resources and capabilities.[23] This reassessment has occurred at a time when Governments of both developed and developing countries have been rethinking their own economic functions in light of political changes and the globalization of the world economy. The most obvious manifestation of this rethinking has been a widespread deregulation and liberalization of markets, the privatization of many State-owned industries and the removal (or reduction of) a wide range of Government-imposed market imperfections (e.g.

subsidies, tariff and non-tariff barriers, price controls and certain rules and regulations).

However, the fact that Governments have lessened their direct intervention in markets does not mean that they have abdicated – or, indeed, should abdicate – their responsibility as *enablers* and *steerers* of wealth-creating activities, or as *facilitators* of the private enterprise system. Indeed, as firm-specific assets become more internationally mobile and others increasingly take on the form of public goods,[24] the role of Governments as coordinators of markets and hierarchies becomes more – rather than less – critical. Moreover, because of the demands of modern technology and competitive pressures, the organization of economic activity has become more pluralistic. This places additional responsibilities on Governments to ensure the synergistic benefits from this new form of capitalism, which Michael Gerlach (1992) called 'alliance' capitalism, are fully exploited.

To a large extent, this remoulded role of national Governments – it is not so much a question of whether or not Governments should intervene in markets, but rather *what kind* of intervention and *for what purpose* – reflects the changes now taking place in the relative efficiency of different modes of organizing economic activity. The market as a systemic organizational entity has been reinstated and upgraded, except in the case of public goods and strategically sensitive products. The current philosophy is that decisions on what is to be produced and how it is produced are best left to the collective will of thousands of firms and millions of consumers. At the same time, this philosophy also presumes that underpinning and sustaining the market as a resource-allocation mechanism is the strong visible hand of Governments. For without the complementary assets of an efficient and up-to-date legal, financial and commercial infrastructure, an educated labour force, an adequate transportation and telecommunications network, a strong anti-monopoly policy, a sound macroeconomic policy and a wealth-creating culture, the market cannot do the job expected of it. Besides its various social and strategic responsibilities, it is the Government's task to cultivate and support – though not necessarily undertake – all of these market-enabling activities.

Possibly, what has been written so far is not contentious. Indeed, the policy implications may seem all too familiar. However, the real challenge facing Governments is how best to implement these policies. The particular point I wish to emphasize is that the globalizing economy of the 1990s is forcing Governments to re-examine their domestic economic strategies in light of the fact that they are competing increasingly for competitiveness-enhancing assets that are much more footloose than they used to be.[25] Macro-organizational policies which, at one time, only affected the domestic allocation and use of resources, are now as likely to affect trade, FDI and cross-border alliances as much as any tariff, exchange-rate change or interest-rate hike. If nothing else, the world economy of the 1990s is obliging Governments to realign their domestic economic strategies more closely to the needs of the international market-place.

It is my strong contention that Governments that are successful in reducing – or helping hierarchies to reduce – the transaction and coordinating costs of economic activity and that best enable their firms to surmount the obstacles to structural change are, *ceteris paribus*, likely to be the most successful, in attracting not only the appropriate kind of FDI, but also at the least real cost. It is surely no accident that countries that have recorded the best economic performances in the past two decades are also those that have designed and implemented a macro-organizational strategy consistent with upgrading the competitiveness and the dynamic comparative advantage of their location-bound resources and have sought to attract a suitable kind of inward FDI.[26]

One final difference between the domestic economic policies now being required of Governments in a world of quicksilver capital and those practised in the 1960s and 1970s is that, except for cultural or strategic reasons, there is little case for discriminatory action by Governments, either in favour of or against inbound TNC activity. Though not always admitted, and except for particular types of incentives and performance requirements, most Governments have downgraded the significance of FDI policies *per se*. Instead, they are preferring to re-examine the appropriateness of their general macro-economic and macro-organizational strategies in light of the globalization of economic activities and the growing mobility of the critical wealth-creating assets, and on the understanding that FDI and trade-related investments are the chief modalities by which countries are linked together. It is, therefore, the interaction between those policies and the strategies pursued by TNCs that determines the extent to which inbound FDI is able to upgrade a country's competitive advantage.

CONCLUSIONS AND SOME CAVEATS

This article has sought to identify the main contributions that inbound FDI can make to the competitiveness of host countries and the conditions that must prevail if that contribution is to be optimized. It has also reviewed the changes that have taken place over the past twenty years in the determinants affecting TNC activity, as well as the attitudes of Governments.

Among the most important of these changes has been the emergence of the global economy and the structural integration of the world's markets and production systems. This new international division of labour, an integral part of which is the growing mobility of intra-firm intermediate products between countries, is demanding a reappraisal of the economic philosophies and policies of national Governments. In particular, the widening locational options of TNCs and the convergence of industrial structures and trade patterns of advanced countries are forcing national administrations to pay more attention to ensuring that the quality of their location-bound resources and capabilities do not fall behind those of their competitors.

In pursuance of these goals, Governments have other critical roles to play, including the elimination of structural and institutional impediments to efficient resource usage; the active implementation of market-facilitating measures; and the encouragement of an ethos of competitiveness among their constituents. The administrations that have gone the furthest in implementing those changes have been the most successful, not only in attracting inbound FDI, but also – much more importantly – in using those investments in a way that best advances their national interests in a globalizing economy.

I would, however, like to conclude by offering a number of caveats. The first caveat refers back to some of the possible costs of FDI as a competitiveness-enhancing vehicle. There is a saying, much beloved by Western economists, that there is no such thing as a free lunch. That means all good things have to be paid for. That is certainly true of FDI; the only question is whether the price attached to it is a fair and reasonable one. One difficulty faced by many Governments in formulating and implementing policies that affect the costs and benefits of inbound FDI is that they either do not have the knowledge, or are uncertain, about what those costs and benefits actually are. This is partly because most decisions, the outcome of which affects the behaviour of foreign affiliates, are taken by their parent companies on the basis of information and expectations known only to them. This is not to say that these globally oriented decisions necessarily work against the interests of host countries; but it does make life more difficult for Governments seeking to optimize the level and pattern of inward FDI and its effects on domestic competitiveness.

The main points made in this article may be summarized by

Table 4.4 Some possible contributions of inbound foreign direct investment to the upgrading of the competitive advantages of host countries

Positive contributions	Negative contributions	Host country characteristics that favour positive contributions
1. By providing additional resources and capabilities, viz. capital, technology management skills, access to markets.	May provide too few, or wrong kind of, resources and assets. Can cut off foreign markets compared with those serviced by domestic firms. Can fail to adjust to localized capabilities and needs.	Availability of local resources at low real cost, particularly those complementary to those provided by foreign firms. Minimal structural distortions or institutional impediments to upgrading of indigenous assets. Development strategies that help promote dynamic comparative advantage.
2. By injecting new entrepreneurship, management styles, work cultures and more dynamic competitive practices.	An inability of foreign entrepreneurship, management styles and working practices to accommodate or, where appropriate, change local business cultures. The introduction of foreign industrial-relations procedures may lead to industrial unrest. The pursuance of anti-competitive practices may lead to an unacceptable degree of market concentration.	The policies pursued by host Governments to promote local entrepreneurship and a keen and customer-driven work ethic; the character and efficiency of capital markets; the effectiveness of appropriate market-facilitating policies. Larger countries may find it easier to introduce some of these conditions than smaller countries.
3. By a more efficient resource allocation, competitive stimulus and spill-over effects on suppliers and/or customers, FDI can help upgrade domestic resources and capabilities, as well as the productivity of indigenous firms, and foster clusters of related activities to the benefit of the participating firms.	Can limit the upgrading of indigenous resources and capabilities by restricting local production to low value-added activities and importing the major proportion of higher value-added intermediate products. May also reduce the opportunities for domestic agglomerative economies by confining its linkages to foreign suppliers and industrial customers.	The form and efficiency of macro-organizational policies and administrative regimes. In particular, the benefits likely to be derived from FDI rest on host Governments providing an adequate legal, commercial and assigning priority to policies that help upgrade human and technological capabilities and encourage regional clusters of related activities, e.g. science and industrial parks.
4. By adding to the host nations' gross domestic product (GDP), via 1–3 above, and by providing additional tax revenue to Governments.	By restricting the growth of GDP via 1–3 above. By transfer pricing or other devices to lower taxes paid to host Governments.	See 1–3 above. Suitable policies of the tax authorities of host Governments to minimize transfer pricing abuse. Countries that have the most to offer TNCs are likely to be the most successful in implementing these policies.

Table 4.4 continued

Positive contributions	Negative contributions	Host country characteristics that favour positive contributions
5. By improving the balance of payments, through import substitution, export-generating or efficiency-seeking investments.	By worsening the balance of payments, through limiting exports and promoting imports and out-competing indigenous firms that export more and import less.	Need to take a long view of importing and exporting behaviour of foreign affiliates. The key issue is not the balance of payments *per se*, but the contribution of FDI to economic efficiency, growth and stability. However, countries with a chronic balance-of-payment deficit may find it difficult to liberalize completely their balance-of-payments policies.
6. By linking better the host economy with the global market-place and helping to advance economic growth by fostering a more efficient international division of labour.	By promoting a division of labour based on what the investing firm perceives to be in its global interests, but which may be inconsistent with dynamic comparative advantage as perceived by the host country.	As 3 above – and, in particular, the extent to which host country Governments can pursue policies that encourage investing firms to upgrade their value-adding activities and invest in activities that enhance the dynamic comparative advantage of indigenous resources. The gains from 6 are particularly important for smaller countries.
7. By more directly exposing the host economy to the political and economic systems of other countries; the values and demand structures of foreign households; attitudes to work practices; incentives; industrial relations and foreign workers; and many different customs and behavioural norms of foreign societies.	By causing political, social and cultural unrest or divisiveness; by the introduction of unacceptable values (e.g. with respect to advertising, business customs, labour practices and environmental standards); and by the direct interference of foreign companies in the political regime or electoral process of the host country.	The extent to which a society is strong and stable enough to adjust smoothly to technological and political change. Also, the strength and quality of Government regulations and norms; the nature of the host country's goals and its perceived trade-off between, for instance, economic growth, political sovereignty and cultural autonomy. The difficulties in optimizing the benefits of the openness induced by FDI will be greatest in countries which are the most culturally distinct from their trading or investing partners.

reference to Table 4.4, which sets out the main costs and benefits of FDI as have been experienced by host countries over the past two or three decades. The balance between the costs and benefits of each kind of contribution varies according to the type of investment (identified in Figure 4.1), a variety of firm- and industry-specific features (some of which have been identified in this article), and the age and nationality of FDI. It will also depend on the characteristics of host countries, especially the policies of host Governments. (Some of these latter characteristics are set out in column 3 of Table 4.4).

A second caveat relates to the nature of a country's competitiveness. The term 'competitiveness' is a relative concept and it is used by analysts to compare the economic performance of firms, industries or countries (or, that of the same firm, industry or country) over time. However, whether a country whose firms are uncompetitive in the production of a particular range of goods or services should encourage inbound FDI to improve its competitiveness is debatable. Very rarely, if ever, can a country expect to be competitive in the production of all goods and services. Obvious examples include growing bananas in Iceland and producing sophisticated electronic equipment in Chad. One of the tasks of the international market-place – backed by the appropriate Government policies – is to allocate resources and capabilities in such a way that each country engages in the kind of economic activities to which it is *comparatively* best suited. Foreign direct investment can play a useful – and sometimes a decisive – part in that process. What, however, it should not be used for is to 'prop-up' activities that can never become internationally competitive. Resources must be directed to where they can be most productively used. After all, one of the functions of trade is to allow a country to import products that it is relatively unsuited to produce for itself and pay for these with products which other countries are relatively unsuited to produce. The success of FDI in upgrading the *competitive* advantage of a country's resources and its *comparative* advantage in the international market-place should be judged by those criteria.

NOTES

1 Of the more substantive studies, those for Canada (Safarian, 1966), Australia (Brash, 1966), Norway (Stonehill, 1965), New Zealand (Deane, 1970), The Netherlands (Stubenitsky, 1970), Kenya (Langdon, 1981), Singapore (Mirza, 1986), the United States (Graham and Krugman, 1989), India (Kumar, 1990), Mexico (Peres-Nuñez, 1990) and Central and Eastern Europe (Artisien *et al.*, 1993) might be mentioned.
2 In 1991, the United Nations Centre on Transnational Corporations (now

the UNCTAD Division on Transnational Corporations and Investment (DTCI) identified over 3,000 books, reports and articles published between 1988 and 1990 alone (UNCTC, 1991).

3 As documented, for example, in the *World Investment Report* (UNCTAD, Division on Transnational Corporations and Investment, 1993, 1994a), and in the *World Investment Directory* (1994b). Since 1981, the annual growth rate of FDI stock has consistently outstripped that of world gross domestic product, gross domestic investment and the exports of goods and non-factor services. Furthermore, it is estimated that, in 1991, foreign affiliates of TNCs generated global sales of more than $4.8 trillion compared with world exports of goods and non-factor services of $4.5 trillion ($3 trillion excluding intra-firm trade; UNCTAD, Division on Transnational Corporations and Investment, 1994a).

4 Some of these changes in attitudes and values are reflected in the publications of the former United Nations Centre on Transnational Corporations since its inception in 1974. In particular, the initial focus on the actions of TNCs that might constrain the sovereignty of national Governments has gradually been replaced by an examination of the ways in which host Governments and foreign direct investors can work together to promote sustainable economic development and the competitiveness of domestic resources and capabilities. The contemporary mood which stresses the complementarity between Governments, firms and markets is also echoed in several of the reports of the World Bank (see, especially, World Bank, 1991, 1993).

5 The expression 'TNC systems' is used deliberately because, although there is a good deal of evidence that uni-national firms – particularly small to medium-sized ones – continue to play an important role in the generation of created assets, sooner or later these firms are forced into a network of complementary activities in which the larger TNCs act as the lead or flagship firms. That idea is further explored in Van Tulder and Junne (1988), Gugler and Dunning (1993), D'Cruz and Rugman (1993) and Harrison (1994).

6 This is especially so in the case of dynamic industries in which product-life cycles are shortening and the urgency to innovate and introduce more cost-effective production techniques is particularly intense.

7 For illustrations of the failures of TNCs to acknowledge the significance of inter-country cultural differences and for ways in which TNCs may, themselves, build upon these differences to their advantage, see an excellent book by the ex-chairperson of Smith Kline Beecham, J. H. Wendt (1993).

8 The gains of spatial agglomeration or clustering of related industries are one of the four critical variables influencing the competitiveness of firms and countries, as identified by Michael Porter (1990).

9 This definition was popularized in the 1930s, when the nature of the firm as an organizational unit was hotly debated among economists in the United Kingdom.

10 These include strategic alliances and long-term contractual relations with suppliers. The widening scope of firms to control at least partially the use of resources and capabilities of other firms in which they have no ownership (and vice versa) is encouraging scholars to return to the

idea of *groups* of related firms as the critical units of micro-economic analysis.

11 Estimates of the universe of TNCs and their affiliates are constantly being revised upwards. The latest estimates by UNCTAD, DTCI (1994a) are at least 37,000 parent firms and 200,000 foreign affiliates in the early 1990s.

12 While this article concentrates on the benefits of inbound FDI, an increasing number of Governments are also reassessing the benefits of outbound FDI. Indeed, as has been stressed frequently – notably in Dunning (1993b) – the globalizing economy is forcing Governments to take a more integrated view of outward and inward TNC activity in exactly the way they do of international trade.

13 As, for example, usually measured by the gross national product (GNP) per head or rate of increase of GNP.

14 For further details, see Dunning (1992). In this latest figure, Porter's 'chance' variable has been replaced by a 'mentality-of-competitiveness' variable; this is believed to be a critical country-specific factor that is not only exogenous to each of the four attributes of the diamond, but also linked closely to the Government and FDI variables.

15 For recent examples, see Wendt (1993).

16 For a summary of these, see Dunning (1993a).

17 Though not necessarily, as much would depend on how the owners of the acquired firm spend the proceeds of the transaction, and how the location-bound resources released by the acquired firm are subsequently deployed.

18 For a recent examination of the structure of FDI in United States research-and-development facilities, see Dunning and Narula (1995).

19 Thus, for example, artificial barriers to trade might encourage defensive market-seeking FDI, but deter efficiency-seeking FDI. Both resource- and efficiency-seeking investors are less interested in the size and character of the local market, which is the main concern of market-seeking investors. Investment incentives and disincentives have been found to be significant in influencing efficiency-seeking FDI, while sequential investors are less likely to be concerned about cross-country ideological, language and cultural differences than first-time market-seeking investors. Strategic asset-seeking investors are unlikely to be influenced by input prices or cross-border transport costs to the same extent as efficiency-seeking investors, while the opportunity to exploit scale economies is likely to be positively correlated with efficiency-seeking FDI and negatively correlated with market-seeking FDI.

20 For example, differences in input requirements; costs of transporting intermediate and final products; the extent to which products need to be adapted to local customer requirements; the advantages offered by networking with local firms; the behaviour of competitors; and the need to be sensitive to Government mandates and policies.

21 Asset portfolios are the accumulated tangible and intangible assets that a firm owns, or to which it has privileged access. It is those portfolios, and the firm's strategic response to them, that determine the kind and range of products a firm produces, the extent to which it is vertically integrated, the number and character of its associations with other firms, and the

geographical distribution of its activities. In turn, the strategy of a firm will be affected by its age, size, organizational competences and long-term objectives.

22 Exceptions include some resource-seeking and manufacturing assembling investments in the poorer developing countries.

23 What might be thought of as a shift from a 'micro-income' to a 'macro-asset' perspective.

24 Examples include many capital- and technology-intensive products and those which, in their exchange, yield external costs and benefits to non-market participants.

25 The idea of competing Governments has a very respectable intellectual heritage. It has been used by public choice economists to explain how individuals by 'voting with their feet', can act as a constraint to Governments in the tax policies and in the services they offer tax payers. See, for example, Brennan and Buchanan (1985). But the same idea could be easily extended to explain how a whole range of actions by Governments that affect the profitability of firms may also influence their locational preferences.

26 There are examples of countries that have attracted FDI, but have not grown and vice versa. But sensible macroeconomic and macro-organizational policies have led to FDI being attracted to the most competitive sections of an economy, or those that are potentially the most competitive.

REFERENCES

Artisien, P. M., Rojec, M. and M. Svetlicic, eds (1993). *Foreign Investment in Central and Eastern Europe* (New York: St Martin's Press).

Brash, D. T. (1966). *American Investment in Australian Industry* (Canberra: Australian University Press).

Brennan, G. and J. M. Buchanan (1985). *The Power to Tax* (Cambridge: Cambridge University Press).

Buckley, P. J. and M. C. Casson (1985). *The Economic Theory of the Multinational Enterprise* (London: Macmillan).

D'Cruz, J. R. and A. M. Rugman (1993). 'Business networks, telecommunications and international competitiveness', *Development and International Cooperation*, 9 (December), pp. 223–261.

Deane, R. S. (1970). *Foreign Investment in New Zealand Manufacturing* (Wellington: Sweet and Maxwell).

Dunning, J. H. (1958). *American Investment in British Manufacturing Industry* (London: George Allen and Unwin, reprinted by Arno Press, New York).

——— (1991). 'Governments, economic organization and international competitiveness', in L. G. Mattson and B. Stymne, eds, *Corporate and Industry Strategies for Europe* (Rotterdam: Elsevier Science Publishers), pp. 41–74.

——— (1992). 'The competitive advantage of countries and the activities of transnational corporations', *Transnational Corporations*, 1 (February), pp. 135–168.

————— (1993a). *Multinational Enterprises and the Global Economy* (Wokingham, United Kingdom and Reading, MA.: Addison Wesley).

————— (1993b). *The Globalization of Business* (London and New York: Routledge).

————— (1994). *Globalization: The Challenge for National Economic Regimes* (The Geary Lecture for 1993) (Dublin: Economic and Social Council).

————— and R. Narula (1995). 'The r&d activities of foreign firms in the US', *International Studies of Management and Organization* (forthcoming).

Gerlach, M. (1992). *Alliance Capitalism* (Oxford and New York: Oxford University Press).

Graham, E. M. and P. R. Krugman (1989). *Foreign Direct Investment in the United States* (Washington, DC: Institute for International Economics).

Gugler, P. and J. H. Dunning (1993). 'Technology based cross-border alliances', in R. Culpan, ed. *Multinational Strategic Alliances* (Binghamton, New York: International Business Press), pp. 123–165.

Harrison, B. (1994). *Lean and Mean: The Changing Landscape of Power in the Age of Flexibility* (New York: Basic Books).

Kogut, B. (1983). 'Foreign direct investment as a sequential process', in C. P. Kindleberger and D. Audretsch, eds, *The Multinational Corporation in the 1980s* (Cambridge, MA: MIT Press), pp. 38–56.

————— and N. Kulatihala (1988). 'Multinational flexibility and the theory of foreign direct investment', Philadelphia, Reginald H. Jones Centre for Management Policy, University of Pennsylvania (mimeo).

Kumar, N. (1990). *Multinational Enterprises in India* (London: Routledge).

Langdon, S. W. (1981). *Multinational Corporations in the Political Economy of Kenya* (London: Macmillan).

Mirza, H. (1986). *Multinationals and the Growth of the Singapore Economy* (New York: St Martin's Press).

Naisbitt, J. (1994). *Global Paradox* (New York: William Morrow and Company).

Peres-Nuñez, N. (1990). *Foreign Direct Investments and International Development in Mexico* (Paris: Development Centre, OECD).

Porter, M. E. (1990). *The Competitive Advantage of Nations* (New York: The Free Press).

Safarian, A. E. (1966). *Foreign Ownership of Canadian Industry* (Toronto: University of Toronto Press).

Stiglitz, J. (1989). *The Economic Role of the State* (Oxford: Basil Blackwell).

Stonehill, A. (1965). *Foreign Ownership in Norwegian Enterprises* (Oslo: Central Bureau of Statistics).

Stubenitsky, F. (1970). *American Direct Investment in Netherlands Industry* (Rotterdam: Rotterdam University Press).

UNCTAD, DTCI (1993). *World Investment Report 1993: Transnational Corporations and Integrated International Production* (New York: United Nations), United Nations publication, Sales No. E.93.II.A.14.

————— (1994a). *World Investment Report 1994.*

————— (1994b). *World Investment Directory, Volume VI, Global Volume.*

UNCTC (1991). *Transnational Corporations: A Selective Bibliography, 1988–1990* (New York: United Nations), United Nations publication, Sales No. E.91.II.A.10.

Van Tulder, R. and G. Junne (1988). *European Multinationals in Core Technologies* (Chichester: John Wiley/IRM).

Wallis, J. J. and D. C. North (1986). 'Measuring the transaction sector in the American economy 1870–1970', in S. L. Engerman and R. E. Gallman, eds, *Long Term Factors in American Economic Growth* (Chicago: University of Chicago Press).

Wendt, H. (1993). *Global Embrace* (New York: Harper Business).

World Bank (1991). *World Development Report* (Oxford and New York: Oxford University Press).

——— (1993). *The East Asian Miracle* (Oxford and New York: Oxford University Press).

5 Foreign direct investment as part of the privatization process*

*Maurice Odle***

Privatization accounts for a significant share of the foreign direct investment that is occurring during the current phase of rapid globalization of the world economy. For a number of cost-cutting, market opportunity and networking reasons, transnational corporations have actively sought to participate in the privatization process. Host countries, for their part, have sought to involve foreign investors in order to tap their vast capital resources and to gain access to their considerable technological, management and marketing skills. This is particularly so in the case of large and complex enterprises in the public sector. This intensive foreign investor role is likely to be sustained over the next few years as a result of the increasing functional convergence of the strategies of transnational corporations and the policies of host Governments.

The upsurge of privatization throughout the world has been matched by an explosion of writings on the subject. The reasons for privatization, the scope of the privatization process in various countries and related social and political constraints, the modes and mechanisms for disposal of state-owned assets, immediate fiscal effects and the hopes for long-term benefits of private managerial efficiency for enterprise performance and industrial development have received considerable attention. While these issues are relevant to all privatizing countries, emphasis in the writings has varied between regions. In the developing countries, a major concern has been the role of privatization in the reduction of both the domestic and external debt and in the development of the stock and capital markets (Ramanadham, 1989). In the developed countries, analysts have tried to assess the economic gains of a conversion from a public to a private monopoly (Vickers and Yarrow, 1991). In the case of the transitional economies of Central

* Reprinted from *Transnational Corporations*, vol. 2, no. 2 (August 1993), pp. 7–34.

and Eastern Europe, commentators have been particularly interested in the fast-track plans and procedures for privatizing virtually a whole economy and the various infrastructural and institutional constraints on the acceleration of this process (Sachs, 1991).

In dealing with privatization, the literature has tended to treat the process as a domestic phenomenon played out between local sellers and buyers. This is probably because of the ideological motivation and social dimensions of the conversion of state-owned enterprises to private entities, whose operations would be determined by the market mechanism rather than Government decision-making. There is more concern with who is selling and what is being sold (industries or firms) and less with distinguishing between the buyers, except for the issue of whether employees have become part-owners ('labour capitalism'), shares have been offered to the general public ('popular capitalism'), or a single buyer or group of buyers has acquired a controlling interest ('institutional capitalism') (Lüders, 1990).

This article attempts to fill a gap in the literature by focusing on the role of foreign direct investment (FDI) in the privatization process. It makes reference to equity and non-equity aspects of foreign involvement and to the experiences of developing and developed countries, and of economies in transition. The introduction describes the general environment. The first section outlines the legal and institutional framework as regards foreign participation in privatization. The second section analyses the incidence of foreign participation in this process. The strategic reasons why transnational corporations (TNCs) participate in the privatization process are discussed in the third part. The final section and the conclusions provide an assessment of why and to what extent countries may want to involve TNCs in the privatization process.

THE ENABLING ENVIRONMENT

The significant degree of foreign involvement in the privatization process has been the result of the considerable liberalization of FDI policies (UN-TCMD, 1992, UNCTAD, 1993) and other macroeconomic reforms that were undertaken within the last ten years. These measures have produced an enabling environment, not only for new investment flows, but also for a participation by TNCs in the privatization of existing assets. Three types of policy measures are particularly noteworthy.

- First, the FDI legislative framework: host countries have relaxed restrictions on investment inflows and introduced measures to attract and facilitate them. These include greater ease of entry and improved rights of establishment, an increase in the foreign ownership share allowed in various sectors and industries, and more generous tax incentives, particularly for export-oriented activities. The streamlining of the implementation of these legislative measures has been achieved via the introduction of 'one-stop shops' and other improvements in the institutional machinery. In addition, many countries have given guarantees, sometimes within the context of bilateral investment treaties, regarding the repatriation of profits and dividends; the expropriation of assets (except in very special circumstances and with adequate compensation); fair and equitable treatment of foreign investors, at least comparable with that accorded to nationals; resort, where necessary, to international arbitration; and protection of intellectual property rights.
- Second, the conducive, but nevertheless passive, legislative framework has been buttressed and supported by a complementary set of pro-active measures. Among other things, host countries have devised information systems and means of accessing international databases for seeking out prospective foreign investors, have undertaken promotion visits abroad to encourage joint-venture partnerships and have organized numerous investment fora and round-tables, sometimes with the aid of embassies, whose functions have become more commercially oriented.
- However, passive and pro-active FDI measures *per se* would not be sufficient. Countries have also liberalized their macroeconomic policies, as part of a general reform and structural adjustment process. Macroeconomic policies include, *inter alia*, a revamping of a country's fiscal policy by reducing corporate and personal income tax rates, a lowering of tariff and non-tariff barriers with respect to the import of intermediate and capital goods, and financial deregulation, allowing foreign investors access to short-term credit in local commercial banks.

These reforms have helped to ensure the success of national privatization programmes and to attract FDI. Successful privatizations have also sent a strong signal that the reforms undertaken are profound and durable. Whereas corporate tax rates, for example, can be altered quite easily, certain types of privatization are very difficult to reverse. Successful privatizations can also boost the confidence of foreigners and serve as a magnet for greater flows of investments in other sectors of the economy.

INCIDENCE OF FOREIGN PARTICIPATION

Data are not available concerning the incidence of foreign participation in the privatization process of host countries. It is estimated that more than 2,000 privatizations have taken place in developing countries (Shirley, 1992) in which a significant proportion involved foreign participation. For example, in Jamaica (which has one of the largest privatization programmes among developing countries), nine out of thirty-eight privatized entities involved the participation of foreigners (Jamaica, National Investment Bank, 1991). In Central and Eastern Europe, the majority of the privatizations that have taken place since the late 1980s consist of sales of enterprises to local investors. In the case of the developed countries, few privatizations involved an outright sale to foreigners, even though, in certain cases, a percentage (usually in the percentage range of 15–20) of the shares was sold in foreign stock markets.

However, the number of privatizations with foreign involvement is not a good indication of the share of foreign direct participation in the privatization process. Foreign direct investment is predominant in large deals in all groups of countries. In Argentina, for example, foreign equity ownership at the end of 1992 amounted to 28 per cent of the $16.5 billion of privatized assets (Table 5.1). In the case of Mexico, the twelve largest foreign participations amounted to approximately 25 per cent of the total value (29.6 trillion Mexican pesos, or about $30 billion) of the 867 enterprises privatized up to November 1991 (Table 5.2). In Poland, of the fifty-two large enterprises that were privatized by the end of 1992, twenty-five had very

Table 5.1 Foreign and other share ownership of privatized assets, Argentina, December 1992

Ownership group	Assets value	
	Millions of dollars	*Percentage*
Foreign companies	4,607.0	27.9
Local companies	6,821.2	41.2
National Government	5,104.5	30.9
TOTAL	16,532.7	100.0

Source: Argentina, Ministry of Economic Affairs.

Table 5.2 Selected large Mexican enterprises sold to foreign corporations, 1991

Mexican enterprises[a]	Transnational corporation	Country	Amount (millions of Mexican pesos)
Interruptores de México	Siemens	Germany	147.4
Renault de México Equipos Automotrices y Automotores Mexicanos	Renault	France	4,699.5
Grupo Garci-Crespo	Pepsi Cola	United States	1,960.0
Envases Generales Continental	Continental Can Co.	United States	1,450.0
Porcelana Euromex	JMP Newcor	United States	6,411.4
Dina Cummins, SA	Cummins Engine Co.	United States	7,920.0
Mecánica Falk, SA	Sundstran Pacific Ltd	Singapore	2,910.8
Cabezas de Acero Kikapoo, SA	Trinity Industries	United States	1,596.6
P. Nacional de Redes	Momoi Fishing Net	Japan	3,407.5
Teléfonos de México	Grupo Carso Southwestern Bell and International France Cable	United States France	6,596,575.8
R. Minerales Mexicanos	E.I. Dupont De Nemours	United States	839.2
Productos Pesqueros	Servac International Ltd	United States	13,000.0
		TOTAL[b]	6,673,887.8

Source: Mexico, Centre for Latin American Monetary Studies (CEMLA), 1991.

[a] The value of this group of enterprises is approximately 25 per cent of the total value (29.63 trillion Mexican pesos) of the 867 enterprises privatized up to November 1991. In January 1992, the exchange rate was $1 = approximately 3,000 Mexican pesos.

[b] Regarding the other enterprises sold to foreigners, in eight cases the Government sold its share to the co-owners, usually the technological partner. In three of these cases the Government had a minor participation in the capital of the enterprise divested. The firms in this situation were: Cia. Mexicana de Radiologia; Sistemas de Energia Autónoma (SEASA); Envases Generales Continental; Cabezas de Acero Kikapoo, SA; Mecánica Falk, SA; Renault de México, SA de CV (closed in 1986); Equipos Automotrices; Dina Cummins, SA.

significant foreign share ownership; more specifically, twelve of these had a foreign ownership share of 80 per cent and ten others had a foreign share of over 50 per cent (Table 5.3). In Hungary, foreigners accounted for about 70 per cent of the approximately $900 million proceeds from the sale of the first 250 privatized enterprises. In the former Czechoslovakia, the share purchased by Volkswagen in the Skoda motor vehicle company amounted to $6.1 billion; the next six largest foreign holdings in Central and Eastern European privatizations were within the $175 million to $106 million range and the next seven were between $83 and $80 million (Table 5.4).

In some countries, FDI inflows resulting from privatization were a significant proportion of total FDI inflows. For example, in Jamaica during 1987–1990, on average, 40 per cent of the $450 million of private foreign capital inflows resulted from privatization (Allen, 1991); in one of these years, 1987, the figure was as high as 94 per cent (Table 5.5). In the Philippines, it is estimated that, for the same period, foreign inflows from privatization amounted to nearly one-third of total private foreign capital inflows (Philippines, Central Bank, 1991).

Besides being involved in the privatization of existing assets, FDI can be used to avoid new capital expenditures by the State. Foreigners may undertake from scratch an investment activity that would normally have been initiated by the State. This type of contracting out to the private sector may occur in the case of infrastructure and utility projects, and it is fundamentally different from turnkey projects, which involve a Government providing the risk capital but retaining ownership. This approach originated on the occasion of the construction of the Channel tunnel. Subsequently, contracting out has taken place in highway projects in Hungary and the Philippines and power-generating projects in Nigeria, Pakistan and Turkey. These projects tend to be large in size and require a considerable amount of capital. Contractors are allowed to build and then operate the plant or project for a specified number of years, until they have fully recouped their capital investment; thereafter, they are contractually required to transfer the asset to the Government. Given the increasing tendency towards downsizing the role of Governments, such 'build, own and operate' (BOT) schemes may remain permanently in private hands, as Governments may decide to sell their repossession rights to the highest bidder.

In addition, there is foreign participation in a number of non-divestiture forms. For example, leasing or management contracts

Table 5.3 Share of foreign investors in Polish privatizations, December 1992

Company's name	Name of foreign investor	Country of foreign investor	Amount paid by foreign investor (millions of dollars)	Foreign investors' share (percentage)
Exbud S.A.	International Trading and Investment	Luxembourg	2.3	17.5
Koszalinskie Zaklady Piwowarski S.A.	AMS Anlagenplanung GmbH	Germany	0.6	30.0
Beloit Fampa S.A.	Beloit Corporation	United States	7.0	80.0
Philips Lighting Poland S.A.	Philips	The Netherlands	21.2	66.7
E. Wedel S.A.	Pepsi Co. Inc.	United States	24.1	40.0
Polfarb S.A.	Basic American Foods	United States	2.3	80.0
Pollena Bydgoszcz-Level Poland S.A.	Unilever	Netherlands/ United Kingdom	19.8	80.0
Pollena Racibórz-Henkel Poland S.A.	Henkel	Germany	3.9	72.4
Pollena Nowy Dwór-Benckiser S.A.	Joh Benkiser GmbH	Germany	2.5	80.0
Alima S.A.	Gerber	United States	6.9	60.0
Pomorska Fabryka Mebli sp. z o.o.	Karl Heinz Klose	Germany	1.9	80.0
Elta sp. z o.o.	Asea Brown Boveri Participations Ltd	Switzerland	9.0	51.0

Table 5.3 continued

Company's name	Name of foreign investor	Country of foreign investor	Amount paid by foreign investor (millions of dollars)	Foreign investors' share (percentage)
Mostostal – Export S.A.	Gerd Bonn	Germany	1.3	28.9
	Kurt Schroder	Germany	3.0	11.1
CPC Amino S.A.	CPC Europe (Group) Ltd.	United States	7.6	80.0
Zaklady Celulozowo-Papiernicze S.A.	International Paper Inc.	United States	120.0	80.0
Fabryka Papieru Malta S.A.	Kronospan GmbH	Germany	1.2	80.0
Przedsiebiorstwo Przemyslu Miesnego w Opolu	Penetex Exp.-Imp. GmbH & Co. KG	Austria	3.2	55.0
Romeo sp. z o.o.	Adolf Ahlers AG	Germany	3.6	80.0
Chifa sp. z o.o.	Aesculap AG	Germany	2.8	80.0
Wydawnictwo Naukowe sp. z o.o.	Cambridge Holding S.A.	Luxembourg	1.0	51.0
Bydgoskie Fabryki Mebli S.A.	Schieder Trading GmbH & Co KG	Germany	2.4	30.0
Tefla S.A.	AT&T Network System International BV	United States	28.0	80.0
MEFTA sp. zo.o.	AEG AG/T.H. Elektrim S.A.	Germany	1.8	60.0
Wizamet S.A.	Gillette Co.	United States	1.5	80.0
Olimex sp. zo.o.	Marga BV (Unilever)	The Netherlands	0.3	70.0

Source: Poland, Information Center of the Ministry of Privatization.

Table 5.4 List of the sixteen largest foreign direct investments in privatized entities in Central and Eastern Europe, 1991

Foreign investor	Home country	Partner	Host country	Industry	Investment amount (millions of dollars)
Volkswagen	Germany	Skoda	Czechoslovakia	Automobiles	6,330
CBC	France	Tourinvest	Czechoslovakia	Hotels	175
General Electric	United States	Tungsram	Hungary	Light bulbs	150
General Motors	United States	Raba-Gyor	Hungary	Cars, engines	150
Pilkington	United Kingdom	HSO	Poland	Glass	140
Guardian	United States	Magyar Uveg	Hungary	Glass	120
Suzuki, C. Itoh	Japan	Ikarus	Hungary	Automobiles	110
Linde	Germany	Technoplyn	Czechoslovakia	Technical gas	106
Electrolux	Sweden	Lehel	Hungary	Refrigerators	83
Hamburger	Austria	Dunapack	Hungary	Packings	82
Ford	United States	Videoton	Hungary	Auto-components	80
Sanofi	France	Chinoin	Hungary	Pharmaceuticals	80
Oberoi	India	Hungar Hotels	Hungary	Hotels	80
U.S. West, Bell	United States	State Authority	Czechoslovakia	Telecommunications	80
Sara Lee	United States	Compack	Hungary	Food	80
ABB	Switzerland	Zamech	Poland	Turbines	50

Source: Wirtschaft (Economy), Wenig Kapital aus dem Westen, 1991.

Table 5.5 Private foreign capital inflows to Jamaica resulting from privatizations, 1987–1990 (millions of dollars)

Item	1987	1988	1989	1990	1987–1990 (total)
Gross private long-term capital	65.70	51.40	133.20	199.40	449.7
of which:					
Privatization[a]	61.95	0.58	52.58	62.89	178.0
(Percentage share)	94.3	1.1	39.5	31.5	39.5

Source: Jamaica, Bank of Jamaica, and Allen (1991).

[a] During the 1987–1990 period, debt – equity swaps amounting to $2.2 million are included.

are prevalent in the hotel industry and land-related development schemes.

Privatization involving TNCs tends to be concentrated in large-scale industries. The enterprises concerned are those in which foreign investors are able to exercise their ownership advantages as sources of capital, technology, management and organizational and marketing skills. Thus, besides consumer products ranging from chocolates to automobiles, TNCs are involved in privatizations of intermediate-goods industries, such as cement, glass, steel, fertilizers and wood and pulp, as well as capital goods industries, such as turbines, transformers, tools and components. Transnational corporations are also increasingly involved in the privatization of enterprises in strategic industries, some of which had been the subject of nationalization only a generation or two ago. The privatization of strategic industries, such as public utilities (including telecommunications, airlines and rail transportation), banking and other sensitive financial institutions, petroleum, mining and other natural resources, and security and defence-related industries, often takes place at a later stage of the privatization process, only after the Government has acquired enough experience in the use of various divestiture modes, mechanisms and procedures (Odle, 1993). Past successes would also have conditioned public acceptance of the privatization of such key industries. Because of the large size of these industries and their technological complexity, there tends to be, paradoxically, an even greater foreign involvement in their privatization than in non-strategic industries.

Among key industries, the incidence of privatization has probably been greatest in telecommunications. The privatization of British

Table 5.6 Foreign equity ownership in privatized telecommunications firms in selected developing countries, 1993

Region/country	Domestic firm	Transnational corporations (percentage ownership)
Asia-Pacific		
Fiji	Fiji International Telecommunications Ltd	Cable & Wireless (49)
Malaysia	Syarikat Telekom Malaysia Berhad	Portfolio (4)
Solomon Islands	Solomon Islands International Telecommunications Ltd	Cable & Wireless (51)
Vanuatu	Vanuatu Telecommunications	France Cable et Radio (49)
Latin America and the Caribbean		
Argentina	ENTEL	Bell Atlantic International in ENTEL North (part of winning Consortia) (32) Telefónica Española in ENTEL South (30)
Barbados	Barbados External Telecommunications Ltd	Cable & Wireless (65)
	Barbados Telephone Company Ltd	Cable & Wireless (65)
Belize	Belize Telecommunications Ltd	British Telecommunications (25)
Chile	CTC	Chase Manhattan Bank (12); Telefónica Internacional (23); and Banco Santander (20)
Dominican Republic	CODETEL	GTE (100)
Guyana	Telephone and Telegraph Ltd	Atlantic Tele-Network Inc. (80)
Jamaica	Telecommunications of Jamaica	Cable & Wireless (59)
	Jamaica International Telecommunications Ltd	Cable & Wireless (49)
Mexico	Teléfonos de México	Southwestern Bell and France Telecom (58)

Region/country	Domestic firm	Transnational corporations (percentage ownership)
St Kitts and Nevis	St Kitts and Nevis Telecommunications Ltd	Cable & Wireless (80)
Trinidad & Tobago	T & T Telephone Co.	Cable & Wireless (49)
Venezuela	CANTV	International Consortium (40) consisting of CTE, Telefónica Española, Electricidad de Caracas, Consorcio Inversionista Mercantil and AT&T
Africa		
Cameroon	FCR	France Cable et Radio (100)
Central African Republic	SOGATI	France Cable et Radio (48)
Chad	Société des Télécommunications Internationales	France Cable et Radio (43)
Djibouti	STID	France Cable et Radio (25)
Equatorial Guinea	GETSA	France Cable et Radio (40)
Madagascar	Société des Télécommunications Internationales de la République Démocratique de Madagascar (STIMAD)	France Cable et Radio (37)
Mali	Télécommunications Internationales du Mali	France Cable et Radio (35)
Nigeria	STIN	France Cable et Radio (23)
Sierra Leone	Sierra Leone External Communications Ltd	Cable & Wireless (40)
Togo	Satelit	France Cable et Radio (45)
Middle East		
Bahrain	Bahrain Telecommunications Company	Cable & Wireless (40)

Source: Based on data in International Finance Corporation (IFC), 1990; The World Bank, 1990; International Telecommunication Union, 1991; and various recent reports.

Telecommunications PLC included the offer of a minority of shares in the Canadian, Japanese and United States stock markets; foreigners were similarly involved in that industry's privatization in Canada, France and New Zealand. Major privatizations in telecommunications in developing countries involving TNCs are listed in Table 5.6. Given the rapid pace of technological change as a result of digital applications, developing countries feel that one way of guaranteeing access to the continually improving technology is to involve TNCs in joint ventures. Also important in developing countries is the need for additional capital to expand and increase the availability of telephone services or simply to reduce the budget deficit.

In the developed countries, the privatization of airlines has sometimes involved foreign investors. British Airways was privatized in 1987, with 15 per cent of the shares being purchased by foreigners. On 14 September 1992, in announcing the $290 million merger of the international carrier Qantas Airways with the domestic carrier, Australian Airlines, the Government indicated that up to 35 per cent of the shares could be offered to either Singapore Airlines, British Airways or Air New Zealand (*The New York Times*, 1992); British Airways eventually won the bid. There has been similar involvement of TNCs in the privatization of the international airlines of a number of developing countries (Table 5.7). As these examples indicate, foreign ownership is usually limited to a minority share so that the airline may still be considered a national carrier and thus be able to continue to receive landing rights in other countries. In the airline industry, the management skills of TNCs and the need to be integrated into their networks are important considerations for a Government in deciding to internationalize (partially) the ownership structure of the airline.

Even highly sensitive industries are beginning to be touched by the privatization process. For example, under the constitution of Mexico, the petroleum industry has to be state owned; but, in a recent decision, TNCs have been allowed to engage in the exploration and development of new oil fields. In the past, FDI had been limited to speciality petrochemicals, rather than to basic petroleum products. In Venezuela, the Government announced in September 1991 that the state oil company will transfer twenty-three out of twenty-eight secondary oil fields to private local and international operators. Likewise, Argentina and Chile have admitted foreign participation in new concessionary areas.[1] Similar developments have taken place in the Nigerian petroleum industry. Ecuador, having recently withdrawn from OPEC, is exploring ways of involving TNCs as a means

Table 5.7 Foreign equity ownership in privatized airlines in selected countries, 1993 (percentage)

Country	Share of foreign ownership
Argentina	30
Australia	35
Chile	35
Costa Rica	10
Czech Republic and Slovak Republic	19
Guatemala	30
Honduras	40
Malaysia	18
Mexico	48
Nicaragua	49
Philippines	30
Peru	49
Russia	31
United Kingdom	15
Venezuela	45[a]

Source: Various reports.

[a] This relates to VIASA, the largest of the three airlines in Venezuela. Since the purchaser, Iberia Airlines of Spain, is state owned, this may not, strictly speaking, constitute a privatization.

of significantly increasing its oil output. In the somewhat less attractive mining, forestry and agricultural industries, foreigners have also begun to return, sometimes in a management capacity.

There are considerable intercountry differences in the incidence of TNC involvement in the privatization process. As will be seen in the next section of this article, these differences are partly a result of host-country policies. Some developing countries, such as Brazil, Malaysia and Mexico, have statutory limitations on the share of foreign ownership of privatized assets. Also, certain countries, like France, Italy, New Zealand and the United Kingdom, have imposed ceilings on foreign shareholdings in strategic enterprises.

In Central and Eastern Europe, TNC participation in the privatization process varies from one country to another, depending on degree of market orientation, FDI policies and strategies adopted. The privatization of medium and large enterprises has been gathering momentum in the Czech Republic, Hungary and Poland, partly because these countries are quite market oriented and possess an institutional framework that is conducive to FDI inflows. In the case of the five new federal States of Germany, massive privatizations have taken place. On the other hand, the members of the New

Independent States and the Baltic States, along with Albania, Bulgaria and Romania, after a hurried enactment of FDI laws, have only recently put into place the basic legislative framework for conducting private business (for example, property laws, company laws, contract laws, bankruptcy laws and income tax laws). As a result, privatization to date involves almost exclusively domestic citizens purchasing assets of small enterprises. For example, in Romania, up to the end of 1992, there were only three privatizations involving foreign investors: a 71 per cent Italian share in a cloth-manufacturing concern, a 49 per cent German acquisition of a brewery and an 81 per cent Swiss holding in a firm manufacturing agricultural products (Romania, National Agency for Privatization, 1993).

The fact that TNCs from most of the major home countries are taking part in the privatization process can have a favourable effect on the selling price of assets, *ceteris paribus*. It was shown above that, of the twelve largest privatization deals in Mexico involving TNCs, seven of the TNCs were from the United States (including one international consortium arrangement), two from France, and one each from Germany, Japan and Singapore. Of the sixteen largest privatizations in Central and Eastern Europe, six involved TNCs from the United States, two each from France and Germany, and one each from Austria, India, Japan, Sweden, Switzerland and the

Table 5.8 Frequency of foreign direct participation, by top ten home countries, in the privatization process in the former German Democratic Republic, end-1992

Home country[a]	Number	Frequency (percentage)
Switzerland	90	15.6
Austria	85	14.7
United Kingdom	78	13.5
France	60	10.4
The Netherlands	54	9.4
United States	54	9.4
Italy	27	4.7
Denmark	25	4.3
Sweden	25	4.3
Canada	7	1.2
Other[b]	72	12.5
TOTAL	577	100.0

Source: Germany, Treuhandanstalt, March 1993.

[a] Excludes the former Federal Republic of Germany.
[b] Includes developing-country investors from Brazil, Guatemala, India, Indonesia, Islamic Rep. of Iran, Israel, the Republic of Korea, Malaysia and Turkey.

United Kingdom. In the five new federal States of Germany, firms from Switzerland, Austria and the United Kingdom head the list of the top ten home countries whose TNCs are participating in the privatization process (Table 5.8).

As with FDI, TNCs from developing countries also play a role, albeit minor, in the privatization process. For example, of the eighteen factories privatized in Cambodia by the end of 1991, eleven were acquired by TNCs from Thailand and by a TNC from Singapore (Cambodia, MOI, 1991). Most of the Cambodian cases involved leases of up to twenty years, rather than outright sales. In Latin America, previously privatized Chilean electricity and gas corporations have been investing heavily in privatizations in Argentina and Peru.

STRATEGIC CORPORATE REASONS FOR TRANSNATIONAL CORPORATIONS TO PARTICIPATE IN PRIVATIZATIONS

A number of the issues related to normal FDI are equally relevant to foreign acquisitions of existing enterprises through privatization. But some concerns are directly relevant to privatization.

Cutting start-up costs

In some instances, TNCs have a choice between greenfield investments and acquiring existing assets. For example, K-Mart (United States) chose to purchase the second largest supermarket (Prior and Maj) in the former Czechoslovakia for $118 million instead of setting up an entirely new enterprise. Such a strategy eliminates a potential rival, exploits appropriate site and locational advantages, avoids any zoning problems, and capitalizes on established local-supplier networks and previous goodwill and name recognition. This captive market strategy also avoids the various approval and licensing difficulties involved in starting up an enterprise in a bureaucratic system that has not yet shed all of the vestiges of central planning. In addition, the acquisition price may be relatively low as the divesting authority may try to compensate TNCs for operating in a still relatively unattractive economic environment (Brezinski, 1992). Similar considerations probably influenced, for example, the decision of Marriott Corporation (United States) to purchase for $20 million the Duna Intercontinental hotel in Budapest, where a shortage of hotel space and prime sites for development exists.

Transnational corporations are frequently not impressed with the enterprise restructuring efforts of Governments prior to privatization. Governments are therefore advised not to engage in costly and time-consuming rehabilitations of plants in the hope of acquiring more favourable selling prices. This relates particularly to export-oriented activities. The reason is that the TNC that wins the bid has not only its own conception of what needs to be done to make the enterprise viable, but also its own understanding of how the newly privatized enterprise fits into its transnational network, what specific product areas and market segments need to be targeted and what others need to be downplayed. The end result is that the TNC may acquire the pre-rehabilitated asset at a relatively low price.

Building regional and global networks

Transnational corporations may view a company to be acquired through privatization not merely as a standalone entity, but as an integral part of a regional or globalized network in which maximizing the profits of a particular affiliate is less important than maximizing the profits of the entire regional or global enterprise (UN-TCMD, 1992; UNCTAD, 1993). For example, when Iberia Airlines of Spain bought into Aerolineas of Argentina, it anticipated triangular flights between Europe, Argentina and the United States, with Buenos Aires, Rio de Janeiro, Sao Paulo, Santiago, Miami, Los Angeles and Madrid linked in the new combined network of planes and schedules. Whereas Iberia could previously fly, for example, a Madrid–Buenos Aires or Madrid–New York route, it could not complete the third leg of the voyage because of lack of landing rights. Iberia hoped to reduce the losses it suffered in 1990 and 1991 by acquiring Aerolineas which had made a profit in those years. Iberia's subsequent purchase of Viasa of Venezuela only served to reinforce this network.

Gaining market share

Maximizing their share of the international market for a particular product (for example, automobiles) or services (such as telecommunications) allows TNCs to maximize long-term profits. Such a strategy sometimes requires a sacrifice of short-term profits. Transnational corporations may acquire assets that are in poor condition and require upgrading and modernization, i.e. assets that may not be immediately profitable. However, if the national market that the privatizing entity serves is large or the international market niche is significant, the enterprise may be integrated effectively into the international production and marketing system of the acquiring TNC. Such an approach is possible even when TNCs acquire less than majority ownership, provided that they succeed in securing management control. For the same reason, TNCs may prefer to maximise their share ownership if profitability prospects are high. Thus, in the case of the Trinidad telecommunications privatization, six of the ten prospective foreign buyers contacted by the consulting firm hired by the Government (Morgan Grenfell) had as a pre-condition majority ownership (Saunders, 1991).

In the automobile industry, when Volkswagen purchased 31 per cent of Skoda (with an agreement for an increase in its shareholding to 70 per cent by 1995), it managed to outbid Renault and Volvo. While the plant is currently geared to supply the Czech Republic and the Slovak Republic, it will probably become increasingly integrated into Volkswagen's network for the whole European market. The alternative, regarded as a second-best solution, would have been to supply Central and Eastern Europe from abroad by expanding the capacity of the plant in Spain, where the inexpensive SEAT model is produced. The market-share and regional-network strategies are twin aspects of long-term strategies pursued by TNCs.

Seeking low-cost investment opportunities

The possibility of acquiring a capital asset at a relatively low price ('bargain basement effect') is an important motivation for TNCs to be involved in privatizations. The recessionary period of the late 1980s and early 1990s has forced TNCs to become more cost sensitive, especially given the increasingly competitive nature of the world economy. Adjustments on the cost side tend to have both a capital and operational aspect.

In countries with privatization schemes, assets may sometimes be priced below market value partly because fiscal and/or foreign-exchange exigencies demand a quick 'fire sale' and inhibit the full exercise of governmental bargaining power. In valuing state-owned enterprises, the true size and earnings potential of local and overseas markets are often not known or not fully taken into account. Of course, the same lack of information could conceivably cause a Government to set too high a price. For example, in the sale of a Hungarian cosmetics company, a prospective buyer, Colgate-Palmolive, originally offered more than any other bidder, but significantly less than the privatization agency's $50 million minimum price. The agency rejected the bid but invited Colgate-Palmolive to continue negotiating; however, the firm decide to withdraw (*The Washington Post*, 1991). In other cases, Governments are eager for share issues to be fully taken up in order to build public confidence in future privatizations; accordingly, share prices can be undervalued. Moreover, international accounting firms and investment banks which sometimes advise Governments and organize the sale of these shares earn generous bonus fees for successful issues.

A dramatic increase in the value of shares and related capital gains frequently occurs soon after privatization. For example, 'at the time of sale of the first tranche of Telmex shares, the market valued the company at $8 billion; at the second sale six months later, it was $14 billion; and a year later when the third tranche was sold, the value was $30 billion' (The World Bank, 1992, p. 11). There are also cases in which a private placement (that does not involve a competitive bidding process) results in an immediate capital gain. For example, Demerara Woods, a forestry enterprise in Guyana, was sold for £9.7 million in 1991 (including a fifty-year lease on 440,000 hectares) to Lord Beaverbrook, who then resold it within a few months for £60 million (*The Guardian*, 1991).

Certain TNCs and creditor banks showed an interest in debt–equity swap arrangements in Latin America partly because of the resulting indirect price discount on the assets earmarked for privatization. In Central and Eastern Europe, TNCs demanded a negative premium or a below-market price for what they perceived as political and social risks, bureaucratic obstacles, repatriation-of-profits difficulties and other economic problems associated with operating in the environment of a transitional economy. In certain developing countries, despite FDI and macro-economic policy reforms, TNCs factor in the adverse effect of current political instability and tend to seek a compensating price reduction to offset the higher rate at which future profits need to be discounted.

Low unit-operating costs of privatized assets are another attractive feature to TNCs. Some state-owned enterprises in developing countries tended to pay lower wages than those in the private sector; this sometimes compensated for the quantity of labour being higher per unit of output. For example, the average wage in the Tungsram Lighting Company in Hungary was one-tenth that of General Electric in the United States. Although the size of the labour force in Tungsram at the time of the purchase was deemed to be too large, labour costs in that company accounted for only one-quarter of the cost of making a light bulb compared with one-half in General

Electric in the United States. It is also possible to shed surplus labour in order to enhance profits, unless employment-performance requirements in the purchase contract explicitly prevent it.

In certain circumstances, TNCs may initially prefer to hold a management contract rather than purchase assets of an enterprise. This allows a TNC to assess the enterprise from an insider position, gaining a bargaining advantage over other potential bidders in the event that the Government eventually decides to divest the assets. For example, certain TNCs adopted this strategy in the mining industry because of either the poor state of the privatized firms or the weakness of the international market for commodities (Greenidge, 1991).

In this regard, the three- to five-year moratorium on the repatriation of profits and the ten- to twelve-year moratorium on the repatriation of capital that are typical of debt–equity swaps, have reduced the attractiveness of low prices of the latter as a mechanism for encouraging TNCs to participate in the privatization process.

CONSIDERATIONS FOR GOVERNMENTS WHEN INVOLVING TRANSNATIONAL CORPORATIONS IN PRIVATIZATION PROGRAMMES

Governments involve TNCs in the privatization process to widen their options, increase the potential price at which the assets can be sold (the higher the number of bidders, the greater the probability of receiving a higher price) and guarantee access to current and future international capital, managerial, technological and marketing resources. At the same time, security concerns are such that Governments sometimes retain some degree of national involvement (in the form of a local private, employee or residual public-sector holding), especially in key enterprises.

Special needs of large-scale privatizations

In those countries in which the savings rates are low, local financial institutions tend to be underdeveloped and other aspects of the capital markets are lacking in absorptive capacity. The ability of the local private sector to purchase state-owned enterprises is therefore limited. At the same time, some Governments may feel that FDI should be a supplement, rather than a substitute, for local capital. Consequently, small and medium-size state-owned enterprises have typically been offered to local investors, and TNC involvement has been restricted mainly to the larger enterprises. For example, in Central and Eastern Europe, only citizens were allowed to participate in the auction of the thousands of 'mom and pop' retail and restaurant businesses. Only in the second round of the auction process were bids from foreigners entertained, although for at least one country it was said that 'many foreigners, mostly Germans, are using Czech fronts to buy property' (*The Chicago Tribune*, 1991). Similarly, there was a tendency for TNCs in developing countries to be denied, *de facto*, the right of entry by the Governments' administrative apparatus with respect to the purchase and sale of small enterprises, partly in an attempt to develop the local private sectors.

For the larger state-owned enterprises, however, there is often a need to tap the reservoir of capital resources that TNCs represent. This would be even more necessary if the State had disposed of a considerable number of enterprises within a relatively short period, and the local capital market had become somewhat saturated. In the developed economies, where state-owned enterprises tend to be large in size, the local capital market has considerable absorptive capacity; however, Governments have often tried to attract TNCs in order to earn higher prices from the increased aggregate demand (Jones, 1991).

Of course, capital is not the only reason for engaging TNCs in the privatization process. Many of the larger enterprises involve complex technologies and are constantly undergoing rapid product or process change. Furthermore, advanced management skills are often in short supply and, in some cases, the effective marketing of a product requires access to the global or regional networks of TNCs.

Reducing the foreign debt has been an additional motivating factor for the increasing involvement of TNCs in the privatization process. Thus a number of important privatizations involved the capitalization of debt, including the Argentine telephone and airline deals, the Chilean telephone transactions, the Philippines airline arrangements and the minority foreign acquisition of the Usiminas steel plant in Brazil. However, some countries, instead of utilizing debt–equity swaps, have preferred to use the proceeds from traditional direct sales to retire existing foreign debt. In addition, a number of countries, Jamaica being a notable example, deliberately chose to sell certain enterprises to foreigners (via a private placement process) in order to acquire quickly foreign exchange, in keeping with the imperatives of the International Monetary Fund and The World Bank restructuring process.

Control measures relating to strategic enterprises

Many Governments decide to retain a certain degree of national involvement in strategic enterprises they choose to privatize. At the same time, they do not want to exercise control, even though they desire to enjoy the financial benefits of substantial ownership. Thus, in the privatizations of Telmex and Mexicana Air, the Government ceded control by retaining non-voting stock in the case of the former, and putting voting shares into a trust in the case of the latter. Thus, the Government was merely interested in exercising influence rather than effective management control. Eastern Europe tends to employ a fairly standard majority/minority/residual formula for foreign, employee and government share-ownership with respect to the privatization of large enterprises. So far, those enterprises have not included what was traditionally classified as strategic enterprises, partly because those countries have not yet reached an advanced stage in the privatization process.

In the developed countries, Governments have sought to retain special voting rights if the foreign investor's share exceeds a certain amount. This approach arose out of the United Kingdom's experience with the privatization of British Aerospace, in which foreigners managed to acquire more shares (in the secondary market) than was originally allotted to them. Under the 'golden share' rule of the United Kingdom, a special rights preference share of one pound allows the Government to intervene if the national interest is deemed to be threatened, as in the case of a TNC securing more than 15 per cent of the shares of an enterprise. The figure is 20 per cent in the case of the 'specific share' provision of the privatization law of France.[2] In New Zealand, the same concept is referred to as the 'Kiwi share'. In the case of the Australian airline privatization, the Government has stated that it plans to introduce a 'golden share' measure in order to be able to commandeer aircraft in the event of a national emergency. In Italy, the golden share rule applies to public utilities.

In addition, Governments have tended to set up public-utility Commissions to protect the public interest with respect to telecommunications, electricity, gas and other such activities. Typically this involves a stipulation of either a maximum rate of return or, even more preferably, a maximum price under which an enterprise being privatized can seek to minimize costs and thus enhance profits. In addition, the Commissions monitor the availability and quality of services. In the case of tradable products, Governments have sought to expose the privatized enterprises to international competition.

Performance requirements

In privatizing strategic industries and other large state-owned enterprises, host countries have sought to gain firm commitments, equivalent to performance requirements, to advance economic development. Such commitments relate primarily to expansion and modernization and are a *quid pro quo* for operating in a large and, frequently, near monopolistic market and for selling a product or service that has an important economic and social impact. To complete a deal, a trade-off is sometimes made by Governments between accepting a lower price in exchange for performance requirements to capture certain external economies. In other situations, incentives are used to offset performance requirements. For example:

- In the case of the 1990 privatization of Mexico's telecommunications enterprise, the Government obtained a binding obligation from the foreign companies to make modernization investments valued at $1 billion a year until the late 1990s (Lieberman, 1991). The new entity is also required to install 4.5 million new lines, amplify rural service by 100 per cent, introduce optical-fibre communication, increase digitalization by at least 65 per cent, upgrade 480,000 obsolete lines and maintain the same price in real terms until 1996, with a 3 per cent annual decrease thereafter.
- Similarly, in the case of the privatization of telecommunications in Chile and Jamaica, commitments were made with respect to modernization plans valued at $250 million and $400 million, respectively.
- The Mexican authorities also obtained certain commitments when privatizing the airline industry. The leading firm in the consortium of foreign investors pledged $3 billion in investment over the next ten years to improve ground facilities, computerize the reservation system, replace aged planes, double the size of the fleet and increase employment from 13,000 to 21,500 (*Business International*, 1990).
- In Chile, SAS of Sweden promised to inject new capital into the privatized airline and thereby won the bid over other foreign airlines.
- In the former Czechoslovakia, Volkswagen managed to win the bidding for the Skoda Motor Company partly because of its commitment to invest $5.3 billion by the turn of the century; double Skoda's annual production to 400,000 cars a year by 1997; help Skoda to develop a new range of models; make avail-

able to Skoda its purchasing and parts network while allowing
Skoda to retain its own identity; and clean up the pollution of
the factory sites (*The Economist*, 1990).

● In the five new federal States of Germany, performance requirements are an integral part of the privatization process across
sectors: 'Price is not the only criterion; indeed an investor who
pledges to inject new capital and management and to keep or
create jobs will be preferred to one who is merely offering more
cash' (Treuhandanstalt, 1991, p. 5).

Certain countries have instituted general regulations with respect to
the level of employment and wages after privatization. Both foreign-
oriented and domestic-oriented privatization are affected. For example, in Malaysia, a retrenchment of employees is not permitted during
the first five years of privatization (Montagu-Pollock, 1990). In
Cambodia, labour is not permitted to be hired for less than $25 per
month in privatized enterprises.

Finally, there is the issue of the appropriateness of performance
requirements in a rapidly liberalizing world of trade and investment
relations. Reference was already made to the possibility of a lower
price for the privatized asset, specific incentives and monopoly-type
conditions being used as counterbalancing factors. Moreover, privatization *per se* constitutes a mere transfer of assets and is not
equivalent to net capital formation. In addition, TNCs have a choice
whether or not to participate in a privatization; this contrasts with a
situation in which a Government imposes performance requirements
on foreign enterprises that are already operating in the country,
without compensatory subsidies.

Preferred forms of foreign participation

The form and degree of foreign participation vary considerably
between countries, partly because of differences in levels of economic development, technological capabilities, availability of local
capital and stock-market maturity, the size of foreign debt and fiscal
burdens, and the political environment of the privatization process.
For example, certain countries seem to be pursuing a 'majority-share-
permissive model' whereby a foreigner is allowed to acquire the bulk
of the equity in a privatizing enterprise. This seems to be the path that
Poland has taken with respect to large enterprises. Foreign investors
are frequently allowed to hold as much as 80 per cent of the equity,
with 20 per cent being reserved for employees. Similarly, in Hungary

and in the former Czechoslovakia, foreigners tend to be offered a majority share, with the remainder divided between employees and the Government.

In developing countries, however, there is no consistent pattern of foreign majority ownership, even in those countries whose privatization policies are foreign-exchange driven. Rather, a 'minority-share-limitation model' seems to be applied, although control frequently resides with the foreign investor (rather than the Government or a local private partner). Moreover, some countries exercise flexibility in implementing their foreign minority ownership policy by not ruling out the possibility of TNCs acquiring majority equity shares during the life of the projects as a result of investment and expansion plans that, in effect, reduce the shares of the local partners. The most extreme manifestations of the minority-equity approach can be found in countries such as Brazil and Malaysia. However, even Malaysia has recently relaxed its ownership restrictions by differentiating between sectors; majority ownership is permitted in export-oriented enterprises and in high-technology industries.

In most developed countries, a 'sector-determined participation model' is rigorously applied by way of the golden share mechanism to limit foreign share ownership severely in public utilities and other strategic enterprises. Most developing countries do not adopt such a rigid approach to their strategic industries. However, all countries deny so far majority ownership to foreign investors in the airline industry.

Finally, in a number of transactions, developing countries have also employed the non-equity form of contracting out the management function. In some cases, these enterprises may be sold outright after the foreign managers make them more profitable and manifestly viable. This 'transitory-management model' is reflected in the privatization practices of such West African countries as Guinea, Côte d'Ivoire, Nigeria and Togo. Leasing and BOT arrangements contain elements of both the transitory-management model and the majority-share-permissive model. A sort of macro version of the transitory management model is the recent 'mass privatization' decision by the Government of Poland to turn over majority of the shares in 600 large state-owned enterprises to twenty national investment/mutual funds to be run (with full powers of restructuring) by Western investment companies for ten years for a fee based upon the performance of the companies under their jurisdiction (*The New York Times*, 1993).

CONCLUSIONS

The involvement of TNCs in privatizations has constituted an important element in the liberalization process. Many strategic industries previously under public ownership, which had excluded (wholly or partly) the local and foreign private sectors, have become more open to both. In addition, there are many other large, though not necessarily strategic, industries, in which, for similar reasons, countries have seen fit to involve TNCs in the privatization process.

This process of intensive foreign involvement is likely to continue, partly because of the continuous movement of macroeconomic philosophy in the direction of greater competitiveness (both within and across borders) and the related change in attitudes towards FDI. The privatization process is not only dynamic but also infectious, and the role of FDI is much greater than has been indicated by the previous literature on the subject. However, the incidence and timing of large-scale privatizations will probably continue to vary across regions and subregions. In certain developed countries, such as the United Kingdom, the process is tapering off, whereas in France, Italy and Sweden, for example, a major phase has just begun. There are similar variations in the developing countries. In a number of Latin American countries, with Brazil as a notable exception, the mature stage of privatizing large enterprises has already been reached. In most countries of Africa and many parts of Asia and Central and Eastern Europe, however, this has yet to occur.

Foreign direct investment plays an important part in the privatization process because it is a critical source of capital. Capital markets in many developing countries are inherently thin; competing against foreign buyers maximizes the selling price of the assets being privatized and improves the performance requirements and other conditions pertaining to their use. Even when local capital is adequate and available, the participation of TNCs can help to bolster foreign exchange (or reduce the level of foreign indebtedness).

In addition, an involvement by TNCs is often seen as a source of technology, management, marketing and organization skills. This helps to explain why, in certain cases, even profitable state-owned enterprises have offered a proportion of their shares to foreign investors. The capital and technological requirements of modern industry are such that a local enterprise frequently cannot survive as a standalone entity in an increasingly competitive environment and in a world of very rapid technological change. The goal of national self-reliance has not been found sustainable and has been replaced by the paradigm of global interdependence.

The benefits that accrue from foreign involvement relate not only to the short-term gains from greater efficiency but depend also on the TNCs' willingness to use their considerable capital, technological and managerial resources to expand and modernize plants, machinery and equipment to meet the challenges of a more competitive international economy. In this regard, the behaviour of a TNC depends partly on how the privatized entity fits into its larger corporate network. Backward and forward linkages may not necessarily be maximized within a single local market. As a result, although TNCs are much more cognizant than they used to be of host-country goals, the imperatives of producing for an international market result sometimes in a conflict of objectives. The privatization process is of a much too recent vintage to have yielded sufficient empirical evidence on the net social gains to a country, even though the long experience with respect to normal FDI and a recent study on the consequences of selling public enterprises (World Bank, 1992) could provide some guidance.

NOTES

** The views expressed here are those of the author and do not necessarily represent those of the United Nations.
1   Subsequently, the Government of Argentina decided to privatize the existing state petroleum enterprise, YPF. A total of $3.04 billion worth of shares, equivalent to over 45 per cent of YPF, were sold on 27 June 1993, with the bulk being taken up by foreign investors.
2   Ministerial approval is required in relation to foreign acquisitions beyond 10 per cent and, in the case of defence-related enterprises, 5 per cent.

REFERENCES

Allen, Mary (1991). Privatization and monetary developments in Jamaica: a preliminary assessment. Paper presented at the 23rd Annual Conference of the Caribbean Regional Monetary Studies Conference, 25–28 November, Belize, mimeo.

Brezinski, Horst (1992). Privatization in East Germany. *Economic Journal on Eastern Europe and the Soviet Union*, 1 (January), pp. 1–21.

Business International (1990). Privatization in Latin America: New competitive opportunities and challenges (December).

Cambodia, Ministry of Industry (1991). (Unpublished data).

The Chicago Tribune (1991). Czechoslovakia's rush to reform becomes a perilous free-for-all (22 October).

The Economist (1990). Volkswagen and Skoda: The people's car heads East (15 December).

Greenidge, Carl (1991). Privatization under structural adjustment in Guyana.

Paper presented at the Ninth Annual Conference of the Trinidad and Tobago Economic Association, 15–16 November, Trinidad, mimeo.

The Guardian (1991). Beaverbrook's £50m. forest deal (1 November).

Jamaica, National Investment Bank Privatization Division (1991). (Unpublished data).

Jones, Susan K. (1991). The road to privatization: the issues involved and some lessons from New Zealand's experience. *Finance and Development*, 28, 1 (March), pp. 39–41.

Lieberman, Ira (1991). Privatization in Latin Ameica: an overview. Paper presented at the Harvard University Development Club Conference on Privatization in Latin America and Eastern Europe, 13 April, mimeo.

Lüders, Rolf (1990). Lessons from massive Chilean privatizations for Eastern European countries. Paper prepared for UN-TCMD, mimeo.

Montagu-Pollock, Matthew (1990). Privatisation: what went wrong. *Asian Business* (August), pp. 32–39.

The New York Times (1992). Merger joins Quantas and Australian Airlines (15 September).

———— (1993). Plan to privatize wins Polish vote (1 May).

Odle, Maurice (1993). Towards a stage theory approach to privatization. *Public Administration and Development*, 13, 1 (February), pp. 17–35.

Philippines, Central Bank (1991). (Unpublished data).

Ramanadham, V. V., ed. (1989). *Privatization in Developing Countries*. London and New York: Routledge.

Romania, National Agency for Privatization (1993). (Unpublished data).

Sachs, Jeffrey (1991). Accelerating privatization in Eastern Europe. World Bank Annual Conference on Development Economics. Washington, DC, 25–26 April, mimeo.

Saunders, Richard (1991). TSTT and the regional telecommunications industry. Paper presented at the Ninth Annual Conference of the Trinidad and Tobago Economics Association, Trinidad, 15–16 November, mimeo.

Shirley, Mary (1992). Privatization: misconceptions, glib answers, and lessons. Guest Lecture No. 8 of the Carnegie Council/DRT International Privatization Project, 8, March.

Treuhandanstalt (1991). The Chance of the 90s: investing in Eastern Germany. Berlin: Treuhandanstalt (August).

———— (1993). The Chance of the 90s: investing in Eastern Germany. Berlin: Treuhandanstalt (March).

UNCTAD (1993). *World Investment Report: Transnational Corporations and Integrated International Production*, Sales No. E.93.II.A.14.

UN-TCMD (1992). *World Investment Report: Transnational Corporations as Engines of Growth*, Sales No. E.92.II.A.24.

Vickers, John and George Yarrow (1991). Economic perspectives in privatization. *Journal of Economic Perspectives*, 5, 2 (Spring), pp. 111–132.

The Washington Post (1991). Flood of foreign investment capitalizes on new Hungary; ventures from overseas overshadow state privatization (10 November).

The World Bank (1992). Welfare consequences of selling public enterprises. Case studies from Chile, Malaysia, Mexico and the United Kingdom. Synthesis of cases and policy summary. Washington, DC, Country Economics Department (June), mimeo.

6 The role of foreign direct investment in the transition from planned to market economies*

*Carl H. McMillan***

This article explores the links between foreign direct investment and economic systems in the experience of the countries of Central and Eastern Europe (including the former Soviet Union). The institutional characteristics of economic systems of the Soviet type dictated an industrialization with virtually no recourse to foreign direct investment. The initiation of processes to dismantle that system has provided the scope for a significant opening of that area's economies. The transition managers' interest in foreign direct investment has been motivated by perceptions of its important potential contributions to industrial restructuring and to the development of the institutions of a market-based economy. The article explores that rationale and assesses it in terms of the initial response of foreign investors. It argues that foreign direct investment is unlikely to play the significant role in the transition originally anticipated.

As the drama in the East continues to unfold, the situation calls for continuing assessment and reassessment. The dust has not settled from the major upheavals of the turn of the decade, but some of the contours of the new landscape are beginning to be discernible. In any assessment of the emerging role for foreign direct investment (FDI) in the Eastern economies, it is important to distinguish the potential from the actual. This article will first set forth the *ex ante*, the desired, role for FDI, which provides the rationale for it as an important element in the transition. It will then use this as a framework for analysing – in a necessarily preliminary way (through 1992) – the *ex post* actual role of FDI.

First, however, it is necessary to address the role of FDI in the

* Reprinted from *Transnational Corporations*, vol. 2, no. 3 (December 1993), pp. 97–119.

period of the Soviet-style economic system. The experience under communism is widely regarded as a past offering little to build upon, therefore necessitating a radical and rapid departure. That past has nonetheless left a legacy of institutions and experiences that inescapably shapes the current transition and influences its outcomes.

THE INHERITANCE

Foreign direct investment played virtually no role in the industrial development of the Eastern economies under traditional state-socialist regimes and central planning.[1] Only as some East European countries began to experiment with modifications of the traditional system did they begin to flirt with the notion that FDI might be useful to the purposes of economic reform.[2] Like the reform measures more generally, these steps to permit FDI were a matter of too little, as well as too late.

The attitude of communist regimes towards such investment was in fact highly ambivalent.[3] They were attracted to it as a means of stimulating the sluggish performance of their economies. Expectations in this regard centred on a perception of the important role that transnational corporations (TNCs) had come to play in the world at large through the international transfer of modern industrial technologies and because of the need to tap into these flows. Expectations tended to be exaggerated by the official rhetoric that typically accompanied a major new policy course and that often took on a momentum of its own. This was most sharply illustrated by the Soviet domestic and international campaign to promote the introduction of 'joint enterprises' in 1987.

At the same time, communist governments, conscious of their fundamental political weakness, were clearly concerned about the potentially destabilizing effects on their official ideologies, planned economic systems and controlled societies of according to foreign firms a major direct role in their economies. These concerns led them to impose severe, initial restrictions on FDI that were only gradually relaxed.

The most powerful constraints, however, lay not in the ambivalence of FDI policy but in the nature of the communist political and economic systems and in their deterrent effects. Restrictions on private economic activity, state-planned and controlled resource allocation and administratively determined wages and prices limited the scope for TNCs to exercise effective control over operations in host Eastern countries. Moreover, the failure of attempts at economic reform under communism to address fundamental systemic deficiencies perpetuated these constraints. It was in fact questionable whether the concept of 'foreign direct investment' in its customary Western usage was even applicable in these circumstances.[4]

Considerations such as these militated towards a self-imposed isolation, one that was externally reinforced by the political divide between East and West that characterized the cold war period. As a result, one of the unique characteristics of the development experience of the Eastern economies was that their industrialization occurred largely without FDI.

Communist rule therefore left a rather poor inheritance, both in terms of the stock of FDI and in terms of the history of accumulated experience with it. The conditions that constrained TNCs had kept it marginal in form, dimension and effect.[5] For the most part, FDI had been a neglected issue, even of external economic policy. Moreover, the fear and suspicion that permeated Eastern FDI policy under communism left a negative psychological legacy. It meant that FDI was not only little known and understood, but also suspect. This in many cases reinforced national psychologies of suspicion of TNCs inherited from earlier historical periods.

The situation had begun to change, however, in the last years of communist rule. The shift in policy towards TNCs, that had begun very gradually in the 1970s, accelerated in the 1980s, especially in the second half of the decade. As a result, by the 1990s, successor Governments inherited the foundations of a legal and regulatory regime for FDI. More importantly, they inherited the momentum for rapid liberalization of the conditions for FDI that had been lately introduced by their predecessors. They also benefited from an already sharply stimulated investor interest in the opportunities opening up in the region, especially in the large, resource-rich Soviet economy.

PRINCIPAL ELEMENTS OF THE POST-COMMUNIST ECONOMIC TRANSITION

The upheavals that led to the fall of communist governments in Central and Eastern Europe (in 1989–1990) and in the former Soviet Union (in 1991) removed the political constraints that had inhibited earlier attempts at reform of their 'command' economies, and made much more radical economic change possible. Successor Governments could act on the basis of a strong political consensus in favour of a major economic transformation: replacement of the now discredited system of comprehensive state ownership and allocation of resources by a market-based, mixed-ownership economy along Western lines. Within this broad consensus, disagreements centred on the desirable extent of marketization and privatization of the economy (basically a question of which Western models to emulate), and on the pace and sequencing of the transition.

An extensive literature has quickly emerged on the post-communist transition.[6] It suffices to recall here its principal aspects in order to provide a framework for an examination of the role of FDI in these processes. The processes of transition will be dealt with under the following broad headings: *stabilization* (both in the fiscal-monetary sense and in terms of broader economic recovery); *marketization* (the dismantling of the system of state planning and control and its replacement by the institutions of the market); *privatization* (a major shift in the ownership structure through denationalization of state assets and the encouragement of new private enterprise); and finally the attendant *restructuring* of domestic production and foreign trade (resulting from both the internal forces of reform and developments in the external economy). Before turning to FDI, some elaboration of each of these four pillars of the transition is necessary.

The most urgent task of the transition in many countries has been *stabilization*. The disruptive effects of the transfer of political power and the dismantling of old institutions of administrative control, against the backdrop of structural imbalances inherited from the previous 'economies of shortage', precipitated budget deficits, generated strong inflationary pressures, permitted the rapid accumulation of bad debts and led to growing imbalances on external accounts. For some countries, the situation attained crisis proportions. Governments came under strong international pressure to pursue comprehensive, macroeconomic stabilization programmes as a condition for external cooperation and assistance in the transition.

In purely economic terms, monetary stabilization can, if necessary, be achieved relatively quickly (although not painlessly) through a package combining austerity measures with institutional reforms required for their implementation. Politically, however, Governments may not be strong enough to sustain, or even to undertake, the 'shock therapy' measures prescribed by domestic and foreign economists.[7] In this event, the stabilization process will be more gradual but not necessarily less painful.

Unfortunately, in the initial years of post-communist adjustment, Eastern Governments have been beset by other, no less severe economic problems that have complicated and slowed the transition. The Eastern economies have suffered harsh shocks from sources other than self-imposed austerity measures, adopted in the interests of near-term stabilization. The collapse of preferential trade under the Comecon system and the disintegration of the Soviet Union, the axis of the regional economy, forced a drastic foreign trade reorientation at a time of world recession. The disjuncture was aggravated by the dissolution of another linchpin in regional economic relations, the former German Democratic Republic. Meanwhile, the rapid decline in Soviet oil production after 1988, which was the culmination of long developing trends in the industry, now exacerbated by national economic and political decline, created a severe energy crisis in the region. Political instability, in some cases spilling over into civil strife, has raised uncertainty, disrupted the course of economic relations and impeded foreign assistance. The list has lengthened of nation states in the area that have not survived the post-communist transition as political entities. Thus economic recovery and political stabilization have overshadowed the restoration of monetary/fiscal balance as urgent policy objectives.

The task of marketization is two pronged. There is the easier (but certainly not painless) dimension of 'liberalization'. This entails the dismantling of the institutions of centralized planning and management that had operated through formally established targets, quotas, taxes and subsidies, as well as through less formal instruments of control. Here, the freeing of prices and wages and the reduction in foreign exchange controls have been among the first measures undertaken in most countries. The more difficult dimension (inevitably slower to achieve) is the establishment of market-based institutions to replace the allocative mechanisms of the old system. As has come to be understood, this involves a staggering task of institution building in the educational, legal and commercial spheres. It means, among other things, the development of new managerial, legal and accounting professions, the creation of a new body of commercial law and the mechanisms for its enforcement, the establishment of a new banking system and related financial markets, the construction of a new system of wholesale trade and the institution of a new tax system, of new systems of social welfare and of mechanisms to foster competitive markets.

The processes of privatization also involve the dismantling of old institutions and the creation of new ones. The objective is to replace the dominant state institutions of ownership with a system that accords primacy to alternative forms, notably private ownership. This involves the restructuring of state enterprises and the transfer of the ownership of their assets to their managers and workers, to the citizenry at large and to foreign owners. This is accomplished through a variety of means, from sale or mass distribution of property rights administered by state property agencies through more haphazard, 'spontaneous' privatizations initiated by enterprise collectives. Bankruptcy laws and procedures provide a mechanism by which state enterprises that are not economically viable can be closed and their assets reallocated. At the same time, the formation of new enterprises by private initiative is permitted and their growth encouraged.

Economic restructuring was on the Eastern policy agenda long before the current transition. Under communism, the Eastern economies were developed not only in relative isolation but also according to political priorities set by the party and state. It became increasingly apparent that party/state preferences had created and perpetuated an industrial structure that was in significant respects inefficient by international standards. Officially, structural problems tended to be viewed as signs of industrial backwardness that could be remedied by periodic 'modernization' drives. As these problems became more intensely felt, however, they were more frankly addressed as central to slowing growth and poor export performance. They were increasingly understood as requiring the restructuring ('perestroika') not only of the economy itself but also of the institutions that had determined its development.

The post-communist transformation is designed to continue and to accelerate this approach. Stabilization will eliminate state subsidies to inefficient enterprises; while privatization and marketization will subject them to the force of economic rather than administrative criteria. For most countries, the resulting industrial restructuring will be the most painful aspect of the transition. The enterprises most affected tend to be large and concentrated in industries long favoured, not only in terms of more generous investment funds but also in terms of higher wages and social benefits to workers. This enlarges the scope of the required structural adjustment and its economic, social and political repercussions. Concerns about these consequences have forced Governments to back away from radical reform policies and to adopt a more gradualist approach to economic restructuring.

Moreover, in many cases, most acutely in that of the former Soviet Union, the problems of restructuring are magnified by the task of demilitarizing the economy. The dismantling of the defence complex adds greatly to the scale of restructuring, and the demobilization of the armed forces compounds the attendant social problems. In Russia, where much of the Soviet defence industry was concentrated, the scale of the problem has made it much more difficult to find the political will to proceed with structural reform.

The shift from plan to market also involves dismantling the monolithic system of state trading and replacing it with a decentralized, diversified and competitive framework for the conduct of external relations. Determination by market rather than by plan would inevitably have led to a major restructuring and reorientation of foreign trade, as competitive forces substituted for administrative criteria. The collapse of the Comecon regional economy and the break up of the former Soviet Union greatly accelerated these processes. The dismantling of the state trading system has liberalized the conditions for trade and reduced the traditional insulation of the Eastern economies from external market forces. The ending of the cold war has eliminated another cause of their international isolation and has created the political conditions that have allowed their incorporation into the organizational framework of the international economy.

In sum, a fundamental dimension of the transition is the opening of relatively closed economies and their reintegration into the world economy. In particular, their opening up to foreign investment has been accelerated.

FOREIGN DIRECT INVESTMENT IN THE TRANSITION

In their approach to FDI, post-communist Governments have been less inhibited by political and ideological concerns than their predecessors. They have more openly sought FDI, in all its forms, and have even competed to establish regulatory conditions attractive to potential investors. Most important, the programmes they have launched, to establish market economies with extensive private ownership, are establishing systemic conditions more favourable to TNCs.

The opening of the Eastern economies to FDI may be viewed simply as the re-establishment of a net capital import position *vis-à-vis* the West. This would be a return to what could be regarded as a more natural relationship, given relative levels of development, and one which state policies in the communist period had artificially distorted. The standard literature on the causes and effects of FDI could then be applied to the analysis.

However, this is not the whole, or even more important, story. In fact, current policies are strongly motivated by a special set of considerations, namely the positive contributions that FDI can make in the transitional period to its reformist aims and processes.[8]

Here, its beneficial effects are perceived to be as significantly institutional as purely economic. Although shared by Eastern reformers, this
viewpoint is perhaps even more strongly held by Western advisers,
and it is a fundamental premise of Western economic assistance to
economies in transition. As the leading international economic organizations in their joint assessment of the Soviet economy maintained
in 1991, 'attracting substantial flows of foreign investment could be
crucial in the transition to a market economy' (IMF, 1991, p. 75). The
United Nations Economic Commission for Europe asserted, more
generally, that 'foreign direct investment is expected to play a
major role in the transformation of the Eastern economies' (United
Nations/ECE, 1992, p. 96). The potential contributions to the major
transitional processes outlined in the preceding section are examined
next.

STABILIZATION AND RECOVERY

Perhaps the aspect of the transition in which FDI has the least obvious
part, given its essentially long-term nature, is in achieving the near-
term goal of monetary stabilization. Inflows of direct investment
capital, especially when involving cash transfers, improve the host-
country's balance-of-payments position. This in turn facilitates
stabilization policy and provides policy-makers greater room for
manoeuvre. In some Central European countries, these FDI-related
financial inflows have begun to be substantial. In Hungary, for
example, the net FDI inflows on a cash basis amounted in 1991 to
about $1.54 billion, which may be compared with convertible cur-
rency reserves at end-1991 of $4.02 billion and a net convertible
foreign debt of $14.55 billion (National Bank of Hungary, 1991).

If stabilization is defined in broader terms as recovery from the
economic shocks that have plagued the Eastern transitions, FDI has a
more direct part to play. Significant inflows of real resources in the
form of capital, technology and know-how can speed up recovery and
thereby accelerate the longer-term processes of transition. The Eastern economies that have shown the first signs of recovery, those in
Central Europe, are in fact those that have benefited from the relatively largest FDI inflows.[9]

MARKETIZATION

It is in the area of institutional transformation, the creation of the
institutional infrastructure that allows markets to function effectively,

that FDI may be especially important to a successful transition. In the first place, it creates pressure for institution building. As has been argued, a liberal regulatory regime is not in itself sufficient to attract FDI on a major scale. The institutional conditions to make it effective and profitable must also be created. For example, as Friedrich Levcik (1991) noted, Governments have been under great pressure to make progress towards currency convertibility in order to accommodate FDI requirements.

Pressures for institution building are generated not only at the level of Government policy, but at the micro-level as well. Foreign investors create a strong and profitable demand for banking, accounting and other business services. At the same time, FDI is a mechanism for improving the supply of such services. Branches of Western banks and accounting firms have rapidly been established in the Eastern countries, and business services generally have been a major target of FDI in the area's economies. Their effects extend beyond the immediate sphere of activity of the foreign investor, spreading indirectly to other areas of the economy.

The operation of foreign affiliates within the host Eastern economies can also contribute, directly and by example, to the development of management skills essential for efficient enterprise behaviour in a market economy. Under central planning, enterprise directors (typically engineers by training) were primarily responsible for the management of production. Moreover, in the conditions of excess demand that resulted from over-full employment planning, the function of managers was essentially superfluous in the areas of product development, quality control, marketing and sales. Since investment planning and financing were largely centralized, the entrepreneurial function was also rendered superfluous.

The development of long-neglected management skills and the institution of related organizational and operational changes within Eastern enterprises (not to mention the general improvement of work habits) are important tasks of the transition. Managerial retraining has accordingly been a particular focus of Western governmental and non-governmental assistance programmes. Foreign investors often organize their own, in-house training for Eastern personnel, managers and workers. Arguably the most effective training is on-the-job, working closely with Western counterparts on a daily basis, according to international standards and procedures introduced through direct foreign involvement in enterprise operations.

Moreover, new business standards introduced through FDI extend through forward and backward linkages beyond foreign affiliates themselves. Perhaps the most celebrated case of the introduction of strict product quality standards, with significant backward linkage effects, is the case of McDonald's. In order to maintain company standards in its operations in Eastern Europe, McDonald's was frequently forced to develop entirely new chains of supply, from the farm to the restaurant.[10]

One might conjecture that the diffusion of new management practices would be more rapid when FDI is undertaken in partnership with a local enterprise than when it is made in a wholly owned branch or subsidiary. In the latter case, on the other hand, it might be possible to introduce international norms more quickly into local management practices.

The direct presence of TNCs can help not only to impart new management skills but also to build a new business ethic. It is generally recognized that the old system failed to encourage a respect for property or to engender a sense of personal economic responsibility. It is therefore not surprising that the dismantling of the traditional system of controls should be succeeded in many instances by a free-for-all, 'wild West' approach to business activity. While some foreign firms may simply join the action, the majority can be expected to help to introduce standards of business ethics that are internationally accepted in the context of a market system.

It is clear from on-the-spot reports that the efforts of TNCs to instill new work habits and ethics may encounter local resistance.[11] Their short-run impact is therefore likely to be limited in many cases. The receptivity of Eastern personnel to new 'foreign' ways will depend upon how deeply old habits were ingrained (older employees, especially at the managerial level, are likely to be more resistant), as well as on other factors determining the cultural gap between foreign and local employees.

Another legacy of the past that must be overcome in the transition, if newly created markets are to function efficiently, is the monopolistic organizational structure of much of the economy. Attempts to dismantle this structure are politically difficult and slow. In these circumstances, the opening up of the economy to FDI can be an effective way to expose monopolistic, domestic enterprises to a more competitive environment, especially when a weak balance of payments makes it difficult to open domestic markets to the competition of imports.

On the other hand, their dominant shares in home markets may constitute much of the attractiveness of large national enterprises to potential foreign investors. The acquisition of a controlling equity in such enterprises has in fact been the objective of many of the major foreign investments to date, especially in Central Europe. The interests of TNCs may therefore conflict with the anti-monopoly objectives of host Government policy.

PRIVATIZATION

The most obvious way in which FDI can contribute to the privatization of the Eastern economies is financial. Private savings in these countries has been greatly eroded by inflation and would in any case have been inadequate in light of the enormity of the privatization task. Foreign financing can help to breach the savings gap. Of course, for this purpose, it need not necessarily be in the form of direct investment. A number of specialized investment funds have been set up in the West to facilitate Western portfolio investment in the Eastern economies, as assets are privatized.[12]

Improvement in the operational efficiency of enterprises has, however, been one of the major aims of Eastern privatizations. If financing is through portfolio rather than direct investment, potentially beneficial effects on the management of the assets are more likely to be diluted. Ways in which FDI can act as a channel for the introduction of new managerial functions and techniques have already been discussed. Direct investment can also raise the efficiency of operations by introducing new productive technology, providing links to new markets and, perhaps most importantly, subjecting Eastern managers to the discipline of commercial rather than administrative criteria.[13] Hence, the influence of TNCs on the management of privatized state enterprises can accelerate their restructuring.

Whether FDI can exercise these potential effects on the efficiency of enterprise operations depends much upon the nature of privatization. Privatization programmes have varied considerably among the Eastern countries.[14] The politically more popular mass distribution of state-owned assets to the citizenry, by means of various voucher schemes and often through the intermediation of newly created investment funds, tends to restrict the participation of foreign investors and hence the potential effects of FDI on enterprise behaviour.[15] It is in those cases (most notably the former German Democratic Republic and Hungary) where state assets have been sold off that FDI is accorded greater scope.[16] So-called 'spontaneous privatizations' have also provided the opportunity for TNCs to undertake major acquisitions even in countries (e.g. the former Czechoslovakia) that have otherwise favoured mass privatization schemes.

The development of a significant private sector hinges not only on the denationalization of state-owned assets but also on the creation of new assets through the growth of private enterprise. The initial, joint-venture phase of FDI in the Eastern economies created entities that were legally independent but operated for the most part within the administrative and operational framework of the local partner, state enterprises. They served, however, to initiate the process of evolution of the hitherto solely state-owned sector towards a more mixed ownership structure. More recently, a second phase, where the acquisition of state-owned assets became possible, has enlisted FDI in privatization of a more direct nature and on a larger scale. A third phase, already legally open, will engage foreign firms increasingly in the task of establishing entirely new ('greenfield') investments.

ECONOMIC RESTRUCTURING

If FDI can thus help to move the ownership structure of the economy from preponderant state ownership towards a more desirable mix, it can also assist in another form of transitional restructuring. This is the restructuring of production, away from a pattern similarly dictated by past, political–ideological priorities towards a structure more firmly based on economic realities. While industrial restructuring is the primary objective, other sectors also come into play. Moreover, restructuring should not be regarded as a task limited to the transition, but an on-going one.

The enormity of the task and the difficult and costly political and social adjustments that accompany economic restructuring were stressed earlier. Foreign direct investment can potentially facilitate restructuring by easing some of the domestic constraints that slow its progress. The most obvious of these is the capital constraint. Capital requirements are enormous and domestic resources are inadequate; they have been reduced by recession and stretched by the multiple tasks of the transition.[17] In such circumstances, the impact of external capital is enhanced, especially if it can be directed to areas where expected, and immediate returns from additional investment are high, such as incomplete investment projects inherited from the previous period (if they are economically sound). Takeovers of existing plant and distribution networks will not increase the net capital stock of the host country unless accompanied by additional, capital-creating investments.

Much has been made in the Western literature of the role of FDI as a channel for the international transfer of technology. This hinges on the notion that proprietary rights can be better safeguarded and more profitably exploited if technology is kept within the firm rather than leased or sold.[18] The acquisition of Western technology has been the primary objective of Eastern policy favouring FDI. It is arguably even more important now, in the transition, given the scale of the currently envisaged restructuring and the notable failure of earlier efforts to close the technology gap.

Moreover, the new international political climate has created much more favourable regulatory conditions. The Western strategic embargo has been curtailed and the COCOM list of restricted technologies scaled down. In these circumstances, there is considerably enlarged scope for technology-based FDI in aid of restructuring. The modernization of Eastern telecommunications and electronic data-processing systems is a prime example. These are technically weak areas of Eastern economies, where Western export controls have been relatively effective in the past. At the same time, they constitute an important part of the infrastructure necessary to the success of the transition.

There are important limits to the potential role of FDI in the processes of industrial restructuring. One of the major impediments to restructuring is the absence of a social safety net to provide unemployed workers with the social benefits that they have traditionally received through their place of work. State enterprises played an important social role, providing housing, food, health and leisure services to employees. Meanwhile, until a new social welfare system is put in place, TNCs will have to be prepared to assume the burden of at least some of these social services or risk a popular backlash. This can act as a deterrent to FDI if the expected costs are high.

The most difficult part of industrial restructuring is the closing down of 'white elephants' inherited from the communist period. The task, as noted earlier, is all the more daunting because the enterprises in question are frequently large and were favoured under the old system. It is doubtful that FDI can do much directly here. It will naturally be attracted to the more profitable enterprises, and there is thus the danger that it will just 'skim off the cream', leaving the problem cases to local resolution (and thereby raising the risk of a political backlash). Foreign direct investment can at best ease the adjustment indirectly by creating alternative areas of growth and employment in the economy.

Perhaps the most straightforward role for FDI in the transition is to establish long-missing links between the Eastern economies and the world economy. As pointed out earlier, the Eastern economies developed in relative isolation, even from each other. The reasons for this isolation had as much (if not more) to do with the nature of the planned economy as with the circumstances of international political economy.[19] The external economic relations of the Eastern countries were comprised largely of merchandise trade, conducted on a state-to-state (or at most Eastern state to Western firm) basis. They were most weakly developed at the level of international, inter-firm relations; and intra-firm linkages existed only through the transnational activities of a few Eastern state enterprises, typically state trading organizations.

The opening up of the Eastern economies to FDI can thus help to fill an important institutional void inherited from the communist past. This is not simply a question of achieving a more diversified and flexible, organizational framework for the conduct of external economic relations, however desirable that may be. It is more importantly a matter of the nature and magnitude of the relations that take place within that framework.

There are theoretical arguments and empirical evidence for regarding FDI flows as trade creating. It is possible that some forms of trade may not take place without the organizational framework of the TNC.[20] In the case of the planned economies, the absence of FDI also contributed to the development of industrial structures that were not oriented to world markets and of enterprises poorly qualified to operate on them. Foreign investment can help to channel resources into branches and enterprises that are potentially capable of competing internationally. Transnational linkages can help them to break into markets to which, with the collapse of Comecon and the dismantling of state trading, their export focus must now be primarily directed.

As the political/administrative criteria that shaped them in the past were removed, the trade relations of these economies have undergone an immediate and drastic geographic reorientation towards the West, especially Western Europe. This has occurred at the price of a collapse in the volume of trade. Ownership ties with Western firms can help to accelerate the recovery, and ensure the longer-term expansion, of trade along these new lines. They provide the channels for the technology, know-how and market access required to boost Eastern shares on Western markets. They also stimulate the intra-firm, intra-industry ties on which so much of the expansion of trade among Western industrial countries has been based in recent decades (Grubel and Lloyd, 1975). Not least importantly, they generate within

Western economies interests in favour of East–West trade expansion through the reduction of long-standing trade barriers.

In these ways, FDI can contribute to the successful future development of the Eastern economies in a more open context. The forced geographic reorientation of Eastern foreign trade has entailed significant immediate changes in its commodity content, but the full restructuring of Eastern foreign trade is necessarily a long-term process. To some extent, it entails a return to pre-communist patterns of specialization; it also requires the creation of new ones. Especially for smaller, more naturally open, Eastern economies, this must be accomplished in harmony with trends in the world economy. Foreign direct investment can potentially provide the organic links to the world economy that will ensure such a more harmonious development of the Eastern economies.

THE ACTUAL VERSUS THE POTENTIAL ROLE OF FOREIGN DIRECT INVESTMENT

Alerted by the dramatic events that led to the opening up of a long-closed area of Europe, TNCs quickly revised their investment strategies to incorporate possible Eastern locations. They are attracted by the relative advantages these locations offer of proximity to European markets (geographically and culturally), skilled (and still relatively cheap) labour and underdeveloped natural resources (especially in the former Soviet Union).

Despite strong investor interest, actual FDI flows to the former communist economies have been far below Eastern or Western expectations; and they have been heavily concentrated in two of them, Hungary and the Czech Republic. The data available on FDI in the Eastern economies are limited in scope and generally poor in quality.[21] They are none the less adequate to demonstrate the general point. The most recent, comprehensive data available – compiled from a variety of sources – are presented in Tables 6.1 and 6.2.

Two kinds of problems lead to variations in the data reported. For most countries, there are major differences between FDI values based on protocols of intent (registrations) and FDI values reflecting actual transfers. This difference is especially wide in the case of the former Soviet Union and its successor states. Values based on the foreign share of the registered capital of joint ventures in the former Soviet Union greatly exceed the share of capital in operating joint ventures. Furthermore, FDI can be made in cash and in kind. Balance-of-payments data on FDI flows – now generally available for the

Table 6.1 Estimated stock of foreign direct investment in Central and Eastern Europe, 1991[a] and 1992 (million dollars)

Country	1991	1992
Bulgaria	350	570
Czechoslovakia (former)	1,200	2,750
Hungary	2,900	5,200
Poland	770	1,450
Romania	270	600
Soviet Union (former)	1,550/4,900	..
Russia	1,300/2,100	1,500/3,000
Yugoslavia[b] (former)	3,080	..
Slovenia	750	1,050

Sources: United Nations/TCMD (1992); World Bank (1992); PlanEcon (1992); and Institute for Economic Policy, Moscow, unpublished data (1992).

[a] Values are for investments made in kind, as well as in cash, wherever possible, and do not include commitments except in the case of the former Soviet Union and Russia where ranges given reflect data on capitalization of both operational and registered investment projects (see explanation in text). For the former Soviet Union and Russia, then, the lower capital figures (operational investments) are more comparable with those given for other countries. Data refer to year-end.
[b] 1991 data for the former Yugoslavia are mid-year.

Table 6.2 Estimated flows of foreign direct investment in Central and Eastern Europe, 1990–1992[a] (million dollars)

Country	1990	1991	1992
Bulgaria	70	250	220
Czechoslovakia (former)	300	690	1,500
Hungary	420	1,900	2,300
Poland	270	400	680
Romania	112	156	331
Soviet Union (former)	480/953	240/n.a.	..
Russia	n.a.	120	200
Yugoslavia[b] (former)	1,381	235	..
Slovenia	333	290	300

Sources: Same as table 6.1.

[a] As in Table 6.1.
[b] 1991 data for the former Yugoslavia represent the first four months of that year.

Central and East European countries – represent only cash transfers through the banking system. They thus understate actual flows. Data on investments in kind are more difficult to obtain and estimates of them vary. Depending on the base used, data on the magnitude and nature of FDI flows can therefore vary greatly.

If the data are messy, their message is nevertheless clear. The end-1991 stock of FDI in the area's economies combined was (using the more conservative figure for the former Soviet Union) $10.1 billion, according to the data presented in Table 6.1. Total flows to the area in that year were about $4 billion. Although these figures represent rapid growth from negligible amounts just three years earlier, they are nevertheless well below expectations and potential. They may be compared with FDI figures for China, which alone recorded a stock in 1991 of well over $20 billion and an inflow of over $3 billion.[22]

Trends are mixed, as Table 6.2 shows. The further growth of FDI flows to the area in 1992 suffered major shocks with the disintegration of 1991 of economies demonstrated to be of particular interest to foreign investors: the former Soviet Union and the former Yugoslavia (and in the case of the latter, the outbreak of civil war). On the other hand, there was a notable increase in flows to the Central European countries, and there is reason to believe that the pace of FDI in Poland will quicken in 1993.[23] The negative impact of the break up of the former Czechoslovakia at the end of 1992 is, however, still to be fully revealed.

Why these disappointing results? Certainly, inadequacies and other negative features of the regulatory framework (including regulations and procedures governing not only the initial investment but also subsequent operations, taxation of revenues and transfer of funds abroad) are a factor – but not the principal one. The institutional legacies of the past, such as the lack of developed input markets and infrastructural deficiencies in areas such as banking and communications, have also been important deterrents. Surveys show, however, that investors have been most concerned about the high degrees of political and economic instability, policy uncertainty and consequent risk that they face in most countries of the region.[24]

The uncertainty and risk are augmented by the evident absence of a broadly based public opinion in the host countries in favour of FDI. On the contrary, much of the public looks upon such investment with resentment and suspicion. These attitudes provide support for those who are philosophically opposed to FDI or whose interests are threatened by it.

These deterrent factors are well illustrated by the case of the Russian oil industry, a case that is all the more important because it is so widely regarded as offering enormous investment potential. Still possessing major, underdeveloped reserves and long closed to FDI, it presents to Western oil companies a kind of last frontier. Moreover, the sharp fall-off in Russian oil output since 1988 has created a strong need for inputs of Western capital, technology and know-how. Despite this potential and despite high expected returns from oilfield operations, actual FDI in Russian oil has been negligible and most has been in service contracts for the workover of existing fields in partnership with Russian enterprises. This seems likely to remain the case, so long as political instability continues to generate great policy uncertainty about the future development of the industry and hence high risks to investors.[25]

Investor response to such uncertainties has been to postpone investment projects, to withdraw from negotiations, or to leave negotiated commitments unrealized. Those investors that have proceeded have typically sought to reduce their exposure by minimizing their 'upfront' capital investment and by making their contributions in kind rather than in cash, or indirectly in the form of loans. Governments in turn have sought to offset the risks that investors face by putting into place official insurance programmes (especially against political risk), but to little effect.

The case of Hungary is the exception that also helps to prove the point. Hungary, one of the smallest of the regional economies, has attracted by far the largest amount of FDI. This is generally explained in terms of Hungary's advantages of national unity and political stability in comparison with its neighbours. Moreover, its relatively progressive history of reform in the communist period left Hungary with the positive legacy of a more investor-friendly business environment than found elsewhere in the region.

CONCLUSIONS

The transition in Central and Eastern Europe has created significant opportunities and requirements for FDI. However, at least in its initial phase, the political, economic and social instability that has accompanied the transition has motivated many investors to take a cautious approach and even to abandon or postpone investment projects.

There is therefore an incongruity between the expectations of transition managers regarding the role that FDI would play in restoring growth and restructuring their economies, and the perceptions of many potential investors of the associated risks and returns. Investment flows to the area, in the crucial first years of the transition, have as a result generally not been of the magnitudes required for FDI to ease domestic resource constraints sufficiently to have an appreciable impact on progress towards a market-based economy. In most cases, the FDI stock is a negligible share of GDP. The sectoral distribution of FDI has been uneven, however. It has been concentrated in a few industries (e.g. automobiles, food processing, hotels and restaurants, business services) where its impact is therefore far greater than average.

Only in Hungary, and perhaps also in the Czech Republic, had FDI by end-1992 attained magnitudes where it might be said to be playing a significant role in economic recovery and transformation. In Hungary, the ratio of FDI stock to GDP in 1992 is estimated to have attained 8.6 per cent.[26] It is not at all clear, however, that future flows to Hungary will continue at past levels. To date, foreign acquisitions of major shares in leading Hungarian enterprises have accounted for the bulk of FDI inflows. That phase of privatization now appears to be ending in Hungary, and with it Hungary's favourable treatment by foreign investors.[27] Greenfield investments will now have to take up the slack, and few such investments on a major scale have been made in Hungary or elsewhere in the region.

In the communist period, FDI was fundamentally limited by the institutional characteristics of the system, even when official policies favourable to it had been adopted. In the post-communist period, the remnants of that system, combined with the political, economic and social problems associated with its replacement, continue to create conditions that hold the actual level of FDI well below the desired. It now seems increasingly unlikely that FDI will play the important role in the Eastern transition that was originally envisaged for it.

NOTES

** This article is based on research supported by a grant from the Ontario Council of International Business. The results were first presented at the thirty-fourth Annual Convention of the International Studies Association, Acapulco, Mexico, March 1993. The author is grateful to K. Morita of Hiroshima University, Japan, for his comments as discussant and to anonymous referees of this journal for their helpful suggestions.
 1 Outward investment did play a limited role in the development of their external economic relations (outside the Comecon system). Eastern enterprises had long been allowed to undertake direct investments abroad, and from the mid-1960s sought to increase the pace and scope of their transnational activities. See McMillan (1987).
 2 The former Yugoslavia was the first, in 1967; then Romania and Hungary, in 1972. Others gradually emulated them; and towards the end of the 1980s, there was what proved to be a last minute rush to follow suit by the more conservative countries, most notably the former Soviet Union. By 1990, all of the Eastern countries had taken the initial legislative steps to allow FDI in their domestic economies. The former

German Democratic Republic adopted enabling legislation only at the very beginning of 1990, just months before its demise as an independent state. Albania was the last, in July 1990. For a full chronology, see United Nations/TCMD (1992, p. 3, table 1).

3 For more extensive discussion of these points, see McMillan (1993).

4 In any case, the term was ideologically 'taboo' in the Eastern countries at the time.

5 A few figures (United Nations/TCMD, 1992) will illustrate the limited extent of FDI, even towards the end of the period of communist rule. By the mid-1980s, the cumulative total of FDI in the Eastern economies combined was estimated to have reached scarcely $1 billion. The former Yugoslavia, with the longest experience and the most open economy, accounted for more than three-quarters of this amount. In the second half of the 1980s, the increased pace of reform in the area economies, most notably 'perestroika' in the former Soviet Union, greatly increased investor interest and opportunities in the region. By the end of the decade, the FDI stock in the Eastern economies had grown by more than 300 per cent to an estimated $3.8 billion, for which the former Yugoslavia and the former Soviet Union together accounted for over four-fifths. Almost all of this investment was in the form of joint ventures; wholly foreign-owned companies were still quite rare.

6 For more detail, the reader is referred to several special journal issues devoted to the economics and politics of the transition: *Journal of Economic Perspectives*, 4, 4 (1991); *Comparative Economic Studies*, XXXIII, 2 (1991); and *East European Politics and Societies*, 6, (1992). See also Islam and Mandelbaum (1993).

7 Two cases of full-scale stabilization programmes of the 'shock therapy' sort were undertaken at the beginning of 1990, in the former Yugoslavia and Poland. In case of the former, the programme was undermined by the growing political crisis which led to the disintegration of the federal state. In the case of the latter, it provoked a prolonged period of political instability.

8 The example of China, and the demonstrable part FDI played in the success of its reforms (especially in the economies of its coastal regions), has been especially important to this perception.

9 The recovery in Poland began in 1992 and GDP growth of 4.5 per cent is estimated for 1993. Hungary's GDP is expected to grow by about 4 per cent in 1993. The Czech Republic experienced positive growth in the second half of 1992, but its further recovery has been delayed by the negative impact in 1993 of the loss of the Slovak market. For details, see *PlanEcon Reports*, IX, 7–12, 1993.

10 J. Hertzfeld (1991) developed this point with regard to McDonald's Russian investment.

11 For a vivid account in the context of the Russian oil industry, see Imse (1993).

12 Investment funds have been created in Europe, North America and Japan to take advantage of these new possibilities. These include the First Hungary Fund, the Austro-Hungary Fund, the Hungarian Investment Company, First Europe Capital Fund and the Central European Development Corporation. On the whole, such funds have been understandably

conservative in their approach, and have proceeded cautiously in acquiring Eastern assets.

13 Through, for example, 'hard' rather than 'soft' budget constraints in the conceptualization of Janos Kornai (1980).

14 Reference here is to 'large' privatizations. David Stark (1992) provided an interesting framework for comparative analysis.

15 Foreign direct investment may, however, play a part in the distribution scheme itself. For example, an Austrian bank, Creditanstalt, has set up one of the larger investment funds in the Czech Republic.

16 Kalman Mizsei (1992) discussed the relationship between privatization and FDI in the context of Poland and Hungary.

17 See Zoethout (1993) for a discussion of the capital requirements of the transition.

18 For example, John Dunning's well known analysis of TNCs is significantly based on this idea; see Dunning (1981).

19 Franklyn Holzman (1976) surveyed these issues.

20 Peter Murrell (1991) has argued this point in the context of East–West trade.

21 The data problems are scarcely surprising given the newness of the phenomenon for the economies concerned and the absence of well-established recording and publication procedures. Moreover, the political and economic chaos in the years concerned has made reliable statistical reporting generally difficult.

22 These values are for actual investment (versus commitments). To render these figures for China more comparable with those for the Central/East European and former Soviet economies, the value of foreign investments in contractual joint ventures in China has been substracted. Preliminary data indicate a tremendous surge of FDI in China in 1992, with an estimated inflow for the year of nearly $5 billion. These data are from Yang (1993).

23 The $2 billion Fiat investment in Poland will be a major factor here, although the treatment of the roughly $1 billion of this that represents Fiat's assumption of the bad debts of the Polish enterprise in which it acquired a 90 per cent stake will be problematic.

24 Survey data indicate the importance of these factors. For investor attitudes towards the area's economies in 1992, see Business International (1992). See Sherr *et al.* (1991) and McMillan (1991) for surveys of investor approaches to the Soviet economy. For a general discussion of the obstacles to FDI in the former Soviet Union, see IMF *et al.* (1991), especially vol. 2, pp. 75ff, and, for Central and Eastern Europe, Artisien *et al.* (1993).

25 Optimistic articles occasionally appear in the business press. These are based on investor interest, not action. They sum up all of the potential investment projects to impressive foreign investment figures but ignore current realities. See, for example, 'Investors see a new star rising slowly in the East', *Financial Times*, 5 January 1993, based on a report in *The East European Investment Monthly* (New York), or 'Oil boom in CIS may attract $85 bln', *Financial Times*, 5 May 1993, quoting *East-West Investment* (Geneva).

26 Calculation based on PlanEcon GDP projection for 1992.

27 This was affirmed by Lajos Csepi, head of the Hungarian State Property
    Agency, who was quoted as adding that many of the best companies have
    now been privatized. See 'Privatization before restructuring says Bank',
    Financial Times, 26 April 1993, and 'Hongrie: privatisation populaire',
    Les Echos, 24 April 1993.

REFERENCES

Artisien, Patrick F. R., Rojec, Matija and Marjan Svetlicic, eds (1993).
    Foreign Investment in Central and Eastern Europe. London: Macmillan
    Press.

Business International and Creditanstalt (1992). *1992 East European Invest-
    ment Survey*. Vienna: Business International.

Dunning, John (1981). *International Production and the Multinational
    Enterprise*. London, Boston: Allen & Unwin.

Grubel, Herbert G. and Peter Lloyd (1975). *Intra-Industry Trade: The Theory
    and Measurement of International Trade in Differentiated Products*.
    London: Macmillan Press.

Hertzfeld, J. (1991). Joint ventures: saving the Soviet from perestroika.
    Harvard Business Review, 69 (January–February), pp. 80–91.

Holzman, Franklyn (1976). *International Trade Under Communism*, New
    York: Basic Books.

Imse, Anne (1993). American know-how and Russian oil. *The New York
    Times Magazine*, 7 March, p. 28.

International Monetary Fund, World Bank, OECD, EBRD (1991). *A Study of
    the Soviet Economy*, three volumes. Paris: OECD Publications.

Islam, Shafiqul and Michael Mandelbaum (1993). *Making Markets:
    Economic Transformation in Eastern Europe and the Post-Soviet States*.
    New York: Council on Foreign Relations.

Kornai, Janos (1980). *The Economics of Shortage*. Amsterdam: North-
    Holland.

Levcik, Friedrich (1991). The place of convertibility in the transformation
    process. In *Currency Convertibility in Eastern Europe*, J. Williamson, ed.,
    Washington, DC: Institute for International Economics, pp. 31–47.

McMillan, Carl (1987). *Multinationals from the Second World*. London:
    Macmillan Press.

——— (1991). *Canada-USSR Joint Ventures: A Survey and Analytical
    Review*. Toronto: Canada–USSR Business Council.

——— (1993). Foreign direct investment flows to the Soviet Union and
    Eastern Europe: nature, magnitude and international implications. *Journal
    of Development Planning*, 23, pp. 305–25.

Mizsei, Kalman (1992). Privatisation in Eastern Europe: a comparative study
    of Poland and Hungary. *Soviet Studies*, 44, 2, pp. 283–96.

Murrell, Peter (1991). The effect of (the absence of) multinationals' foreign
    direct investment on the level of Eastern European trade. *Economics of
    Planning*, 24, 3, pp. 151–60.

National Bank of Hungary (1991). *Annual Report*. Budapest.

PlanEcon (1993). *PlanEcon Reports*. Washington, DC: PlanEcon.

Sherr, Alan B. *et al.*, eds (1991). *International Joint Ventures: Soviet and Western Perspectives*. New York: Quorum Books.

Stark, David (1992). Path dependence and privatization strategies in East Central Europe. *East European Politics and Societies*, 6, 1, pp. 17–54.

United Nations, Economic Commission for Europe (1992). *Economic Bulletin for Europe*, 44.

United Nations, Transnational Corporations and Management Division (TCMD) (1992). *World Investment Directory: Volume II, Central and Eastern Europe*. Sales No. E.93.II.A.I.

World Bank (1992). *Foreign Direct Investment in the States of the Former USSR*. Studies of Economies in Transformation Paper No. 5 (Washington, DC: The World Bank).

Yang, Canlong (1993). Wholly foreign-owned enterprises: benefits and recommendations. Paper presented to a UNDP-sponsored seminar at the Research Institute for International Economic Cooperation, Ministry of Foreign Trade and Economic Cooperation, Beijing.

Zoethout, Tseard (1993). Financing Eastern Europe's capital requirements. *RFE/RL Research Report*, 2, 7.

7 Foreign direct investment and international migration*

*Karl P. Sauvant, Padma Mallampally and Persephone Economou***

International migration that arises from differences in economic conditions among countries is becoming an issue of increasing concern for migration-receiving countries, in view of the adjustment problems involved. But the link between economic development and migration has not been sufficiently explored. The present article examines one aspect of that link, namely the relationship between foreign direct investment (which serves, in theory, as an alternative to labour movement) and migration. It suggests that, to the extent that transnational corporations contribute to economic growth in migrant-seeking countries and that this growth leads to a reduction in poverty, foreign direct investment can reduce – in the longer term and on balance – the necessity to migrate, especially because of poverty. In the short term, foreign direct investment can help to reduce migratory pressures through the creation of employment, which, though tending to be small in the aggregate, can be sizeable in some countries and industries. Furthermore, training and career prospects, often associated with employment in foreign affiliates, create the potential for upward mobility and improvements in status, which may mitigate the desire to migrate of those seeking better opportunities. Policies need to aim more at facilitating foreign direct investment and at promoting employment creation and upward mobility through transnational corporations.

INTRODUCTION

International migration is likely to be one of the key issues of the 1990s. As a result of striking changes in the direction and composition of migration flows because of shifting demographic, economic and

* Reprinted from *Transnational Corporations*, vol. 2, no. 1 (February 1993), pp. 33–69.

political conditions in various regions, prospects for large and unregulated migration flows have increased, creating concern among receiving countries. Both developing and developed countries are affected, including, among the latter, each of the Triad members, that is the European Community, the United States and Japan. In addition, temporary movements of labour and skilled professionals are taking place on an increasing scale, not only between developing and developed countries but also between developing countries themselves, in response to human-resource needs and surpluses in different countries. In total, some 75 million legal and illegal migrants, transient workers, refugees and displaced persons from developing countries were not residing in their own countries at the beginning of the 1990s.

It is generally agreed that the lack of economic development is one of the principal causes of emigration. Little is known, however, about the interrelationships between development and migration, although interest is beginning to focus on that relationship.[1] The present article examines *one* aspect of that relationship, namely the link between foreign direct investment (FDI) and economic migration, focusing particularly on how FDI may influence migration from developing countries.

Economic migration refers to migration determined by differences in economic conditions between countries. Such differences range from differences in access to the means of survival to differences in economic opportunity of various kinds, including the opportunities for gainful employment, improved remuneration and conditions of work and upward mobility in terms of occupational status and responsibility. In other words, the economic factors leading to migration represent a continuum, characterized at one end by the *push* of poverty and economic hardship, and at the other by the *pull* of opportunity and attaining an advanced standard of living. While the boundaries between migration motivated by economic and non-economic considerations (including cultural, social and political factors) are not clear-cut, that economic factors are an important force determining international migration is quite clear.

The discussion below focuses, first, on the growing importance of FDI in the world economy; second, on the impact of FDI on migration, by contributing to economic growth in the long run; third, on the role of FDI in the creation of improved opportunities, through generating employment and opportunities for advancement in employment; and, finally, on some policy implications.

FACTOR MOBILITY, TRADE AND THE IMPORTANCE OF FOREIGN DIRECT INVESTMENT

Economic theory suggests that if factors of production – broadly defined as land, labour and capital – are mobile among countries, differences in their earnings would decrease. In reality, there are limitations to the mobility of capital, labour and, of course, land. International trade in goods and services can, in theory, act as an alternative to the movement of factors of production. Thus, under competitive conditions, if factor endowments of countries differ, but technologies are the same and factors are not mobile, the differences in factor endowments will be reflected in the differences in relative prices of products among countries; countries will therefore find it profitable to export goods that use their relatively abundant factor of production more intensively, and to import those that require a more intensive use of their scarce factor. As a result, the scarce factor in each country becomes somewhat less scarce, and the abundant factor becomes relatively less abundant. In that fashion, labour-abundant countries export their labour in the form of labour-intensive goods and import capital in the form of capital-intensive goods. In theory, the result is the equalization of factor prices, or at least a movement towards an equalization of factor prices. To what extent the actual pattern of trade follows factor proportions depends on the technologies used, transportation costs, market structure and the availability of information. But the basic theoretical principle remains, namely that trade in goods (and services, to the extent that they are tradable) can work as a substitute for the movement of land, labour and capital.

There is no doubt that international trade has contributed during the past century to compensate for differences in factor endowments and the lack of mobility of factors. Its impact in reducing economic disparities due to imbalances in factor availabilities has, however, been only partly effective. Part of the reason is protectionism. A further liberalization of trade could thus contribute to a further reduction of the pressure for migration due to economic differences caused by imbalances between labour and capital availabilities in many developing countries.

Flows of trade, however, even on a vastly liberalized scale, cannot fully address the problems of poverty, low incomes and/or limited economic opportunities that underlie the decisions of many who migrate from less-developed countries. First, the existence of non-traded goods and services limits the extent to which international cross-border trade can work as a substitute for the movement of

factors of production. Second, it is clear that patterns of trade are determined not only by factor endowments, but also by differences in technologies, skills, income levels and political factors that affect the grants of preferential trade status. Third, flows of trade work indirectly, and their ability to compensate for factor movements depends upon factor-market conditions as well. In other words, unless the technological and human resource gaps between developed and developing countries, as well as income disparities, are reduced, and unless markets, including labour markets, function perfectly, trade can act only partially as a substitute for the movement of capital and labour, or production factors more narrowly defined.

Flows of capital or finance can act directly to reduce differences in factor proportions between countries and to bring relative factor prices and incomes of countries closer together. Capital is perhaps the most mobile factor in terms of freedom from regulatory constraints, but capital does not always flow in the direction of countries in which it is most scarce. The reasons include institutional factors, that is the lack of markets and instruments to channel portfolio investments into capital-scarce developing countries, as well as the fact that it is not capital alone, but a package of capital, technology, managerial know-how and market access, along with the institutions that support economic activity, which is required to put labour to productive, or more productive, use.

Both trade and capital movements, therefore, work imperfectly to equalize or bring together factor proportions, or wages and incomes, between countries with large differentials. The movement of labour thus has an important role to play. Contrary to what might be expected, given the existence of national boundaries and immigration laws, extensive movements of labour take place to locations where labour and skills shortages exist and where new capital is accumulating alongside innovation, technical progress and entrepreneurial development. In fact, labour may well be the most mobile factor, not only within regions and between neighbouring countries, but also on a wider scale internationally, driven as it is by individual or household decisions requiring little institutional support. There are, however, limits to the extent to which labour can move, not only because of the financial, physical and psychological costs of moving to the migrant, but also because of the costs of adjustment and absorption within the receiving societies and, sometimes, within the sending countries as well. The strong and widespread restrictions by many countries on inward labour movement testify to those limits.

Given the limitations on the movement of capital as well as of

labour, the role of FDI, or of the investment made directly in an enterprise in a foreign country in order to acquire a lasting interest and control in the enterprise, deserves attention. It is a distinguishing characteristic of FDI that it combines capital, technology, training and trade in order to organize and create production capacity. In other words, the transnational corporations (TNCs) that are responsible for FDI bring an integrated package of tangible and intangible assets to host countries, which can serve as an alternative to labour movement, as well as a stimulus to development. The package acts not only to supplement domestically available factors of production that create opportunities for employment and income generation, but also to stimulate growth through transfer of technology, training, interlinkages with the rest of the economy and access to foreign markets.

Indeed, the role of FDI in international economic transactions has increased in importance during the 1980s. Foreign-direct-investment flows, undertaken by an estimated 36,000 TNCs with over 170,000 affiliates abroad (of which about 70,000 are in developing countries), grew faster than both exports and domestic output during the period 1986–1990, to reach a stock of about $1.9 trillion in 1991 (Table 7.1). World-wide sales by foreign affiliates, estimated at $5.5 trillion in 1990, have become more important than exports, valued at $3.3 trillion, for delivering goods and services to markets. The strategies of TNCs play an important role in decisions regarding the location of activities and discrete functions along the value-adding chain of production. Increasingly, the role of TNCs is to integrate and coordinate those functions, which has led to the emergence of an integrated international production system. In other words, international production by TNCs is becoming more interdependent, with linkages between parent companies and affiliates, as well as among affiliates, increasing in number and complexity, and becoming more integrated on a regional or even global scale. Indeed, the increasing regionalization of the world economy in terms of trade and investment blocks – and the regional core strategies of TNCs underlying the process of deep integration associated with the formation of regional investment blocks – could create an environment within which the cross-border flow of migrants is facilitated, even in the absence of formal integration schemes.

Most FDI outflows originate from and are directed to developed countries. Five home countries (France, Germany, Japan, the United Kingdom and the United States) account for 67 per cent of total outflows (Table 7.2), estimated at $180 billion in 1991 (UN, TCMD, 1993). About 50–55 per cent of world-wide outflows from

Table 7.1 World-wide foreign direct investment and selected economic indicators, 1991, and growth rates for 1981–1985, 1986–1990 and 1990–1991 (billions of dollars and percentages)

Indicator	Value, 1991 (current prices in billions of dollars)	Annual growth rate, 1981–1985	Annaul growth rate, 1986–1990	Annual growth rate, 1990–1991
Foreign-direct- investment outflows	180	4	24	−23
Foreign-direct- investment stock	1,900	5	11	11
Sales of transnational corporations	5,500[a]	2[b]	15	..
Gross domestic product at factor cost	22,300[b]	2	9	−6[c]
Gross domestic investment	5,100[b]	1	10	..
Exports	3,500	2	10	4
Royalties and fees receipts	30[c]	−1	20	−1

Source: United Nations, Transnational Corporations and Management Division (1993).

[a] For 1990.
[b] For 1982–1985.
[c] Estimate.

those countries during the second half of the 1980s were in the services sector. In recent years, developing countries have received, on average, less than 20 per cent of world-wide FDI inflows. In fact, the share of average annual investment inflows in developing countries fell from 26 to 17 per cent between the periods 1981–1985 and 1986–1990. (The proportion rose to 25 per cent in 1991, however, as a result of increasing flows to developing countries and decreasing flows to developed countries.) As loans from private sources to capital-importing developing countries declined during the 1980s, FDI has become the principal source of foreign savings from private sources for those countries, accounting for about 75 per cent of total long-term capital flows from private sources.

Table 7.2 Outflows of foreign direct investment from the five major home countries, 1987–1992

Country	1987	1988	1989	1990	1991	1992[a]	Share in world total (percentage)			Growth rate (percentage)		
			(billions of dollars)				1981–1985	1986–1990	1991	1981–1985	1986–1990	1991
France	9	14	19	35	24	17[b]	6	10	13	−17	45	−31
Germany	9	13	18	28	21	16[c]	9	9	12	13	27	−24
Japan[d]	20	34	44	48	31	16[e]	11	19	17	8	32	−36
UK	31	37	36	18	18	16[c]	19	17	10	−2	2	2
United States[f]	26	14	26	29	29	50[c]	23	13	16	−5	16	−0.4
Total[g]	95	112	143	158	123	115	68	68	67	0.01	23	−22

Source: United Nations, Transnational Corporations and Management Division (1993).

[a] Based on preliminary estimates.
[b] Estimated based on outflows in the first two quarters of 1992.
[c] Estimated based on outflows in the first three quarters of 1992.
[d] Data for Japan do not include reinvested earnings.
[e] Estimated based on outflows in the first quarter of 1992.
[f] Excluding outflows to the finance (except banking), insurance and real estate industries of The Netherlands Antilles. Also excludes currency-transaction adjustments.
[g] Totals may not add up due to rounding.

FOREIGN DIRECT INVESTMENT, GROWTH AND MIGRATION

As mentioned earlier, substantial economic differentials among countries play an important role in creating the potential for international migration. The persistence of income differentials between developing and developed countries highlights the fact that economic growth in developing countries during recent decades, with a few striking exceptions, has been relatively low. In part because economic growth has not kept pace with rapid population growth, the income gaps between many developing countries and the developed economies have persisted and, in absolute terms, widened. The average annual per capita income of countries classified as low-income economies by the World Bank increased in real terms (1987 dollars) from $180 in 1970 to $350 in 1990, while in the high-income economies, including developed countries and oil-exporting countries, it increased from $11,150 to $17,150 (The World Bank, 1992, table 2). It has been estimated for a group of major potential migrant-sending countries of Eastern Europe and North Africa that GNP rates of growth of 6 per cent to 8 per cent would be required to equalize their per capita GNP to that of France in fifty years (Tapinos, 1991, p. 6). There is a widespread recognition therefore that, unless appropriate policies are pursued at national and international levels for promoting the growth of developing countries, the existing income differentials causing migration are unlikely to narrow (Appleyard, 1991, p. 14). To put it differently, unless rapid growth is set in motion in the developing countries, as well as the countries of Central and Eastern Europe, economic pressures for movements of people to developed countries, driven by hardship or by relatively greater opportunity abroad than in their own countries, are likely to increase.

It is in this context that the role of FDI in promoting growth becomes relevant. The potential of FDI to contribute to growth is being increasingly recognized, reflecting, on the one hand, an awareness of the limitations with respect to the flows of private lending and official development assistance and, on the other, the favourable experience of countries, such as some of the economies of East and South-East Asia, which have achieved high rates of growth with a substantial involvement of TNCs and associated resources.

Economic growth is a complex process involving the interrelationship between a number of factors, many economic, others political and social. Classical political economy emphasized the importance of expanding the quantity of the basic factors of production: capital, land (including natural resources) and labour, as well as the importance of the role of expanding markets to improve efficiency. More recently, research has shown the important contribution of technical change to economic growth, over and above the contribution from expanding quantities of productive factors, and the role that can be played by elements such as improvements in the organization of production and exchange (Solow, 1957; Denison, 1985). Even more recently, economists have emphasized the role of qualitative improvements in the labour force of an economy, improvements that come about from better health, increased education and greater access to training. Investment in human resource development has become an important component of growth and development strategies for both developed and developing economies.

Thus, economic growth can occur in a variety of ways and be driven by different features of an economy. Growth may be stimulated by investment that augments and improves the productivity of national physical resources. It can be driven by innovation and technological change, which not only improve the productivity of existing activities, but also create competitive advantages in new ones. The development of labour skills, or investment in human resources, has grown in importance as a source of economic growth. International trade can promote growth by allowing countries to exploit their existing comparative advantages and develop new ones, encouraging a faster and more efficient utilization of domestic resources and enabling countries to reap the benefits of economies of specialization and participation in the international division of labour.

Transnational corporations can contribute to each of these sources of growth:[2]

● Transnational corporations are a major channel for transferring *capital* across borders. Foreign direct investment that adds to the physical capital stock of a host country directly affects host-country growth. Even in those developing countries where FDI constitutes a small share of gross domestic capital formation, it is usually a larger share in key industries, such as advanced-technology manufacturing industries. In the Republic of Korea, for example, FDI inflows during 1986–1989 accounted for 1.6 per cent of gross domestic capital formation, but foreign affiliates contributed about one-half of new capital in the electrical-machinery and transportation-equipment industries during 1984–1986 (UN, TCMD, 1992, p. 118). Furthermore, TNCs can stimulate local production through linkages with the domestic economy, especially in those developing countries where local businesses have developed sufficiently to serve the needs of these firms. For example, in 1988, local procurement by Japanese affiliates in Latin America and Asia was 30 per cent and 44 per cent, respectively; in manufacturing, the corresponding figures were 52 per cent and 47 per cent.

- The presence of TNCs that invest in host economies may be more critical for the development of those economies than the direct contribution of FDI to capital formation indicates, since these firms create several channels through which economic impulses can be transmitted. One of these channels is the development of *technology*. The transfer of technology from TNCs to developing countries is an important channel through which technology can be acquired by these countries. For many developing countries, in fact, FDI may be the only way of gaining access to the latest technology or to key technologies. Foreign direct investment can foster technological change in developing countries through its contribution to higher factor productivity, changes in product and export composition and the introduction of organizational innovation. Other indirect means of transferring technology to developing countries include the provision of technical assistance to local firms to which foreign affiliates have subcontracted the supply of parts, leading to the upgrading of the technological level of supplier industries.

- Transnational corporations can also contribute to growth in host developing countries through their effect on the *quality of human resources*, especially with respect to the improvement of management capabilities. Improving managerial capabilities can take place through formal as well as informal learning. The latter consists of on-the-job training through short courses or assignments to the parent company, career development provided by TNCs, as well as the informal transmission of values, attitudes and beliefs embedded in the organizational culture of these corporations that foster entrepreneurship and enhance productivity.

- Transnational corporations also affect growth in developing countries through their effects on international *trade*. Transnational corporations play an important role in international trade (for the United States, for example, 80 per cent of the combined exports and imports in 1989 was undertaken by TNCs). A significant portion of international trade – perhaps as much as 30–40 per cent – consists of intra-firm transactions. Given their importance in international trade (for example, exports of foreign affiliates accounted for 30 per cent of total exports of the Republic of Korea and manufacturing exports of foreign affiliates accounted for 44 per cent of total manufacturing exports of Brazil), TNCs can have a significant impact on the growth of developing countries through the improvement of export performance and by inducing a structural shift in exports of developing countries towards technologically advanced products, such as electrical machinery and transport equipment.

Transnational corporations are likely to have a stronger impact upon growth through some of the channels outlined above – and their components – than through others; in some instances, the importance of TNCs may be small. More than the direct contribution of TNCs to the growth of host developing countries through each channel, it is the synergistic nature and interaction between these channels, as well as the development of linkages with the domestic economy, that strengthens their overall contribution to growth. From that perspective, the actual size of investment capital brought to a host country is only a small part of the total package of assets that TNCs bring to a host country.[3] The actual impact of TNCs on the host-country economy, however, depends on a number of factors, including the stage of development of the country, which determines how effectively countries are able to attract FDI flows and absorb the opportunities offered by these corporations. It also depends on the effectiveness of host-country policies in avoiding or minimizing costs that arise on account of business practices of TNCs and on host-country capabilities available for negotiating with TNCs. Finally, it must also be recognized that, unless growth leads to a reduction in poverty and hardship, the indirect effect of FDI on growth will have little impact on migratory pressures.

To conclude, FDI brings capital, technology, skills and expertise to host countries and, in this manner, contributes to increasing the productivity and the rate of growth of the host economies; it also contributes indirectly through trade linkages to world markets and backward and forward linkages to domestic firms. There is considerable evidence to show that these impacts can be significant, although the extent of such contributions depends principally upon the economic conditions and policies of the FDI-receiving host country on the one hand and the strategies of TNCs on the other. The relationship between FDI and migration is, therefore, indirect and complex, since it depends upon the impact of FDI on economic development and economic opportunity and upon the responsiveness of potential migrants to increased incomes and opportunities. Foreign direct investment is likely to act as an important complement to domestic investment for stimulating growth in the long run, thereby reducing the necessity for emigration from the host country due to poverty or lack of economic prospects.

Effects on migration are, however, likely to emerge only in the long run. The immediate impact of growth may well be to increase the supply of outward migrants, in particular by raising the ability to meet the costs of migration. Moreover, FDI may also establish linkages between industrialized and developing countries that subsequently serve as bridges for international migration. It has been observed, for example, that, paradoxically, FDI and the promotion of export-oriented growth in developing countries and the central role played by the United States in this process seem to have had the effect of encouraging immigration to the United States from the countries involved (Sassen, 1989, p. 814). The inflow of migrant workers from Asian developing countries into Japan for the first time in that country's history, in the 1980s, has also been attributed, at least partly, to the linkages created by the growing presence of Japanese TNCs in the migrants' home countries (Sassen, 1993, p. 16).

Although it is quite possible that the creation of new economic linkages between countries through FDI adds to the complex set of factors influencing positively the supply of migrants from developing to developed countries, it is likely that both the factors mentioned above operate primarily in the short run. In the long run, sustained development works to stem migration by raising incomes as well as generating the expectation of improved economic prospects in the future, eventually turning migrant-sending countries into net immigration ones. The size and composition of migratory flows can be expected to vary with the rate, stage and nature of economic development of a country, as is evident from the experience of developed countries as well as newly industrializing economies.[4]

FOREIGN DIRECT INVESTMENT, EMPLOYMENT AND MIGRATION

As discussed in the preceding section, the contribution of FDI to economic growth – and, with it, its impact on migration – is not immediate. But the employment opportunities arising from FDI are immediate. Furthermore, the opening of possibilities for upward mobility and career advancement within foreign affiliates can also act as an incentive for potential emigrants seeking better opportunities to remain at home. Thus, by stimulating economic growth, FDI widens the range of economic opportunities and thereby reduces the incentive for migrants to leave their countries. Moreover, the very engagement of TNCs in a country, especially on a large scale, their contributions to domestic growth and the improvements in future growth prospects that this signals, strengthens the perception that new opportunities are emerging at home, thus further discouraging the outflow of opportunity-seeking migrants.

Employment

The creation of employment opportunities is one of the consequences of the package of tangible and intangible assets that TNCs bring into a host country. More importantly, the establishment of foreign affiliates in a host country has a direct and immediate impact on the employment situation of that country, reducing at least one of the economic incentives for outward migration.

By one estimate, world-wide employment by TNCs in parent firms and foreign affiliates stood at about 6.5 million at the end of the 1980s (International Labour Office, 1992, p. 49). In terms of magnitudes, however, direct employment created by TNCs in host developing countries is relatively small, estimated at about 7 million in the mid-1980s (less than 1 per cent of the economically active population of these countries); indirect employment is estimated to be two to three times that figure (UN, TCMD, 1992, p. 183). Moreover, overall employment by foreign affiliates of TNCs from major home countries was fairly stagnant during the 1980s, increasing by about 6 per cent annually between 1981 and 1989 for Japan, 5 per cent between 1984 and 1990 for Germany and remaining unchanged for the United States (Table 7.3). A similar trend can be observed for employment by manufacturing foreign affiliates of these countries, which also grew slowly or remained stagnant. This is supported further by evidence from some developing countries, which shows that employment by foreign affiliates has been declining. Labour-replacing technological advances and the increase in capital intensity of some investments partly account for that decrease.

In the light of the above, then, the creation of employment by foreign affiliates can, *overall*, play only a limited role in counteracting migration. Still, in those host countries in which there is unemployment (or underemployment), the creation of employment by foreign affiliates may ease immediately at least some of the push

Table 7.3 Employment by foreign affiliates of transnational corporations from Germany, Japan and the United States (thousands)

Country	Total[a]	Manufacturing	Services	Developed countries	Developing countries
Germany					
1984	1,697.0	1,237.0	445.0	1,206.0	445.0
1985	1,789.0	1,312.0	461.0	1,262.0	483.0
1986	1,788.0	1,276.0	496.0	1,241.0	506.0
1987	1,881.0	1,336.0	528.0	1,326.0	517.0
1988	1,974.0	1,395.0	563.0	1,414.0	525.0
1989	2,172.0	1,518.0	636.0	1,562.0	567.0
1990	2,328.0	1,638.0	674.0	1,700.0	570.0
Japan[b]					
1981	738.5	626.3	83.6	160.2[c]	578.4
1985	709.5	558.1	124.1	200.5[c]	509.0
1987	961.8	753.6	171.6	349.4[c]	612.4
1989	1,156.6	922.3	205.9	539.0[c]	617.6
United States[d]					
1977	7,196.7	..	..	..	..
1982	6,640.2	4,432.9[e]	1,972.5[e]	4,536.1[e]	2,236.2[ef]
1983	6,383.1	..	..	..	..
1984	6,417.5	..	..	..	..
1985	6,419.3	..	..	..	..
1986	6,250.2	..	..	..	..
1987	6,269.6	..	..	..	..
1988	6,403.5	..	..	..	..
1989	6,622.1	4,196.8[e]	2,271.5[e]	4,166.6[e]	2,586.0[ef]
1990	6,706.3	..	..	..	..

Sources: United States Department of Commerce (1985, 1992); Mataloni (1992); Germany, Deutsche Bundesbank (1992); Japan, Ministry of International Trade and Industry, various issues.

[a] Total includes sectors and regions other than those shown separately.
[b] Ending in March of that year. Data are based on surveys of affiliates and cover a different universe of affiliates in each year.
[c] Includes Oceania.
[d] All affiliates of non-bank United States parent firms.
[e] All affiliates of all United States parent firms.
[f] Includes employment in international affiliates; that is, those that have operations in more than one country and are engaged in petroleum shipping, other water transportation, or operating movable oil and gas drilling equipment.

for outward migration in search of jobs. On the other hand, for host countries facing tighter labour-market conditions, the creation of new jobs by foreign affiliates could initially raise wages and improve job opportunities, thus acting as an incentive for potential migrants not to seek better opportunities of work and living else-where; in fact, these countries could become attractive for immigrants from elsewhere.

In those economies (for example, Malaysia, Hong Kong, Singapore) in which FDI has been particularly important to the domestic economy, the employment impact of TNCs has been considerable. For example, the share of employment by majority-owned foreign affiliates in the manufacturing sector of Singapore in total employment was 60 per cent in 1988 (UNCTC, 1992a; ILO and UNCTC, 1988, chapter 3). In addition, TNCs are the primary source of employment in export-processing zones. It was estimated that, by the end of the 1980s, more than 200 export-processing zones were in operation in developing countries, employing over 1.5 million workers, with another 150 under construction or in the planning stage; the number of employees in export-processing zones of developing countries is anticipated to reach 2.5 to 3 million by the mid-1990s (UNCTC, 1990a, chapter 1). (It should be noted, however, that most export-processing zones never live up to the expectations with which they were created, and that many have failed.) Export-oriented manufacturing assembly operations in Mexico, the Caribbean Basin and Mauritius, established mainly by TNCs from the United States, have been a dynamic source of employment opportunities in these countries. As a result, foreign affiliates in export-processing zones of developing countries may account for a substantial share of total employment by all foreign affiliates in a given country, as well as of total employment. For example, employment by *maquiladoras* in Mexico was estimated to be about 470,000 in 1991, which was about half of all employment by foreign affiliates in Mexico and about 16 per cent of Mexican manufacturing employment (Martin, 1992, p. 4; UN, TCMD, 1994). Similarly, in 1986, assembly operations accounted for about 62 per cent of total manufacturing employment in Barbados, 35 per cent in Haiti, 25 per cent in the Dominican Republic and 11 per cent in Mexico (Schoepfle and Perez-Lopez, 1991). In addition, jobs were created through backward linkages with supplier industries. Most affiliates in export-processing zones engage in low-skill labour-intensive manufacturing production (mostly assembling, light manufacturing and data processing), and pay low wages. Still, by providing employment, affiliates in export-processing zones can relieve some of the pressure for outward migration. But the fact that the foreign affiliates in such zones usually employ workers with low levels of skill (mostly women) may not keep relatively skilled workers from seeking better employment opportunities elsewhere.

The success of export-oriented investments in labour-abundant economies in generating employment and stemming migration depends significantly on the prospects for trade. Mexico is an example. Taking advantage of low labour costs and proximity to the North American market, employment by the Mexican affiliates of General Motors, Ford and Chrysler grew from 22,000 in 1980 to 80,000 in 1988, while employment in the automobile industry in the United States fell by 150,000 between 1978 and 1989 (Koechlin and Larudee, 1992, p. 20). The conclusion of the North American Free Trade Agreement (NAFTA) in 1992, and the free trade access which the treaty (when ratified) provides producers in Mexico to the United States and Canada, is likely to play an important role in further stimulating the flow of FDI to Mexico. By one estimate, the increase in employment between 1992 and 2000 in Mexico as a result of United States FDI directed into Mexico is expected to be between 400,000 and 680,000 (Koechlin and Larudee, 1992, p. 24). Considering the influx of FDI from other countries into Mexico, as well as the dynamic growth effects of NAFTA on the domestic economy, employment creation by inward FDI would actually be much higher. It would include, among other things, employment created for skilled workers in the domestic services sector resulting from an increase in demand for professional services (accounting, advertising, legal services, etc.) by newly established foreign affiliates and domestic firms subject to increased international competition.[5] More generally, according to an estimate by Sherman Robinson *et al.* (cited in Hufbauer and Schott, 1993, pp. 19–20), a 1 per cent increase in the Mexican capital stock can reduce the level of permanent migration to the United States by about 44,000 workers. Thus, an increase in FDI in Mexico of $31 billion between 1992 and 2000 ($3.5 billion each year) (Koechlin and Larudee, 1992, p. 23) as a result of NAFTA could raise the stock of domestic capital, estimated to be about $500 billion, by 6 per cent and create employment opportunities leading to a reduction in permanent emigration to the United States of about 260,000 workers (Hufbauer and Schott, 1993, p. 20).[6]

In some developing countries, furthermore, the role of FDI – and hence its job-creating potential – may be particularly important in certain key industries. For example, in the Republic of Korea, FDI has been particularly significant in electrical machinery and transportation equipment in terms of its contribution to capital formation. In Thailand, assets of foreign affiliates account for over 85 per cent of total assets in mechanical and electrical equipment. In the Philippines, assets of foreign affiliates accounted for over 40 per cent of assets in chemicals and electrical equipment. Employment in these industries may be particularly rewarding, as these industries are central to economic development and have a strong future orientation.

Important in this context is also that wages offered by foreign affiliates in host developing countries are often higher than wages offered by domestic firms. To the extent that that is the case, there will be less incentive to migrate because of wage differentials, although, in the case of structural unemployment, the flow of migrants in search of employment may still occur. On average, the annual nominal wage offered by majority-owned non-bank affiliates of non-bank United States parent firms in developing countries increased by almost 50 per cent between 1982 and 1989, to $12,500 (United States, Department of Commerce, 1985, 1992). There is evidence indicating that compensation payments offered by foreign affiliates in services in developing countries are higher than those offered by domestic service companies in those countries. To illustrate, in the case of Kenya, the average wages paid by foreign service affiliates exceed those paid by domestic service companies by 75 per cent (UNCTC, 1989, pp. 16–17). Moreover, wages offered by foreign affiliates in the services sector in developing countries are similar to the prevailing wage in developed countries, since the same technology is used, and the same skills are required, in both groups of countries (UNCTC, 1989, pp. 16–17). Concerning wages in export-processing zones, it was found that wages for workers in such zones in Sri Lanka were considerably higher than wages of similar workers in the rural areas or the informal sector (ILO, 1986, p. 68). In the Caribbean, wages in export-processing zones are generally higher than average wages in industry outside these zones (Long, 1986, p. 29). Higher wages offered by foreign affiliates may therefore encourage those migrants seeking better employment opportunities to remain in their country of origin – although, as pointed out earlier, the total number of jobs in foreign affiliates is limited.

Finally, where labour markets are already tight, substantial inward FDI can further increase pressures on the domestic supply of labour, creating upward pressures on wages and strengthening incentives for workers to upgrade their skills and increase their productivity. Several newly industrialized economies in Asia fall into this category. In fact, partly as a result of their labour shortages, some of them have become substantial outward investors (UNCTC, 1991). To alleviate their labour shortages, inward migration of skilled labour seeking better work opportunities has sometimes been encouraged by these countries. Thus, about 25,000 of the 150,000 foreign workers in

Singapore in 1990 were skilled or professional workers, and the Government of Singapore has a clear policy to encourage such settlers (Lim, 1991, pp. 25 and 49). The Governments of Thailand and Malaysia, as well as of other newly industrialized countries, in fact, financially assist inward migration. Increased numbers of migrants were required to complement capital flows in these countries and to oversee the operations of TNCs; indeed, the ethnic composition of migrants has changed, reflecting the composition of foreign investment (Appleyard, 1991, p. 40).

In sum, with the exception of those countries in which FDI is important in relation to the size of the domestic economy and, to a certain extent, export-processing zones in which foreign affiliates are a significant source of employment, the scope of TNCs to generate employment is fairly narrow if compared with the economically active population. The creation of employment in host developing countries by TNCs can, therefore, contribute only to a limited extent to a reduction of outward-migratory pressures. Furthermore, in countries with tight labour markets, the entry of TNCs may induce inward migration.

Upward mobility

Prospects for upward mobility within foreign affiliates are a potentially important impact of FDI – not necessarily in terms of the number of top managerial positions that are available, but in terms of the hope and expectation to achieve status through merit-based advancement in firms that are often regarded as more stable and promising than domestic ones. The prospect, expectation and reality of upward mobility within foreign affiliates may diminish the incentive for those seeking improved economic opportunities to leave, by offering greater scope for career advancement at home. This is further enhanced by the availability of training, which improves the prospects for professional advancement in foreign affiliates in comparison with domestic companies. It should be noted, however, that the scope for such advancement depends on the type of activities in which these affiliates are involved.

Foreign affiliates can positively affect managerial capabilities in host developing countries: directly through non-formal training and indirectly through the transfer of values conducive to enhancing entrepreneurial and managerial capabilities. Foreign affiliates usually undertake vocational training of locally hired employees to provide them with the skills necessary for the functioning of the affiliates. The training of unskilled and semi-skilled workers accounts for a substantial part of all training efforts by foreign affiliates in terms of the number of workers trained. However, their greatest contribution lies in the development of management capabilities in host developing countries. A few large foreign affiliates have established their own training programmes for high- and medium-level managerial staff and key technical personnel. In terms of the share of training expenditure of TNCs, the training of skilled labour accounts for a large share. Transnational service corporations in particular invest heavily in training, since much of services technology is embodied in human beings. In general, foreign affiliates spend at least as much as domestic firms for the training of skilled workers. In the case of Turkey, for example, expenditures of foreign affiliates for executive training of host-country nationals, as a share of payroll, exceeded those for executive training in domestic firms by a factor of two (Erden, 1988). The availability of training schemes as well as informal training of employees by foreign affiliates (often in industries that are central to economic development) and the possibility of merit-based promotion can create perspectives for local employees that counteract pull factors from elsewhere.

Those counteracting forces are further strengthened by the fact that the overwhelming majority of employees in foreign affiliates – including a substantial share of employees at the management level – is locally recruited (and, as mentioned in the preceding paragraph, locally trained). In other words, prospects for career development in foreign affiliates are favourable: workers can advance within foreign affiliates by assuming greater responsibilities and, eventually, even reach the highest managerial levels. Data on the number of expatriates working in foreign affiliates bear this out. For example, evidence from Japanese and United States TNCs shows that the number of expatriate workers in foreign affiliates is, indeed, small: the combined number of expatriates for these two countries was less than 57,000 in 1989 or about 1 per cent of employment in foreign affiliates. In the case of United States TNCs, there has even been a marked decline in their share of employment in foreign affiliates (Table 7.4). Thus, the great majority of employees of foreign affiliates are, indeed, hired locally.[7]

It should furthermore be noted that career possibilities are not necessarily limited to advancement within foreign affiliates. Since these affiliates are part of larger transnational corporate systems, career development increasingly can also include assignments elsewhere, including, of course, in developed countries. The emergence

Table 7.4 Expatriate employment in foreign affiliates of United States and Japanese transnational corporations (number of and percentage share of home-country citizens in total employment)

Item	United States[a]		Japan	
	1982	*1989*	*1981*	*1989*
Number of expatriates	41,200	19,700	15,181	36,800
Sector (percentage share)				
All industries	0.8	0.4	2.0	3.0
Mining	5.3[b]	2.6[b]	1.2	2.5
Manufacturing	1.9	0.2	1.0	1.7
Services	1.3	0.5	..	..

Source: United Nations, TCMD (1992, p. 178); United States, Department of Commerce (1985, 1992); Japan, Ministry of International Trade and Industry.

[a] Data are for majority-owned non-bank affiliates of non-bank United States parent firms.
[b] Petroleum.

of an integrated international production system and the greater specialization and cooperation that this implies within the framework of corporate networks spanning several countries further increases the possibilities of career development beyond national borders, especially for professional, technical and kindred personnel.

Looked at from a different perspective, TNCs and their affiliates constitute a mechanism through which FDI internalizes the migration of skilled personnel at both the professional and upper-echelon managerial levels within their international production systems. This is facilitated, moreover, by the fact that official impediments to migration (the transaction costs of migration) are likely to be much smaller for TNC-sponsored transfers of personnel for well-defined positions than for independent migration efforts (Dunning and Gray, 1991). Foreign-direct-investment flows may therefore instigate the movement of managerial and technical staff from one country to another. This is particularly likely in the case of service industries. Furthermore, expatriate personnel need not necessarily come from the country of the parent company; there is some indication that trained managerial personnel from third countries are attracted. For example, expatriates from other countries in Asia (particularly, India and the Philippines) are finding employment as middle-level managers and accountants in foreign affiliates in Indonesia, which has a shortage of such personnel.[8] It is also conceivable – as mentioned above – that some of the locally hired staff may be transferred abroad including to the country of origin of the investment. Overall, however, the figures involving this type of outward migration are relatively small. What is more important is probably that the possibility of upward mobility of this kind can have an important psychological effect which becomes an input in the decision-making processes of potential migrants when deciding whether or not they need to move elsewhere in their search for advancement.

FOREIGN DIRECT INVESTMENT AND MIGRATION: AN ASSESSMENT

Transnational corporations deliver a package of assets to host econo-mies and link together various elements that determine growth. The overall impact of these various elements is likely to be greater than the sum of their individual effects. Indirect effects through interactive synergies on unrelated domestic firms in the host economy must also be taken into account. This positive contribution of TNCs to the growth of developing economies can be expected to have some impact in the long term in reducing the push for outward migration created by poverty and economic hardship.

Foreign direct investment can also reduce directly the immediate desire for emigration by providing employment to those seeking employment or improved economic opportunity. Although the con-tribution of foreign affiliates to overall employment is small, it is not negligible, and it is particularly significant in economies in which FDI accounts for a fairly high share of total investment, as well as in export-processing zones and other export-oriented activites; more-over, employment is often concentrated in key, future-oriented indus-tries. Partly as a result, employees in foreign affiliates often also enjoy higher incomes than their counterparts in domestic firms. Furthermore, affiliates of TNCs also provide opportunities for local managerial, professional and technical personnel for professional development and advancement through training programmes and advancement within the foreign affiliate – and, in fact, even outside the affiliate. The creation of these opportunities is likely to have some impact in terms of reducing outward migration, particularly if one takes into account the improved perspective that growth itself, and the presence of TNCs, is likely to provide.

It must be recognized, however, that the impact of FDI may be greater for middle- and high-income developing countries than for low-income countries. This is not only because low-income coun-tries receive very little FDI, but also because the key requirements for growth in those countries, such as increasing agricultural productivity, improving basic infrastructures and increasing educational and nutritional standards, are generally not areas of TNC participation.

Thus, a threshold level of domestic development may be required to benefit most from the potential for growth that FDI provides. On the other hand, some low-income countries are able to attract FDI on the basis of large domestic markets because of large populations, or natural resource endowments. Moreover, FDI by TNCs, whatever its size, releases other resources, both domestic and foreign, for investments in the important areas mentioned earlier. It thus serves to supplement, in low-income countries, domestic investment and development assistance in reducing the pressure to migrate. In the middle- and higher-income countries, the growth- and opportunity-producing impact of FDI and, hence, the impact of migration, are likely to be much greater.

POLICY ISSUES

The previous sections emphasized the contributions that FDI can make by reducing the economic pressure to migrate, by promoting the long-term development prospects of migrant-producing countries as well as through the immediate creation of employment opportunities and improvements of employment conditions and job-upgrading possibilities. The share of many developing countries, as well as Central and Eastern European countries, with a migration potential in FDI world-wide is, however, low (Table 7.5). It is important, therefore, to increase the share of these countries in FDI flows. It is also important to create conditions and incentives conducive to maximizing the contributions of TNCs to growth through technological development, human resource development and trade in the host countries, both directly and through linkages with domestic enterprises, and to promote employment generation and the availability of higher-level jobs available to host-country nationals. Since the objectives of TNCs are not necessarily identical with those of host countries and, moreover, the objectives of home and host countries of TNCs may also differ, the challenge is to structure policies in such a way that TNCs, in pursuing their corporate strategies, contribute the maximum in the above respects to host developing countries.

This is not an easy challenge to respond to, since, to date, FDI policies have not been used as a tool of migration management – in other words, the migration effects of FDI have not been taken into account by host countries, home countries or the international community when formulating policies towards FDI. This is not surprising, since many of the links between FDI and migration are indirect, and since the factors influencing migration are complex and involve a wide array of both domestic and foreign economic policies. Nevertheless, coordinated policies by host countries, home countries and the international community directed towards increasing investment flows as well as towards strengthening their contributions to development on a sustained basis would serve to alleviate outward migration by improving economic conditions and prospects for the future, as well as by creating employment opportunities. Furthermore, policies directed specifically towards enhancing the contribution of FDI to employment generation and the creation of higher-level job opportunities would contribute directly to reducing the pull of more plentiful and better employment abroad. It needs to be emphasized, however, that the issue is not migration *per se* but rather the broadening of choices facing potential migrants.

Policies for strengthening the contribution of foreign direct investment to growth

Policies to stimulate FDI for growth that would assist in reducing outward migration must focus on increasing FDI flows and enhancing its contribution to growth through the various channels discussed earlier. Studies on the determinants of FDI suggest that economic conditions in host countries – including, especially, the size and growth of domestic markets and a minimum level of human and physical infrastructure – are important factors.[9] Many poor countries lack these attributes. However, many of them do have specific locational advantages, such as particular natural resources endowments or an abundance of low-cost labour. Given the general economic conditions and specific locational conditions, however, the existence of a congenial investment environment is essential for TNCs to invest. Potential host countries, therefore, need to strengthen their efforts to improve the climate for FDI by reviewing their FDI policy regimes relating to such issues as the exclusion of sectors or industries from FDI, restrictions on local borrowing, the purchasing of shares in local markets and the repatriation of earnings by TNCs. While strategic interventions in the area of FDI – usually implemented through investment incentives and performance requirements and/or restrictions on FDI, with a view to increasing long-term benefits or ensuring local control – may have a role to play, such interventions should be highly selective and based on a careful assessment of cost and benefits.

Table 7.5 Foreign direct investment in selected migrant-sending countries

Country	Average annual FDI inflows, 1986–1990 (million dollars)	Ratio of FDI inflows to GDCF, 1986–1990 (percentage)	Employment in foreign affiliates (thousands)	Number of emigrants[a] (thousands)
Africa				
Algeria	9.2	(0.04)	..	..
Benin	..	..	..	..
Botswana	60.9	(25.7)	35.0(1989)	..
Burkina Faso	1.5	..	..	..
Egypt	1,067.8	(8.1)	..	..
Ethiopia	2.1	..	..	..
Malawi	0.02	..	..	..
Mali	3.8	..	..	..
Morocco	95.6	(1.4)	..	23.8[e]
Somalia	..	..	..	..
Sudan	0.7	(0.2)	..	..
Tunisia	74.0	(3.7)	..	..
Asia				
Bangladesh	2.2	(0.1)	..	..
India	160.5	(0.2)	..	..
Rep. of Korea	676.0	(1.6)	315.0(1978)	415.8[c]
Pakistan	174.8	(2.0)	..	..
Philippines	492.6	(8.5)	156.0(1988)	438.2[d]
Central and Eastern Europe				
Albania	..	..	..	..
Bulgaria	..	..	..	..
Czechoslovakia	..	..	..	28.7[l]
Hungary	..	..	..	1,690.4[k]
Poland	28.6	(0.01)	85.3(1990)	278.8[j]
Former USSR	..	..	103.7(1990)[m]	..
Europe				
Turkey	388.2	..	..	..
Yugoslavia	15.7	..	..	..
Latin America and the Caribbean				
Bolivia	8.2	(0.0)	..	..
Colombia	454.6	(0.3)	..	69.1[f]
Ecuador	77.4	(0.05)	..	2,901.7[g]
El Salvador	14.8	(0.0)	..	2,709.8[h]
Haiti	7.4	(0.0)	..	..
Jamaica	46.4	(0.03)	87.0(1988)	..
Mexico	2,606.4	(1.7)	940.5(1987)	782.9[i]
Western Asia				
Jordan	24.5	(2.4)	..	..
Syrian Arab Republic	67.3	..	..	1,597.6[b]

Source: TCMD, *World Investment Directory*, various volumes; United Nations (1978, 1986, 1990).

[a] Cumulative flows of short- and long-term emigrants during 1977–1988 as reported by migrant-sending countries.
[b] Long-term emigration data cover 1977, 1980, 1981; short-term emigration data cover 1980, 1981.
[c] Long-term emigration; data cover 1983–1988.
[d] Long-term emigration; data cover 1970, 1972–1973, 1975–1976, 1983, 1986–1988.
[e] Long-term emigration; data cover only 1970–1973 and 1980.
[f] Long-term emigration; data cover 1980 and 1981.
[g] Long-term and short-term emigration; data cover 1979–1988.
[h] Long-term emigration; data cover only 1979–1982 and 1984.
[i] Long-term emigration data cover 1970–1973, 1976–1985; short-term emigration data cover 1976–1985.
[j] Long-term emigration.
[k] Long-term emigration.
[l] Long-term emigration.
[m] Data are for the Commonwealth of Independent States.

Maintaining a credible and stable policy environment, once it is put in place, is also important. Administrative structures and practices must be aligned with policies, so that disparities between practice and policy do not deter prospective investors. Host countries also need to pay attention to the efficiency of their public administrations in dealing with matters relating to FDI.

Host-country policies can influence the contribution of FDI to growth not only through their direct addition to investment capital, but also through the various other channels, discussed earlier, by which growth is enhanced. In many instances, this requires policies to reinforce and strengthen the capabilities of host-country institutions and coordinate investment policies with macroeconomic and trade policies. Some of the measures necessary include the following:

- Measures to support and encourage local entrepreneurship, including the removal of administrative restrictions on the formation of new businesses, the establishment of programmes to provide training in business skills and greater scope for TNCs operating in special enterprise zones to purchase locally. Such policies can stimulate local investment through linkages as suppliers to TNCs.

- Policies to create an adequate human resources base through education and training and appropriate incentives, in order to maximize the contributions of FDI and other forms of TNC participation to the transfer and development of technology and to human resource development.

- Improved coordination between trade and investment policies. An export-oriented trade strategy, for example, is likely to be more effective if it is supplemented by an open policy with respect to FDI, so that the latter may contribute directly to trade. In a competitive environment, trade and FDI policies should be aimed at providing incentives for both domestic and foreign firms to develop new areas of comparative advantage.

- Policies to strengthen the operation of markets and ensure competition, so that domestic consumers, producers and factors of production can benefit from competition and linkages with TNCs. This is particularly important if the efficiency benefits from the entry of FDI are to be achieved.

Home-country policies to facilitate FDI by their firms in developing countries with high migratory pressures could also contribute to the growth of those countries and to a reduction of potential migration. Such measures include fiscal and financial incentives, including development finance at the bilateral level, bilateral investment treaties and investment-guarantee schemes (UNCTC, 1990b, pp. 29–35). There are also a number of trade-related measures providing preferential access to developing country exports that are also conducive for encouraging FDI in developing countries. For example, under the Caribbean Basin Initiative, the United States encourages its firms to enter into manufacturing arrangements with Caribbean Basin firms, guaranteeing duty-free access to the products manufactured in the region. Additional policy areas to encourage investment by TNCs in migrant-producing developing countries that deserve the attention of home countries include the removal or relaxation of all forms of restrictions on outward investment; tax exemptions or higher tax concessions; financial assistance for investments; strengthened information and promotion services; and additional or improved preferences and the removal of impediments to exports from the countries concerned.

Regional and multilateral measures to promote FDI in developing countries include financial assistance schemes or funds (such as, for example, the NORSAD Fund between the Nordic countries and the South African Development Co-ordination Conference member States); multilateral information and promotion services (such as the Centre for the Development of Industry created by the first Lomé Convention between the members of the European Community and the African–Caribbean–Pacific (ACP) States); and multilateral investment arrangements such as the ICSID and MIGA. Regional and multilateral trade arrangements also give preferences to developing country exports, and therefore encourage export-oriented investments. Many of these measures could also be examined with a view to further encouraging FDI in developing countries with significant potential for outward migration.

Finally, it has been proposed that, given the highly uneven distribution of FDI among countries despite bold policy changes in many developing countries to attract FDI, serious consideration should be given to the establishment of a multilateral FDI facility, as a tripartite venture between host and home countries and TNCs, with a view to providing loans to developing countries to promote development through FDI and alleviating the persistent imbalance in FDI flows (UN, TCMD, 1992, chapter 11). Such a facility could contain a special window for assisting countries in which hardship or severe lack of economic opportunities leads to significant pressures for outward migration.

Policies to promote employment and upward mobility through transnational corporations

Policies to enhance economic growth by encouraging FDI inflows can be expected to contribute to employment generation in host countries as well, although the extent of employment generation depends upon the nature of the investments. Policies may also, however, focus directly on maximizing the employment impact of FDI by encouraging investment in labour-intensive industries. Such policies include, among others, the establishment of export-processing zones and other export-oriented activities, such as offshore assembly operations. They also include incentives and facilities for the establishment of affiliates in labour-intensive services, such as data processing and tourism. Such policies are likely to impact directly on employment opportunities. However, policy makers should recognize the limitations of labour-intensive investment for promoting long-term growth and attempt to maintain a balance between employment and development objectives in the formulation of policies.

In addition to policies for increasing employment opportunities, countries also need to implement policies to encourage human resource development, professional development and the advancement of local personnel in foreign affiliates. Fiscal and financial incentives to foreign investors could encourage such development. Policies to strengthen the education and skills of local staff through education or training programmes implemented by host countries are relevant to attract FDI in labour-intensive activities, as well as to encourage professional development and advancement. Host countries, as well as home countries, could encourage training abroad by facilitating exit and entry regulations and visas.

Countries ought to consider targeting specific functions of TNCs for attracting jobs suited to their specific labour and skill endowments. In targeting investments for specific activities, special attention should be paid to FDI in services. The growing tradability of information-intensive services because of the increased use of computer-communication links has increased the prospects for foreign production and outsourcing of services involving data processing as well as professional skills. Data entry, transaction processing, database creation or updating as well as software and accounting services are examples of activities that are gradually moving to countries with relatively low-cost educated and skilled labour. Policies could be formulated to promote FDI in such activities and exploit the potential of services tradability. To encourage these as well as other investments, it may be necessary for host countries to strengthen the infrastructure that is needed for the location of certain jobs; for example, the establishment of accounting or software affiliates or regional headquarters may require an upgrading of telecommunication facilities.

If finally enacted, the General Agreement on Trade in Services (GATS) could stimulate both FDI and the movement of skilled services personnel, potentially creating job opportunities for workers in service industries as well as facilitating intra-firm mobility of services personnel. The draft final text of GATS (contained in Sauvant and Weber, 1992) imposes a general obligation of most-favoured-nation treatment (or non-discrimination across foreign services or service suppliers) and specific obligations (or obligations applicable only to services included in the schedules of contracting parties, subject to whatever conditions are listed) of market access and national treatment upon all signatories as regards services supplied through four modes of supply, namely cross-border supply of a service; provision implying movement of the consumer to the location of the supplier; services sold by legal entities that establish a presence in the territory of one party, but originate in the territory of another party; and provision of services requiring the temporary movement of natural persons. Thus, affiliates of TNCs in services as well as service suppliers or persons employed by suppliers who are nationals of a country that is party to the agreement are covered by the obligations, although the extent to which specific modes are covered will depend upon the activities included in a country's list of commitments.

Regional cooperation and integration arrangements could have similar impacts by generating employment and career opportunities for workers and professionals by stimulating investment in export-oriented manufacturing industries, or directly by including investment liberalization in their provisions. At present, the only such arrangement that includes both developed and developing countries, thus holding out the prospects for significant flows of FDI, is the North American Free Trade Agreement (NAFTA). NAFTA also makes allowance for the reciprocal temporary entry of business persons (business visitors, traders and investors, intra-company transferees and professionals), easing some of the restrictions in their cross-border movement. Apart from formal regional cooperation or integration arrangements, the increasing regionalization of the world economy into trade and investment blocks, and the regional core strategies of TNCs associated with such blocks, are factors that must be taken into account in the formulation of policies.

Cooperation between migration-receiving and migration-sending countries

Policies to strengthen the contribution of FDI to migration management through economic growth, employment generation and the creation of enhanced opportunities for professional development could be supported by cooperation between migrant-receiving and migrant-sending countries to monitor trends in FDI, trade and development as they relate to migration. Such cooperation could be implemented through the establishment of informal bilateral committees comprising representatives from the two groups of countries, as well as representatives of TNCs and the private sector and trade unions from each of the countries. These committees could periodically review matters relating to migration, FDI, trade and development, in light of current trends, and propose appropriate measures and actions to sustain FDI flows and their contribution to the development of the migrant-sending countries. Such measures could include not only support for the policies discussed earlier, but also greater coordination between investment and trade policies and regional cooperation on matters relating to FDI, trade, development and migration.

CONCLUSION

Foreign direct investment by TNCs has a role to play in reducing economically motivated emigration pressures. But two caveats have to be made. First, the effect of FDI is (a) long-term and indirect; (b) small as regards the creation of employment in the short term; and (c) partly based on the expectations generated regarding the future. Second, FDI needs to be seen in the broader context of development. Furthermore, it should be kept in mind that migration *per se* is not an undesirable phenomenon but rather has an important part to play in increasing global economic efficiency.

The principal manner in which FDI helps to reduce emigration is by contributing to growth, assuming that growth is translated into a reduction of poverty and inequality. Foreign direct investment can play this role not only by providing capital, but, perhaps more importantly, through technology transfer, human resource development, providing access to markets and creating various backward and forward linkages with the economies in which foreign affiliates are established. At the same time, the onset or acceleration of growth may well be accompanied by an increase in outward migration. But, on balance, and over time, to the extent that TNCs contribute to economic growth, emigration pressures – especially of the kind that are more poverty related – should be reduced.

In the short term, furthermore, FDI can alleviate migratory pressures by creating employment. However, while the employment-creating effect is important in some countries and industries, overall it is small. At the same time, employment in foreign affiliates is often associated with higher wages, better training and favourable career prospects (including postings in other countries). In brief, employment in foreign affiliates is associated with upward mobility and higher status and, therefore, can become a factor in the decision-making process especially of opportunity-seeking potential migrants.

Finally, both the growth- and opportunity-enhancing effects of FDI can create positive perspectives about development which may influence the attitudes of potential migrants and induce them to stay. Thus, it is not only the concrete impact on growth and employment of FDI, but also its role in engendering optimistic expectations regarding the development and career prospects that need to be taken into account.

For these reasons, it would be desirable, when formulating FDI policies, to pay attention to the effects that such investment can have on migratory pressures. This should be done not only in terms of increasing flows of FDI to countries with large emigration potential due to economic factors, but also in terms of trying to target policies in such a manner that makes them particularly relevant from a migration perspective. Perhaps it would be useful for this purpose to strengthen cooperation between migration-receiving and migration-sending countries, including through the creation of informal bilateral mechanisms comprising representatives from the two groups of countries, as well as representatives of TNCs and trade unions, to monitor matters relating to FDI, trade, development and migration.

This last observation leads to the second caveat, namely that the relationship between FDI and migration needs to be seen in the broader context of development. Neither in the long term nor in the short term can FDI *alone* play a lead role in reducing economically motivated migratory pressures; in fact, FDI can even lead to some migration. Foreign direct investment is only *one* mechanism, and an indirect one at that, affecting migratory pressures; its role is of a contributory nature. This draws attention to the need to pursue proper development strategies (including proper FDI, trade and technology policies), and the need to create the proper national and international frameworks within which such strategies can be implemented optimally. Only when the root cause of economically motivated migration – poverty and the associated lack of options – is reduced substantially, can one expect large-scale migratory pressures to ease.

Of necessity, these conclusions are of a general and tentative nature because, as noted earlier, little research has been done on the relationship between development and migration, and even less has been done on that between FDI and migration. The agenda for research needed is, therefore, long indeed. Such research might begin with the development of a methodological framework for analysing the reasons determining the decision of individuals to migrate and the way in which FDI impacts that decision. This implies combining what is essentially a decision-making process based on household behaviour with the perceived impact of TNCs on the domestic economy. Other areas for research include distinguishing between different types of FDI (mergers and acquisitions versus greenfield investment), different industries and different motivations for investing abroad (efficiency-seeking, market-seeking, export-oriented investments) and how these relate to migration. In terms of the employment-creating impact of TNCs, for example, most FDI in developing countries tends to be greenfield investment which adds to the stock of capital and to the availability of employment opportunities. On the other hand, the size of chronic unemployment or underemployment in some countries may be too large to be considerably reduced by any type of FDI. Related to that, and given the changing strategies and structures of TNCs, what is the employment-generating effect of foreign affiliates likely to be in the future? Also, since TNCs internalize, at least to a certain extent, part of the international labour market, especially as regards skilled personnel, the question arises as to the extent of this internationalization, and whether it is likely to grow in the future. Finally, what FDI-related policies could be developed that are targeted to reduce migratory pressures? These are just a few of the areas that need further research – preferably as part of a broader enquiry into the relationship between migration and development.

NOTES

** The views expressed here are those of the authors and do not necessarily represent those of the United Nations. The authors gratefully acknowledge comments on an earlier draft by John H. Dunning, Jean-Pierre Garson, Bimal Ghosh, Peter Gray, Inge Kaul, J. D. McBain, Thierry Noyelle and Sharon Stanton Russell. An earlier version of the paper was presented to OECD Conference on 'Migration and International Cooperation: Challenge for OECD Countries', Madrid, 29–31 March 1993.

1 Recent meetings and conferences reflect this interest; for example, the International Conference on Migration organized by the OECD in Rome, 13–15 March 1991, and the Tenth IOM Seminar on Migration, organized by the International Organization for Migration in Geneva, 15–17 September 1992, which focused, in part, on the links between migration and development. The Transnational Corporations and Management Division of the United Nations Department of Economic and Social Development, in collaboration with UNCTAD and IOM, is implementing a project focusing on the interrelationships between foreign direct investment, trade and migration. See also Papademetriou and Martin (1991) and United States Commission (1990).

2 For a detailed analysis of the impact of TNCs on economic growth of developing countries, see United Nations, Transnational Corporations and Management Division (1992).

3 It has been noted that, for a number of countries in Asia, the amount of FDI that would be needed to compensate for the loss of migrants' remittances received by these countries, based on present levels of investment, would have to be significantly higher – twenty-five times the current amount of investment flows in the case of the Philippines, for instance (UNDP, 1992, p. 59). Such estimates ignore precisely the fact that TNCs bring to the host country an integrated package of tangible and intangible assets. The multiplier effect of the investment capital on the domestic economy and the positive externalities that are associated with TNCs can generate income streams and benefit the host country beyond what the actual amount of investment suggests.

4 For a discussion of the evolution of migratory flows in relation to the development process, see Appleyard (1989, chapter 1). See also United States Commission (1990).

5 On the other hand, NAFTA is expected to result in a rise of unemployment in agriculture (ranging between 800,000 and 2,000,000) as a result

of the removal of trade barriers and subsidies to corn producers, which would be too large to be absorbed by the *direct* job creation through FDI (Koechlin and Larudee, 1992, p. 21).

6 The annual average inflow of FDI to Mexico during 1987–1991 was \$3.3 billion. In 1991, FDI flows to Mexico were \$4.8 billion (UN, TCMD, 1994). Although an inflow of FDI of that magnitude may be partly in anticipation of NAFTA, whose impact on FDI could subside after some time, it is not unreasonable to believe that FDI inflows in excess of \$3 billion can take place.

7 While host-country nationals account for the majority of employees in foreign affiliates, at the senior level, expatriates typically do account for a higher percentage. There may also be differences in the use of expatriates in senior management positions among United States, European and Japanese affiliates in developing countries, with Japanese ones relying more heavily on home-country nationals (Kobrin, 1989; Scullion, 1991; Zeira and Banai, 1985). To a certain extent, however, this may reflect the newness of the bulk of Japanese FDI. It can be expected that, as the stock of FDI matures, an increasing number of management positions in Japanese foreign affiliates will be taken over by nationals of the host country, as has been the case in foreign affiliates of United States and European TNCs, if only because expatriates typically are very expensive for their parent firms.

8 'MNCs in Indonesia look to Asian expats to fill management posts', *Business Asia*, 11 May 1992, p. 159.

9 For a review of these studies, see UNCTC (1992b).

REFERENCES

Appleyard, Reginald, ed. (1989). *The Impact of International Migration in Developing Countries*, Paris: OECD.

——— (1991). *International Migration: Challenge for the Nineties*. Geneva: International Organization for Migration.

Denison, Edward F. (1985). *Trends in American Economic Growth, 1929–1982*. Washington, DC: The Brookings Institution.

Dunning, John H. and H. Peter Gray (1991). Foreign direct investment and migration. Paper prepared for the seminar on *International Migration: The Impact of Employment Policies, Trade and Foreign Direct Investment* sponsored by the Friedrich Ebert Foundation in cooperation with UNCTC, UNCTAD and IOM, 21–22 November.

Erden, D. (1988). Impact of multinational corporations on host countries: executive training programs. *Management International Review*, 28, pp. 39–47.

Germany, Deutsche Bundesbank (1992). Die Kapitalverflechtungen der Unternehmen mit dem Ausland nach Ländern und Wirtschaftszweigen, Beilage zu *Statistische Beihefte zu den Monatsberichten der Deutschen Bundesbank*, 3, 4 (April).

Hufbauer, Gary C. and Jeffrey J. Schott (1993). *NAFTA: An Assessment*. Washington, DC: Institute for International Economics.

International Labour Office (1986). Proceedings of the South Asian Symposium on Multinationals and Social Policy, New Delhi, 3–5 December.

——— (1992). World Labour Report. Geneva: International Labour Office.

——— and United Nations Centre on Transnational Corporations (1988). *Economic and Social Effects of Multinational Enterprises in Export Processing Zones*. Geneva: International Labour Office.

Japan, Ministry of International Trade and Industry of Japan, *Kaigai Toshi Tokei Soran: Kaigai Jigyo Katsudo Kihon Chosa*, various issues.

Kobrin, Stephen J. (1989). Expatriate reduction in American multinationals: have we gone too far? *ILR Report*, 27, 1 (Fall), pp. 22–29.

Koechlin, Timothy and Mehrene Larudee (1992). The high cost of NAFTA. *Challenge*, 35, 5 (September–October) pp. 19–26.

Lim Lin Lean (1991). International migration in Asia: patterns, implications and policies. Paper presented at the UNFPA/ECE Expert Group meeting, Geneva, July.

Long, Frank (1986). Employment effects of multinational enterprises in export processing zones in the Caribbean. Geneva: International Labour Office Working Paper No. 42.

Martin, Philip (1992). Foreign direct investment and migration: the case of Mexican *maquiladoras*. Paper presented at the 10th IOM seminar on migration, Geneva, 15–17 September.

Mataloni, Raymond J. Jr (1992). U.S. multinational companies: operations in 1990. *Survey of Current Business*, 72, 8 (August), pp. 60–78.

MNCs in Indonesia look to Asian expats to fill management posts. *Business Asia*, 11 May 1992, p. 159.

Papademetriou, Demetrios G. and Philip L. Martin, eds (1991). *The Unsettled Relationship: Labor Migration and Economic Development*. New York: Greenwood Press.

Sassen, Saskia (1989). America's immigration 'problem'. *World Policy Journal* (Fall), pp. 810–831.

——— (1993). The weight of economic internationalization: comparing the new immigration in Japan and the United States. Paper presented at the Association of Japanese Business Studies, New York, 8–10 January.

Sauvant, Karl P. and Joerg Weber, eds (1992). *The International Legal Framework for Services*. Dobbs Ferry, New York: Oceana Publications.

Schoepfle, Gregory K. and Jorge F. Perez-Lopez (1991). Employment implication of export assembly operations in Mexico and the Caribbean Basin. In *Migration Impacts of Trade and Foreign Investment*, Sergio Diaz-Briquets and Sidney Weintraub, eds, Boulder, Colorado: Westview Press, pp. 15–52.

Scullion, Hugh (1991). Why companies prefer to use expatriates. *Personnel Management*, 23, 11 (November), pp. 32–35.

Solow, Robert M. (1957). Technical change and the aggregate production function. *Review of Economics and Statistics*, 3 (August), pp. 313–320.

Tapinos, George Photios (1991). Development assistance strategies and emigration pressure in Europe and Africa. Washington, DC, Commission for the Study of International Migration and Cooperative Economic Development, Working Paper.

United Nations (1978). *1977 Demographic Yearbook*. Sales No. E.F.78.XIII.I.

———— (1986). *1985 Demographic Yearbook*. Sales No. E.F.86.XIII.I.

———— (1990). *1989 Demographic Yearbook*. Sales No. E.F.90.XIII.I.

United Nations Centre on Transnational Corporation (1989). *Transnational Service Corporations and Developing Countries: Impact and Policy Issues*. Sales No. E.89.II.A.14.

———— (1990a). *The Challenge of Free Economic Zones in Central and Eastern Europe*. Sales No. E.90.II.A.27.

———— (1990b). *Foreign Direct Investment, Debt and Home Country Policies*. Sales No. E.90.II.A.16.

———— (1991). *World Investment Report 1991: The Triad in Foreign Direct Investment*. Sales No. E.91.II.A.12.

———— (1992a). *World Investment Directory 1992, Vol. 1, Asia and the Pacific*. Sales No. E.92.II.A.II.

———— (1992b). *The Determinants of Foreign Direct Investment: A Survey of the Evidence*. Sales No. E.92.II.A.2.

United Nations Development Programme (1992). *Human Development Report 1992*. New York and Oxford: Oxford University Press.

United Nations, Transnational Corporations and Management Division (1992). *World Investment Report 1992: Transnational Corporations as Engines of Growth*. Sales No. E.92.II.A.19.

———— (1993). *World Investment Report 1993: Transnational Corporations and Integrated International Production*. New York: United Nations. Sales No. E.93.II.A.14.

———— (1994). *World Investment Directory 1992, Vol. IV, Latin America and the Caribbean*. New York: United Nations. Sales No. E.94.II.A.10.

———— and The World Bank (1994). *Liberalizing International Transactions in Services: A Handbook*. New York and Geneva: United Nations. Sales No. E.94.II.A.11.

United States Commission for the Study of International Migration and Cooperative Economic Development (1990). *Unauthorized Migration: An Economic Development Response*. Washington, DC: Government Printing Office.

United States, Department of Commerce (1985). *U.S. Direct Investment Abroad: 1982 Benchmark Survey Data*. Washington, DC: Government Printing Office.

———— (1992). *U.S. Direct Investment Abroad: 1989 Benchmark Survey, Final Results*. Washington, DC: Government Printing Office.

World Bank, The (1992). *World Tables, 1992*. Washington, DC and Baltimore, Maryland: Johns Hopkins University Press for the World Bank.

Zeira Yoram and Moshe Banai (1985). Selection of expatriate managers in MNCs: the host environment point of view. *International Studies of Management and Organization*, 15, 1, pp. 33–51.

8 The North American Free Trade Agreement and foreign direct investment*

*Michael Gestrin and Alan M. Rugman***

The North American Free Trade Agreement substantially liberalizes the North American investment regimes. The Agreement establishes a clear, rules-based framework for the impartial treatment of foreign direct investment and places strict limits upon the use of performance requirements. It also establishes dispute-settlement mechanisms specifically designed to deal with investment issues. With the added clarity and security that these provisions provide to foreign investors in North America and the drastic reduction of Mexico's tariffs on regionally originating goods, transnational corporations will be encouraged to rationalize the organization of their North American operations and to increase substantially foreign direct investment in Mexico. In addition to these rules and procedures, however, the North American Free Trade Agreement also contains significant discriminatory measures. Several industries have been exempted by the signatories from key investment provisions of the Agreement. Other industries, such as automobiles, textiles and apparel and segments of the electronics industry, will be protected from import competition by strict rules of origin.

INTRODUCTION

This article describes and analyses the provisions of the North American Free Trade Agreement (NAFTA) in tems of their impact upon the North American investment regimes.[1] The principal aims of NAFTA investment provisions[2] are to encourage foreign direct investment (FDI) in North America and to create an integrated North American market. These aims are pursued through the establishment of rules that reduce the scope for the adoption of discretionary and

* Reprinted from *Transnational Corporations*, vol. 3, no. 1 (February 1994), pp. 77–95.

discriminatory policies with respect to FDI by the signatory Governments, as well as rules of origin that encourage North American value-added activity in several industries.[3]

While NAFTA's investment provisions are meant to contribute to a less discriminatory North American investment environment, they also reflect the protectionist demands of several powerful North American industries. Numerous exceptions to the investment provisions serve to potect regionally based producers from foreign competition through the targeted 'grandfathering' of discriminatory measures that were in place before the Agreement came into effect, as well as through the establishment of a few new discriminatory measures. In addition, the rules of origin are highly restrictive in some industries and are therefore likely to result in trade and investment diversion in these cases.

The next section describes NAFTA's new investment rules. The Agreement's discriminatory measures and their potential impact upon intra- and interregional investment patterns for particular industries are examined in the section that follows. The last section concludes with a summary of the main findings and some observations concerning the viability of NAFTA as a model upon which investment agreements in other regional forums might be based in the post-Uruguay Round era.

INVESTMENT PROVISIONS OF THE NORTH AMERICAN FREE TRADE AGREEMENT

The North American Free Trade Agreement can affect FDI regimes in North America through two types of provisions. The first type deals explicitly with FDI issues. These appear in chapter 11 of the Agreement (in which the basic rules for the treatment of FDI and the resolution of disputes between investors and States are outlined), chapters 12 and 14 (in which investment issues related to the provision of services and financial services are dealt with, respectively), and chapter 17 on intellectual property rights. The second type consists of investment-related trade measures. These include the rules of origin and measures related to duty drawback and deferral.[4]

THE INVESTMENT MEASURES

The investment and services chapters

The national treatment provisions (articles 1102, 1202, 1405 of the Agreement) stipulate that each party[5] must accord to investors and investments from the other NAFTA parties 'treatment no less favorable than that it accords, in like circumstances, to its own investors' (article 1102.1). The national treatment provisions constitute the conceptual cornerstone of NAFTA. Several provisions of the Agreement, however, move beyond national treatment either by establishing common norms for the treatment of FDI among the three signatories (e.g. articles 1105 and 1110, described below), or through the adoption of measures based upon reciprocity (e.g. the so-called 'tit-for-tat' reservations in the annexes, also explained below).

The most favoured-nation treatment provisions (articles 1103, 1203, 1406) stipulate that each signatory must accord to investors from the other signatories to NAFTA 'treatment no less favorable than that it accords, in like circumstances, to investors of any other Party or of a non-Party' (article 1103.1). The most-favoured-nation provisions confer upon foreign investors based in North America the best possible treatment among all foreign investors in instances where one of the parties has chosen to hold a reservation against the national treatment provisions. Under the terms of the United States–Canada Free Trade Agreement, this added security was not available.

The minimum standard of treatment provisions (article 1105) mainly reflect the concerns of United States and Canadian firms that the national treatment and most-favoured-nation provisions might not provide adequate protection in Mexico. Article 1105 attempts to commit the parties to a performance 'floor', reflecting the unique concerns arising from the negotiation of an economic agreement between economies at such disparate levels of development. Similarly, the expropriation and compensation provisions (article 1110) also seek to establish a minimum North American standard. The acceptance of these articles by Mexico is historically significant in so far as these represent a weakening of the Calvo doctrine.[6]

The performance requirements provisions (article 1106) contain a list of requirements that the parties may not impose upon investors of other parties or of non-parties with respect to the establishment or operation of an investment. These include export requirements; domestic-content requirements; import requirements;

trade-balancing requirements; the linking of domestic sales to export levels or foreign-exchange earnings; technology-transfer require- ments (except when required to remedy violations of domestic com- petition laws); and requirements that a firm act as 'the exclusive supplier . . . to a specific region or world market'. In addition, article 1106 forbids the linking or the conferral of an advantage (such as a subsidy or a tax advantage) to domestic-content requirements, domes- tic-input requirements, trade-balancing requirements; and the linking of domestic sales to export levels and/or foreign-exchange earnings. Article 1106 does permit Government support to be linked to the location of production, the provision of particular services, the train- ing and employment of workers, the construction or expansion of particular facilities and the conduct of research and development.

The limits of NAFTA upon the use of performance requirements are more stringent than those included in the Uruguay Round Final Act in two respects.

- First, the Uruguay Round Final Act prohibits trade balancing and local-content requirements (with respect to both right of estab- lishment and conferral of advantages). The North American Free Trade Agreement also prohibits those requirements, as well as the technology and exclusive supplier requirements, with respect to establishment.
- Second, the Final Act allows developing countries a five-year phase-out period (seven years for the least developed countries), as well as several broad exceptions, such as the use of prohibited performance requirements to protect infant industries. In this respect, Mexico has committed itself to much stricter limits on the use of such measures under the terms of NAFTA than those of the developing countries under the terms of the Final Act.

The Denial of Benefits provisions (article 1113) establish the rights of non-North-American investors who are established in one NAFTA country and who want to expand their operations into another NAFTA country. The key feature of the article is that it accords full NAFTA rights to outside investors as long as they have 'substantial business activities in the territory of the Party under whose law (the business) is constituted or organized' (article 1113.2).

Finally, NAFTA's investment chapter expands upon the types of investment covered by the Agreement beyond the coverage offered by the United States–Canada Free Trade Agreement. Indeed, whereas the United States–Canada Free Trade Agreement covers only foreign direct investment, NAFTA also protects portfolio investments. This additional coverage is significant, albeit difficult to quantify. Of interest, however, is the lack of coverage for the growing number of strategic business alliances.[7] Given the increasingly important role of these alliances in international business and their implications for capital movements, that omission is noteworthy.[8]

The Investor–State Dispute Settlement Mechanism

The North American Free Trade Agreement also sets out rules for the settlement of disputes between investors and signatory Governments. The Investor–State Dispute Settlement Mechanism consists of a set of rules that create an interface between NAFTA and either of two international arbitration conventions, namely the International Convention for Settlement of Investment Disputes (ICSID) and the arbitration rules of the United Nations Commission on International Trade Law (UNCITRAL).

The Investor–State Dispute Settlement Mechanism establishes the conditions under which an investor can take a NAFTA member-state to arbitration, the functions of NAFTA's Commission during disputes,[9] the forms of compensation that the arbitration panels can award, enforcement mechanisms available to the disputing parties, and exclusions from the Dispute Settlement Mechanism.

The Dispute Settlement Mechanism is important in several regards. First, and from a historical perspective, the introduction of the Investor–State Dispute Settlement Mechanism based upon the existing international conventions and rules highlights the depth of Mexican reforms that have been under way since the mid-1980s. The Dispute Settlement Mechanism of NAFTA is binding and based upon international law; as such it runs counter to the Calvo doctrine upon which Mexican (and most other Central and South American) policy towards foreign investors has been based since the nineteenth century. It also reflects the extent to which NAFTA goes beyond being based purely upon national treatment. In effect, NAFTA has enhanced the role of supra-national rules and administrative structures in the governance of the FDI regimes of North America.[10]

Intellectual property protection

The protection of intellectual property in North America has been significantly improved with the adoption by the Mexican Government of stringent intellectual property laws in 1991. NAFTA adds to this improvement in marginal ways, namely by establishing clear rules and expectations for investors operating across borders in North America and by turning Mexico's domestic intellectual property reforms into international commitments. Furthermore, investors are able to make use of NAFTA dispute settlement mechanisms when disputes over intellectual property issues arise. Some areas are likely to continue to give rise to conflicts due to divergent domestic policy approaches among the signatories, the protected cultural industries of Mexico and Canada being a prominent example. The agreement on intellectual property rights under the Uruguay Round is comparable with NAFTA intellectual property provisions in terms of achievements. However, NAFTA provides more protection with regard to intellectual property than the Uruguay Round Final Act in several respects. For example, NAFTA protects pharmaceuticals in the process of being developed, while the Uruguay Round Final Act provides only limited protection under those circumstances.

INVESTMENT-RELATED TRADE MEASURES

The rules of origin

The rules of origin establish procedures for determining whether products traded within NAFTA are originating within the member countries and therefore are eligible to enjoy the benefits of NAFTA tariff reductions. These rules have been formulated to encourage production in North America and to avoid the establishment of export platforms by non-regionally based firms in any member country of NAFTA.

The rules of origin[11] contain two types of requirement that are applied in different combinations to different products. The basic requirement is for imported intermediate inputs to undergo a change in tariff classification. The second requirement (sometimes applied in addition to the change in tariff classification) is that products must contain a minimum regional value content. For those products to which the minimum regional value content applies, the exporter can choose between one of two methods to calculate that value: the first is based upon a transaction value test and the second is based upon a net cost test. The transaction value test uses the selling price of the good. The net cost test uses the producer's total cost less the cost of sales promotion, marketing, after-sale service, royalties, shipping and packaging and certain interest costs.

For several important sectors, NAFTA rules of origin are considered to be stricter than those of the United States–Canada Free Trade Agreement. The rules have been tightened in terms of the change in tariff classification requirements, the regional value content requirements and, in some cases, requirements that specific sub-assemblies be produced in North America. The potential impact of the rules of origin for investment patterns in several industries is considered in the section on discriminatory aspects of NAFTA investment provisions.

Restrictions upon duty drawback and deferral programmes

The North American Free Trade Agreement places restrictions on duty drawback and deferral programmes. These programmes allow producers duty waivers on intermediate inputs if the final product is subsequently exported, or if pre-specified minimum levels of domestic value added are achieved. The restrictions that NAFTA places upon these programmes have a similar impact upon FDI as the rules of origin. Indeed, these restrictions are intended to promote regional sourcing and to avoid the establishment of export platforms. As such, they affect Canada and Mexico, both of which have maintained such programmes in the past to encourage production for export to the United States market.

The elimination of duty drawback (after a transition period of seven years for Mexico–Canada and Mexico–United States trade and two years for Canada–United States trade), combined with stricter rules of origin, will potentially have dramatic effect upon the trade and investment patterns in some industries. These effects are considered together with the analysis of the impact of the rules of origin in the next section.

THE EXCEPTIONS TO THE NORTH AMERICAN FREE TRADE AGREEMENT INVESTMENT PROVISIONS

The previous section described the main provisions of NAFTA that form the basis for the treatment of FDI by the signatory Governments once the Agreement comes into effect. These rules centre upon the principles of national treatment, most-favoured-nation treatment, as well as upon certain supra-national norms and regulations (i.e. the minimum standard of treatment provisions and the Investor–State Dispute Settlement Mechanism). Foreign-direct-investment regimes in North America under NAFTA are also shaped by investment-related trade measures, such as the rules of origin and restrictions upon duty drawback and deferral programmes. The principal goal of the investment-related trade measures is to ensure that NAFTA benefits and promotes North American producers and production.

This section examines discriminatory measures of NAFTA that run counter to either the letter or the spirit of the investment provisions described in the previous section. These measures reflect the concerns of politically important industries in the North American economies that, for one reason or another, have sought and obtained protection from global competition. Four sections of the Agreement stand out in this regard: the annexes, the broad national security exemption (article 2102), the automotive annex, and the rules of origin.

The annexes

The Free Trade Agreement grandfathered all measures and laws that were in effect prior to its ratification and that ran counter to aspects of that Agreement. The appeal of the grandfathering instrument was its simplicity. However, given the complexity and discriminatory nature of the Mexican investment regime relative to its Canadian and United States counterparts, grandfathering all past Mexican legislation would have effectively defeated the purpose of negotiating a free trade agreement with Mexico. As a result, grandfathering was replaced with negative lists. These lists consist of reservations – existing measures and/or laws[12] that run counter to one or more provisions of the Agreement. One of the main advantages of these lists is that they have made discrimination in the investment regimes of the signatories much more transparent.

The function of the annexes[13] is to exclude 'sensitive' industries in each of the signatory economies from the main investment and trade provisions of NAFTA (subject to the 'existing measure' constraint). The Canadian and United States reservations do not contain many economically significant industries since the investment regimes of both countries are already very liberal. Historically sensitive sectors in both countries have been accorded reservations such that while each regime remained largely open to FDI, NAFTA negotiations did not produce any substantive advances in terms of further liberalization.[14] The most important Canadian exclusion from the main NAFTA investment provisions is its cultural industries. The most important United States exclusion is its maritime industry.

The Mexican lists are much longer than those of Canada or the United States. However, most of Mexico's reservations in the manufacturing sector are subject to complete phase-out provisions. For example, although foreign ownership of an enterprise of the autoparts industry will be limited initially to 49 per cent that restriction will be completely lifted five years after the Agreement comes into effect. Seven years after the Agreement comes into effect, the export requirements imposed upon investors under the ALTEX and PITEX decrees will be completely eliminated. From 1 July 1995, investors based in Canada and the United States will be allowed to own 100 per cent of enterprises engaged in the provision of value-added telecommunication services.

Annex 3 is unique to Mexico and covers industries whose control is reserved for the Mexican State and is enshrined in the Mexican constitution. Eleven industries are covered in that annex: petroleum and derivative products, electricity, nuclear power and materials, satellite communications, telegraph services, radiotelegraph services, postal services, railroads, the issuance of currency, control over maritime and inland ports, and control over airports and heliports. Phase-outs do not apply to any of these reservations.

One of the most important Mexican reservations consists of constraints placed upon FDI in the energy industry. While foreign participation is permitted in petrochemicals up to 49 per cent, the energy industry remains in the hands of the State. The concern raised by this particular reservation is that energy could become a bottleneck in the Mexican economy as the manufacturing sector expands in response to NAFTA liberalization measures. In the absence of an infusion of foreign capital, the inefficient State-run energy industry will probably not be able to keep up with projected increases in demand.[15]

The Agreement does contain some liberalizing measures in the energy industry. For example, it allows for increased foreign involvement in Government procurement contracts and for expanded foreign involvement in the generation of electricity for own and other nonpublic use. Ultimately, the impact of the Mexican energy restrictions depends upon the extent to which the Mexican Government chooses to exercise its right to exclude foreign participation.

In addition to the specific sectoral reservations, the annexes also contain 'all sector' reservations. These reservations apply to particular groups, regions or procedures. They include the foreign investment review processes of Canada and Mexico. For acquisitions[16] above specified amounts ($150 million in Canada and $25 million in Mexico, subject to a 'phase-up' schedule which will bring the Mexican review threshold to $150 million by the year 2003), Government approval is necessary. The most notable feature of these exclusions is that the outcomes of the review processes in both countries are not subject to challenge under the terms of NAFTA dispute settlement procedures. This being said, however, the high thresholds will ensure that most acquisitions will not be subject to review.

In sum, the annexes identify sensitive industries in each of the signatory economies and describe the measures that each of these economies has chosen to maintain in order to protect these industries. In Canada and the United States, the annexes serve to maintain the status quo. In Mexico, the annexes will serve gradually to open most of the manufacturing sector to full foreign participation. However, several industries of the Mexican economy (most notably, energy) will remain off-limit to FDI, largely for political reasons.

The national security exemptions

The United States also maintains investment review procedures, but these are not described in the annexes. The reason for this is that the United States review of the FDI is based upon national security considerations and, therefore, falls under the terms of NAFTA's broad national security exclusion (article 2102). The review of FDI in the United States is conducted by the Committee on Foreign Direct Investment in the United States and the procedures for the conduct of the review are based upon the Exon–Florio amendment (Section 721) of the Omnibus Trade and Competitiveness Act of 1988 (Graham, 1991; Graham and Ebert, 1991).

The scope of the United States investment review process is much less clearly specified than it is in Canada and Mexico. Concern over the United States review procedures stems partially from amendments to the Exon–Florio legislation in 1992 stipulating that the need for United States technological leadership in industries related to defence should serve as a legitimate basis for blocking foreign acquisitions (greenfield investments are excluded from review by the Committee). Since most advanced technologies have military and civilian use, the discriminatory potential of the Exon–Florio legislation is considerable. While this potential has not yet been realized, the continued erosion of the United States position in high-technology manufacturing[17] could give rise to calls for a more active role for the Committee on Foreign Direct Investment – and no rewriting of the Committee's mandate would be necessary.

Furthermore, it is not clear whether outcomes of the United States review process are subject to challenge under the terms of NAFTA dispute settlement procedures. The United States position is that all national-security-related decisions are not subject to dispute resolution under the terms of NAFTA. However, article 1138 of the investment chapter states that only the decision to allow or disallow an investment on the basis of national security considerations is excluded from the review process. The Canadian position is therefore that, apart from the specific exclusion of article 1138, any other matter related to article 2102, such as the question as to what constitutes a legitimate national security concern in the first place, is subject to the Agreement's dispute settlement provisions. Since Canada and the United States do not see eye to eye on this point, the issue will only be resolved if a case is brought before the NAFTA Commission.

Another exception to the principal investment rules of NAFTA that does not appear in the annexes concerns the funding by the Government of the United States of high-technology consortia that exclude participation by foreign firms. The best known example is Sematech, a consortium comprising United States computer chip producers. Again, the exclusion is omitted from the negative lists because it falls under the auspices of the national security clause (for a brief but thorough history of Sematech, refer to *The Economist*, 1994, pp. 77–79).

The strengthening of the Committee on Foreign Direct Investment in 1988, the relaxation of anti-trust policy beginning in the early 1980s and the increased financial support for high-technology consortia beginning in the late 1980s are signposts marking a shift in United States policy towards its trading partners and towards FDI in high-technology industries (Rugman and Warner, 1994). With respect to NAFTA, these developments serve to highlight the importance of the national security article (2102) to FDI in high-technology industries and the potential – as yet unrealized – of that article for allowing discriminatory treatment of FDI in the United States.

The North American Free Trade Agreement automotive provisions

The history of the North American automotive industry is one of managed trade and investment.[18] Trade and investment have been administered through the 1965 Automotive Agreement between Canada and the United States; a series of voluntary export restraint agreements[19] on Japanese automotive products beginning in 1981; five Mexican Automotive Decrees beginning in 1963; and, to a lesser extent, the Caribbean Basin Initiative of 1982 (establishing a 35 per cent local-content requirement for products entering the United States).

The main features of NAFTA automotive provisions from an investment perspective are the complete opening up of the Mexican automotive industry to North American investment over the Agreement's first ten years, the establishment of tighter rules of origin and tracing requirements to encourage more regional sourcing, and various advantages conferred upon 'incumbent' producers.

In terms of opening the Mexican automotive industry to North American investment, NAFTA phases out the numerous performance requirements and investment restrictions left over from the 1989 Automotive Decree by 1 January 2004. NAFTA allows for full foreign participation in the automotive parts industry, eliminates all sourcing restrictions on the five existing Mexican assemblers,[20] and completely phases out the trade-balancing requirements for parts and finished vehicles.

The opening of the Mexican automotive regime, however, has been accompanied by a tightening of the rules of origin. For automobiles and light trucks and their engines and transmissions a regional value content requirement of 62.5 per cent applies under NAFTA. Automobile producers, unlike producers in other industries, cannot choose between the transaction value and net cost tests – they must use the net cost test (the same restriction applies to the footwear sector). The reason is that the net cost test reflects better regional content when there is extensive vertical integration that largely eliminates market-determined prices along the value-added chain for automobiles.[21]

The rules of origin have also been tightened through the introduction of a 'tracing' requirement that is intended to deal with the problem of 'roll-up'. Roll-up occurs when intermediate inputs, containing materials that do not originate within NAFTA, but that meet the regional value content and change in tariff classification requirements, are treated as if they originate within NAFTA when introduced to the next stage of assembly in another NAFTA member. Tracing seeks to overcome this problem by requiring manufacturers to keep track of materials not originating in NAFTA members that would otherwise 'disappear' along the various stages of production as sub-assemblies are granted 'originating' status. The ultimate effect of tracing is to raise the regional value content requirement of automotive production, since non-NAFTA-originating materials that would otherwise be rolled-up in the absence of tracing now count against regional value content.

Although not explicitly discriminatory, the tightened rules of origin and the new tracing requirement constitute an attempt to promote regional sourcing in the automotive industry. As an instrument of industrial policy, however, rules of origin are extremely blunt and usually costly from an economic welfare perspective. In this case, the greatest efficiency loss to which NAFTA is likely to give rise is associated with the diversion of parts sourcing away from efficient Asian suppliers.

In terms of the effect of these rules upon investment patterns, Peter Morici (1993, p. 247) suggested that, 'given the number of stages in the transformation of basic components into automobiles, the use of non-North American parts by transplants should be substantially reduced'. In addition, the restrictions which NAFTA places upon duty drawback programmes for new producers suggests that future investments by these companies will be predominantly located in the United States.

Finally, NAFTA, by grandfathering the United States–Canada Auto Pact and the Free Trade Agreement revisions to it, distinguishes between Auto Pact and non-Auto Pact producers and confers specific advantages to the former. Existing producers are defined as those producing vehicles prior to model year 1992. That distinction, and the associated differences in treatment based upon it, runs counter to national treatment. Indeed, article 1 of the automotive annex (annex 300-A) stipulates that 'existing' producers must be granted 'treatment no less favorable than (is accorded) to any new producer' (article 1, annex 300-A). In contrast to the national treatment provision, which is intended to protect foreign producers, the 'foreign treatment' provision of the automotive annex allows for the conferral of advantages on incumbent assemblers. One significant reservation in this regard can be found in Canada's extension of duty waiver programme for the Big Three and Volvo (annex 1, p. C-17).

On balance, NAFTA is beneficial for the North American automotive industries. The Mexican automotive and autoparts industries, in particular, stand to benefit as investment is expected to increase by over 16 per cent (USITC, 1993, p. x). Furthermore, the North American automotive industry will become more competitive globally as a result of the increased scope for rationalizing production and the heightened regional competition to which NAFTA will give rise. However, these efficiency gains will be partially offset by the trade and investment diversion caused by the extremely strict rules of origin. Asian parts manufacturers stand to lose the most in this regard.

The rules of origin and sectoral adjustment

The North American Free Trade Agreement's rules of origin are intended to discourage the establishment of export platforms within NAFTA and encourage regional production in industries for which the regional value content requirements are high. Although these rules are not discriminatory in the same way as the measures contained in the annexes or in the national security exclusion provisions, they do constitute a form of industrial policy aimed at reorganizing productive capacity along regional lines through administrative and, hence, arbitrary incentives (as in the case of the automotive rules of origin outlined above).[22]

In addition to automobiles, several other industries in North America have been conferred considerable competitive advantages with respect to non-regionally based producers through tighter regional-content requirements (usually in combination with restrictions upon duty drawback and related programmes). These include electronics, textiles and apparel, home appliances and measuring and testing equipment (USITC, 1993, p. 3).

The rules of origin for electronics embody the explicit strategic objective of increasing regional production of high-technology components (USITC, 1993, p. 5–4). For numerous electronic products containing non-NAFTA-originating materials, the rules of origin are complex, involving change in tariff classification and regional value content requirements, as well as the requirement that certain sub-assemblies be completely produced in North America. These rules have been applied to encourage more regional production of parts related to the production of high-definition televisions, flat-panel displays and printed circuit sub-assemblies, among other products (USITC, 1993, p. 5–3). These products and, especially, the technologies upon which they are based have been at the centre of the current policy debate in the United States over the erosion of its competitiveness in high-technology industries.

In addition, the rules have also been tightened for more mature technologies. In particular, the rules of origin aim at increasing the regional production of television tubes. Televisions made in North America with regionally produced tubes will enjoy duty-free access into any NAFTA market. Televisions made with foreign tubes are subject to a 5 per cent duty in the United States. Furthermore, duty drawback restrictions increase the duties on Asian tubes that previously entered Mexican *maquiladoras* from 0 to 15 per cent. Thus, the rules of origin in the electronics industries explicitly aim at increasing regional production. The tight rules of origin will encourage an increase in productive capacity for television tubes in the United States, largely at the expense of Asian producers. The latter have been effectively shut out of the North American market. The effects of tighter rules of origin and restrictions upon duty drawback, however, are not always as clear. Indeed, in a few cases, producers might find it in their best interests to move the production of sub-assemblies completely offshore in response to the duty rate differentials created by the combination of the elimination of duty drawback and deferral benefits, tight rules of origin and the level of the external tariff (USITC, 1993, p. 3-5; Peter Morici (1993) also considers this potential problem in greater detail).

The rules of origin for textile and apparel producers are based upon the concepts of 'yarn forward' and 'fibre forward'. To qualify for NAFTA treatment, goods must be made in North America from the yarn and fibre stages onward (the two rules apply to different types of material). These rules have been described as 'ultrastrict' by Gary Hufbauer and Jeffrey Schott (1993, p. 44) and as an example of rules of origin 'at their worst' by Peter Morici (1993, p. 241). Indeed, they are likely to have significant investment implications. In particular, since NAFTA substantially liberalizes trade in textiles and apparel between Mexico and its NAFTA partners, low-wage producers of apparel for export to North America stand to experience at least some investment and trade diversion to Mexico (to the extent that it is possible to talk about trade diversion at all in an industry in which trade and investment patterns are already highly administrative in nature). The Caribbean Basin Initiative economies are particularly concerned about this possibility (Hufbauer and Schott, 1993, p. 46). The increase in apparel production in Mexico that NAFTA will bring about is also likely to lead to decreases in North American imports from Asia (USITC, 1993, p. 8-2).

The Uruguay Round Agreement's proposed phase-out of the Multi-Fibre Arrangement and the gradual incorporation of the global textile and apparel industry into the GATT of most-favoured-nation-based tariff system mean that global production patterns will be shaped increasingly by market forces. Mexico stands to benefit from the Multi-Fibre Arrangement, as well as from the enhanced market access afforded by NAFTA. Apparel producers located in Mexico are likely to expand their share of the North American market significantly as a result of the Uruguay Round Agreement and NAFTA.

Machine tools is another industry in which the rules of origin have been tightened. The rules for that industry stipulate that non-NAFTA-originating parts may not be used in sub-assemblies, and they impose strict limits upon the use of non-NAFTA-originating motors, pumps, electrical control panels, lasers and 'major castings, weldments, and fabrications' (NAFTA, article 401, section B and USITC, 1993, p. 6–2). The United States International Trade Commission estimates that the United States machine tools industry might respond to the stringent rules of origin (in combination with the relatively low external tariff on these products) by moving more production offshore (USITC, 1993, p. 6-2).

CONCLUSIONS

On balance, NAFTA treatment of FDI is impressive. New ground has been broken in terms of establishing clear rules, enforceable dispute settlement mechanisms and increased transparency in the discriminatory regimes of the signatories. NAFTA is therefore likely to stimulate FDI and give rise to efficiency gains as TNCs rationalize their operations across the three signatory economies.

This being said, the Agreement is not simply an exercise in trade and investment liberalization. It establishes discriminatory measures for particular industries and practices at the national and regional level. At the national level, each member of NAFTA has chosen to exempt particular industries from various investment provisions (usually some combination of the national treatment, the most-favoured-nation and the performance requirements articles). The most notable exemptions are the energy industry in Mexico, the maritime industry in the United States and the cultural industries in Canada.

At the regional level, the extremely tight rules of origin for particular industries (although technically consistent with national treatment) will probably give rise to some trade and investment diversion and will also serve to disadvantage new producers in North America whose traditional supplier networks are located in other regions. In essence, these rules seek to reduce import competition (on an interregional basis) for automobiles, textiles and apparel, electronics (particularly, television) and certain machine tools. Provisions that distinguish between incumbent and new producers and accord preferential treatment to the former on the basis of this distinction act as protective complements to the rules of origin. While the rules of origin reduce import competition, the preferences accorded to incumbents soften transplant competition. Such use of this type of derogation from national treatment is concentrated in the automotive industry.

The numerous positive precedents set by NAFTA concerning FDI will invariably influence the negotiation of future regional trade and investment agreements (not to mention any extension of NAFTA itself) and will probably serve as benchmarks for future investment-related negotiations in the World Trade Organization. The tight rules of origin in the industries discussed above will not significantly detract from the positive contribution of NAFTA to the FDI regimes in North America, mainly because the United States external tariff on many of these products is already low (which means that the diversion effects of the rules will be low as well).

Rules of origin are necessary for the functioning of free trade agreements. However, as these agreements come to constitute an increasingly significant element in the administrative structure of global trade, especially among developing countries, their potential to serve protectionist goals and a beggar-thy-neighbour type of quest for manufacturing capital and employment should be considered more carefully. Within the context of NAFTA, the rules of origin are extremely tight only in a limited number of industries, such as automobiles, textiles and apparel and electronics. Furthermore, the pernicious diversion effects of tight rules of origin are reduced to the extent that the external tariff on the products to which these rules apply is already low in the biggest NAFTA market – the United States. The 2.5 per cent tariff for automobiles and most autoparts into the United States, for example, is helpful in this regard (although the failure of the Uruguay Round to have this rate further reduced is a disappointment). Unfortunately, NAFTA, in addition to all of the positive precedents it establishes in the area of international investment, also sets a dangerous example for future regional trade agreements in its limited, but obvious, use of rules of origin to support particular industries.

NOTES

** The authors are grateful for the insightful comments and suggestions received by an anonymous referee on earlier drafts of this article.

1 Throughout this article 'North America' refers to Canada, Mexico and the United States.

2 Investment provisions in this article refer to all investment-related provisions in the Agreement, including investment-related trade measures.

3 For a theoretical analysis of the impact of NAFTA investment provisions

on the strategic behaviour of TNCs operating in North America, see Rugman and Gestrin (1993).

4 For an overview of the theory of TNC activity and the relationship between environmental factors and TNC behaviour, see Dunning (1993), Rugman (1981) and Rugman and Verbeke (1990b).

5 The term 'party' is hereafter used to refer to the signatory Governments to NAFTA.

6 The Calvo doctrine was enunciated in 1868 by Carlos Calvo (1824–1906) of Argentina. The doctrine stipulates that foreign investors will be subject to domestic laws and that disputes can only be resolved in domestic courts (Power, 1993, p. 12).

7 These are defined as medium- to long-term cooperative ventures between two or more TNCs, in which the contractual relationships between these firms usually fall somewhere in between arm's-length relationships that characterize market transactions and fully internalized relationships, such as joint ventures or mergers. In other words, a part of the value of the relationship is intangible in so far as it involves the combination and reorganization of the existing capital of the partners, without necessarily involving changes in the ownership structures of the firms in question.

8 For an in-depth discussion of networks and their impact upon the global economy, see OECD (1992).

9 The Commission consists of cabinet-level representatives from all parties whose mandate is to oversee the Agreement's implementation and to provide interpretation of sections of the Agreement, when required, within the context of the Dispute Settlement Mechanism (article 2001).

10 A more detailed analysis of the dispute settlement procedures is found in Graham and Wilkie (1994).

11 For a more detailed explanation of the rules of origin, see Johnson (1993).

12 Formally defined, an existing measure is one that was in effect before the Agreement came into effect. However, to avoid the possibility that industry groups in any of the signatory ecomonies might pressure their Governments to slip in new protectionist measures before 1 January 1994, an informal agreement between the three signatories established the cut-off date for the definition of an existing measure as 7 October 1992, when the draft text of the Agreement was initialled by Ministers from each of the parties.

13 The annexes which contain reservations against investment provisions are 1, 2, 3 (unique to Mexico, encompassing that country's constitutional retrictions upon FDI) and 7 (financial services). For a detailed analysis of the annexes and the reservations they contain, refer to Gestrin and Rugman (1993).

14 For a detailed discussion of the Canada–United States trade and investment relationship, refer to Rugman (1990).

15 For a detailed examination of NAFTA energy provisions, see Plourde (1993) and Hagen *et al.* (1993).

16 Greenfield investments are not subject to review.

17 Estimates by the Organization for Economic Co-operation and Development, based upon the STAN database, show that the United States share of high-technology exports from OECD countries declined from 31.1 to

26.3 per cent and that import penetration for high-technology products (imports as a share of domestic consumption) increased from 4.2 to 18.4 per cent between 1970 and 1990 (OECD, 1993, p. 87, table 16).

18 Two excellent analyses of the impact of NAFTA upon the North American automotive industry are Eden and Molot (1993) and Johnson (1993).

19 For an analysis of the empirical record of the use of United States trade laws, see Rugman and Gestrin (1991) and Rugman and Verbeke (1990a).

20 The Big Three automobile producers (General Motors, Ford and Chrysler), plus Nissan and Volkswagen.

21 In 1982, intra-firm trade in the transportation-equipment industry accounted for 44, 45 and 50 per cent of total trade for that industry in the United States, Japan and the United Kingdom, respectively (OECD, 1992, p. 220).

22 The rules of origin do not, strictly speaking, derogate from national treatment unless, as in the case of provisions for the automobile industry, they confer upon established producers preferential rules of origin.

REFERENCES

Dunning, John H. (1993). *Multinational Enterprises and the Global Economy* (Wokingham, United Kingdom and Reading, MA: Addison Wesley).

The Economist (1994). 'Uncle Sam's helping hand', 331 (2 April), pp. 77–79.

Eden, Lorraine and Maureen Appel Molot (1993). 'The NAFTA's automotive provisions: the next stage of managed trade', *C. D. Howe Institute Commentary*, 53, November (Toronto: C. D. Howe Institute).

Gestrin, Michael and Alan M. Rugman (1993). 'The NAFTA's impact on the North American investment regime', *C. D. Howe Institute Commentary*, 42, March, (Toronto: C. D. Howe Institute).

Graham, Edward M. (1991). 'Foreign direct investment in the United States and U.S. interests', *Science*, 254, 20 (December), pp. 1740–1745.

───── and Michael Ebert (1991). 'Foreign direct investment and U.S. national security: fixing Exon-Florio', *World Economy*, 14, pp. 245–268.

───── and Christopher Wilkie (1994). 'Multinationals and the investment provisions of the NAFTA', *The International Trade Journal*, 8, 3 (Spring), pp. 945–982.

Hagen, Daniel, Steven Henson and David Merrifield (1993). 'Impact of NAFTA on energy markets', in Alan M. Rugman, ed., *Foreign Investment and NAFTA* (Columbia: University of South Carolina Press), pp. 228–248.

Hufbauer, Gary Clyde and Jeffrey J. Schott (1993). *NAFTA: An Assessment* (Washington, DC: Institute for International Economics).

Johnson, Jon R. (1993). 'NAFTA and the trade in automotive goods', in Steven Globerman and Michael Walker, eds, *Assessing NAFTA: A Trinational Analysis* (Vancouver, Canada: The Fraser Institute), pp. 87–129.

Morici, Peter (1993). 'NAFTA rules of origin and automotive content requirements', in Steven Globerman and Michael Walker, eds, *Assessing NAFTA: A Trinational Analysis* (Vancouver, Canada: The Fraser Institute), pp. 226–250.

Organization for Economic Co-operation and Development (1992). *Technology and the Economy: The Key Relationships* (Paris: The Technology/ Economy Programme, OECD).

———— (1993). *Economic Surveys: United States* (Paris: OECD).

Plourde, Andre (1993). 'Energy and the NAFTA', *C. D. Howe Institute Commentary*, 46, May (Toronto: C. D. Howe Institute).

Power, Michael E. (1992). *The Work of Nations* (New York, Vintage).

———— (1993). 'Foreign investment protection agreements: a Canadian perspective', Working Paper Series No. 14 (April), mimeo.

Rugman, Alan M. (1981). *Inside the Multinationals: The Economics of Internal Markets* (New York: Columbia University Press).

———— (1990). *Multinationals and Canada–United States Free Trade* (Columbia: University of South Carolina Press).

———— and Michael Gestrin (1991). 'U.S. trade laws as barriers to globalization', *World Economy*, 14, 3, pp. 335–352.

———— and Michael Gestrin (1993). 'The strategic response of multinational corporations to NAFTA', *Columbia Journal of World Business*, 28, 4 (Winter 1993), pp. 18–29.

———— and Alain Verbeke (1990a). *Global Corporate Strategy and Trade Policy* (London and New York: Routledge).

———— and Alain Verbeke (1990b). 'Multinational corporate strategy and the Canada–U.S. Free Trade Agreement', *Managment International Review*, 30, 3, pp. 253–266.

———— and Mark Warner (1994). 'Competitiveness: an emerging strategy of discrimination in U.S. antitrust and R&D policy?', *Law and Policy in International Business*, forthcoming.

United States International Trade Commission (1993). *Potential Impact on the U.S. Economy and Selected Industries of the North American Free-Trade Agreement* (Washington, DC: United States International Trade Commission), publication 2596.

9 East Asian investment and trade

Prospects for growing regionalization in the 1990s*

*Carlos A. Primo Braga and Geoffrey Bannister***

This article analyses the extent to which economic proximity in East Asia has increased because of the fast growth of intra-Asian trade and foreign-direct-investment flows in the 1980s. Several indicators of economic proximity are discussed in order to provide insights into the evolving patterns of economic interdependence in the region. The article analyses the extent to which trade and foreign-direct-investment flows in East Asia have been characterized by a growing intraregional bias in the 1980s. It also discusses how FDI and trade flows are linked, with special attention to the role of Japanese transnational corporations in this process, and explores the role of foreign direct investment in services in East Asia. The article concludes with a discussion of the proposition that growing integration in East Asia may lead to the emergence of a large discriminatory trading bloc in the region. In this context, it argues that regionalism as a market-driven process will continue to characterize East Asian trade and foreign-direct-investment relations. Preferential trade liberalization, however, should continue to play a secondary role in the developing strategy of the countries in the region.

INTRODUCTION

During the 1980s, countries in East Asia and the Pacific[1] displayed an impressive performance, leading the developing world in terms of economic growth, trade expansion and poverty reduction (The World Bank, 1993). Although the region encompasses countries that are quite heterogeneous in terms of size, population and natural endowments, the most successful of them share a common feature: all of them have adopted outward-oriented policies. As a corollary, it is

* Reprinted from *Transnational Corporations*, vol. 3, no. 1 (February 1994), pp. 97–136.

argued that the region has an important stake in the stability of an open multilateral trade system, that is the system built around the General Agreement on Tariffs and Trade (GATT).

The difficulties faced regarding the completion of the Uruguay Round and the proliferation of regional (minilateral) arrangements have led to a renewed interest for regional integration in East Asia. Prospects for a formal trading bloc encompassing Japan and other Asian countries do not seem particularly promising. Geopolitical considerations, memories of the pre-Second World War era, the dependence of the region on other markets for its exports and the apparent lack of enthusiasm of Japan for such a strategy constrain the minilateral route.[2] Still, market-led economic integration (i.e. a natural process that promotes stronger economic ties within a region) seems to continue to evolve in the absence of an institutional apparatus.[3] It has been argued, for example, that flows of foreign direct investment (FDI) from Japan and the East Asian newly industrializing economies are paving the way for an 'Asian bloc', ahead of developments at the institutional level (UNTCMD, 1992, p. 39). The dynamism of FDI flows in the region and their potential influence on trade patterns make this proposition worth considering.

This article analyses the extent to which 'economic proximity' in East Asia has increased because of the fast growth of intra-Asian trade and FDI flows in the 1980s.[4] Several indicators of economic proximity are discussed below in order to provide insights into the evolving patterns of economic interdependence in the region. The next section analyses the extent to which trade and FDI flows in East Asia have been characterized by a growing intraregional bias in the 1980s. The following section discusses how FDI and trade flows are linked, with special attention to the role of Japanese transnational corporations (TNCs) in this process. The final section explores the role of FDI in services in East Asia. This article ends with a discussion of the proposition that growing integration in East Asia may lead to the emergence of a large discriminatory trading bloc in the region.

Table 9.1 Intraregional and interregional trade in East Asia, the European Community and North America, 1970, 1980, 1985, 1990 (billions of dollars and percentage)

Item	Billions of dollars				Share of total (percentage)			
	1970	1980	1985	1990	1970	1980	1985	1990
East Asia[a]								
Total trade	61.32	514.10	594.02	1,179.58	100	100	100	100
of which:								
Intraregional trade	14.36	151.23	167.18	402.50	23	29	28	34
X+M from North America	18.81	118.00	180.34	310.92	31	23	30	26
X+M from EC12	7.74	58.55	63.72	180.53	13	11	11	15
X+M from EFTA	1.27	9.27	11.59	28.94	2	2	2	2
X+M from Australia/New Zealand	3.10	19.19	23.12	37.88	5	4	4	3
X+M from Latin America	2.23	15.54	15.93	23.90	4	3	3	2
X+M from rest of Asia	1.53	13.46	15.14	22.51	3	3	3	2
X+M from rest of the world	12.28	128.86	117.01	172.40	20	25	20	15
EC12[b]								
Total trade	240.49	1,456.14	1,303.76	2,754.71	100	100	100	100
of which:								
Intraregional trade	124.13	763.15	701.11	1,637.51	52	52	54	59
X+M from North America	28.13	124.14	137.65	233.29	12	9	11	8
X+M from East Asia	7.40	59.81	63.01	181.89	3	4	5	7
X+M from EFTA	24.25	141.80	124.44	274.19	10	10	10	10
X+M from Australia/New Zealand	3.70	10.54	11.47	18.35	2	1	1	1
X+M from Latin America	8.54	38.24	29.63	44.69	4	3	2	2
X+M from rest of Asia	2.16	11.36	11.62	22.95	1	1	1	1
X+M from rest of the world	42.18	307.10	223.83	341.85	18	21	17	12

Table 9.1 continued

Item	Billions of dollars				Share of total (percentage)			
	1970	1980	1985	1990	1970	1980	1985	1990
North America^c								
Total trade	115.74	619.01	765.60	1,184.65	100	100	100	100
of which:								
Intraregional trade	45.47	205.25	293.09	439.49	39	33	38	37
X+M from EC12	26.82	113.81	136.55	218.52	23	18	18	18
X+M from East Asia	17.94	114.05	182.77	298.63	15	18	24	25
X+M from EFTA	3.59	16.59	18.57	31.01	3	3	2	3
X+M from Australia/New Zealand	2.38	9.50	11.00	17.51	2	2	1	1
X+M from Latin America	10.02	52.28	49.18	65.28	9	8	6	6
X+M from rest of Asia	1.71	5.81	7.71	11.61	1	1	1	1
X+M from rest of world	7.81	101.73	66.72	102.60	7	16	9	9
Memo item:								
China^d								
Total trade	..	..	69.42	115.44	..	..	100	100
of which:								
X+M from East Asia	..	..	38.84	68.54	..	..	56	59
X+M from North America	..	..	8.31	13.84	..	..	12	12
X+M from EC12	..	..	4.91	13.69	..	..	7	12
X+M from EFTA	..	..	1.15	1.76	..	..	2	2
X+M from Australia/New Zealand	..	..	1.40	1.98	..	..	2	2
X+M from Latin America	..	..	2.22	1.49	..	..	3	1
X+M from rest of Asia	..	..	1.10	2.22	..	..	2	2
X+M from rest of world	..	..	11.49	11.90	..	..	17	10

Source: United Nations, Series D, Comtrade tapes.

[a] East Asia: Japan, Republic of Korea, Hong Kong, Singapore, Taiwan Province of China, Indonesia, Malaysia, Thailand and the Philippines.
[b] EC12: Belgium, Denmark, France, Germany, Greece, Ireland, Italy, Luxembourg, The Netherlands, Portugal, Spain and the United Kingdom. Data for Germany reflect trade relations of the former Federal Republic of Germany.
[c] North America comprises the United States, Canada and Mexico. Latin America excludes Mexico.
[d] These figures, based on Chinese updated trade statistics, understate Chinese imports and exports to the extent that they do not include Chinese trade through Hong Kong.

TRADE AND FOREIGN-DIRECT-INVESTMENT FLOWS IN EAST ASIA: IS THERE A GROWING INTRAREGIONAL BIAS?

Trade flows

A common measure of the importance of intraregional trade is the proportion of such trade in the total trade of the countries of that region (sometimes called the trade-dependence ratio). Table 9.1 shows the relevant shares for East Asia, the European Community and North America (encompassing Canada, Mexico and the United States) from 1970 to 1990. The focus of the analysis concentrates on these regions because they are the three main trading 'blocs' in the world economy. As already noted, preferential trade is not a major characteristic of the East Asian trading bloc – in contrast, for example, with the European Community – given the limited coverage of the main integration arrangement in the region, the Association of South-East Asian Nations (ASEAN). None the less, the share of intraregional trade increased from 23 to 34 per cent between 1970 and 1990. The European Community, which, by 1970, already had a much higher share of intraregional trade (52 per cent), also saw an increase in its intraregional trade share over the 1980s to 59 per cent by 1990. North America, in turn, experienced a slight decrease in its share, from 39 per cent to 37 per cent over the 1980s.

At first sight, these numbers seem to support the proposition that international trade is becoming regionalized with the formation of three large trading blocs. The movement towards greater dependence on intraregional trade seems particularly pronounced for the European Community and the East Asian countries. In the former, this trend is often associated with the single-market initiative, a clear example of policy-led preferential regionalization. The East Asian case, on the other hand, can be considered as an example of nondiscriminatory market-led integration.

There are, however, a number of criticisms of the share of intraregional trade as an indicator of trade bias, Kym Anderson and Hege Norheim (1993), for example, pointed out that the intraregional trade share is affected by the number of countries included in the region, even if they all have uniform patterns of trade. Further, as the case of East Asia exemplifies, the size of countries in a region also affects the share of intraregional trade independent of trade bias. The trade-intensity index, suggested by A. J. Brown (1949) and popularized by P. Drysdale (1988), attempts to address these problems by dividing the share of a country's exports going to a particular region by that region's share in world markets. Formally, the index can be written as follows:

$$l_{ij} = x_{ij/m_j} = x_{ij}/[w_j/(l - w_i)], \tag{9.1}$$

where x_{ij} is the share of country j in country i's exports, m_j is the share of country j in the total market for country i's exports, and w_i and w_j are country i and country j shares in world imports. (The share of country i in world imports is subtracted from the denominator of m_j because country i cannot export to itself.) When the value of the index exceeds one, it indicates the existence of a positive trade bias between countries (regions) considered; that is, country (region) i trades with country (region) j more intensively than j trades with the rest of the world.

Our calculations of the trade-intensity index for the East Asian economies are presented in Table 9.2 for several years during the 1970–1990 period. The indices for trade within the East Asian region are higher than those for trade with other regions, indicating a positive intraregional bias. Still, for most of the economies in the table (with the exception of Hong Kong and Singapore), the intensity of intraregional trade has declined between 1970 and 1990.[5]

The results presented in Table 9.2 seem to indicate that, for most individual countries within the East Asian region, trade has become more diversified during the 1970s and 1980s. Globalization, rather than regionalization, seems better to describe trends in international trade for several East Asian countries. This conclusion is consistent with the findings of Anderson and Norheim (1993), who, working with an all-encompassing definition for Asia, found that, from 1973 to 1990, the intraregional trade intensity index fell from 2.88 to 2.31. According to the same authors, the intraregional trade-intensity index for North America also fell from 3.93 to 3.5, while the index for Western Europe increased from 1.54 to 1.6.

Summing up, the perceived build-up of an East Asian trade bloc with Japan at its core has not translated into a growing intraregional trade bias over the 1980s. Actually, if one relies only on trade patterns to judge the evolution of economic interdependence in the region, the concept of an East Asian bloc seems inadequate.[6] True enough, the second half of the 1980s witnessed an increase in the trade-intensity index of Japan with East Asia. Moreover, the growing outward orientation of the Chinese economy has significantly biased the trade orientation of Hong Kong, given its role as an entrepôt centre for China. Still, for most East Asian countries, intraregional trade intensity has declined over the 1980s.

Table 9.2 Trade-intensity indices for East Asian countries, all commodities, 1970, 1980, 1985, 1990

Partner[a]	China 1970	China 1980	China 1985	China 1990	Hong Kong 1970	Hong Kong 1980	Hong Kong 1985	Hong Kong 1990	Indonesia 1970	Indonesia 1980	Indonesia 1985	Indonesia 1990	Japan 1970	Japan 1980	Japan 1985	Japan 1990
North America	..	..	..	0.462	2.355	2.188	2.003	1.582	0.732	1.207	0.924	0.698	1.717	1.491	1.560	1.667
European Community	..	..	..	0.192	0.536	0.625	0.445	0.383	0.356	0.160	0.179	0.280	0.283	0.301	0.281	0.375
European Free Trade Area	..	..	..	0.110	0.540	0.719	0.592	0.512	0.018	0.011	0.028	0.059	0.348	0.380	0.342	0.411
Australia and New Zealand	..	..	..	0.580	2.074	2.523	1.808	1.240	1.908	1.590	0.747	1.351	1.924	2.443	2.077	1.932
Latin America (except Mexico)	..	..	..	0.408	0.390	0.643	0.346	0.484	0.059	0.857	0.525	0.089	0.953	1.101	1.054	0.939
East Asia	..	..	..	4.202	0.943	0.850	0.761	0.961	5.566	5.374	5.802	4.048	1.969	1.762	1.402	1.670
East Asia plus China	..	..	..	3.937	0.912	0.969	1.558	2.137	5.248	4.999	5.022	3.989	2.130	1.933	1.709	1.687
Rest of Asia	..	..	..	1.880	1.153	0.289	0.339	0.439	0.047	0.293	0.531	0.763	1.674	1.659	1.439	1.214
Rest of the world	..	..	..	0.396	0.610	0.660	0.245	0.068	0.516	0.141	0.184	0.257	0.448	0.525	0.306	0.442
World	..	..	..	0.990	0.991	0.987	0.993	0.974	0.997	0.993	0.998	0.995	0.951	0.979	0.912	0.945

Partner[a]	Republic of Korea 1970	Republic of Korea 1980	Republic of Korea 1985	Republic of Korea 1990	Malaysia 1970	Malaysia 1980	Malaysia 1985	Malaysia 1990	Philipines 1970	Philipines 1980	Philipines 1985	Philipines 1990	Singapore 1970	Singapore 1980	Singapore 1985	Singapore 1990
North America	2.565	1.727	1.650	1.667	0.792	1.027	0.573	0.900	2.183	1.769	1.574	2.009	0.655	0.819	0.914	1.115
European Community	0.150	0.352	0.272	0.288	0.553	0.470	0.437	0.345	0.216	0.441	0.377	0.410	0.465	0.326	0.304	0.322
European Free Trade Area	0.158	0.294	0.520	0.368	0.091	0.090	0.075	0.100	0.068	0.115	0.203	0.113	0.126	0.163	0.149	0.213
Australia and New Zealand	0.553	1.168	0.822	1.190	1.507	1.449	1.159	1.359	0.235	1.396	1.286	0.923	2.096	4.594	2.732	2.028
Latin America (except Mexico)	0.082	0.481	1.006	0.838	0.216	0.074	0.116	0.182	0.043	0.209	0.107	0.321	0.268	0.458	0.512	0.416
East Asia	3.539	2.428	2.307	2.202	4.979	4.172	5.330	3.487	4.801	3.406	3.415	2.305	1.729	3.245	3.518	2.745
East Asia plus China	3.336	2.259	1.983	2.063	4.820	4.008	4.663	3.393	4.527	3.228	3.063	2.205	1.772	3.139	3.136	2.662
Rest of Asia	1.246	1.408	1.734	1.096	1.158	3.004	3.426	2.953	0.306	0.585	0.399	0.193	7.448	5.315	4.845	4.316
Rest of the world	0.215	0.609	0.488	0.467	0.512	0.404	0.368	0.338	0.181	0.423	0.347	0.385	0.929	0.500	0.462	0.418
World	0.993	0.992	0.986	0.982	0.997	0.993	0.995	0.992	0.995	0.995	0.997	0.996	0.993	0.989	0.989	0.984

Table 9.2 continued

Partner[a]	Taiwan Province of China				Thailand			
	1970	1980	1985	1990	1970	1980	1985	1990
North America	2.250	2.237	2.150	1.761	0.710	0.802	0.885	1.228
European Community	0.158	0.307	0.227	0.349	0.515	0.747	0.566	0.513
European Free Trade Area	0.066	0.172	0.134	0.275	0.136	0.410	0.306	0.366
Australia and New Zealand	0.817	2.289	1.641	1.565	0.303	0.886	1.157	1.285
Latin America (except Mexico)	0.158	0.720	0.535	0.522	0.021	0.133	0.240	0.418
East Asia	3.599	2.298	2.367	2.354	5.547	3.142	3.154	2.310
East Asia plus China	3.393	2.138	2.035	2.206	5.230	3.071	3.009	2.234
Rest of Asia	2.292	0.407	0.434	0.648	2.829	1.575	1.869	1.420
Rest of the world	0.278	0.476	0.324	0.417	0.493	0.686	0.594	0.589
World	0.990	0.991	0.990	0.985	0.996	0.996	0.996	0.991

Source: Calculated by the authors, based on United Nations, Series D, Comtrade tapes.

[a] Regional definitions as in Table 9.1.

It remains true, however, that the region trades more intensively with itself than with the rest of the world, as attested by trade intensity ratios that are significantly greater than unity. This result highlights the strength of market forces that work in favour of regional integration in East Asia. Moreover, the high level of intra-regional FDI flows that characterized the second half of the 1980s has led some analysts to suggest that regional integration trends may become stronger in the 1990s (Young, 1993). In order to discuss this possibility, we look in greater detail at the available information on FDI flows in East Asia during the 1980s.

Foreign-direct-investment flows

Table 9.3 presents data on the cumulative flows of FDI into East Asia for the periods 1980–1984 and 1985–1989.[7] The column showing flows to the East Asian region as a whole illustrates how the sources of these flows have changed during the past decade. For the first half of the 1980s, the main source of flows was North America with 42 per cent of the total, followed by East Asia with 36 per cent. During the second half of the 1980s, these positions were reversed, with a large increase in the share of inflows from East Asia to 57 per cent, and a decline in the North American share to 21 per cent. Most of that increase is attributed to the surge in FDI from Japan and Taiwan Province of China.

To keep things in perspective, however, it is worth examining this evidence in conjunction with Japanese flows of FDI to other regions in the world. Table 9.4 presents the distribution of Japanese outward FDI flows for selected years from 1980 to 1991, and cumulative flows from 1951 to 1991. While flows to East Asia made up between 12 per cent and 14 per cent of all Japanese FDI from 1989 to 1991, flows to North America made up between 45 per cent and 50 per cent. And even though the share of Japanese FDI to East Asian countries has been increasing steadily since 1988, this growth can be viewed simply as a return to the historical norm (as suggested by the higher share of East Asia in cumulative Japanese FDI flows from 1951 to 1991 *vis-à-vis* recent shares in FDI flows).

There is, however, evidence of a significant intraregional bias with respect to FDI originating from the Asian newly industrializing economies. A large proportion of the increase in the share of flows of FDI into East Asia came from Hong Kong, Singapore and Taiwan Province of China (Table 9.3). Although FDI from the Republic of Korea also increased in the late 1980s, it remained substantially

Table 9.3 Cumulative foreign-direct-investment flows into East Asia[a] by source region, 1980–1984 and 1985–1989 (millions of dollars and percentages)

Source/host country	Taiwan Province of China 1980–1984	1985–1989	Malaysia 1980–1984	1985–1989	Japan 1980–1984	1985–1989	Singapore 1980–1984	1985–1989	Philippines 1980–1984	1985–1989
(Million dollars)										
Western Europe	186	1,185	434	1,426	598	2,459	835	1,087	593	73
North America	820	1,553	248	482	1,195	5,331	1,206	1,440	1,883	363
Australia/New Zealand	0	8	145	96	0	0	0	0	60	12
East Asia	996	3,046	928	4,456	189	239	848	1,845	672	195
Japan	615	2,027	472	1,895	0	0	848	1,845	441	103
Hong Kong	203	799	88	312	180	239	0	0	203	68
Indonesia	0	4	42	54	0	0	0	0	0	0
Malaysia	0	27	0	0	0	0	0	0	0	1
Philippines	28	62	45	1	0	0	0	0	0	0
Republic of Korea	0	1	16	99	0	0	0	0	7	2
Singapore	150	110	176	713	0	0	0	0	20	7
Taiwan Province of China	0	0	39	1,345	9	0	0	0	0	15
Thailand	0	15	50	27	0	0	0	0	0	0
China	0	0	0	11	0	0	0	0	0	0
Latin America	0	252	5	83	15	0	0	0	35	11
World	2,002	6,044	1,760	6,554	1,997	8,029	2,889	4,371	3,242	654
(Percentage)										
Western Europe	9	20	25	22	30	31	29	25	18	11
North America	41	26	14	7	60	66	42	33	58	55
Australia/New Zealand	0	0	8	1	0	0	0	0	2	2
East Asia	50	50	53	68	9	3	29	42	21	30
Japan	31	34	27	29	0	0	29	42	14	16
Hong Kong	10	13	5	5	9	3	0	0	6	10
Indonesia	0	0	2	1	0	0	0	0	0	0

Table 9.3 continued

Source/host country	Taiwan Province of China		Malaysia		Japan		Singapore		Philippines	
	1980–1984	1985–1989	1980–1984	1985–1989	1980–1984	1985–1989	1980–1984	1985–1989	1980–1984	1985–1989
Malaysia	0	0	0	0	0	0	0	0	0	0
Philippines	1	1	3	0	0	0	0	0	0	0
Republic of Korea	0	0	1	2	0	0	0	0	0	0
Singapore	7	2	10	11	0	0	0	0	1	1
Taiwan Province of China	0	0	2	21	0	0	0	0	0	2
Thailand	0	0	3	0	0	0	0	0	0	0
China	0	0	0	0	0	0	0	0	0	0
Latin America	0	4	0	1	1	0	1	0	1	2
World	100	100	100	100	100	100	100	100	100	100

Source/host country	Indonesia		Hong Kong		Republic of Korea		Thailand		Philippines	
	1980–1984	1985–1989	1980–1984	1985–1989	1980–1984	1985–1989	1980–1984	1985–1989	1980–1984	1985–1989
(Million dollars)										
Western Europe	1,978	2,945	190	283	83	367	261	439	2,586	4,880
North America	884	1,398	778	176	216	722	402	545	5,558	5,319
Australia/New Zealand	26	149	16	74	0	5	18	10	239	204
East Asia	3,062	4,985	420	645	184	1,371	655	2,571	4,709	14,133
Japan	1,593	1,678	341	596	150	1,284	369	1,571	3,238	9,321
Hong Kong	1,286	836	0	0	34	75	148	436	678	1,692
Indonesia	0	0	0	5	0	0	1	2	44	64
Malaysia	1	49	0	1	0	0	16	5	16	35
Philippines	0	8	40	6	0	0	1	–2	113	67
Republic of Korea	39	769	0	–1	0	0	2	23	25	123
Singapore	141	514	26	15	0	11	115	157	487	1,013
Taiwan Province of China	0	1,094	13	7	0	1	4	360	57	1,728
Thailand	2	37	0	12	0	0	0	0	50	54
China	0	0	0	5	0	0	0	20	0	36

Table 9.3 continued

Source/host country	Indonesia 1980–1984	Indonesia 1985–1989	Hong Kong 1980–1984	Hong Kong 1985–1989	Republic of Korea 1980–1984	Republic of Korea 1985–1989	Thailand 1980–1984	Thailand 1985–1989	Philippines 1980–1984	Philippines 1985–1989
Latin America	66	158	0	−21	−17	21	82	−36	104	310
World	6,016	9,635	1,404	1,162	466	2,485	1,418	3,550	13,197	24,882
(Percentage)										
Western Europe	33	31	14	24	18	15	18	12	20	20
North America	15	15	55	15	46	29	28	15	42	21
Australia/New Zealand	0	2	1	6	0	0	1	0	2	1
East Asia	51	52	30	55	39	55	46	72	36	57
Japan	26	17	24	51	32	52	26	44	25	37
Hong Kong	21	9	0	0	7	3	10	12	5	7
Indonesia	0	0	0	0	0	0	0	0	0	0
Malaysia	0	1	0	1	0	0	1	0	0	0
Philippines	0	0	3	0	0	0	0	0	1	0
Republic of Korea	1	8	0	1	0	0	0	1	0	0
Singapore	2	5	2	1	0	0	8	4	4	4
Taiwan Province of China	0	11	1	1	0	0	0	10	0	7
Thailand	0	0	0	1	0	0	0	0	0	0
China	0	0	0	−2	0	0	0	−1	0	0
Latin America	1	2	0	1	−4	1	6		1	1
World	100	100	100	100	100	100	100	100	100	100

Source: UNCTAD, Division on Transnational Corporations and Investment data base.

a See Table 9.1 for regional definitions. Western Europe includes EC12, Austria, Finland, Norway, Sweden and Switzerland.

Table 9.4 Japanese outflow of foreign direct investment by region[a]
(percentage)

Host region	1980	1985	1989	1990	1991	Cumulative 1951–1991
North America	34.0	45.0	50.2	47.8	45.3	44.0
Latin America	12.5	21.4	7.8	6.4	8.0	12.4
Asia	25.2	11.8	12.2	12.4	14.3	15.2
East Asia	24.8	10.7	11.9	12.2	14.2	15.1
Other	0.4	1.1	0.3	0.2	0.1	0.1
Middle East	3.4	0.4	0.1	0.0	0.2	1.0
Europe	12.3	15.8	21.9	25.1	22.5	19.5
Africa	3.0	1.4	1.0	1.0	1.8	1.9
Pacific Islands	9.6	4.3	6.8	7.3	7.9	6.1
Total	100	100	100	100	100	100

Source: Japan, Ministry of Finance.

[a] Regional definitions as in Table 9.1, except that Europe includes EC12, Austria, Finland, Norway, Sweden and Switzerland.

smaller than that from the other newly industrializing economies. The primary host countries for FDI from these economies were the ASEAN–4 countries and China.

Unfortunately, consistent FDI information for China is limited to the second half of the 1980s. The data for that period seem to amplify the trend in question. From 1985 to 1988, 80 per cent of all FDI into China came from East Asian countries. Of this, by far the majority was from Hong Kong (65 per cent) with Japan coming in second (14 per cent). It is worth noting that Hong Kong's FDI into China is magnified by flows of FDI from other sources (e.g. Taiwan Province of China and developed countries), which use Hong Kong companies as conduits for their investments (UNTCMD, 1993a).

The analysis so far has been carried out in terms of shares of FDI flows by region. In order to explore further the issue of intraregional bias, the following index of FDI intensity was calculated:

$$B_{ij} = f_{ij}/i_{wj} \qquad (9.2)$$
where $f_{ij} = (\text{FDI}_{ij}/\text{FDI}_{iw})$
and
$i_{wj} = (\text{FDI}_{wj} - \text{FDI}_{ij})/(\text{FDI}_w - \text{FDI}_{iw})$.

In the above equations, subscript i refers to the home country, subscript j refers to the host country and subscript w refers to the world: f_{ij} represents FDI from country i to country j as a share of total FDI from country i; and i_{wj} represents the share of FDI from the rest

Table 9.5 Investment intensity index, East Asia[a]

Host/home country/region	Taiwan Province of China 1980–1984	1985–1989	Malaysia 1980–1984	1985–1989	Japan 1980–1984	1985–1989	Singapore 1980–1984	1985–1989	Philippines 1980–1984	1985–1989
Western Europe	0.192	0.445	0.615	0.507	0.803	0.805	0.764	0.603	0.420	0.229
North America	1.937	2.020	0.458	0.463	4.159	11.539	1.999	2.867	3.866	7.280
Australia/New Zealand	0.000	0.068	5.387	0.772	0.000	0.000	0.000	0.000	1.135	0.953
East Asia	6.495	4.488	7.319	9.382	0.685	0.136	2.724	3.226	1.714	1.877
Japan	3.482	2.653	2.874	2.138	0.000	0.000	3.260	3.840	1.236	0.978
Hong Kong	9.834	13.917	4.571	4.566	8.633	2.802	0.000	0.000	5.836	10.527
Republic of Korea	0.000	0.160	9.162	17.408	0.000	0.000	0.000	0.000	2.108	2.729
Singapore	50.929	17.376	70.191	113.879	0.000	0.000	0.000	0.000	3.944	9.904
Taiwan Province of China	0.000	0.000	32.118	20.333	6.353	0.000	0.000	0.000	0.000	1.900

Host/home country/region	Indonesia 1980–1984	1985–1989	Hong Kong 1980–1984	1985–1989	Republic of Korea 1980–1984	1985–1989	Thailand 1980–1984	1985–1989	East Asia 1980–1984	1985–1989
Western Europe	0.920	0.802	0.293	0.588	0.410	0.316	0.423	0.257	0.458	0.445
North America	0.481	0.991	3.473	1.046	2.400	2.389	1.104	1.059	2.031	1.588
Australia/New Zealand	0.261	0.817	0.692	3.521	0.000	0.101	0.786	0.147	1.109	0.430
East Asia	6.795	4.736	2.798	5.508	4.277	5.433	5.633	11.604	3.637	5.808
Japan	2.826	1.109	2.518	5.540	3.711	5.617	2.759	4.172	2.551	3.149
Hong Kong	23.693	8.678	0.000	0.000	6.863	2.843	10.138	12.792	4.722	6.664
Republic of Korea	6.393	98.433	0.000	-1.126	0.000	0.000	1.116	7.271	1.855	5.654
Singapore	15.125	52.615	11.761	12.193	0.470	4.123	55.605	43.159	24.172	39.620

Table 9.5 continued

	Indonesia		Hong Kong		Republic of Korea		Thailand		East Asia	
	1980–1984	1985–1989	1980–1984	1985–1989	1980–1984	1985–1989	1980–1984	1985–1989	1980–1984	1985–1989
Taiwan Province of China	0.000	10.089	13.498	0.446	0.000	0.030	3.827	8.894	6.049	5.880

Memo item:

	China 1985–1989
Western Europe	0.062
North America	0.452
Australia/New Zealand	0.284
East Asia	3.535
Japan	0.436
Hong Kong	51.441
Republic of Korea	0.000
Singapore	4.271
Taiwan Province of China	0.000

Source: Authors' calculations, based on UNCTAD, Division on Transnational Corporations and Investment data base.

[a] Regional definitions as in Table 9.1. Western Europe includes EC12 + Austria, Finland, Norway, Sweden and Switzerland.

of the world to country j, as a share of total FDI from the rest of the world. Thus, B_{ij} is an indicator of the importance of country j as a host for country i's FDI relative to its importance as a host for FDI from the rest of the world.

The indices of FDI intensity for the two sub-periods of the 1980s mentioned earlier are presented in Table 9.5. They confirm that the Republic of Korea, Singapore and Taiwan Province of China increased their FDI orientation towards East Asia significantly more than the rest of the world over the past decade. Hong Kong's outward investment pattern was dominated by the growing importance of China as an FDI destination. Finally, the regional bias of Japanese FDI actually declined over the 1980s, a result that complements the growing diversification of the Japanese economy already identified with respect to trade.

THE RELATIONSHIP BETWEEN TRADE AND FOREIGN DIRECT INVESTMENT

Review of the theory

There have been a few attempts to derive broad normative propositions for FDI policies focusing on the trade–FDI link. According to K. Kojima (1973, 1985), trade-oriented FDI occurs when the home country invests in those industries in which it has a comparative disadvantage.[8] Trade-oriented FDI is characterized as being welfare improving. It has been pointed out that Kojima's neo-classical framework is unable to capture the role of firm-specific advantages in determining FDI flows (Dunning, 1988). Accordingly, his normative recommendations are criticized as relying on a model that does not take into account relevant aspects of contemporary FDI flows. Moreover, the trade–FDI link is also affected by the type of TNC activity, as well as by the stage of development of the host and the home country, as illustrated by the product-cycle approach (Vernon, 1966).

Still, the concept of trade-oriented FDI is a useful reference for the analysis of trade–FDI links in East Asia. It is well known that a good part of FDI in the developing countries of East Asia has a clear export orientation (Riedel, 1991; King and Roc, 1992). Comparing Asia and Latin America, for example, Kenji Takeuchi (1990, p. 32) showed that Japanese affiliates in Asia presented a much stronger export orientation (as measured by the ratio of exports to total sales) than Japanese affiliates in Latin America (45 per cent versus 20 per cent in 1986).[9] And recent FDI flows from the newly industrializing economies into other countries in the region have also been characterized by a high proportion of firms that are export oriented – the so-called 'mobile exporters' (Wells, 1992).

The trade–FDI link in East Asia has often been modelled in the context of the 'flying-geese' hypothesis that focuses on the relationship between changes in industrialization and comparative advantage (Akamatsu, 1962; Ozawa, 1990). According to this hypothesis, the dispersion of technologies that influence trade patterns in particular commodities is transmitted through FDI from the lead country to the follower countries. Lead-country firms, in an attempt to continue exploiting the ownership advantages of their technology combined with the factor-cost advantages of the host countries, move production of their 'second tier' products offshore to the follower countries. The combination of FDI and relatively cheaper domestic factors of production helps to raise the competitiveness of the products on the world market and leads to an increase in exports from the follower country. The expected image of this process over time is that the revealed comparative advantage (or relative export concentration) of the lead country in a particular product declines as its production moves overseas, while the corresponding revealed comparative advantage in the follower countries increases. In the usual description for East Asia, Japan is the lead country, followed by the newly industrializing economies, which are, in turn, followed by the ASEAN-4 and, more recently, by China. In short, the flying-geese pattern is seen as contributing to a 'virtuous cycle' of FDI–trade expansion in which industrial restructuring evolves in synchrony with comparative advantage trends.

The implications of the flying-geese pattern for regional integration, however, are less straightforward. Although intraregional FDI flows are bound to increase economic proximity (e.g. by promoting convergence in business practices), it does not necessarily follow that they will increase the intraregional bias of trade flows. As the data reviewed earlier suggest, the flying-geese pattern is quite compatible with globalization, as East Asian exporters target markets outside the region. It has been argued, however, that as mobile exporters move from lead to follower economies in the flying-geese pattern (reflecting, for example, growing labour costs in the home country), networking activities tend to grow, promoting regional integration (UNTCMD, 1993c, pp. 49–50). In such a scenario, one would expect a significant increase in intra-industry and intra-firm trade within the region (as a sign of growing networking), alongside the evolving globalization process. Moreover, the recent burst in intraregional

FDI should be expected to deepen further existing intraregional networks in the 1990s.

The hypothesis that, under the wings of a flying-geese formation, regionalization is being nurtured is discussed below. First, we analyse the extent to which the flying-geese hypothesis has been relevant in explaining trade–FDI patterns in East Asia in the 1980s. Following that, recent trends in intra-industry and intra-firm trade are analysed.

Evidence of links between trade and foreign direct investment at the regional level

The flying-geese hypothesis was initially tested following the method suggested by Rana (1990). We calculated revealed comparative advantage (RCA) indices for an average of three years at the beginning of the decade (1979–1981) and at the end of the decade (1989–1991) for Japan, the newly industrializing economies and the ASEAN-4 for three-digit SITC categories.[10] For each follower country, those manufactured products in which RCA indices increased between the two periods were selected. The change in the RCA index for these products was then tested to see if it was significantly correlated with the change in the related RCA indices for Japan. A negative and significant correlation was considered evidence in favour of the flying-geese hypothesis. The results of this exercise (Table 9.6A), provide moderate support for that hypothesis. Spearman rank correlation coefficients were significant and negative, as expected, for Indonesia, the Philippines, the Republic of Korea and

Table 9.6A Results of revealed comparative advantage: Spearman rank correlations with Japan

	(Observations)	*Japan*
Hong Kong	57	−0.04479
Republic of Korea	44	−0.37223[a]
Singapore	31	−0.24718
Taiwan Province of China	51	−0.17285
Indonesia	57	−0.27262[a]
Philippines	47	−0.31071[a]
Thailand	52	−0.30266[a]
Malaysia	50	−0.11587[a]

Source: Own calculations.

[a] Significant at the 5 per cent level.

Table 9.6B Results of related comparative advantage: Spearman rank correlations, ASEAN-4 with the newly industrializing economies

	Hong Kong	*Republic of Korea*	*Singapore*	*Taiwan Province of China*
Indonesia	−0.12244	−0.37205[a]	−0.35351[a]	−0.1999
Philippines	−0.33182	−0.25081[b]	−0.16212	0.02128
Thailand	−0.11312[a]	0.02222	−0.03714	0.01588
Malaysia	0.00548	−0.09782	0.04989	−0.29268[a]

Source: Own calculations.

[a] Significant at the 5 per cent level.
[b] Significant at the 10 per cent level.

Thailand. For the other countries, the coefficients were not significant.

Table 9.6B presents results for the second tier of the flying-geese relationship. Here, positive changes in RCAs for the ASEAN-4 countries were compared with changes in RCA indices for the newly industrializing economies. The results also provide some support for the second-tier hypothesis, with significant negative correlations for Indonesia *vis-à-vis* the Republic of Korea and Singapore, the Philippines with respect to Hong Kong and the Republic of Korea, and Malaysia with respect to Taiwan Province of China.

An alternative test of the flying-geese hypothesis was performed using the available information on FDI flows at the industry level. A possible interpretation of the flying-geese hypothesis is that comparative advantage in the follower countries (newly industrializing economies or ASEAN) in a particular industry is negatively related to comparative advantage in that industry in the lead country (Japan), and positively related to outward FDI from the lead country to the follower country. In order to test this proposition, we ran the regression below, using pooled data over nine manufacturing industries and eight East Asian countries (newly industrializing economies and ASEAN-4):

$$RCA_{ij} = a + b_1 JRCA_i + b_2 JFDI_{ij} + e_{ij} \qquad (9.3)$$
where
$i = 1 \ldots 9$ (industries)
$j = 1 \ldots 8$ (countries),

and where $JFDI_{ij}$ is the aggregated flow of Japanese FDI to each country and each industry from 1980 to 1988.[11] $JRCA_i$ is the revealed

Table 9.6C Regression results of flying-geese model of foreign direct investment

Variable	Parameter estimate	Standard error	t-statistic
Intercept	1.667	0.2500	6.673
JRCA	−0.621	0.2930	−2.118[a]
JFDI	−0.001	0.0016	−0.625

Observations: 72
Adjusted R^2:0.0428
F-test value 2.788[a]

Source: Own calculations.

[a] Significant at the 5 per cent level.

comparative advantage index for Japanese exports from industry i and RCA_{ij} is the revealed comparative advantage index of industry i in host country j (both calculated for the average level of trade over the 1987–1989 period). Following the flying-geese hypothesis, our expectation was that b_1 would be negative and b_2 would be positive.

The results of the regression analysis are presented in Table 9.6C. A joint F-test of the significance of the parameters rejects the hypothesis that all parameters except the intercept are zero at the 95 per cent level. However, the adjusted R^2 is very low at 0.04. The coefficient on the Japanese RCA index is significantly different from zero and of the expected sign, but the coefficient on Japanese FDI is not. Several factors might account for this disappointing result. First, the relatively high level of aggregation of the data may obscure the relationship between trade and FDI observable at a finer industry level. Second, RCA indices reflect not only changes in the export structure of a country, but also changes in world trade in a particular industry. This 'world industry trade' effect may dominate the changes in RCA indices, in which case we would not expect them to be highly correlated with changes in FDI (alternative specifications of regression (9.3) using export levels as the dependent variable did not generate better results, however). Third, pooling the data for all countries may not be appropriate given the possibility of different supply responses in countries at different levels of development. Moreover, the lag structure between FDI flows and changes in comparative advantage may differ from the one assumed in equation (9.3).

Summing up, there is some evidence that countries in the region have continued to follow the flying-geese pattern in the 1980s as far as trade-specialization patterns are concerned. The role played by FDI flows in shaping those patterns, however, could not be established based on FDI information at the two-digit ISIC level.

INTRA-INDUSTRY TRADE

Kiichiro Fukasaku (1992, p. 24) pointed out that the flying-geese model is built upon the assumption that trade patterns fostered by FDI flows tend to evolve according to inter-industry specialization. It can be argued, however, that trade-oriented FDI will also promote intra-industry trade.

Intra-industry trade is defined as exports and imports of goods and services from the same product category between two countries (regions). Interest for intra-industry trade developed in response to empirical findings that economic integration among developed economies was mainly characterized by more intra-industry trade rather than by inter-industry specialization (Balassa, 1963). Following these findings in the early 1960s, there was a flurry of empirical and theoretical work focusing on the phenomenon of intra-industry trade.

On the empirical front, there was a lively debate on the extent to which intra-industry trade was simply a statistical 'mirage' created by inadequate industry definitions,[12] leading to the development of alternative ways to measure intra-industry trade (Greenaway and Milner, 1986). On the theoretical front, two main lines of research evolved. First, there were attempts to show that intra-industry trade might be explained by differences in factor proportions among products classified in the same industry. In this context, it was established that intra-industry trade was not necessarily at odds with conventional Heckscher–Ohlin predicitons (Falvey, 1981). Second, new models were developed that are able to explain intra-industry trade in a non-Heckscher–Ohlin world. The role of differentiated products (Krugman, 1979; Lancaster, 1980), product cycles (Grubel and Lloyd, 1975), oligopolistic markets (Brander and Krugman, 1983) and the emergence of TNCs (Agmon, 1979) have been explored in this context.

Intra-industry trade can be viewed as an indicator of 'economic proximity'. The smaller the difference in per capita income between two countries (regions), for example, the higher would be the level of intra-industry trade between them. The above hypothesis relies on the following assumptions: (i) similarities in demand conditions (or

Table 9.7 Intra-industry trade indices for East Asia

		Japan	Newly industrializing economies	ASEAN-4	East Asia	China	United States	European Community (EC12)	World
Japan	1980	. .	0.258	0.075	0.206	0.100	0.308	0.369	0.261
	1990	. .	0.324	0.184	0.291	0.250	0.367	0.428	0.358
Hong Kong	1980	0.097	0.297	0.456	0.241	0.177	0.255	0.252	0.453
	1990	0.111	0.225	0.371	0.216	0.315	0.288	0.314	0.502
Indonesia	1980	0.011	0.152	0.212	0.089	0.001	0.014	0.036	0.083
	1990	0.076	0.277	0.301	0.198	0.027	0.071	0.073	0.178
Malaysia	1980	0.090	0.516	0.539	0.332	0.020	0.619	0.261	0.425
	1990	0.272	0.631	0.545	0.591	0.203	0.534	0.352	0.581
Philippines	1980	0.111	0.271	0.122	0.218	0.080	0.089	0.080	0.166
	1990	0.167	0.276	0.491	0.290	0.061	0.243	0.203	0.304
Republic of Korea	1980	0.354	0.262	0.093	0.467	. .	0.273	0.267	0.396
	1990	0.425	0.488	0.267	0.577	. .	0.370	0.298	0.485
Singapore	1980	0.085	0.444	0.498	0.566	0.089	0.450	0.362	0.658
	1990	0.266	0.685	0.628	0.661	0.379	0.479	0.358	0.716
Taiwan Province of China	1980	0.207	0.269	0.165	0.477	. .	0.209	0.209	0.352
	1990	0.366	0.399	0.281	0.604	n/a	0.326	0.296	0.483
Thailand	1980	0.046	0.315	0.260	0.196	0.072	0.175	0.087	0.262
	1990	0.169	0.579	0.461	0.360	0.076	0.373	0.242	0.397
China	1980	. .	. .	. .	. .	. .	. .	. .	. .
	1990	0.231	0.578	0.224	0.572	. .	0.189	0.212	0.498

Source: Calculated by the authors, based on United Nations, Series D, Comtrade tapes.

overlap in consumer tastes) tend to be higher the greater the proximity in terms of levels of economic development between the trade partners, and (ii) an overlap of tastes enhances the potential for intra-industry trade in differentiated products. The importance of demand influences as a source of intra-industry trade has often been translated into the presumption that intra-industry trade is mainy an attribute of trade patterns among developed countries.

As several analysts have shown, however, levels of intra-industry trade involving developing countries are not always negligible and have been rising over time (Balassa, 1979; Havrylyshyn and Civan, 1983). Table 9.7 presents the Grubel–Lloyd indices of intra-industry trade for selected countries in East Asia with their major trading partners in 1980 and 1990.[13] There is a significant increase in the level of intra-industry trade between Japan and the other East Asian countries betwen 1980 and 1990. This is also true for trade between our selected countries (with the exception of Hong Kong) and the newly industrializing economies, as well as the ASEAN-4 (shown in the second column of Table 9.7).[14] It is worth noting that intra-industry trade has been increasing not only at the regional level, but also with respect to all major trading partners of East Asia. The rate of growth of intra-industry trade at the regional level has been, in most cases, substantially higher (particularly in Malaysia, Singapore and Thailand) than that with non-regional trade partners. This trend is even stronger when intra-industry trade levels with China are also considered.

For most East Asian countries, the overall growth in intra-industry trade can be partially explained by their success in sustaining above-average rates of economic growth, a phenomenon that has placed them on a convergence path with the developed countries. Based on the previous discussion of the patterns and trade orientation of FDI flows in East Asia, however, it is worth exploring the extent to which the growing activity of TNCs in the region has also influenced the observed growth in intra-industry trade flows.[15]

In the case of vertically integrated TNC networks (i.e. networks that coordinate different stages of production across countries), the link between their expansion and the growth of intra-industry trade will occur if intermediate products and finished products are lumped together in the same industrial classification. On the other hand, it is clear that the expansion of these networks will be closely associated with the growth of intra-firm trade (i.e. international trade in goods and services between a parent company and its affiliates). Still, an increase in intra-industry trade, even if characterized by a regional bias, is not incompatible with a globalization strategy (i.e. rationalization and integration of manufacturing activities being pursued as a means to achieve greater competitiveness at the global level).

Foreign direct investment that leads to the formation of horizontally integrated TNC networks (i.e. networks in which each firm specializes in a particular product range) also tends to promote intra-industry trade. A product-cycle rationale may be used to explain the appearance of these networks, as parent firms in the lead country maintain production of high-quality products (i.e. closer to the technological frontier) and shift the production of lower-quality (more standardized) items to their affiliates in follower countries.

In order to test the extent to which Japanese FDI in the 1980s has promoted intra-industry trade in East Asia, the following regression was estimated:

$$\text{IIT}_{it} = a + b_1\text{RPCI}_{it} + b_2\text{JFDI}_{it} + b_3\text{DIST}_i + b_4\text{DUM}_i + u_{it}, \quad (9.4)$$

where:
$i = 1 \ldots 9$ countries,
$t = 1980, 1990,$

and where, IIT_{it} is the Grubel–Lloyd index for intra-industry trade between country i and Japan in year t: RPCI is a measure of the per capita income difference between country i and Japan, defined as: $\text{RPCI}_i = |\text{PCI}_{\text{Japan}} - \text{PCI}_i| / [(\text{PCI}_{\text{Japan}} + \text{PCI}_i) / 2]$. JFDI_{it} is total Japanese FDI in manufacturing in country i in year t, DIST_i is the distance between the capital of country i and Tokyo, and DUM_i is a dummy variable for country i. Dummy variables were used for Hong Kong and Singapore, to capture the effects of their geographic location on their propensity for entrepôt trade, and for Indonesia, to capture any differences in trade patterns due to the high concentration of resource-driven FDI.

The results of the regression analysis are presented in Table 9.8. The coefficients of all the variables are significant and of the expected sign, except for the dummy variables for Indonesia and Singapore.[16] The coefficients of RPCI and DIST are negative, confirming the conventional result that geographic and economic proximity induce a greater degree of intra-industry trade. The coefficient of JFDI is positive, suggesting a pro-intra-industry trade effect from Japanese FDI. The coefficient of the dummy variable for Hong Kong is negative, but its magnitude must be calculated relative to the intercept term, since the two are not independent. When this is taken into account, the 'Hong Kong effect' is also positive.

The complementarity between Japanese FDI and intra-industry

Table 9.8 Results of regressions on intra-industry trade

	Parameter estimate	Standard error	t-statistic
Intercept	0.6799	0.1898	3.581[a]
RPCI	−0.2135	0.1116	−1.913[a]
JFDI	0.0004	0.0001	3.261[a]
Hong Kong dummy	−0.3704	0.1290	−2.871[a]
Indonesia dummy	−0.0678	0.0751	−0.903
Singapore dummy	−0.1782	0.1287	−1.384
Distance	−0.0005	0.0001	−3.206[a]

Observations: 18
Adjusted R^2: 0.6162
F-test value: 5.549[a]

Source: Own calculations.

[a] Significant at the 5 per cent level.

trade suggests that Japanese TNC networks have contributed to the promotion of regional economic proximity. It is worth noting that, in the case of the United States TNCs, using data for 1970, Richard Caves (1981) found a negative sign for United States FDI as an explanatory variable for intra-industry trade, but a positive sign for the level of intra-firm trade. These results were interpreted as meaning 'that FDI captures the substitute relation between international trade and direct investment while AFFL [intra-firm trade] picks up its complementary aspect' (Caves, 1981, p. 219). The results obtained here in the case of Japanese FDI seem to indicate that intra-firm trade (associated with vertical integration) in East Asia not only shows up as intra-industry trade, but also domintes the conventional substitution effect between trade and FDI. Unfortunately, Japanese data on intra-firm trade are not available in a format that would allow a more formal test of this proposition. In the section below the available information on intra-firm trade by Japanese TNCs is analysed in more detail.

INTRA-FIRM TRADE

Intra-firm trade accounts for a significant proportion of world trade flows.[17] Intra-firm trade data have to be handled with care given the role of transfer-price mechanisms and accounting practices in influencing the recorded value of these transactions. There is evidence, however, that intra-firm trade tends to increase with the degree of coordination required for efficient interaction between trade partners, a phenomenon that is particularly relevant in the case of research-and-development-intensive industries (Siddharthan and Kumar, 1990).

Intra-firm trade is the most narrow definition of TNC-related trade.[18] For the parent company, it secures greater control over input by suppliers and downstream markets than arm's-length transactions and it enhances the possibilities for economic coordination across national frontiers. Accordingly, growing levels of intra-firm trade within a region can be interpreted as another indicator of increased economic proximity. An increase in the levels of intra-regional intra-firm trade led by Japanese parent companies would be a possible explanation for the complementarity between FDI and intra-industry trade identified above.

In order to investigate intraregional trends in intra-firm trade, we used data from surveys of the Ministry of International Trade and Industry covering business activities of Japanese parent companies. It is important to note that the coverage of these data is limited and that comparisons between years are not necessarily valid, given changes in the number of companies participating in the survey from year to year.[19] Despite this shortcoming, this data set provides at least some information on the evolving trends in Japanese intra-firm trade at the regional level during the 1980s.

Tables 9.9 and 9.10 present information on trade flows associated with Japanese parent companies for recent fiscal years. Information at the regional level is available only for the fiscal years 1986 and 1989. The regional aggregation used in the Ministry of International Trade and Industry surveys differs somewhat from the one adopted in this article (see notes to the tables). In the case of Asia, however, the vast majority of Japanese affiliates is concentrated in the 'East Asia plus China' region; as a consequence, no significant distortion is introduced by the use of this broader regional definition in assessing intra-firm trade trends. Keeping in mind that the available time series is quite sketchy and that changes in the coverage of the survey qualify the validity of comparisons between different fiscal years, the following considerations are pertinent.

On the export side, the intra-firm ratio of Japanese parent companies followed a consistent upward trend over the 1983–1990 period (at least for the manufacturing sector).[20] Intra-firm exports within Asia grew significantly, even though the region continued to display a much lower intra-firm export ratio than that which characterizes the pattern of Japanese exports to other markets in developed countries.

Table 9.9 Exports shipped by Japanese parent companies, by industry and region, various years (billions of yen and percentage)

	Total exports shipped by Japanese parents (billions of yen)	Destination (percentage) North America[a]	Asia	Europe	Exports shipped by Japanese parents to their affiliates (billions of yen)	Intra-firm export ratio[b] (percentage) Total	North America	Asia	Europe
Fiscal year 1990									
All industries, of which:	52,440	..	..	..	16,086	30.7	..	..	..
Manufacturing, of which:[c]	32,868	..	..	..	14,162	43.1	..	..	..
General machinery	2,089	..	..	..	723	34.6	..	..	..
Electrical machinery	10,398	..	..	..	5,097	49.0	..	..	..
Transport equipment	12,236	..	..	..	5,866	47.9	..	..	..
Precision instruments	1,761	..	..	..	1,206	68.5	..	..	..
Wholesale and retail trade	18,595	..	..	..	1,893	10.2	..	..	..
Fiscal year 1989									
All industries, of which:	47,560	35.8	27.3	25.4	15,533	32.7	52.2	15.9	30.5
Manufacturing, of which:[c]	24,121	38.1	27.2	22.4	9,912	41.1	63.4	17.8	43.1
General machinery	1,364	32.5	27.0	26.2	597	43.8	67.2	21.4	47.8
Electrical machinery	7,876	39.7	24.6	26.9	4,008	50.9	65.5	25.4	59.8
Transport equipment	8,857	45.4	17.1	19.1	3,639	41.1	64.6	22.1	23.2
Precision instruments	1,031	39.6	21.3	33.4	544	52.8	72.6	32.5	50.4
Wholesale and retail trade	22,894	32.8	27.1	30.6	5,569	24.4	34.7	21.4	20.2
Fiscal year 1986									
All industries, of which:	44,965	39.2	26.2	19.2	14,372	32.0	54.1	8.3	36.0
Manufacturing, of which:[c]	24,641	42.1	22.2	20.6	9,658	39.2	60.7	11.8	42.6
General machinery	1,582	28.6	30.1	18.8	509	32.2	64.9	11.8	44.3
Electrical machinery	6,434	43.7	17.5	25.1	2,789	43.3	58.7	15.9	50.6

Table 9.9 continued

	Total exports shipped by Japanese parents (billions of yen)	Destination (percentage)			Exports shipped by Japanese parents to their affiliates (billions of yen)	Intra-firm export ratio[b] (percentage)			
		North America[a]	Asia	Europe		Total	North America	Asia	Europe
Transport equipment	11,418	52.3	14.0	18.3	4,991	43.7	62.6	17.8	33.7
Precision instruments	1,245	52.7	8.4	30.6	743	59.7	64.9	34.8	61.4
Wholesale and retail trade	19,937	37.1	29.6	18.0	4,666	23.4	43.7	5.3	24.4
Fiscal year 1983									
All industries, of which:	46,093	..	..	..	10,910	23.7	..	..	..
Manufacturing, of which:[c]	23,477	..	..	..	7,000	29.8	..	..	..
General manufacturing	1,880	..	..	..	236	12.6	..	..	..
Electrical machinery	5,744	..	..	..	1,425	24.8	..	..	..
Transport equipment	9,582	..	..	..	4,343	45.3	..	..	..
Precision instruments	431	..	..	..	167	38.7	..	..	..
Wholesale and retail trade	21,244	..	..	..	3,873	18.2	..	..	..

Source: Japan, MITI, various years.

[a] Only Canada and the United States are included in North America.
[b] Intra-firm exports to total exports.
[c] Leading technology- or human capital-intensive industries.

Table 9.10 Imports shipped to Japanese parent companies, by industry and region, various years (billions of yen and percentage)

	Total imports shipped to Japanese parent firms (billions of yen)	Destination (percentage)			Imports shipped to Japanese parent firms by their affiliates (billions of yen)	Intra-firm export ratio[b] (percentage)			
		North America[a]	Asia	Europe		Total	North America	Asia	Europe
Fiscal year 1990									
All industries, of which:	32,370	..	..	..	3,411	10.5	..	..	..
Manufacturing, of which:[c]	10,092	..	..	..	2,064	20.5	..	..	..
General machinery	102	..	..	..	31	30.4	..	..	..
Electrical machinery	1,691	..	..	..	527	31.2	..	..	..
Transport equipment	973	..	..	..	156	16.0	..	..	..
Precision instruments	168	..	..	..	39	23.2	..	..	..
Wholesale and retail trade	21,692	..	..	..	1,269	5.9	..	..	..
Fiscal year 1989									
All industries, of which:	38,752	29.5	22	29.6	11,128	28.7	24.4	53.8	8.9
Manufacturing, of which:[c]	9,823	27.8	28.2	7.8	3,037	30.9	14.0	36.3	49.2
General machinery	92	22.9	47.1	19.9	31	33.7	9.9	65.0	2.2
Electrical machinery	2,173	44.7	47.1	4.7	779	35.8	8.4	65.5	16.0
Transport equipment	1,696	59.1	13.4	19.0	610	36.0	35.1	63.3	13.1
Precision instruments	97	34.1	51.3	14.2	37	38.1	24.0	56.0	8.6
Wholesale and retail trade	28,496	30.3	19.2	37.8	8,061	28.3	33.5	71.0	4.9

Table 9.10 continued

	Total imports shipped to Japanese parent firms (billions of yen)	Destination (percentage)			Imports shipped to Japanese parent firms by their affiliates (billions of yen)	Intra-firm export ratio[b] (percentage)			
		North America[a]	Asia	Europe		Total	North America	Asia	Europe
Fiscal year 1986									
All industries, of which:	16,585	29.4	27.2	15.2	4,313	26.0	50.1	16.7	22.2
Manufacturing, of which:[c]	3,055	30.9	23.0	12.1	716	23.4	24.2	40.0	15.7
General machinery	122	43.3	20.4	25.0	15	12.3	3.2	53.0	0.3
Electrical machinery	395	56.5	36.6	6.3	194	49.1	5.6	122.4[d]	18.7
Transport equipment	158	52.4	10.3	16.9	35	22.2	20.8	69.3	24.9
Precision instruments	74	53.3	23.8	21.4	27	36.5	14.4	78.3	40.7
Wholesale and retail trade	13,330	29.2	28.1	16.2	3,553	26.7	57.9	11.5	23.7
Fiscal year 1983									
All industries, of which:	18,246	..	..	..	5,053	27.7	..	..	..
Manufacturing, of which:[c]	4,867	..	..	..	1,018	20.9	..	..	..
General machinery	90	..	..	..	18	20.0	..	..	..
Electrical machinery	322	..	..	..	135	41.9	..	..	..
Transport equipment	69	..	..	..	24	34.8	..	..	..
Precision instruments	24	..	..	..	8	33.3	..	..	..
Wholesale and retail trade	12,849	..	..	..	3,932	30.6	..	..	..

Source: Japan MITI, various years.

[a] Only Canada and the United States are included in North America.
[b] Intra-firm exports to total exports.
[c] Leading technology- or human capital-intensive industries.
[d] Result suggests non-matching coverage in the survey between firms reporting total imports and those reporting intra-firm imports.

Moreover, as a destination of intra-firm exports, the region's share reached only 13 per cent by 1989. On the import side, the data suggest that intra-firm imports within Asia expanded vigorously, while decreasing in other key markets. By 1989, Asian countries had become the main source of intra-firm imports shipped to Japanese parent firms.

A closer examination of the data shows that the main factor behind these trends was the significant increase in intra-firm trade by Japanese trading companies in Asia. These companies play a large role in determining Japanese intra-firm trade flows. This is particularly true with respect to imports, a result that may be construed as more evidence of the competitive advantage of these companies in penetrating the Japanese market.[21] Still, the extent to which intra-firm imports are a response to vertical specialization remains an empirical question.[22]

One possible interpretation of these trends is that Japanese TNCs are increasing their control of Japanese trade within Asia, while keeping a more stable ratio of intra-firm trade *vis-à-vis* their transactions with the rest of the world. In this context, the perception of an Asian trade 'bloc' being formed could be explained by the ongoing qualitative change in regional trade patterns led by the strategic behaviour of Japanese TNCs. On the other hand, it can be argued that the increase in intra-firm trade in Asia may reflect the impact of changing trading practices (e.g. once a trading company establishes an affiliate in a given country, an arm's-length trade transaction may become intra-firm simply because the affiliate purchases the goods in the host economy and then ships them to the parent firm).

In any event, it is quite clear that Japanese intra-firm trade within Asia presents a much larger share of sales from affiliates to parent firms than is the case for Japanese intra-firm transactions in North America (excluding Mexico) and Europe (Table 9.11). In developed countries, Japanese intra-firm exports are at least three times larger than intra-firm imports. In contrast, intra-firm imports from Asia by Japanese parent companies were more than twice as large as their exports to affiliates in that region in fiscal year 1989. In other words, while intra-firm trade between Japan and other developed countries is organized mainly as a downstream process (from parent firms to affiliates), in Asia it has a much larger upstream component (from affiliates to parent firms).

This result is not particularly surprising. After all, a similar pattern (see memorandum item in Table 9.11) can also be identified in intra-firm transactions between United States parent firms and their affili-

Table 9.11 Ratio of intra-firm exports to intra-firm imports of Japanese parent companies, various years

Year/region	World	North America[a]	Asia	Europe
FY1990	4.71	..	..	..
FY 1989	1.40	3.18	0.45	3.60
FY 1986	3.33	3.89	1.29	5.53
FY 1983	2.16	..	..	..

Memo item	World		East Asia[c] plus China	EC-12
United States TNCs[b] 1990	1.18		0.64	2.38
			Japan 3.94	

Sources: Japan, MITI, various years; United States Department of Commerce (1992).
[a] United States and Canada.
[b] Only majority-owned affiliates are included in intra-firm trade in the case of United States TNCs.
[c] East Asia not including Japan.

ates in East Asia (excluding Japan). If, however, as suggested by Dennis Encarnation (1992, 1993), Japanese affiliates in East Asia have better access to the Japanese market than their competitors, it can be argued that this trend will foster an intraregional trade bias to the extent that Japanese parent companies control a substantial share of Japan's imports.

FOREIGN DIRECT INVESTMENT IN SERVICES IN EAST ASIA[23]

Over the 1983–1990 period, FDI outflows increased at a much faster pace than either global trade or world output. Investment outflows – which had increased in nominal terms at an annual average growth rate of 8.7 per cent per year over the 1970–1983 period – grew at a yearly rate of 27.8 per cent from 1983 to 1990. Lately, this trend has slowed down, reflecting the decrease in FDI outflows from France, Germany and, particularly, Japan over the 1991–1992 period.[24] Still, with annual outflows from the five major home countries (United States, Japan, United Kingdom, France and Germany) still being over $100 billion, FDI continues to play a central role in the ongoing process of internationalization of economic activities.

A major force behind the fast expansion of FDI flows in the 1980s was the dynamism of FDI in services.[25] By 1980, 38 per cent of the outward stock of FDI from the major home economies[26] was in the tertiary sector; ten years later, the share of the tertiary sector was 50 per cent (UNCTAD, Division on Transnational Corporations and Investment, 1993, p. 62). The main recipients of these flows were developed economies:[27] 48 per cent of their inward stock of FDI was in the tertiary sector by 1990, against 38 per cent in 1980 (UNCTAD, Division on Transnational Corporations and Investment, 1993, p. 62). It is worth noting that the share of inward FDI stock in the tertiary sector for the main host developing economies[28] also increased, from 23 per cent in 1980 to 30 per cent in 1990 (UNCTAD, Division on Transnational Corporations and Investment, 1993, p. 62). Still, most of the expansion of services FDI occurred in developed economies. Actually, the European Community was the single most important destination of services FDI in the 1980s, a phenomenon usually attributed to the effects of the single market initiative and its programme of services deregulation.

Japanese FDI also became increasingly services oriented during the 1980s. By 1976, 40 per cent of Japan's stock of outward FDI was in the tertiary sector. By 1990, this share had evolved to 67 per cent (UNTCMD, 1992, p. 18). As in the case of other major home economies, most of these investments went to developed countries. Yet, the composition of Japanese FDI in developing countries also assumed a clear services orientation in the 1980s: FDI in tertiary activities accounted for 31 per cent of the FDI stock in these countries by 1980; ten years later, this share had grown to 62 per cent.

The relevance of the growing services orientation for future trade patterns is not easy to assess. After all, a significant proportion of these investments occurred in real estate, offshore financial centres and in countries offering flags of convenience. In the case of East Asia, however, the continuous expansion of FDI in trading affiliates and in miscellaneous services, which include professional services, suggests that these investments have a strong trade nexus.

Investment decisions in services are affected by some of the same variables that influence investment decisions in manufacturing (UNTCMD, 1993b). The size of the market, the openness of the host economy, cultural proximity, oliogopolistic reaction and political risk are often mentioned as relevant variables in this context.[29] In the case of services, however, to the extent that proximity between providers and consumers is often required, FDI decisions are also influenced by the need to follow affiliates of home-country clients. In this context, the dynamism of Japanese services TNCs in the region could be interpreted as a natural by-product of the historical engagement of Japanese manufacturing TNCs in East Asia.

This explanation, however, is at best incomplete. As the contrast between the Japanese FDI profile in Indonesia (the country with the largest stock of Japanese FDI in Asia) and Hong Kong illustrates, the characteristics of the host economy (particularly its regulatory environment) also shape FDI trends. The magnitude of Japanese FDI in services in the Asian newly industrializing economies in the 1980s, for example, underscores the role of 'thick-market' externalities (concentration of economic activities) associated with manufacturing in fostering the demand for producer services. By 1990, the sectoral distribution of Japanese FDI in newly industrializing economies was similar to the one prevailing in developed economies, with a clear orientation towards services. In Indonesia, in contrast, Japanese FDI in tertiary activities accounted for a meagre 9 per cent of the total stock by 1990.

It is also worth noting that, in the 1986–1990 period, the newly industrializiing economies attracted approximately 12 per cent of all Japanese FDI going into trading activities around the world, doubling their historical share for the 1951–1985 period as a destination for this type of investment. The surge in the activities of Japanese trading companies in the region was focused primarily on Hong Kong and, to a lesser extent, on Singapore. In the past, Japanese trading companies played an important role in establishing trade networks in association with some manufacturing TNCs (e.g. those in the textile industry).[30] The current expansion suggests that these companies are positioning themselves to explore further the growing role of Hong Kong and Singapore as service hubs for East Asia and China.

This scenario could be interpreted as a new stage in the flying-geese pattern of development in East Asia. While outward investments from the newly industrializing economies and Japan expand manufacturing export platforms in the region (particularly in ASEAN-4 countries and China), Japanese FDI in the newly industrializing economies presents a services bias with investments that support regional networking (e.g. trading, professional services, transportation) playing an important role in this context. Japanese FDI should also be expected to increase its involvement in infrastructure projects (e.g. electric power and telecommunications) and the provision of related services in the region. This development, however, will be contingent on further liberalization of the regulatory environment in the region.

CONCLUDING REMARKS

This article presented evidence that 'economic proximity' among East Asian countries (and China) is increasing. Intraregional trade dependence is on the rise and will probably continue to increase, if (as expected) the region sustains a growth rate above the world average. However, this trend will not necessarily imply an increase in the intraregional trade bias (as measured by the trade-intensity index), as the experience of the 1980s illustrates. In sum, globalization (i.e. production for markets outside the region) will remain an important facet of the trade orientation of East Asia and China.

The surge in intraregional FDI flows in the 1980s put in motion additional forces fostering economic integration. Flows of FDI from the newly industrializing economies, for example, are characterized by a strong intraregional bias, and this trend should carry on into the 1990s. Japanese FDI, in turn, is promoting intra-industry trade and vertical integration among manufacturing bases in East Asia. In this context, Japanese affiliates in East Asia seem to be in a privileged position to gain market access to the Japanese market via intra-firm transactions. Moreover, the continuous expansion of Japanese trading companies in Hong Kong and Singapore suggests that regional networks, organized in the flying-geese style, will continue to thrive in East Asia.

Against this background, a relevant question is whether East Asian countries should pursue formal economic integration through a preferential trading arrangement as a way to accelerate market-led integration. This question reflects the following considerations: (i) there are limits to market-driven integration and, in order for this process to continue, some sort of harmonization of domestic policies is required (this would be particularly true with respect to FDI policies and services liberalization); and (ii) a regional arrangement may be the most effective response for East Asia to the proliferation of discriminatory trading arrangements in the rest of the world.

It seems clear that, given East Asia's dependence on non-regional markets, regionalism should be pursued not as a substitute for the multilateral trade system, but as a mechanism to support multilateral liberalization. The argument that an East Asian bloc could provide an effective deterrence to the development of a 'fortress' mentality in Europe and North America requires that Japan be a member of this minilateral arrangement. As discussed above, however, Japanese firms have already secured strategic positions in the region independent of preferential arrangements. Moreover, Hong Kong and Singapore (the most important locations for regional Japanese networks) are characterized by liberal trade and FDI policies. And to the extent that tariffs and formal non-tariff barriers in Japan for manufactured products are already low, it is difficult to envision market-access negotiations that would be particularly appealing to other Asian countries.[31] In short, the feasibility of a regional bloc with Japan at its core seems weak at best.

Still, it can be argued that alternative minilateral initiatives should be pursued as a necessary condition for 'deep integration' at a more limited regional level.[32] Obvious sub-regional candidates for 'deep integration' are the southern provinces of China with the economies of Hong Kong and Taiwan Province of China, and the so-called 'growth-triangle' linking Singapore, the Malaysian state of Johor and Indonesia's Riau province. The potential benefits for transnational harmonization and cooperation in trade, FDI and labour policies in these regions seem self-evident. What is not clear is the extent to which new minilateral initiatives are needed to address these issues.

With respect to Hong Kong and China, *de facto* integration is expected to be confirmed by *de jure* integration with the return of that economy to Chinese rule in July 1997. Growing economic ties between Taiwan Province of China and China have already led to bilateral negotiations focusing on investment guarantees (Jones *et al.*, 1992, p. 16). Discussions around a more ambitious minilateral arrangement, however, will remain subject to the evolution of bilateral relations on the political front.

In the case of the 'growth triangle', it is important to note that the countries involved are already members of ASEAN, which offers several preferential programmes designed to promote investment and cooperation among its member countries (e.g. the ASEAN Industrial Projects Programme). The 'growth triangle', however, has not been contingent on their existence.[33] Actually, developments at the bilateral level, with Singapore as the hub, are being closely observed as potential lessons for ASEAN as a whole (Yuan, 1991). In other words, there does not seem to be a need for a new minilateral initiative to advance integration in the area.

Summing up, we find that regionalism as a market-driven process is bound to continue to evolve in East Asia. Preferential liberalization should continue to play a secondary role in the development strategy of the countries in the region. Minilateral initiatives focusing on cooperation and harmonization of FDI policies may also play a positive role in the region. It seems clear, however, that the need and feasibility of an all-encompassing preferential trading arrangement to advance this agenda is debatable. Regionalism in East Asia is unlikely to develop into a discriminatory East Asian trading bloc.

NOTES

** The authors are indebted to the former United Nations Transnational Corporations and Management Division (now the UNCTAD Division on Transnational Corporations and Investment) for providing access to its data base. Comments, suggestions and help with the data from Ramgopal Agarwala, Kenji Takeuchi and Alexander Yeats, as well as from anonymous referees of this journal, are also gratefully acknowledged. Research assistance was provided by Yuko Kinoshita. The findings, interpretations and conclusions are the authors' own. They should not be attributed to the World Bank, its Board of Directors, its management or any of its member countries.

1 This article focuses on a sub-set of countries in the East Asian and Pacific region: Japan, the four newly industrializing economies (Hong Kong, Republic of Korea, Singapore and Taiwan Province of China) and four members of the Association of South-East Asian Nations (ASEAN-4), namely Indonesia, Malaysia, the Philippines and Thailand. In the text, this group of countries is referred to as East Asia. Whenever data for China are available, figures for an 'East Asia plus' (East Asia plus China) region are also provided.

2 For a summary analysis of potential new minilateral trade arrangements in the 1990s, see Primo Braga and Yeats (1992).

3 See Lorenz (1992) for a discussion of this concept.

4 Economic proximity is bigger the lower the costs arising from geographic distance (mainly transport and communication costs), 'cultural' distance (differences in culture, language, business practices, etc.) and regulatory barriers (both border and non-border measures) that hamper the international movements of goods, services and factors of production. GATT (1990) used the term 'economic distance' to convey the same concept.

5 The trend for the 1980s is essentially the same, with a decline in the trade-intensity indices with East Asia for all economies, except Hong Kong and Taiwan Province of China.

6 For a similar conclusion, see Frankel (1991).

7 The data on FDI are from the data base of the UNCTAD Division on Transnational Corporations and Investment. There are some caveats that should be mentioned with respect to the quality of the data. First, FDI figures were collected from a number of national sources that do not necessarily follow a common methodology. For example, different countries consider different levels of purchases of a domestic company's shares by a TNC as indicating a controlling interest for the purposes of foreign investment. In addition, for the most part, the data are in terms of approvals and not actual investments. Nevertheless, the trends identified are broadly consistent with data on FDI in East Asia from other sources, such as those cited in Lim and Fong (1991), from the Organiza-

tion for Economic Co-operation and Development (OECD) and the World Bank.

8 In a related proposition, it has been suggested that Japanese firms follow FDI strategies that are more trade enhancing than those of United States firms (Kojima, 1973). Encarnation (1992), however, showed that, when confronted with similar political and economic environments, United States and Japanese TNCs follow comparable strategies (the export orientation of United States and Japanese TNCs in East Asia, for example, has not been significantly different in the 1980s).

9 It is worth noting that the export orientation of TNCs is also affected by the character of prevailing trade policies in the host country. Accordingly, this result is, in part, a by-product of the more inward-oriented style of development followed by Latin American countries. One should expect these differences to diminish in the 1990s if Latin America continues to pursue trade liberalization.

10 The revealed comparative advantage index is calculated following Balassa (1965) as: $(X_{ij}/X_j)/(X_i/X)$, where X_{ij} is the value of exports in industry i from country j, X_j is the value of total exports of manufactured products from country j, X_i is the value of world exports in industry i, and X is the value of total world manufactured exports.

11 The data were obtained from the Japanese Ministry of Finance (two-digit International Standard Industrial Classification).

12 The main outcome of this debate was the recognition that although 'categorical aggregation' (i.e. inappropriate classification of products and activities in the same 'industry') affects intra-industry trade estimates, it cannot explain the totality of intra-industry trade flows. Categorical aggregation tends to diminish when trade data are disaggregated more narrowly, but even at the seven-digit SITC level trade overlap is observed. It is worth noting that most analysts rely on three-digit SITC as an appropriate approximation for an industry in the context of intra-industry trade analyses. For further details, see Finger (1975) and Greenway and Milner (1983).

13 The Grubel–Lloyd index is calculated as:

$$\text{IIT} = 1 - [\Sigma_i \Sigma_j \Sigma_k \, |X_{ijk} - M_{ijk}|/\Sigma_i \Sigma_j \Sigma_k (X_{ijk} + M_{ijk})],$$

where X_{ijk} and M_{ijk} are exports and imports, respectively, from country i to country j of products in industry k, and $|\,|$ indicate absolute value. For the analysis pursued in this article (particularly the question of trends in intra-industry trade), the use of the unadjusted Grubel–Lloyd index was considered appropriate. For a discussion of the possible bias that affects this index if the country's total commodity trade is imbalanced see Aquino (1978) and Tharakan (1983).

14 Similar results were found by Lee (1989, 1992) and Fukasaku (1992).

15 Formal models linking the presence of TNCs to intra-industry (and intra-firm) trade are presented in Helpman and Krugman (1985). It is shown, for example, that in the case of single-product firms, FDI and intra-industry trade tend to be complements rather than substitutes, as long as the capital-rich country (in a two-country world) remains a net exporter of manufactures.

16 The basic results of the regression (i.e. signs, significance of variables,

adjusted R^2) are not significantly altered if the dummies for Indonesia and Singapore are dropped.

17   John H. Dunning (1993, p. 409) offered the following figures for the importance of intra-firm trade for different countries/years. For each country the first figure represents the share (in percentage points) of intra-firm transactions in total exports and the second figure the related share for imports: Japan, 1983 – (31, 18); United States, 1986 – (36, 36); United Kingdom, 1984 – (29, 51); Sweden, 1975 – (29, 25); Belgium, 1976 – (53, 48); Portugal, 1981 – (31, 34).

18   For comprehensive analyses of all modalities of TNC-related trade, see Hipple (1990) and Cantwell (1992).

19   Working with the data of the Ministry of International Trade and Industry of Japan for fiscal year 1989, OECD (1993a, p. 20) pointed out that it 'is impossible to determine the share of intra-firm trade in total Japanese trade, given the official published data. What can be determined is the share of intra-firm trade in total foreign trade involving the companies covered by the survey. 'Of the 3,331 Japanese parent companies contacted in the *Fourth Survey*, 1,562 (46.9 per cent) answered the questionnaire. The number of overseas affiliates contacted was 8,804 of which 6,362 (72.3 per cent) responded. It is worth noting, however, that usually more than 90 per cent of the major corporations respond to these surveys.

20   Data for 1990 are puzzling with respect to the role of trading companies in Japanese trade. According to the published information, there was a dramatic decrease in the amount of intra-firm trade conducted by these companies in fiscal year 1990, particularly with respect to imports. This result, however, could simply reflect a more limited coverage of large trading companies in the 1990 edition of the survey.

21   For more on this, see Lawerence (1991).

22   K. Kojima and T. Ozawa (1984) argued that trading companies have been instrumental in persuading manufacturing firms losing comparative advantage to locate abroad and to serve the Japanese market through exports. In this fashion, their growing activity in Asia could be interpreted as compatible with the vertical-integration hypothesis.

23   Parts of this section rely on Primo Braga (1994).

24   For details about the recent performance of Japanese FDI, see Rutter (1993).

25   A broad definition of the services sector encompasses professional, community, social and personal services, trade and finance, transport and communication, public administration and defence, as well as construction and public utilities.

26   Australia, Canada, France, Germany, Italy, Japan, The Netherlands, United Kingdom and the United States.

27   These figures refer to the same countries mentioned above, plus Spain.

28   The main developing host economies considered in this context were: Argentina, Brazil, Chile, China, Colombia, Hong Kong, Indonesia, Malaysia, Mexico, Nigeria, Philippines, Republic of Korea, Singapore, Taiwan Province of China, Thailand and Venezuela.

29   Indicators of cultural proximity have been built using Hofstede's indicators of differences among national value systems, based on informa-

tion collected from IBM affiliates around the world. See Hofstede (1980) and Kogut and Singh (1988).
30 For a description of these alliances, see Yoshihara (1978).
31 It is also a foregone conclusion that Japan would not be interested in negotiating structural impediments to trade at the regional level. Labour movements would be the 'wild card' in this, as long as Japan and Asian labour-exporting countries could find grounds for substantive negotiations on this issue.
32 'Deep integration' arrangements address not only trade in goods, but also trade in services, movements of labour and capital and the harmonization of regulatory regimes. Moreover, these arrangements usually adopt supranational dispute-settlement mechanisms.
33 For a brief discussion of these programmes, see OECD (1993b).

REFERENCES

Agmon, T. (1979). 'Direct investment and intra-industry trade: substitutes or complements?', in H. Giersch, ed., *On the Economics of Intra-Industry Trade* (Tubingen: J. C. B. Mohr), pp. 49–62.

Akamatsu, K. (1962). 'An historical pattern of economic growth in developing countries', *Developing Economies*, 1 (March–August), pp. 17–31.

Anderson, Kym and Hege Norheim (1993). 'History, geography and regional economic integration', in K. Anderson and R. Blackhurst, eds, *Regional Integration and the Global Trading System* (London: Harvester-Wheatsheaf), pp. 19–51.

Aquino, A. (1978). 'Intra-industry trade and inter-industry specialization as concurrent sources of international trade in manufactures', *Weltwirtschaftliches Archiv*, 114, pp. 756–762.

Balassa, Bela (1963). 'European integration: problems and issues', *American Economic Review*, Papers and Proceedings, 53, pp. 175–184.

———— (1965). 'Trade liberalization and "revealed" comparative advantage', *The Manchester School of Economic and Social Studies*, 33, pp. 99–123.

———— (1979). 'Intra-industry trade and the integration of the developing countries in the world economy', in H. Giersch, ed., *On the Economics of Intra-industry Trade* (Tubingen: J. C. B. Mohr), pp. 245–270.

Brander, J. A. and P. Krugman (1983). 'A reciprocal dumping model of international trade', *Journal of International Economics*, 13, pp. 313–321.

Brown, A. J. (1949). *Applied Economics: Aspects of the World Economy in War and Peace* (London: George Allen and Unwin).

Cantwell, John (1992). 'The relationship between international trade and international production', mimeo.

Caves, Richard E. (1981). 'Intra-industry trade and market structure in the industrial countries', *Oxford Economic Papers*, 33 (July), pp. 201–223.

Drysdale, P. (1988). *International Economic Pluralism: Economic Policy in East Asia and the Pacific* (New York: Columbia University Press).

Dunning, John H. (1988). 'The eclectic paradigm of international production: a restatement and some possible extensions', *Journal of International Business Studies*, 19 (Spring), pp. 1–32.

—————— (1993). *Multinatinal Enterprises and the Global Economy* (Workingham, United Kingdom and Reading, MA: Addison Wesley).

Encarnation, Dennis J. (1992). *Rivals Beyond Trade: America Versus Japan in Global Competition* (Ithaca, New York: Cornell University Press).

—————— (1993). 'A common evolution? A comparison of United States and Japanese transnational corporations', *Transnational Corporations*, 2 (February), pp. 7–31.

Falvey, R. E. (1981). 'Commercial policy and intra-industry trade', *Journal of International Economics*, 11, p. 495–511.

Finger, J. M. (1975). 'Trade overlap and intra-industry trade', *Economic Inquiry*, 13, pp. 581–589.

Frankel, Jeffrey A. (1991). 'Is a yen bloc forming in Pacific Asia?', in Richard O'Brien, ed., *Finance and the International Economy* (Oxford: Oxford University Press for the AMEX Bank Review), pp. 4–21.

Fukasaku, Kiichiro (1992). *Economic regionalization and intra-industry trade: Pacific-Asian perspectives* (Paris: OECD).

General Agreement on Tariffs and Trade (1990). *International Trade, 1989–90* (Geneva: GATT).

Greenaway, David and Chris Milner (1983). 'On the measurement of intra-industry trade', *Economic Journal*, 93, pp. 900–908.

—————— (1986). *The Economics of Intra-Industry Trade* (Oxford: Basil Blackwell).

Grubel, Herbert G. and P. J. Lloyd (1975). *Intra-Industry Trade* (New York: John Wiley & Sons).

Havrylyshyn, O. and E. Civan (1983). 'Intra-industry trade and the stage of development: a regression analysis of industrial and developing countries', in P. K. M. Tharakan, ed., *Intra-Industry Trade: Empirical and Methodological Aspects* (Amsterdam: North-Holland), pp. 111–140.

Helpman, Elhanan and Paul R. Krugman (1985). *Market Structure and Foreign Trade: Increasing Returns, Imperfect Competition, and the International Economy* (Cambridge, MA: The Massachusetts Institute of Technology Press).

Hipple, F. Steb (1990). 'The measurement of international trade related to multinational companies', *The American Economic Review*, 80 (December) pp. 1263–1270.

Hofstede, Geert (1980). *Culture's Consequences* (Beverly Hills, CA: Sage Publications).

Japan, Ministry of International Trade and Industry (MITI) (1986). *Dai nikai kaigai jigyo katsudo kihon chosa: Kagai tooshi sooran* [The Second Basic Survey on Overseas Investment Activities: Comprehensive Statistics] (Tokyo: Keibun Shuppan).

—————— (1989). *Dai san-kai kaigai jigyo katsudo kihon chosa: Kaigai tooshi sooran* [The Third Basic Surevy on Overseas Investment Activities: Comprehensive Statistics] (Tokyo: Keibun Shuppan).

—————— (1991). *Dai yon-kai kaigai jigyo katsudo kihon chosa: Kaigai tooshi sooran* [The Fourth Basic Survey on Overseas Investment Activities: Comprehensive Statistics] (Tokyo: Keibun Shuppan).

—————— (1992). *Dai nijuichi-kai wagakuni kigyo no kaigai jigyo katsudo* [The 21st Survey of the Overseas Business Activities of Japanese Enterprises] (Tokyo: Ministry of Finance Printing Bureau).

Jones, Randall, Robert King and Michael Klein (1992). *The Chinese economic area: economic integration without a free trade agreement* (Paris: OECD).

King, Timothy J. and Catherine Roc (1992). 'Intra-Asian foreign direct investment: South East and East Asia climbing the comparative advantage ladder', *Asian Economies*, 80 (March), pp. 5–34.

Kogut, Bruce and Harbir Singh (1988). 'The effect of national culture on the choice of entry mode', *Journal of International Business Studies*, 19 (Fall), pp. 411–432.

Kojima, Kiyoshi (1973). 'A macroeconomic approach to foreign direct investment', *Hitotsubashi Journal of Economics*, 14 (June), pp. 1–21.

———— (1985). 'Japanese and American direct investment in Asia: a comparative analysis', *Hitotsubashi Journal of Economics*, 26 (June), pp. 1–35.

———— and T. Ozawa (1984). *Japan's General Trading Companies: Merchants of Economic Development* (Paris: Development Centre, OECD).

Krugman, Paul (1979). 'Increasing returns, monopolistic competition and international trade', *Journal of International Economics*, 9, pp. 469–479.

Lancaster, K. (1980). 'Intra-industry trade under perfect monopolistic competition', *Journal of International Economics*, 10, pp. 151–176.

Lawrence, Robert Z. (1991). 'How open is Japan?', in P. Krugman, ed., *Trade with Japan: Has the Door Opened Wider?* (Chicago: The University of Chicago Press), pp. 9–37.

Lee, Young Sun (1989). 'A study of the determinants of intra-industry trade among the Pacific Basin countries', *Weltwirtschaftliches Archiv*, 125, pp. 346–358.

———— (1992). 'Intra-industry trade among the Pacific-Basin countries and its implication for regional cooperation', *Asian Economic Journal*, 6, pp. 213–229.

Lim, Linda Y. C. and Pang Eng Fong (1991). *Foreign direct Investment and Industrialization in Malaysia, Singapore, Taiwan and Thailand* (Paris: OECD).

Lorenz, Detlef (1992). 'Economic geography and the political economy of regionalization: the example of Western Europe', *American Economic Review*, Papers and Proceedings, 82, pp. 84–87.

Organization for Economic Co-operation and Development (1993a). *Intra-Firm Trade* (Paris: OECD).

———— (1993b). *Regional Integration and Developing Countries* (Paris: OECD).

Ozawa, T. (1990). 'Multinational corporations and the ''flying geese'' paradigm of economic development in the Asian Pacific'. Paper presented at the 20th Anniversary World Conference on Multinational Enterprises and 21st Century Scenarios, in Tokyo, 4–6 July 1990.

Primo Braga, C. A. (1994). 'International transations in services: a primer'. Background paper for the United Nations and The World Bank, *Liberalizing International Transactions in Services: A Handbook* (Washington, DC: The World Bank).

———— and Alexander J. Yeats (1992). 'The simple arithmetic of existing minilateral trading arrangements and its implications for a Post-Uruguay

Round world', Policy Research Working Paper No. 974 (Washington, DC: The World Bank).

Rana, Pradumna B. (1990). 'Shifting comparative advantage among Asian and Pacific countries' *The International Trade Journal*, 4 (Spring), pp. 243–258.

Riedel, James (1991). 'Intra-Asian trade and foreign direct investment', *Asian Development Review*, 9, pp. 111–146.

Rutter, John (1993). *Recent trends in Japanese direct investment abroad: the end of an era?* (Washington, DC: United States, Department of Commerce).

Siddharthan, N. S. and N. Kumar (1990). 'The determinants of inter-industry variations in proportion of intra-firm trade: the behaviour of US multinationals', *Weltwirtschaftliches Archiv*, 26, pp. 581–591.

Takeuchi, Kenji (1990). *Does Japanese direct foreign investment promote Japanese imports from developing countries?* (Washington, DC: The World Bank).

Tharakan, P. K. M. (1983). 'The economics of intra-industry trade: a survey', in P. K. M. Tharakan, ed., *Intra-Industry Trade: Empirical and Methodological Aspects* (Amsterdam: North-Holland), pp. 1–34.

UNCTAD, Division on Transnational Corporations and Investment (1993). *World Investment Report 1993: Transnational Corporations and Integrated International Production* (New York, United Nations), United Nations publication, Sales No. E.93.II.A.14.

United Nations Centre on Transnational Corporations (1991). *World Investment Report 1991: The Triad in Foreign Direct Investment* (New York, United Nations), United Nations publication, Sales No. E.91.II.A.13.

———— (1992). *World Investment Directory 1992, Volume 1, Asia and the Pacific* (New York, United Nations), United Nations publication, Sales No. E.92.II.A.11.

United Nations, Transnational Corporations and Management Division (1992). *World Investment Report 1992: Transnational Corporations as Engines of Growth* (New York, United Nations), United Nations publication, Sales No. E.92.II.A.19.

———— (1993a). *Transnational Corporations from Developing Countries: Impact on Their Home Countries* (New York, United Nations), United Nations publication, Sales No. E.93.II.A.8.

———— (1993b). *The Transnationalization of Service Industries: An Empirical Analysis of the Determinants of Foreign Direct Investment by Transnational Service Corporations* (New York, United Nations), United Nations publication, Sales No. E.93.II.A.3.

———— (1993c). *Foreign Direct Investment and Trade Linkages in Developing Countries* (New York, United Nations), United Nations publication, Sales No. E.93.II.A.12.

United States, Department of Commerce, Bureau of Economic Analysis (1991). *Direct Investment Abroad: 1989 Benchmark Survey, Preliminary Results* (Washington, DC: United States Government Printing Office).

———— (1992). *U.S. Direct Investment Abroad: Operations of Parent Companies and their Foreign Affiliates, Preliminary 1990 Estimates* (Washington, DC: United States Government Printing Office).

Vernon, Raymond (1966). 'International investment and international trade in the product cycle', *Quarterly Journal of Economics*, 80 (May), pp. 190–207.

Wells, Louis, T. Jr. (1992). 'Mobile exporters: new foreign investors in East Asia'. Paper presented at the National Bureau of Economic Research Conference on Foreign Direct Investment Today, 15–16 May 1992.

World Bank, The (1993). *Sustaining Rapid Development. East Asia and the Pacific: Regional Development Review* (Washington, DC: The World Bank).

Yoshihara, Kunio (1978). *Japanese Investment in Southeast Asia* (Honolulu: University Press of Hawaii).

Young, Soogil (1993). 'East Asia as a regional force for globalism', in K. Anderson and R. Blackhurst, eds, *Regional Integration and the Global Trading System* (London: Harvester-Wheatsheaf), pp. 126–143.

Yuan, Lee Tsao, ed. (1991). *Growth Triangle: The Johor-Singapore-Riau Experience* (Singapore: Institute of Southeast Asian Studies).

Part III

10 The growing interdependence between transnational corporations and Governments*

*John M. Stopford***

The rapid growth of foreign direct investment has brought the transnational corporation centre-stage in the international political economy. Foreign direct investment has significantly increased the economic interdependence of nations and has made key factors of production more mobile. These developments challenge the traditional assumption of comparative advantage. Rather than concentrating on natural endowments, attention needs to be focused on *created assets*. This article, using the concept of 'triangular diplomacy, argues that a greater degree of partnership in wealth creation between transnational corporations and nations is possible, provided that both parties understand each other's requirements more fully. In particular, the article argues the need to consider policy and policy coordination in terms of a positive-sum game, not the zero-sum game that has dominated so much Western thinking.

The optimism that greeted the fall of the Berlin Wall has proved to be short lived. The hope was for an acceleration of progress towards a liberalized world economy, in which the beneficial impetus to world growth from intensifying global competition could be given free rein. Instead, the removal of the common threat of communism has had the perverse effect of releasing pent-up economic rivalry in the form of increasingly bitter trade fights. The long delay in completing the Uruguay Round of Multilateral Trade Negotiations, combined with symptoms of a world of adversarial trade blocs, suggest a new mood of national self-interest.

Trade frictions are caused in part by the fact that the pace of building an increasingly interdependent world economy through

* Reprinted from *Transnational Corporations*, vol. 3, no. 1 (February 1994), pp. 53–74.

investments is continuing at an unprecedented rate. Mobile investments and intensifying global competition affect the source and nature of the associated trade flows. How to capture more of the benefits within a country has become a pressing issue for Governments. What national policies can induce firms – both domestic and foreign – to invest for production and exports and thereby increase national wealth? Within the past two years, this question has emerged centrally in the political debate in Sweden, the United Kingdom, the United States and, more recently, Germany. There, the Solidarity Pact talks among politicians, trade unions and industry have been aimed at ensuring the competitiveness of Germany as an investment location in the 1990s. Regional issues are taking a back seat in the national debates. The same debates have taken place in many developing countries, as a prelude to adopting far-reaching policies of liberalization and privatization.

Yet, Governments' responses to international economic developments are inherently ambiguous. They want the benefits of foreign direct investment (FDI) and are increasingly prone to intervene to increase their share, but fear the consequences when other nations do the same. They also fear possible losses of national sovreignty. For example, some policy makers in the United Kingdom see no inconsistency in simultaneously espousing the cause of market forces and opposing European integration on issues that threatened the country's ability to determine its own future. Those fears are most acute in high-technology industries, such as aircraft, semi-conductors, super-computers, high-definition television and the like, regarded by many as crucial for their national security and for the strength of their national industries.[1] How Governments resolve the dilemmas bred of ambiguity is a matter that no transnational corporation (TNC) can afford to ignore.

This article argues that managers need to look beyond their products and markets when calculating their global strategies. They need to develop a greater understanding of the forces driving change in the 'global political economy' if they are to be spared surprise. What game is really being played, under whose rules? The answers involve more than the effect of domestic political influences on individual project negotiations. The rules of the game are, in effect, determined by the outcomes of a three-way tug of war: domestic political imperatives pull one way; international economic imperatives can pull in another; and firms' global competitive imperatives can add a third dimension. Conventional perspectives and calculations do not readily capture the dynamic interactions at work and may blind many to the reality of new sources of risk.

In particular, risks are created as two quite different perspectives about how to build competitiveness come increasingly into conflict. Though rather oversimplified, firms can be regarded as being engaged in a race to create and accumulate new resources that change the structures of competition and fuel further interdependence across borders. This dynamic perspective on a positive-sum game of wealth creation is shared by many Governments in Asia. By contrast, Governments of countries in Europe and North America can be regarded as espousing more static policies to promote and protect indigenous firms. Their actions can directly affect the location of production and thus the welfare of nations in a 'beggar-thy-neighbour' zero-sum game.

To make the case, the evidence on growing economic interdependence and the central role of TNCs in that process is summarized first. Then, some of the political and policy issues are explored that are involved in the building of a simple model of triangular diplomacy that illustrates the form of interactions affecting both States and firms. Because Government calculations are often made on the basis of static and increasingly out-dated notions of the Ricardo/Heckscher–Ohlin theory of comparative advantage, some attention to theory will help to explain why frictions in policy choice are likely to continue.[2] The aim is to illuminate the sources of friction and risk and to suggest that firms should raise their voice in influencing the policy debates.

GROWING ECONOMIC INTERDEPENDENCE

Is the world moving towards the 'ideal' state of a global economy in which growth is fuelled by close economic interdependence among the leading nations in trade, investment and cooperative commercial relations, combined with relatively little restriction on cross-border transactions or discrimination against foreign-owned entities? There are two parts to this depiction of an ideal: economic interdependence, as well as harmonization of policy among leading nations. If one looks only at the first part, the evidence might be used as support for K. Ohmae's (1990) claim that strategy should be based on the presumption of a 'borderless world' and that Governments' powers to dictate terms to the market are in terminal decline.[3] Discussion of the second part provides an alternative conclusion, but that is deferred until after considering why Ohmae and others are making the claims they do.

Growing economic interdependence can be seen in the evidence that world trade has been growing faster than world GDP. Even more impressively, FDI has been growing four times faster than trade since 1982, despite a downturn during the recent recession. Deregulation of capital markets has fuelled an equal boom in cross-border financial flows. Daily transactions across the foreign-exchange markets now routinely exceed $900 bilion, a figure that dwarfs national acounts of annual current deficits or surpluses.

Central to this growth has been the role of TNCs in reshaping the world economy (Caves, 1982; Dunning, 1993). Their expansion has four notable features, some of which are indicated in Table 10.1:

- First is the growth of output of TNCs. At some point during the 1970s, the output from assets located in one country, but owned and controlled in another, exceeded the volume of world trade for the first time. That output is highly concentrated: just 420 of the largest of the 37,000 or so parent TNCs account for over half of the total output.[4] The implications for Governments are far reaching, for it is much harder to control foreign investors within a country than to control trade flows at the border. And controlling large firms and harnessing their resources effectively demands particular skills and resources that few nations possess in large quantities.

- A second feature is the growing share of TNCs in exports, both from their home countries and from many of their host countries. Transnational corporations manage about three-quarters of world trade in manufactured goods, over a third of which is inter-affiliate trade. For example, United States-owned affiliates abroad now sell more than twice what the whole of the United States exports. Leading the impetus for the North American Free Trade Agreement (NAFTA), Mexican-based affiliates of United States firms already account for over 40 per cent of Mexico's trade with the United States, its largest trading partner (UNTCMD, 1992).

- A third indicator of the significance of TNCs relates to technology. Transnational corporations are the primary source of privately funded research and development and dominate the international trade in technology payments that is estimated to exceed $30 billion a year. The vast bulk of this trade is in the form of transfers among affiliates in the same group. Understanding the decisions of TNCs about where to locate their innovation effort deserves more attention than has been given so far.[5]

- A fourth indicator of the importance of TNCs is the growth of both

Table 10.1 Foreign direct investment and selected economic indicators, 1981–1991 (billions of dollars and percentage)

Indicator	Value, 1991 (billion dollars, current prices)	Annual growth 1981–1985 (per cent)	Annual growth 1986–1990 (per cent)	Annual growth 1990–1991 (per cent)
FDI outflows	180	4	24	−23
FDI stock	1,900	5	11	11
Foreign sales of TNCs	5,500[a]	2[b]	15	n.a.
GDP at factor cost	22,300[b]	2	9	−6[c]
Gross domestic investment	5,100[b]	1	10	n.a.
Exports	3,800	2	10	4

Source: UNCTAD, DTCI (1993).

[a] For 1990.
[b] For 1982–1985.
[c] Estimate.

strategic alliances among these firms and of other non-equity forms of collaboration with local firms. Alliances can change the structures of competition and challenge the powers of national and regional competition regulations: the economic unit of competition can become wider than that defined by the legal boundaries of a single firm. Moreover, the constantly evolving bargains within an alliance underscore the dynamism of the race to acquire resources. As one study concluded, 'companies that are confident about their ability to learn may even prefer some ambiguity in the alliance's legal structure. Ambiguity creates more potential to acquire skills and technologies' (Hamel *et al.*, 1989, p. 139).

The growth of local, contract-based collaboration has far-reaching, often subtle implications for the transfer of technology and other resources. For example, General Motors' policies of collaboration with local parts suppliers in Brazil have required hundreds of engineers to spend long periods in Brazil and to incur costs that far exceed the formal value of their assets there. Yet, neither alliances nor contracts are well recorded in the official statistics of FDI. In other words, the official indicators of the reach of TNCs are understated and ignore many other, hidden aspects of growing and deepening economic interdependence.

Firms' motivations to pursue growth vary considerably, but can be grouped in three, well-known basic categories. One is market-seeking growth to gain greater returns on the resources, technical or managerial, already developed. Another is resource-seeking, to gain access to natural resources or the human and technical resources in other countries. The third – efficiency-seeking – is growing fastest at present, as firms seek new ways to link together previously separate operations so as both to lower total system costs and to increase their abilities to respond to changes in demand anywhere in the world. In some cases, all three motivations guide policy choices simultaneously in different parts of a single enterprise.

These motivations have taken various forms that have reflected the delicate balance that needs to be struck between gaining scale efficiencies from global integration on the one hand and maintaining responsiveness to local differences on the other. As C. A. Bartlett and S. Ghoshal (1989) demonstrated, firms are attempting to create a variable geometry of organization that is both appropriate to their strategies and capable of being managed effectively.[6] For the purposes of this argument, one can depict the evolution of the strategies of many TNCs as a combination of market- and resource-seeking

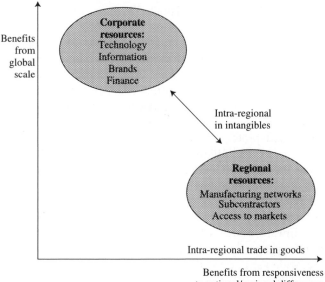

Figure 10.1 The differentiated global network

policies occurring within regions where there are efficiencies to be gained by specialization of production and trade in products. Simultaneously, they are building world-scale efficiencies in functions such as technology and information systems, and their trade across regional boundaries is growing in the intangibles of knowledge and finance.

The effect of these developments is to transform some firms' structures in the way depicted in Figure 10.1. The implication is that at least some TNCs have already developed their strategies in ways that provide them options for responding to possible trade wars among the trade blocs of NAFTA, the European Union and in East Asia. The implication is also that they are becoming much harder to control within any one nation.

GOVERNMENT RESPONSES

Given that investment is one of the keys to economic growth, Governments are motivated to seek as many sources of new investment as possible. Small wonder that so many have been putting out the welcome mat to TNCs and fattening the incentive packages on offer to bias firms' location decisions. Within Europe, there are constant contests both among nations and among regions within nations to attract mobile wealth-creating capital. More generally there has been a general liberalization of investment policy in many, especially developing, countries. And the pace of liberalization has accelerated. Of eighty-two policy changes adopted by thirty-five countries during 1991, eighty reduced restrictions on foreign investors. Furthermore, sixty-four bilateral investment treaties for the promotion and protection of FDI were signed during the first eighteen months of the 1990s, compared with 199 such treaties signed during the 1980s (UNTCMD, 1992, p. 3). Privatization and deregulation of communications, as well as of financial markets, have also helped extend the sense of greater mobility of critical resources.

One needs, however, to put the investment contribution of TNCs into context. Inward FDI – a form of transfer of world savings – is only a marginal proportion of total national capital formation. There is, of course, wide variation in this figure. Some of the poorer nations, especially in Africa, attract virtually no foreign capital. At the other end of the scale, Singapore relied on TNCs for over 35 per cent of its capital formation during the period 1986–1989 (UNTCMD, 1992). In the same period, that figure was over 12 per cent for the United Kingdom and 7 per cent for the United States. In almost all countries, these shares have risen significantly above the levels obtained in the early 1970s (UNTCMD, 1992). Though relatively small in value, the composition of inward FDI can be crucial. The United Kingdom, for example, relies on TNCs for infusions of new technologies in industries such as electronics (including consumer electronics) and automobiles.

Enhancing the investment function by promoting inward FDI is, however, a double-edged sword. It can create growth and add needed skills, but it can also hinder growth.[7] Moreover, there are growing concerns about trade consequences. Many foreign affiliates import much more than local firms. For example, in the United States, they import twice as much per worker in the same industry, thus partially or wholly offsetting export gains (Krugman, 1990, p. 127). Such evidence has led to calls to revise the generally liberal trade policy of the United States and has added to the sense of ambiguity in the general policy response.

There are added concerns that inward FDI can create strategic vulnerability. One example is the European debate about the growth of alliances in politically salient industries such as electronics. As one Olivetti executive put it:

In the 1990s, competition will no longer be between individual companies but between new, complex corporate groupings. A company's competitive position no longer (solely) depends on its internal capabilities; it also depends on the type of relationships it has been able to establish with other firms and the scope of those relationships.

(Financial Times, 29 May 1990)

The electronics industry in Europe is not, therefore, the same as the European electronics industry. Calculations of an appropriate response have sparked a prolonged debate. Some argue that Europe should focus on creating conditions that enhance its value-adding capability regardless of ownership. Others disagree and argue that ownership matters, because it shapes future prospects in any one region: firms give preference to the home territory, making the burden of adjustment to adverse trading conditions fall at the periphery of the system.

Similar fears of dependency and vulnerability have been voiced in the United States, coupled with a more general concern that the United States is losing out in the race to accumulate resources (Reich, 1991; Thurow, 1992). Government persistence in supporting local, high-technology players in Japan, Europe and some developing countries like the Republic of Korea, Taiwan Province of China and Brazil has sparked serious trade frictions with the United States. The reasons are not hard to find. These are industries in which the returns from technical advance create beneficial spillover effects in related industries and create new barriers to entry that can protect first movers. These are also industries in which a nation's competitive position is clearly not determined by factor endowments. Instead, the competitive position is created by the strategic interactions among domestic firms and their home Governments and among domestic and foreign firms and Governments.

Oligopolistic competition and these strategic interactions have effectively replaced the invisible hand of market forces and 'violate the assumptions of free trade theory and the static economic concepts that are the traditional basis for US trade policy' (Tyson, 1992, p. 3). The growing relationship between trade and FDI has provoked a fierce debate among economists about the welfare effects of free trade. Some analyses have suggested that free trade is not automatically the best policy for high-technology industries.[8] National intervention can promote local welfare when it provides spillover effects to local related industries and trade barriers can be used to shift oligopolistic rents from foreign to domestic locations of production.

Even though proponents of such arguments have themselves shown that Governments are poor at picking winners and that the unilateral gains from interventionist support of automobiles, semi-conductors and commercial airlines have been meagre (for example, Baldwin, 1988), the arguments can carry great political weight in domestic policy debates. There are clear signs that the current administration in the United States is responding to them and starting to put in place more directly interventionist policies that might provoke retaliation elsewhere. Moreover, there is a real danger that these responses will extend to other industries, as in the current disputes over countervailing duties, tax policies for foreigners and the rules for public procurement.

Further distortions and impediments to trade are created by national differences in the rules governing competition, even in those high-technology industries characterized by an international dispersion of manufacturing and a separation of the location of research from manufacture (Yoffie, 1991). Such impediments are so deeply embedded in national structures that attempts to negotiate their removal meet stubborn resistance, as the faltering progress of the United States–Japan Structural Impediments Initiative talks indicates. Japan has acceded to *gaiatsu* (pressure from abroad) on those agenda items, such as infrastructure spending, where self-interest matched foreign desires. But where Japan sees no national gain – for example, loosening *keiretsu* trading relationships and ending exclusionary business practices – it has dragged its feet.

TRIANGULAR DIPLOMACY

The competing national and international forces can be represented in a simple model of triangular diplomacy (Figure 10.2). One side of the triangle represents competition among firms for shares of the global market-place. Another represents the agenda of bargaining between firms and Governments. The third represents competition among Governments, in terms of trade policy, the web of bilateral and multilateral treaties and domestic policies that have international repercussions. As diplomacy shifts from competition for power from more territory towards a competition for wealth as a means to gain power, TNCs have a more direct influence on the conduct of intergovernmental relations. Connecting all the three sides of the

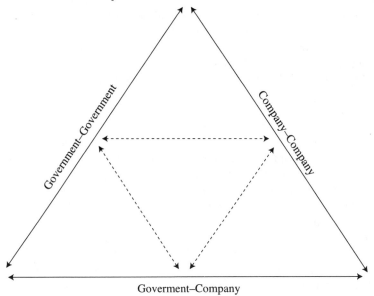

Figure 10.2 Triangular diplomacy
Source: Stopford and Strange (1991).

triangle are interlocking bargains that together shape the operating rules of the game.[9]

The impact on individual States depends on the relative importance of international and purely national transactions, the types of goods and assets traded and the forms of agreement created to support a State's objectives. The great variation of national size and resources, the state of development and so on, suggest that the outcomes are likely to vary enormously. Growing interdependence does not mean a convergence of outcomes – but diversity. This adds pressure on managers to understand the fine grain of the interplay of forces in each region and to ensure that their options for response are indeed as flexible as some now claim them to be.

Triangular diplomacy can be seen at work among the East Asian economies. Led by Japanese firms, East Asian economies are becoming more interconnected, even without a formal trade pact. The Asian regional developments are clearly being influenced by the extent to which Japan can export its ideological preference for lending the invisible hand a bit of administrative guidance to other, similarly inclined, neighbours.

Japanese firms enjoy access to official support from at least two sources. One is the Japanese International Development Organization, set up in 1989 by the Keidanren (an association of large Japanese employers), with about one-fifth of its capital supplied by the Government. This agency provides financial assistance for investment in developing countries, especially in Asia. The other source is the Japanese aid programme that concentrates on infrastructure projects and provides over half of all aid to the Association of South East Asian Nations and to China. Though official policy is that there are no ties between the public and the private purse, critics point to outcomes that seem more than coincidental. For example, Japanese firms won over a third of the aid contracts in the year up to 31 March 1992. The link between public and private capital is well illustrated by China's Liaoning Province, where Japanese investment was modest until 1988, when $145 million was pledged to finance a dam. 'This spurred a flood of private cash. The biggest project was a $155 million cement plant . . . and . . . half of the foreign investment in Liaoning now comes from Japan'. (*The Economist*, 24 April, 1993, p. 80).

The possibility of ties is also suggested by apparent biases in the direction of Japan's outward FDI in Asia that cannot be wholly explained by market forces alone. Matsushita, for example, now relies on Asia for 59 per cent of all its overseas production, up sharply from the beginning of the 1990s. Already, one-tenth of Matsushita's Asian production is exported to Japan, and that proportion is growing. The simultaneous drives for both market-seeking and efficiency-seeking investments seem enhanced by tacit Government support. The resulting advantages in such products as air-conditioners and compressors, as well as in consumer electronics, will increasingly affect trade elsewhere in the world.

The export of administrative guidance could have repercussions far beyond the region, with serious consequences for Western investors. Consider, for example, the impact on world financial markets as Asia continues to grow at much faster rates than elsewhere. Asia commanded 14 per cent of central bank reserves in the early 1980s, a share that has now risen to 43 per cent. One forecast is that the growing interconnections in the region could boost the emerging Asian bond market to the scale of the Eurodollar market. The most favourable terms exist for Asian countries and for Western countries operating in those countries. Capital availability for the United States and others could become increasingly dependent on Asian sources, and on Asian terms.[10] The implications for corporate strategy are clear and at odds with much recent corporate behaviour, for many United States firms have reduced, relatively or absolutely, their investment in the region since 1985.

A further manifestation of triangular diplomacy is that, when Governments clash in one industry, the repercussions can be felt in others. One example can serve to make the point. While the fourth round of negotiating the terms and conditions of the Multi-Fibre Arrangement was taking place, the United Kingdom unilaterally reduced its import quota for Indonesian T-shirts. Looking for retaliation against 'perfidious Albion', Indonesia embargoed a chemical project that was being built locally by a United Kingdom firm. A value of £100 million of assets was put at risk because of a conflict over less than £5 million of annual trade. Who in the plant construction business would routinely track developments in the textile trade? Yet, a close understanding of all the principal influences on a Government might have given better advance intelligence of looming problems and, perhaps, might have suggested some measures to protect the project.

RICARDO REVISITED

One symptom of a Government clinging to Ricardian notions of comparative advantage is when it measures national competitiveness primarily in terms of trade performance, as shown in the balance of payments (particularly the current account), and the presumed effect on the exchange rate. For long, in many Western countries, trade and money have been considered central. Where TNC behaviour and influence on trade performance appeared at odds with received wisdom, they were dismissed as a curiosity worth at best a footnote. Those footnotes, however, are now appearing in the main text. Ricardian notions cannot explain why Sony (Japan) exports televisions from the United Kingdom while national producers have all but disappeared, or why Malaysia is one of the world's largest exporters of semi-conductors.

The problem is that the central tenet of the theory – the immobility of assets across borders – no longer holds true. Not only does capital move in the place of goods, but also other factors of production, especially the created, intangible assets of technology and organizational skill, are increasingly mobile within firms. The growth of intra-industry trade and investment reflects such mobility. Moreover, it is increasingly apparent that costs at the level of the firm are not the same as those for the nation and that foreign investors can enjoy new advantages as they transfer their systems of production across borders. The lean production systems of the Japanese automobile producers give their transplant assembly operations an edge over local firms and allow for greater exporting opportunity, even though they have the same costs of labour, transport and other infrastructure factors.[11]

These increasingly important manifestations of a new order are drawing attention to the need to distinguish productive assets that are created from those that are natural endowments.[12] Created assets are primarily in the form of human capital – the stock of knowledge, technological and organizational capacity, infrastructure and governing policies. Endowments, primarily land, mineral resources and labour, remain immobile, but are of decreasing importance in determining outcomes. Richly endowed countries like the former Soviet Union or Zaire can remain relatively poor if they fail to enhance their human capital as fast as their competitors. In other words, policy makers need to concern themselves with the inputs to future competitiveness, not just react to outcomes after the event.

Some policy makers have well understood the new realities. The Governor of the Central Bank of the Republic of Korea once said: 'Don't listen to ''comparative advantage'' advice. Whenever we wanted to do anything the advocates of comparative advantage said ''we don't have comparative advantage''. In fact, we did everything we wanted, but whatever we did we did well' (Alagh, 1989, quoted in Wade, 1992, p. 270). The Republic of Korea's growing ability to create new resources and transform its competitiveness was not recognized by the World Bank's first mission there in the early 1960s. Holding conventional views of the static nature of resources, that mission dismissed projections of rapid growth as ludicrously optimistic because performance had been so poor in the 1950s. Much the same could be said for the post-war development of Japan. The State, it would seem, can have a positive role in influencing market forces in ways that help its constituent firms to grasp the lightning rod of innovation. That is precisely what the present debate is now about in the United States and Europe.

Consider the issue of labour. It used to be thought that the possession of a large pool of low-cost labour conferred an advantage on a nation. Today, direct labour costs are becoming a relatively minor part of the total costs of production in many industries. In electronics, they can be as low as 3 per cent and, according to a recent IFC study, even in standardized automobile components (coil springs, piston rings and valves) companies report that direct labour costs are only

10–15 per cent of total manufacturing costs and falling (Miller, 1993). Similarly, indirect labour costs are falling as a proportion of total costs. The old argument is losing its power and the issue is focused on the possession of trained labour and how skills in one country can be transferred to another by firms, rather than by national educational policies. For example, General Motors and Ford have trained the local work-force as part of their successful transfer of advanced engine manufacturing to Mexico.

The same issues affect the shifts of location of TNCs among developed countries. There is much evidence that, within Europe, inward investors are avoiding locations of relatively low skill and eschewing the cash advantages of investment incentives. Instead, they are preferring locations where they can have ready access to a pool of highly trained labour, even though the short-term costs may be higher. The argument is that the ability of the work-force to upgrade itself to satisfy the demands of next-generation products will determine by how much total long-run costs can be lowered to enhance the durability of the firm's competitiveness.

Increasingly, national competitiveness is coming to depend on the abilities of people and firms to innovate – to create new products and services, to lower the real costs of supply by increasing productivity and to build relationships with customers at home and abroad – and of society to organize its affairs effectively. The innovative assets are a central part of the created assets of a State. They are intangible and primarily the property of firms, especially in those industries in which the costs of research exceed the capacity of individuals or, in some cases, even Governments, to fund. This means that firms, not the State, have the right, within the constraints of the law, to exploit these assets wherever and however they choose. Rising scale for innovation means that TNCs will provide increasingly the well-spring for progress, the outcome of which is measured in terms of trade flows, income levels and income differentials.

It is perhaps curious that Michael Porter (1990) ignored many of these developments in his recent, influential book. He gave little weight to the role of TNCs or multilateral agencies and ignored the effects of inter-State bargaining. He seemed to regard domestic resource creation as the dominant determinant of competitiveness, considering global influences as little more than interesting additions to his domestic 'diamond' of factors. Indeed, recent analysis has demonstrated that Porter's implied policy prescriptions are muddled and sometimes inappropriate (e.g. Cartwright, 1993). Part of the difficulty is that Porter, like many Government officials, assumed that firms are conditioned by local factors before they go abroad. He undervalued the intangible advantages TNCs possess in terms of their ability to lower the transaction costs of the global market and thus work towards integrating country-specific factors as they transform their internal resources.

Moreover, the imperatives of competition now mean that competitors in a global industry resemble one another more closely. Previous notions of fundamental differences in terms of enterprises' national origin – United States firms behave differently from Japanese ones, and so on – have to be revised (Vernon, 1992). The implication is that a more productive way to address the issues may be to start from a clearer depiction of the forces in the international political economy and then work backwards to consider how specific national conditions fit into the whole and are shaped by the changing motivations of the key investors. Only then might one be able to see and understand the causes of the diversity of the outcomes.

POLICY COORDINATION

The globalization of markets does not mean that Governments lose control of their economic destinies. But to retain control, they must revise their approaches to capture the benefits from new, innovative sources of advantage within their own borders. A central issue is the extent of coordination – perhaps even, on occasion, integration – of policy, both domestically across ministerial departments and across national borders. Even though the domestic organization, both private and public, controls most of the ingredients needed to foster greater created sources of advantage, no State today can be wholly self-sufficient in commanding all the resources it needs. Transnational corporations provide complementary, but not substitutive, resources that can accelerate progress. Their extending reach means that their influence on national and international policy is moving away from the periphery of special-interest pleading towards a more central position on the stage.

There are many obstacles to be overcome before effective policy coordination can be achieved. Not only must policy makers shift from a static, defensive posture and come to grips with the global dynamics, but they must also have to understand more fully how the interplay of regulatory and competitive forces impacts on industries in different ways. A general policy that makes economic sense for one industry may be disastrous for another. Furthermore, short-run domestic political agendas can deny them the commitment to build for longer-run strength. One recent study concluded that 'the competitiveness of a country rests both on the ability of its firms to organize and utilize their own assets efficiently and also on the ability of Government to ensure that the markets in which firms compete are the least distorted. In order to achieve these objectives, Governments need to restructure their own internal systems of management so as to gain the maximum benefits from an integrated system of governance' (Dunning, 1992, p. 44). At the very least, this requires harmonization of a diverse agenda ranging from tax and competition policy to common environmental standards.

It is seldom clear what is the optimum degree of domestic policy coordination, let alone what defines the best constituent policies. The difficulty is that the calculus of optimality is in constant flux, not just because of competition, but also because States keep changing their expectations. 'A state has objectives that are multiple . . . . It wants to be efficient and competitive and to preserve social peace and the cohesion of the state with society. It wants autonomy and the freedom to chose its own path to economic development and access to advanced technology and overseas markets' (Stopford and Strange, 1991, p. 135). Success in managing these domestic dilemmas may be a necessary condition for progress, but is not a sufficient condition for managing the wider web of relationships in the international economy.

The domestic uncertainties are multiplied across borders, raising the important question of whether it is either beneficial or, indeed, possible to achieve international policy coordination. The case for coordination rests on the fact that national policies affect others, both at the macro level of, say, currency intervention and at the micro level of industrial policy. The case is also based on the premise that coordination increases the chances that Governments will achieve individual and collective economic goals. The case against coordination rests on the fact that uncertainties and shocks are so severe as to wipe out any possible gains.[13]

A recent study reviewed all such arguments and, on the basis of some carefully crafted simulations for the United States economy, concluded that some forms of coordination were possible and, despite obvious risks, were more desirable than independent approaches (Ghosh and Masson, 1993). The authors argued that uncertainty provides an incentive to cooperate and that coordination is beneficial, provided that policy makers' perceptions of how the economy works are not unduly flawed and are revised to take account of experience. They went further to argue that coordination in the form of simple, non-activist policies are cautious and respond only imperfectly to macroeconomic developments may be better than attempts to find and agree on fully optimal policies. They also addressed the familiar argument that the greatest gains are likely to arise from information sharing among the major industrial nations. They showed that information sharing alone, free of any policy commitment, can be valueless and may even lower welfare: the temptation to mislead can make information about policy intentions less credible. Given the arguments earlier in this article, caution and simplicity seem essential ingredients of fruitful attempts to achieve some gains from the uncertainties bred of the rapid changes in the rules that shape the form of the deepening economic interdependence of nations.

TRANSNATIONAL CORPORATIONS AS DIPLOMATS?

If TNCs are truly moving more centre-stage in affecting the emerging rules, then the question naturally arises as to whether their influence is helpful to the cause of policy coordination or a hindrance. The corollary is to ask how the managers of these enterprises are responding to their new responsibilities and whether they may be expected to change their behaviour in ways that might add impulses for further change in the underlying relationships.

Relationships between States and TNCs are necessarily based on bargaining, for there are mutual hostages to be exchanged. But when the rules are in flux, one must ask such questions of managers as 'Can they afford to wait for Governments to sort out new rules, domestically and internationally?' or 'Should they actively intervene in the debates?' The available evidence suggests that the answers are diverging according to the position of individual firms, but in roughly predictable ways. The difficulty for Governments, though, is that these responses are often hard to decode, for firms hold quite different attitudes as to the nature and extent of their engagement in the public debate. Some seem unwilling to engage in the debate at all, fearful of attracting criticism that they are intervening in politics. Others openly espouse the cause of greater liberalization of the rules for managing cross-border transactions of all kinds. Yet others are busily lobbying Governments for greater degrees of protection.

If one looks behind the façade of these debating positions one can discern that much of the response has to do with the economics of the business involved. Those United States managers whose international business is primarily through FDI have tended to greet the debate with a big yawn (Wells, 1992). The same has been true for many Europeans in the same sorts of industries. Both appear to consider that their configuration of invested assets gives them adequate insurance against continuing trade frictions. Those whose international business is primarily through trade take the opposite view. They are deeply concerned to have some voice in the debate, for they have more at stake.

There is, however, an added consideration affecting the response: the competitive strength of the business. Those who are relatively weak are more prone to invoke the support of home or regional Governments.[14] Consider, for example, the European automobile industry. Some executives, like M. Calvet of Peugeot (France), argue passionately that a liberalization of investment and trade restrictions should be delayed for as long as possible for fear of destroying the existing European producers. There is an alignment of interests between the Government of France and French producers for deep integration of local policy, but also for protectionism at the borders to impede international integration. That sense of alignment is not, however, shared by the United Kingdom, which has argued equally strongly that a liberalization and integration of markets is essential if the United Kingdom is to retain its share of world automobile production. For it, the local presence of United States and Japanese producers is vital in the aftermath of the failure of British Leyland (now the Rover Group).[15]

The weakness of the European electronics industry creates a similar diversity of views and introduces dilemmas that seem incapable of solution by rationality alone. None of the obvious options is wholly satisfactory. Further protection shows no sign of arresting the decline and would merely maintain higher prices. Besides, the consequential inward FDI flows would threaten the incumbents more directly. The dilemma of existing protection is illustrated by Regulation No. 288/89 [OJL 33, of 4 February 1989] that requires the diffusion process for semi-conductor manufacturing to be located in a member State to guarantee free circulation within the European Community. Many think that this restriction will create inefficiency and hurt local buyers. Selective encouragement for some segments does not appear to have helped in the past, because of technical changes that have eroded the protectability of the segment boundaries. Moreover, mergers to gain greater scale do not provide a clear solution. Rather than encouraging any Europe-wide administrative guidance, the dilemmas mean that it is a case of *sauve qui peut*.

The sense of dilemma can cause leading industrialists to make inconsistent statements. For example, one top official in Philips, the troubled leader at the centre of the storm, reaffirmed his support for free trade, but then went on to argue for policies that would oblige Governments to buy European (Van der Klught, 1986). Moreover, Philips successfully argued for European price protection for video tape recorders to maintain inefficient local production. The extra margins awarded to the Japanese had the perverse effect of adding to their cash-flow capability to fund the development of next-generation products faster than the protected Europeans could achieve.

To whom then should Governments listen? The evidence from many industries indicates there is a growing divergence in positions taken by leading TNCs from the European Union in responding to shifts in global competition and regionalization. There is a dilemma in the sense that industry's voice in the debate is likely to be one sided. Weak firms are much more vociferous in lobbying both their national Governments and the European Community than are most of the strong players. Strong leaders in investment-intensive industries have been relatively silent, reflecting perhaps their confidence and sense of indifference to changes in trade policy. Few have gone as far as British Petroleum, which stated in 1990 that 'as an international company, BP's commercial success is crucially dependent on . . . the maintenance and enhancement of the GATT-based multilateral trading system'.

If firms fail to rise to the challenge of acting more as diplomats and continue to act on the basis of short-run perceptions of shareholder requirements, they may provoke policy responses that are the opposite of longer-run shareholder interests. The short-termism debate, especially as it affects the workings of the capital markets, cannot be excluded from the debate. But the issue of time perspective in managing adjustments in a turbulent global economy introduces further dilemmas for States and firms alike. Though TNCs (and, indeed, the official position of the European Union) may, in general, resist protectionism, there are so many special cases of weakness, especially in trade-oriented industries, that the fears of a 'Fortress Europe' developing selectively may prove to be justified. Precisely the same effect could develop within NAFTA and across East Asia.

IS PARTNERSHIP POSSIBLE?

All of the foregoing suggests at least two alternative scenarios for future development. The optimistic scenario is that the silent majority of strong TNCs will have a crucial and more overt role in nudging Governments towards adopting policies that reflect more appropriately the present competitive realities. Should that happen, one might see faster progress towards the twin ideal of a liberalized global economy with growing economic interdependence, matched by moves to erode, or even eliminate, domestic distortions to the terms and conditions of operating across borders in developing and developed countries alike. One recent forecast of possibilities in this scenario is for a fourfold real increase in FDI flows by the year 2020, with the fastest growth occurring in developing countries, where the marginal returns to fresh capital transfers are likely to be greatest (Julius, 1993). As DeAnne Julius (1993, p. 7) argued, 'to bring about such a scenario requires long-term commitment. Companies must commit their [resources] to develop distant markets. Governments must commit to continuing the politically difficult process of economic liberalization . . . . If such commitments can be made and kept, then together we can reap the growth potential from building an increasingly integrated world community'.

The pessimistic scenario is that weaker Western firms will continue to be tempted to bargain for political solutions for their troubles. The effect might be to add further muddle to an already confused set of signals to Governments at regional and national levels. If, simultaneously, Governments preserve outdated notions of static comparative advantage, it is unlikely that North America and Europe will pay sufficient attention to building jointly the created assets needed for future competitiveness.

Of the many possible shocks that could move the world towards this pessimistic scenario, the impact of FDI and further economic interdependence on welfare – both within and across countries – stands out as a cause of dangerous instability. Transnational corporations are not the benign engines of growth the United Nations is now suggesting (UNTCMD, 1992). The growing concentration of investment flows within the Triad markets of the United States, Europe and Japan – for quite understandable competitive reasons – affects the international division of labour and makes it more difficult for latecomer countries to break into the charmed circle of development. The expected rapid growth of population in poor countries is storing up trouble for the next generation. Already, the phenomenon of economic refugees is causing trouble on some frontiers, and could add further pressures for States to strengthen their policies of national self-interest. Even within countries, the wealth effects of inward FDI are skewed in their distribution.

Wholly market-based competition does not necessarily promote social justice.

It is perhaps the sheer pace of change that makes it so hard for many States to develop the administrative capacity needed to manage the multiple dimensions of the task simultaneously. How to train officials to comprehend the new realities adequately and to abandon old shibboleths? How to build internal resources as fast as competing States? How to harness TNC skills and resources in durable bargains? Very few nations have the political will to build indigenous resources ahead of demand, as the Republic of Korea has done in its long sustained policies of education, technology enhancement and institution building. Yet even the Republic of Korea is finding that, to maintain its momentum of growth, it has to change and accord foreigners a greater role than hitherto.

To support the development of such national capacity for intelligent bargaining and to provide some form of insurance against welfare and other shocks, the global economy needs a stronger international polity to foster greater clarity, consistency and credibility in policy development. Progress will only be made possible by strong States that understand the new competitive realities and that are prepared to develop the needed new resources. Markets alone are unlikely to assist that process.

The real gains from policy coordination are unlikely to be reaped until there is a stronger basis for partnership between Governments and firms, regardless of nationality of origin. Both need to adjust their behaviour to understand the other side better. Because they cannot make forecasts to choose among the possible scenarios – that would defeat the purpose of making scenarios – managers, thus, need to pay increased attention to the mentalities of Governments, to be alert to indicators of their emerging policy responses in a post-Ricardian world and to calculate how action in other industries may affect them for good or ill. To maintain a narrow perspective on one's own products, markets and proximate competitors is to take undue risks. Firms cannot afford to ignore their diplomatic role in influencing how Governments determine effective policies that will influence the attractiveness of any one location for investment. Failure to confront the tensions and frictions of conflicting perspectives will serve to worsen the fears of trade wars and impede the recovery of the global economy.

NOTES

** An earlier version of this article was presented at a symposium in Stuttgart, Germany, sponsored by the Carnegie-Bosch Institute, April

1993. The author acknowledges with gratitude the support of that Institute.
1 An eloquent statement of the threat to one nation from other Governments' interventions in high-technology industries is provided in Tyson (1992).
2 For an excellent summary of the theory and economists' subsequent modifications, see Findlay (1991).
3 This sense that economic determinism was eroding Government power was foreshadowed by Raymond Vernon (1971) in his classic treatise, *Sovereignty at Bay*, though he later modified his position.
4 For details, see Stopford (1992a). John H. Dunning (1993) has challenged the UN-TCMD (1992) estimate of 37,000 parent TNCs and proposed a lower, but still substantial, population estimate.
5 One exception is Cantwell (1993).
6 For equivalent evidence that few TNCs have become global in all functions, see Morrison *et al.* (1991).
7 Some data from developing countries indicate that as much as 30 per cent of foreigners' investment projects can inhibit growth. See Encarnation and Wells (1986).
8 For a summary of recent developments in strategic trade theory, see Baldwin (1985), Krugman (1987) and Ernst and O'Connor (1992).
9 For a full exploration of the model, see Stopford and Strange (1991).
10 Data and forecast provided by Ken Courtis, Senior Economist, Deutsche Bank Capital Markets Asia, at a Business Week conference, Palm Beach, April 1993.
11 For a careful exploration of the new economics of automobile production across borders, see Womack *et al.* (1990).
12 Economic growth theory has been emphasizing the growth-enhancing role of technology and human capital accumulation, as well as the possibilities of increasing returns to scale at the aggregate level. See, for example, Romer (1987), Helpman (1992) and Dennison (1985).
13 Coordination can range from formal, institutionalized rules for an international monetary system to *ad hoc* bilateral agreements. For an extensive review of possibilities, see Horne and Masson (1988).
14 For a fuller exploration of the combined effects, see Stopford (1992b), from which some of the general arguments presented here are drawn. See also Milner (1988) for an exploration of TNC influence on the politics of international trade.
15 The sale of 80 per cent of Rover to BMW, its German competitor, in early 1994 has upset the arrangements with Honda (Japan) and has created another round in the endless speculation about whether the consolidation of the world automobile industry will proceed along continental lines, heavily influenced by Government support policies, or whether a few individual firms will transcend continental borders to build a truly global oligopoly. Speculation about such structural dynamics is beyond the scope of this article.

REFERENCES

Alagh, Yoginder (1989). 'The NIEs and the developing Asian and Pacific region: a view from South Asia', *Asian Development Review*, 7, 2, pp. 113–27.

Baldwin, Robert E. ed. (1988). *Trade Policy Issues and Empirical Analysis* (Chicago: Chicago University Press).

———— (1992). 'Are economists' traditional trade policy views still valid?', *Journal of Economic Literature*, 30 (June), pp. 804–829.

Bartlett, C. A. and S. Ghoshal (1989). *Managing Across Borders* (Boston, MA: Harvard Business School Press).

Cantwell, John, ed. (1993). *Transnational Corporations and Innovatory Activities: United Nations Library on Transnational Corporations* (London: Routlege).

Cartwright, Wayne R. (1993). 'Multiple linked diamonds: New Zealand's experience', *Management International Review*, Special issue, 33, pp. 55–70.

Caves, Richard E. (1982). *Multinational Enterprises and Economic Analysis* (Cambridge, MA: Cambridge University Press).

Dennison, Edward F. (1985). *Trends in American Economic Growth 1929–1982* (Washington, DC: The Brookings Institution).

Dunning, John H. (1992). 'The global economy, domestic governance, strategies and transnational corporations: interactions and implications', *Transnational Corporations*, 1, 3 (December), pp. 7–45.

———— (1993). *Multinational Enterprises and the Global Economy* (Reading, MA: Addison Wesley).

Encarnation, D. J. and L. T. Wells, Jr (1986). 'Evaluating foreign investment', in T. H. Moran, ed., *Investing in Development: New Roles for Private Capital?* (Oxford: Transaction Books), pp. 61–86.

Ernst, Dieter and David O'Connor (1992). *Competing in the Electronics Industry: The Experience of Newly Industrialising Countries* (London: Routlege).

Findlay, Ronald (1991). 'Comparative advantage', in John Eatwell, Milgate Murray and Peter Newman, eds, *The New Palgrave: The World of Economics* (London: Macmillan), pp. 99–107.

Ghosh, Atish R. and Paul R. Masson (1993). *Economic Cooperation in an Uncertain World* (Oxford: Basil Blackwell).

Hamel, G., Y. L. Doz and C. K. Prahalad (1989). 'Collaborate with your competitors – and win', *Harvard Business Review*, 67 (January–February), pp. 133–139.

Helpman, Elhanan (1992). 'Endogenous macroeconomic growth theory', *European Economic Review*, 36 (April), pp. 237–267.

———— and Paul R. Krugman (1985). *Market Structure and Foreign Trade: Increasing Returns, Imperfect Competition and the International Economy* (Cambridge, MA: MIT Press).

Horne, Jocelyn and Paul R. Masson (1988). 'Scope and limits of international cooperation and policy coordination', *IMF Staff Papers*, 35, 2 (June), pp. 259–296.

Julius, DeAnne (1993). 'Liberalisation, foreign investment and economic growth', Shell Selected Paper, March, mimeo.

Krugman, Paul R. (1987). 'Is free trade passé?' *Journal of Economic Perspectives*, 1 (Fall), pp. 131–144.

———— (1990). *The Age of Diminished Expectations* (Cambridge, MA: MIT Press).

Miller, Robert R. (1993). 'Determinants of US manufacturing investment abroad', *Finance and Development*, 30, 1 (March 1993), pp. 16–18.

Milner, Helen V. (1988). *Resisting Protectionism* (Princeton, NJ: Princeton University Press).

Morrison, A. J. *et al.* (1991). 'Globalization and regionalization: which way for the multinational?', *Organizational Dynamics*, 19, 3 (Winter), pp. 17–29.

Ohmae, K. (1990). *The Borderless World* (New York: Harper Business).

Porter, Michael (1990). *The Competitive Advantage of Nations* (London: Macmillan).

Reich, Robert (1991). *The Work of Nations* (New York: Knopf).

Romer, Paul R. (1987). 'Crazy explanations for the productivity slowdown', in *NBER Macroeconomic Annual* (Cambridge, MA: National Bureau of Economic Research).

Stopford, John M. (1992a). *Directory of Multinationals* (London: Macmillan).

————— (1992b). 'Offensive and defensive responses by European multinationals to a world of trade blocs', OECD Development Centre Technical Paper No. 64 (Paris: OECD).

————— and Susan Strange (1991). *Rival States, Rival Firms* (Cambridge: Cambridge University Press).

Thurow, Lester (1992). *Head to Head: The Coming Economic Battle Among Japan, Europe and America* (New York: William Morrow).

Tyson, Laura (1992). *Who's Bashing Whom? Trade Conflict in High-Technology Industries* (Washington, DC: Institute for International Economics).

UNCTAD, Division on Transnational Corporations and Investment (1993). *World Investment Report 1993: Transnational Corporations and Integrated International Production* (New York: United Nations), United Nations publication, Sales No. E.93.II.A.14.

United Nations, Transnational Corporations and Management Division (1992). *World Investment Report 1992: Transnational Corporations as Engines of Growth* (New York: United Nations), United Nations publication, Sales No. E.92.II.A.19.

Van der Klught, C. J. (1986). 'Japan's global challenge in electronics – the Philips' response', *European Management Journal*, 4, 1 pp. 4–9.

Vernon, Raymond (1971). *Sovereignty at Bay* (New York: Basic Books).

————— (1992). 'Transnational corporations: where they are coming from, where they are headed', *Transnational Corporations*, 1, 2 (August), pp. 7–35.

Wade, Robert (1992). 'East Asia's economic success: conflicting perspectives, partial insights, shaky evidence', *World Politics*, 44 (January), pp. 270–320.

Wells, Louis, T., Jr (1992). 'Conflict or indifference: US multinationals in a world of regional trading blocs', OECD Development Centre Technical Paper No. 57 (Paris: OECD).

Womack, J. P., D. T. Jones and D. Roos (1990). *The Machine that Changed the World* (New York: Rawson Associates).

Yoffie, David B. (1991). 'Technology challenges to trade policy'. Paper presented at the National Academy of Engineering Symposium on 'Linking trade and technology-policies: an international comparison', Washington, DC, June 1991.

11 Trade and foreign direct investment policies

Pieces of a new strategic approach to development?*

*Manuel R. Agosin and Francisco J. Prieto***

In recent years there has been a fundamental rethinking of development strategies. This re-examination has many and complex ramifications and causes. This article is concerned mainly with trade and foreign direct investment (FDI). In the trade-policy field, a large and growing number of developing countries have introduced or are introducing liberalization programmes that include the total or partial dismantling of non-tariff measures and reductions in the levels and dispersion of tariffs. As regards FDI policies, these have also undergone substantial change. From a distrust of transnational corporations (TNCs) and an approach that relied mostly on a host of restrictions and prohibitions, Governments in developing countries are now coming to appreciate what foreign investors can contribute to development. As a consequence, policies in this field have also been substantially liberalized, and many countries are in outright competition with each other to attract FDI.

A JOINT STRATEGIC TRADE AND FOREIGN DIRECT INVESTMENT POLICY APPROACH

The case for an organic policy approach

The new approach to development arises not simply from a conversion to liberal ideals, although a greater appreciation of the limits of Government and the possibilities offered by markets certainly has played a role. The main factor behind this sea-change in attitudes is the realization by policy makers that development, in today's world economy, implies attaining international competitiveness in a grow-

* Reprinted from *Transnational Corporations*, vol. 2, no. 2 (August 1993), pp. 63–86.

ing number of industries. This new approach reflects itself in a growing emphasis on exports as an engine of growth and on technological transformation in the domestic economy. Pure import substitution at any cost is a thing of the past.

This rethinking of development strategies arises out of the trends that can be observed in the international economy and, in turn, contributes to it. These trends are well described by the term 'globalization', which can be characterized by four stylized facts:

- International trade in both goods and services is growing faster than domestic output in most countries and certainly in the world economy as a whole.
- Foreign direct investment is growing faster than national investment.
- International financial flows are growing at a much faster rate than domestic financial transactions.
- International trade, investment and finance are all occurring at the same time and through the same agent, the transnational corporation.[1]

Globalization has direct implications for both the activities of TNCs in developing countries and the objectives that Governments of developing countries have in seeking to attract them. Whereas in the early post-war period, the wave of FDI into (mostly) Europe and Latin America was oriented fundamentally to domestic markets, over the past decade or so, the motivation for FDI in developing countries has slowly shifted from producing for the domestic market to using the host economy to manufacture a part or component of a product for world or regional markets. This is partly because production and distribution are increasingly being carried out within world-wide, and increasingly complex, networks of firms (UNCTAD, 1993). Therefore, except for the largest host countries, the objective of penetrating the markets of individual nation states has taken a backseat to planning for global or regional markets.

It also is related to the changes in development strategies, to which mention has already been made. As development strategies have shifted from import substitution to export orientation, trade barriers have come down, enabling TNCs to consider the advantages offered by a growing number of sites in the developing countries. In T. Ozawa's (1992) terminology, the shift from an inward-oriented import-substituting strategy to an outward-oriented export-promoting one fosters comparative-advantage advancing FDI, which comes to replace FDI in industries in which a developing country has comparative disadvantages. By eventually bidding up wages, this very process tends to erode eventually the labour-cost advantages host countries have, gradually transforming them into foreign investors in lower-wage economies.

These stylized facts fit well the situation that one finds in the economies of East and South Asia, which are well on the way to constituting a closely knit regional grouping forged through trade and FDI links. It also describes recent developments in Mexico, as it becomes more integrated economically with North America. In this case, the close economic links already existing between Mexico and the United States will be intensified with the coming into effect of NAFTA.[2] The reforms undertaken by other Latin American countries may eventually push them into a similar relationship with each other. Not only are trade barriers rapidly coming down in most countries, but a number of bilateral and plurilateral free trade agreements have been signed between them in the 1990s, and this process is likely to accelerate. The eventual extension of NAFTA southward would also stimulate hemisphere economic integration. Moreover, the lowering of barriers towards FDI has attracted considerable flows to some of the countries of the region, particularly Argentina, Brazil, Chile, Mexico and Venezuela (Calderón, 1993). Trade agreements in the hemisphere would accelerate the trend towards larger FDI flows of recent years.

However, most parts of the developing world have yet to be incorporated into the globalization or regionalization processes. This may be due to a variety of factors, including the incipient stage of their economic reforms and the possession of few assets of interest to TNCs.

As regards an individual developing country wishing to attract FDI, the new strategy of TNCs involves an increasing export orientation of their activities. It also implies that FDI is considerably more footloose, that TNCs view increasingly individual countries as alternative sites and that FDI is becoming more difficult to attract and to keep. If, indeed, TNCs are in process of changing their investment strategies and are 'going more global', this would mean that trade policies of potential host countries will become increasingly important in efforts to attract and keep FDI.

While the benefits of international competitiveness in a growing range of activities have come to be recognized as a key ingredient for development, what is less appreciated is the need to develop an integrated approach to development policy. In particular, globalization is clearly pointing to the need to consider trade and FDI policy jointly. This article argues in favour of a *joint strategic trade and FDI policy package*. A pure trade policy ignoring other areas (in the case of this article, FDI) is clearly suboptimal in a world in which TNCs are among the principal producing and trading agents.

Lessons from the new trade and growth theories

The case for selective trade policies has been well rehearsed. Left to its own devices, the market is particularly inefficient in identifying long-term, potential comparative advantage, which, in J. Dunning's (1992) apt characterization, depends on increasing the ratio of created assets to natural assets. This is especially so in the developing world, where the private sector and market institutions are weak. Under these conditions, there is an important role for government intervention in identifying industries with long-run promise, steering investment resources in their direction, acting to complete or create markets and investing in the creation of complementary assets in which the private sector is likely to under-invest (because of the public-good nature of those assets). This will involve, *inter alia*, both trade and FDI policies.

The new trade theories (Krugman, 1987, 1990; Ocampo, 1991) stress the characteristics of modern economies that violate the assumptions needed for incentive neutrality to be the optimal trade policy. The most relevant notions for developing countries derived from the new theories are those related to learning effects, economies of scale and external economies. In fact, the validity of the concept used above – that of potential, or acquired, comparative advantage – depends on the existence of at least one of these phenomena. Comparative advantage can be acquired if an activity has learning effects, that is if costs decline as workers and managers become more familiar with new technologies, management or marketing methods. Or, in the case of economies of scale, average costs decline as the scale of production rises, permitting firms to become internationally competitive. Externalities are particularly relevant to developing countries because the social benefits of acquiring any new technology, management method or marketing expertise are likely to be much higher than the private benefits. And private costs are unlikely to be recouped by individual firms investing in these activities. New production or marketing methods spread from innovating firms to other firms in a variety of ways, including franchising and licensing, the migration of labour and management, imitative behaviour, or through supplier/

purchaser relationships. Therefore, spillover effects can help a whole segment of an economy to *acquire* comparative advantage.

At the same time, the new endogenous growth literature has stressed the importance of investment in human capital and in the stock of knowledge as determinants of growth (Romer, 1990, 1993). In this conceptual framework, the most important contribution that FDI can make to the economic growth of host developing economies is not in the form of capital; rather, it can relax the key constraint of knowledge with an economic value (what can loosely be identified with technology). An economy that is closed to FDI deprives itself of ideas that are the proprietary knowledge of TNCs and which, because of the economic value of exploiting these assets internally, TNCs are unwilling to license or sell at arm's length. As recently stated in UNCTAD (1993, chapter XI), 'given international knowledge spillovers, it is more important to host technology than to own it'. By contrast, an economy with liberal policies towards TNCs will be able to take advantage of a stock of knowledge that is vastly superior to that available to its own productive factors. And, as already noted, given the 'non-rival' nature and difficult appropriability of technology (and of any idea), the siting in a host developing country of foreign firms may have large and positive spillover effects. Therefore, policies that are favourable to FDI and other activities of TNCs are more likely to lead to a transfer of technologies and knowledge to host countries than policies that put undue emphasis on domestic control over productive activities. Indigenous capabilities are more likely to be developed through welcoming than through restrictive FDI policies.

However, this does not mean that no effort should be made to steer FDI into particular sectors or to influence the activities that they carry out in a host economy. As an economy moves from dependence on natural resources as its basis of comparative advantage to a greater dependence on *created* assets, TNCs can play a major role *and can be deliberately encouraged to do so* by specific government action.

One of the policy implications that has been emphasized in the literature on the new trade theories is that there is ample scope for government intervention in trade in order to maximize development impacts. It has not been equally stressed that there are as well important FDI policy implications, nor that, in the context of globalization, strategic trade and FDI policies need to be considered jointly. This article emphasizes two policy implications of the new trade and growth theories that are germane to the issue of the complex of trade and FDI policies. One had already been discussed: the identification of sectors in which a country can reasonably expect to acquire comparative advantage and the promotion of production in such sectors. The other is the promotion of activities with large externalities for the rest of the economy. This will normally involve not only domestic investment, but also – and in some cases primarily – FDI and other forms of TNC activities.

The question arises as to what are the best methods to pursue selective intervention in an economy. According to J. Bhagwati (1988, pp. 98–100), the successful Far Eastern export-oriented economies managed their policy interventions and strategic decision making through *prescriptive* rather than *proscriptive* methods. Under proscriptive regimes, activities that are not specifically permitted tend to be prohibited. Thus, for example, such regimes typically make heavy use of licensing (e.g. for imports or domestic and foreign investment) and rely on high and differentiated tariffs. By contrast, the use of quantitative controls and prohibitions is much less widespread under the prescriptive approach, which instead tends to rely more on incentives (particularly production, export or interest-rate subsidies) and on moral suasion.

This distinction is even more germane to FDI policy than to trade policy: if the argument is correct that open FDI policies are more conducive to the development of indigenous capabilities than restrictive policies, the most successful approaches to FDI policy will be those that emphasize incentives to do the 'right' things and undertake desired activities, rather than prohibitions or limitations on activities perceived to be undesirable, which tend to discourage *all* investment.

THE DEVELOPMENT OF AN INTEGRATED POLICY PACKAGE

The linkage between trade and foreign direct investment

If countries are to succeed in changing the manner in which they participate in the international economy, it is important that the linkages between trade and FDI be recognized explicitly. Trade policy has *always* affected FDI flows. In fact, there is a little understood interaction between the way that TNCs tend to look at the international economy and the trade policies in vogue in developing countries. In the post-war period, up to the 1980s, TNCs tended to view national markets as discrete, and their investment decsions in one market were connected to those made in another only by the overall constraints of their managerial or financial resources and not by the integration of production decisions on a global or regional basis. Developing-country Governments tended to foster this attitude through trade policies that favoured import substitution and market-seeking FDI. In turn, the trade policies of developing countries were inward-looking partly because policies of import substitution produced results in terms of attracting FDI.[3]

In more recent years, a gradual shift in the strategies of TNCs has taken place (UNCTAD, 1993). Transnational corporations themselves have grown into international networks of firms producing for world or regional markets. Thus, FDI decisions in one country have become more organically linked to FDI decisions in other locations within a network. Accordingly, FDI in developing countries of the labour-seeking or component-sourcing variety has gained in importance.[4] As a consequence of this trend and contributing to it, trade policies in developing countries have been considerably liberalized.

Under current circumstances, TNCs are likely to be interested not only in a liberal FDI policy (a necessary but not sufficient condition for investment) but in whether a country is suitable for inclusion in their networks. It is in this sense that trade policies acquire particular relevance. Policies for attracting TNCs that are regionally or globally oriented are likely to include the establishment of well-functioning export-processing zones, the availability of facilities such as effective and administratively easy-to-use tariff-drawback schemes for foreign inputs going into production for export and a stable exchange rate that is favourable to the production of tradables (and, therefore, encourages the sourcing in the country of value-added activities oriented to foreign markets).

It is becoming increasingly understood that liberal policies *per se* will not necessarily yield outward-oriented development, and that more pro-active and organically linked trade, investment and industrial policies are necessary. And export-oriented trade policies can be significantly enhanced by linkages to TNCs with access to markets and whose networks themselves constitute channels to international markets. It is often difficult to obtain access to international markets outside the channels of TNCs, both because international markets are intrinsically difficult to penetrate (e.g. information on consumer tastes or specifications may be difficult to obtain, national firms may not produce goods of desired quality) and because trade barriers tend to discriminate against national firms from exporting countries and in favour of foreign affiliates of home-country TNCs.

Moreover, the blending of suitable trade policies with investment policies (of which FDI policies are a subset) is more likely to yield results than export-promoting trade policies just by themselves. Investment policies are needed to overcome the scarcity of competitiveness-enhancing assets, with export-promoting trade policies playing a supportive role. Finally, the trend in international trade negotiations at both the multilateral and regional levels is towards the placement of increasing restrictions on the ability of Governments to subsidize their exports, even when those exports represent a small share of world markets (Agosin and Tussie, 1993). This means that the way to go is through stimulating investment in sectors in which countries can acquire comparative advantage, and FDI policy has a clear role to play in this context.

Towards a new policy paradigm

Traditionally, foreign trade was considered to be the main link between the domestic and the international economies. As a result, policy makers, in their efforts to improve the integration of their countries into the international economy, were mainly concerned with the consistency of trade policy and its desired impact on trade flows. With the growing importance of TNCs as agents for gaining access to international markets and technologies, issues relating to FDI and how to attract it have gained in prominence. New instruments, norms and regulations have become far more relevant to such 'deep integration' than the traditional 'border measures' (Lawrence, 1993). The new policy mix requires a far more complex set of instruments than the traditional discussion of tariffs and non-tariffs measures *cum* exchange-rate policy. For developing countries, the challenge is to devise an integrated policy package aimed at achieving a more dynamic insertion into the world economy.

Although it would be senseless to attempt to design a 'generic' package that could fit all countries and all their particular needs, it is certainly possible to identify some key concepts that have been brought to the centre of international discussions under a new light and that might help one to develop a new conceptual framework for the planning, implementation and evaluation of economic policy in an integrated fashion.

Three major principles of international economic relationships have been redefined in the effort of the world community to strengthen economic interdependence and promote world economic growth. These principles are most-favoured-nation (MFN) treatment, enhanced market access and national treatment. Although these principles have for long been recognized as the basis of merchandise trade relationships, in recent years they have taken on new dimensions, and an effort has been made to extrapolate them to other realms of international policy making and to transform them into the cornerstones for a deep integration of the world economy. An example of these new goals can be found in the multilateral negotiations that are taking place in the Uruguay Round, especially in the areas of services, intellectual property rights and trade-related measures.

A fourth category of measures that needs to be taken into account in the design of a trade–FDI policy package are measures to enhance international competitiveness. These measures do not fit easily into the other categories and have become the subject of intense trade disputes in the past. They also go well beyond the border measures of concern to traditional trade policy.

The first three principles being discussed have, for long, constituted a desirable goal of international economic negotiations in the area of merchandise trade. Few countries, if any, do actually conform completely to each and every one of these principles. Most countries have chosen to depart partially from them in order to allow for certain discretionalities in the handling of their own economies. Such departures are, in some cases, an answer to domestic political pressures or, in others, the result of differing perceptions of how to attain given development goals. In fact, the careful choice of such departures should be the key to a development strategy that is selective in its approach and integrates trade and FDI elements.

Most-favoured-nation treatment

This principle is at the heart of multilateralism and constitutes the cornerstone of the GATT. The purpose of the MFN clause is to eliminate all sources of discrimination in the treatment granted by one individual country to the rest of its trading partners. Its scope of application was – up to now – limited to merchandise trade and basically to the application of tariff barriers. In spite of many declarations of adherence to this clause, reality shows that countries do in fact discriminate in their trade relations with different countries. Generalized systems of preference (GSP) schemes, preferential trade agreements, trade zones, economic unions and a number of special arrangements do in fact violate the MFN commitment. Departures from this key principle are normally justified whether with the argument of compensating the asymmetries prevailing among different countries (like in the case of GSP schemes), on the basis of economic, cultural, political or geographical affinities (the case of the European Community), or to promote faster rates of liberalization among 'similarly minded' countries (the case of NAFTA).

But the commitment to MFN treatment rarely went beyond covering some border measures affecting merchandise trade. As regards the international movement of factors of production and other non-border issues, substantial discrimination in the treatment granted to different countries is the rule. Wide use is made of bilateral or otherwise limited fiscal agreements of a discriminatory nature (e.g. double taxation treaties). Also, many countries have signed bilateral investment agreements, and many special cooperation agreements cover discriminatory arrangements in the fields of labour mobility and harmonization and the recognition of professional services. Moreover, a number of preferential schemes exist for the transfer and use of technology, access to government procurement, the use of subsidies, access to credit and foreign exchange and the implementation of just about every possible economic instrument, norm or regulation pertaining to economic activities. The internationalization of areas as diverse as banking, insurance, medical services, agricultural production, the automobile industry, entertainment and cultural activities, computers, maritime, air and road transportation and so on, are all affected at various levels by a complex network of special international arrangements. *Reciprocity* rather than *non-discrimination* seems to be the rule in the handling of international economic relations in matters that go beyond the border measures that affect merchandise trade.

The recognition of this fact gives us a clue as to the first critical question in the design of an integrated package or policy mix, and this is: what is the size and location of the particular economic space in which an individual country wishes to evolve? Obviously, there will not be a single economic space that suits the needs of all countries, independently of how much political will there is in a given country to promote multilateralism at a world scale. The definition of such a space will have to take into account a number of relevant considerations, such as the geographical location of the country in question; its relative stage of development; its technological, capital, physical and human resource endowment; the identification of its 'revealed' comparative advantages, as well as those the country wishes and is able to create; and its social, cultural and political specificities. The selection of the individual countries that may constitute such a space will look closely into the degree of complementarity that may be generated through preferential arrangements with those potential associates. In other words, as much as entrepreneurs follow discretionary and highly selective approaches when seeking new partners to develop their projects, countries need to follow a similar strategy in the definition of the economic space in which they wish to interact so as to maximize the development impact of such integration.

It is interesting that most new bilateral or plurilateral free trade agreements that have been signed in the recent past (or are actively under negotiation) include investment provisions. This is as true of the Canada–United States Free Trade Agreement, as of NAFTA or the agreements that are being signed in Latin America (e.g. MER-COSUR or the Chile–Mexico agreement signed in 1991). The high degree of trade integration achieved between Japan and the newly industrializing economies of South and East Asia, rather than being promoted by formal government integration efforts, owes more to market forces and to FDI decisions, first by Japanese corporations and more recently by those of the more industrialized developing econo-mies of the region; however, the specific encouragement of Govern-ments has also played an important role (Ozawa, 1992; UNTCMD, 1992). For example, the Government of Japan has aided the process of internationalization of Japanese corporations by providing finan-cing to developing countries in the region for the construction of complementary infrastructure.

Recent evidence indicates that integration policies at the trade level can play a great role in stimulating FDI. In the case of Mexico, the recent huge increase in FDI owes a great deal to NAFTA. It seems that corporations are beginning to see Mexico as part of North America and are in the process expanding into Mexico as a way of penetrating the North American market. It is also true that, without the reassessment of FDI policies that Mexico has undertaken since the mid-1980s, it would not have been possible for the country to take advantage of the many opportunities that the NAFTA will eventually open (UNCTC, 1992). Mexico has followed a two-pronged approach: on the one hand, it has sought greater economic integration into the North American market and, on the other, it has very significantly liberalized its trade and FDI policies towards the world. Both approaches are supportive of each other.

A similar strategy may be in the making in the rest of Latin America. Most countries in the area have removed barriers to trade and FDI (some more successfully than others). At the same time, Argentina, Brazil, Paraguay and Uruguay have moved towards form-ing a common market (MERCOSUR), and there has been a spate of free trade agreements between differenct countries in the region (Lahera, 1992). Several countries, in particular Chile, have expressed their enthusiasm for a free trade agreement with the United States. The basic objective behind these movements is not primarily that of reaping the static gains from customs unions emphasized in the trade literature. Rather, it is hoped that the creation of larger economic spaces (most of them regional), in the context of generally liberal trade and FDI policies, would encourage a substantially enlarged flow of FDI for regional markets.

Market access

It is obvious that very little would be achieved in the area of world economic interdependence with the mere application of the MFN principle on a world scale if all countries decided to deny market access on a non-discriminatory basis. Domestic economies would remain closed and the benefits of international trade would fail to accrue to the world community. But once again, this principle is far from being a general rule, even in the area of merchandise trade, for most countries. Although tariff barriers have declined over the years, a number of non-tariff barriers and so-called 'grey-area' measures such as voluntary export restraints and orderly marketing agreements have proliferated almost *pari passu* with declining tariffs.

The concept of market access has been limited, up to now, to the removal of border measures that would facilitate the cross-border flow of goods at the international level. The deepening of economic interdependence would require the removal of all internal measures that discriminate against the provision of goods and services by foreign suppliers, *even when permanent establishment in the domestic market* is required by such suppliers. On the other hand, certain temporary limits to market access might be beneficial for the country imposing them, if such limits assist it in developing new capabilities in industries subject to strong learning effects or with important externalities for the rest of the economy.

Generally, the smaller the domestic market of a country, the more important will be the market access it is granted by others. For example, access to the European Community for clothing has been a fundamental factor in determining the location of foreign firms in Mauritius' export-processing zones. Likewise, as already noted, the negotiation of a free trade agreement or a common market among a group of countries will make all the participating countries more attractive to TNCs.

Certain market-access decisions in services may also have important trade effects that need to be considered. Two competing considerations need to be taken into account in deciding the extent of market access in services that a country wishes to offer foreigners. On the one hand, market access can be curtailed in services such as banking and insurance in order to provide domestic suppliers a 'breathing space' to become competitive. On the other, policy makers need to be aware of the fact that the competitiveness of goods may be crucially affected by the availability of low-cost, high-quality producer services (such as telecommunications), which TNCs are frequently better equipped to provide than national firms. In some cases, the entry of TNCs may render domestic markets more competitive and lower unit costs. Likewise, locational decisions by goods-producing TNCs may depend on the availability of low-cost producer services. Some of these considerations have been important in recent privatizations and the opening up to foreign investors of utilities, telecommunications and financial services industries in several countries in Latin America.

The decision will depend on the economic development strategy of individual countries. In this respect, the critical question is: in which industry can a country expect to develop international competitiveness in a reasonable period of time? In other words, where does dynamic comparative advantage lie and how can policies towards FDI in services contribute to it?

The notion of market access is relevant to other measures as well. Some of these are directly related to TNC activities. Examples of market-access measures in the broad sense are restrictions on FDI or on foreign equity participation, restrictions on the movement of personnel, limitations on market shares for foreign companies and conditionality for the acquisition or transfer of technology and know-how. As can be adduced by the line of argument developed in the first part of this article, fairly broad market access is more desirable.[5]

National treatment

The application of full national treatment represents the ultimate stage of world economic integration. An old aspiration of merchandise trade agreements, it has been substantially realized in the area of cross-border goods trade. The application of full national treatment to foreign capital, labour, technology and services presents a far more complex case. The basic issue relating to the concept of national treatment is that policy makers need to be conscious of the ways in which their decisions affect the treatment that foreign goods, services, corporations or persons receive and the objectives that any departure from national treatment pursues. As a general principle, national treatment ought to be the rule. But in selected circumstances, it may be necessary to bar foreign firms from benefits open to national ones (because national firms are at a 'structural' disadvantage) or to offer them benefits to which nationals do not have access (in cases in which foreign corporations clearly provide assets that are particularly scarce in the national economy). In some cases, it may be appropriate to mix both approaches.

There are a number of policy instruments that affect the operations of companies located within a country and that can be applied using three criteria: discriminatory treatment in favour of domestically owned companies; full national treatment; and treatment more favourable to foreign-owned companies. The instruments involve, among others, procedures for the collection of taxes, tax rates, access to domestic and foreign credit, access to subsidies and tariff-draw-back schemes, access to government procurement, price intervention, research and development subsidies and subsidized interest rates for certain activities. As already noted, in today's economic environment, national treatment for foreign producers in the area of access to competiveness-enhancing measures (export or training subsidies, tariff-drawback schemes) is likely to be an important determinant of TNCs' locational decisions.

Competitiveness-enhancing measures

This category relates mainly to those measures that seek to improve an economy's international competiveness. In the first place, there are subsidies of various types, not only to exports but to production, labour training or technological upgrading. Government spending or subsidies to private spending on particular kinds of education, the building of infrastructure needed to export, the provision of producer services of various types (in particular, telecommunications) and efforts to improve the operation of domestic capital and credit markets are also part of such policies. The locational decisions of TNCs are likely to be increasingly affected by policies of this nature (in particular, export-processing zones and administratively simple tariff-drawback schemes) than by the existence of protected national markets.

It should be kept in mind that such policies, if they are to be successful, should be highly selective (in the sense of few in number). Government failure is as prevalent in developing countries as market failure: the capabilities of effective action by Governments are severely limited; and, as pointed out by many analysts (e.g. Bhagwati, 1982; Krueger, 1974), policies that seek to skew market prices lend themselves to abuse and unproductive rent seeking. The avoidance of rent seeking can be ensured by tying all incentives to the delivery of specific performances, as the East Asian newly industrializing economies have successfully done.[6]

It should also be noted that competitiveness-enhancing measures are not synonymous with a policy of 'picking the winners'. The latter is open to the criticism that policy makers are less likely than the private sector to know which are the activities with potential comparative advantage, and that mistakes can be particularly costly.[7] Competitiveness-enhancing measures can apply to broad types of activity (non-traditional exports, research and development expenditures, training of local staff), and can be written into tax laws and regulations that are automatic and non-discretionary. In other words, they could take the form of a 'performance-based tax system' for business income. What is no longer at issue is the need for a competiveness strategy and its operationalization through appropriate policies. As Dunning (1992, p. 8) observes:

> Any Government that . . . pursues a 'hands-off' or 'leave-it-to-the-market' strategy is likely to be as negligent in promoting the welfare of its citizens, as were its predecessors of the 1960s and 1970s, that sought to replace the discipline of the market by socialist or centrally planned macro-organizational strategies.

It should be noted that subsidies that directly or indirectly encourage exports, and remedies for the damage they may cause to domestic producers in importing countries, have become a focus of contention in international trade negotiations. If successfully concluded, the new disciplines that will emerge as a result of the Uruguay Round include important restrictions on all but the poorest countries on the ability of developing countries to subsidize exports (Tussie, 1993; Ocampo, 1992). Therefore, greater care than in the past must be taken in the design of such policies.

Impacts of different policy packages on foreign direct investment

As can be seen in Table 11.1, which presents a very selected sample of possible options, a wide variety of trade and investment policies can have an impact on the volume and quality of FDI flows. The table

Table 11.1 Selected 'old' and 'new' trade and investment measures and probable impact on foreign direct investment

I. Measures affecting most-favoured-nation treatment
1. Trade agreements: Expanded market size for certain products and services; encourages FDI for regional markets.
2. Free trade agreements and common markets: Expanded market size for all products and services produced in the domestic economy; encourages FDI for regional markets and promotes inclusion by TNCs in the regional rationalization of production.

II. Measures affecting market access
Traditional border measures
3. Tariffs, quotas, technical standards, voluntary export restraints: Preserves the domestic market for domestic producers; encourages market-seeking FDI while discouraging labour-seeking and component-sourcing FDI; may discourage resource-seeking FDI, if exchange rate is overvalued as a result of import substituting policies.

Non-traditional ' inside-the-border' measures
4. Prohibitions to operate in domestic market: Preserves market for domestic producers.
5. Limited access to joint ventures: Preserves acquisition of technology and know-how for domestic producers; restricts market access to foreign producers; restricts FDI in services.
6. Full access to domestic markets for services producers: Encourages FDI in services; may contribute to technological and know-how diffusion if allied to 'realistic' performance requirements and/or targeted incentives. May encourage labour-seeking, component-sourcing and resource-seeking FDI in service-using industries.
7. Visa requirements for temporary labour movements: Discourages FDI in professional and other services; preserves domestic market for national producers.
8. Obligation to use domestically produced inputs: Discourages FDI of all kinds.

III. Measures affecting national treatment
9. Full national treatment for all foreign investors: Encourage all FDI; may adversely affect national firms with reasonable prospects of becoming internationally competitive.
10. Preferential tax treatment for TNCs with certain attributes: Encourages FDI with desirable attributes (e.g. access to foreign markets, technology transfer).
11. Preferential tax treatment for TNCs in exchange for selected performance requirements: May contribute to upgrading of economy's international competitiveness through spillover effects; encourages FDI with desirable characteristics.
12. Discriminatory treatment for TNCs (special performance requirements not imposed on local firms and with no compensating incentives, barring access to domestic credit markets, government procurement, foreign exchange, or incentives available to domestic

firms such as tariff drawback schemes or export subsidies): May discourage FDI in certain circumstances; however, may be necessary in economies with strong disequilibria or to compensate domestic firms for certain disadvantages in relation to TNCs (e.g. access to international credit markets, better access to export markets).

IV. Competitiveness-enhancing measures
  13. Export-processing zones: Encourages labour-seeking and component-sourcing FDI.
  14. Export subsidies: Encourages labour-seeking, component-sourcing and (to a lesser extent) resource-seeking FDI; in certain cases, they may *discourage* export-orientated FDI (e.g. when they substitute for needed currency devaluation and when they are granted by Governements against which importing countries are expected to countervail).
  15. Tariff drawback schemes: Encourages labour-seeking and component-sourcing FDI.
  16. Stable exchange rate: Encourages all kinds of FDI.
  17. Investment in physical and social infrastructure: Encourages all kinds of FDI; can be used as *quid pro quo* to attract desired FDI from specific companies.

---

is purely illustrative, but serves to drive home the points that trade policy can have powerful impacts on FDI and that FDI policy can have powerful impacts on trade outcomes; and that both sets of policy tools need to be considered together. It should also be stressed that no measure, or group of measures, in and of itself, will encourage FDI in the desired quantity and in the industries preferred by policy makers. The attractiveness of a particular location to foreign investors depends on a large variety of factors, some of which are intangible (economic and political stability, for example) (UNCTC, 1992).

A very important set of variables refers to the macroeconomic environment. Macroeconomic stability, both internal and external, are likely to be important considerations to foreign investors. With regard to the exchange rate, it is an essential condition that its level be such that it makes production for export internationally competitive. It is also essential that extreme fluctuations in the real exchange rate be avoided. Such fluctuations discourage all investment for export markets, foreign and domestic alike.

In fact, FDI is likely to be even more fickle than domestic investment, because in most cases it has alternative sitings that domestic investors will not – or are not in a position to – consider. Thus, the conditions of macroeconomic stability and microeconomic competitiveness that must prevail are likely to be more exacting when it comes to foreign investments than what would be required for those of a purely domestic nature.

Institutional and legal arrangements and their stability are also essential determinants of the quantity and quality of FDI. In this regard, instruments such as the foreign investment regime and the institutional arrangements related to competition policy (the effectiveness of anti-trust laws, institutional supervision of the financial sector, consumer-protection mechanisms and environmental protection laws) are particularly relevant.

The policy dilemma

The basic policy dilemma that developing countries have to face is that, on the one hand, the attainment of development goals may imply the need for some restrictions on the full sway of the principles of MFN and national treatment and on unfettered market access, while, on the other hand, TNCs are tending to favour increasingly the least number of such restrictions. Before the era of globalization, foreign affiliates were oriented towards serving domestic markets and favoured trade restrictions that reserved markets to them. Today, they are increasingly integrated into global or regional networks of firms. Therefore, they are considerably more footloose than they used to be, *and more footloose than purely domestic firms in host economies*. The implication is that economic policies (including trade policy) in host countries could have large effects on trade flows, FDI, employment and output, since they have decisive effects on the siting of TNC activity.

It may be true that the removal of barriers affecting market access and the granting of full national treatment would make countries far more attractive to foreign investors than those showing limitations in those areas. Yet two things should be taken into account:

● First, it is obvious that the mere removal of such barriers is not a sufficient condition for attracting FDI. Political and social stability, the quality of the labour force and of the physical infrastructure available in a country, its natural resource endowment, its geographical location and the size of its domestic market may all be factors at least as important as the degree of openness and deregulation prevailing in the country. In fact, the higher the rating a country shows with respect to these factors, the greater its bargaining power to extract development-enhancing performance from TNCs in exchange for market access and national treatment.

● Second, the free and unchecked movement of factors of production at the international level *does not* guarantee development *per se*. In fact, this is certainly not the case within national borders, where almost perfect mobility of goods, services and factors of production does not, automatically, solve domestic regional imbalances with respect to development. This is not only true in developing countries but in developed ones as well.

It is important, then, to make explicit which are the objectives of a particular country wishing to become more integrated into the global economy. In other words, why do countries go global? This should help policy makers define what they expect from TNCs and how to calibrate the degree of market access and MFN and national treatment each country wishes to grant to foreign products, services and factors of production.

GLOBALIZATION AND OPTIMAL FOREIGN DIRECT INVESTMENT POLICIES

Some of these considerations can be used in determining the exact content of the trade-cum-FDI policy mix. Of course, optimal policies are highly country specific, and the notions developed below should be considered to be only illustrative. It is assumed that the objective of the country in question is the attainment of international competitiveness and it is orienting its trade and FDI policies accordingly. This section attempts to answer the question of how FDI policies can themselves support the attainment of this objective. The discussion will deal with general FDI and with FDI policies for specific industries.

Optimal FDI policies

As already noted, one characteristic of globalization is that it has increased the proportion of economic activity that is footloose (Dunning, 1992). Therefore, the optimal FDI policies in the era of globalization (in which there is intense locational competition for such investment) are those that are most transparent, non-discretionary and stable over time. As already noted, proscriptions tend to discourage all FDI. Likewise, case-by-case approvals of specific incentives and lengthy delays in investment approvals are likely to divert investments to neighbouring countries that are close locational substitutes. Frequent changes in the rules discourage investment.

With the exception of large investments (the size of which is determined on a country-by-country basis) and investments in industries which the Government wishes to promote (and, hence, which will receive privileged treatment), investment proposals should receive automatic approval. As regards industries in which FDI is permitted, use should be made of a negative list; the closed industries should be as few as possible. Transnational corporations should be able to remit their profits and even repatriate their investment (after a minimum period of, say, one to three years in order to discourage speculative capital flows) with ease. Joint venture requirements should be selective and restricted to certain strategic industries, where they can be used as a counterpart for higher-than-average incentives. These are undoubtedly the kinds of policies that allow TNCs to focus on the underlying economic rationale for investing in a particular country.

Should Governments offer investment inducements, such as tax rebates, outright cash grants or production or export subsidies? This is a difficult question to answer in the abstract, as it will depend on a variety of factors, not least what other competing countries are offering. In order not to engage in bidding wars that result in giving away to the investing corporations the rents that Governments expect will accrue to their countries, it is important that countries exchange information on their FDI policies, as a first step towards harmonizing them. This will be particularly important in countries establishing free trade arrangements. At any rate, generalized investment incentives should be moderate, for both budgetary considerations and in order not to shift the rents accruing from FDI to the investors.

Foreign investors with an orientation towards world or regional markets are more likely to be interested in the general policy framework for FDI and in *trade policies* than in investment incentives. These will be discussed in the next section.

Steering FDI into specific industries

The new trade theories suggest that there is ample scope not only for strategic trade policy in developing countries but also for strategic FDI policy – or, more generally, strategic investment policy, pure and simple, be it foreign or domestic. In fact, strategic trade policy has a large component of strategic investment policy: the orientation of investment resources to industries in which comparative advantage can be created or to activities that have large externalities for the economy as a whole or for parts of it, such that it is possible to create competitive clusters of activities over a reasonable period of time.

As regards FDI, strategic investment policy in developing countries boils down to three issues. The first one is whether investment incentives should be differentiated industry-wise. The second issue is whether incentives and performance requirements should be used to stimulate activities by TNCs that have large externalities (e.g. the training of skilled labour). The third issue revolves around the desirability of performance requirements (particularly of the export variety) as a way of steering TNCs towards export markets.

If a Government has identified specific industries or activities (e.g. non-traditional exports or on-the-job training) it wishes to encourage through differentiated incentives, TNCs investing in them alongside domestic producers should be given national treatment, that is they should be entitled to the same incentives. In some cases, TNCs are the only firms operating in these areas, and incentives amount, in effect, to preferential treatment for TNCs. Such encouragements are entirely justified and should form part of the panoply of policy tools of a Government in implementing a strategic trade and investment policy. However, such inducements should be moderate, their economic rationale should be clear and they should be offered to a small number of activities only. How to choose them depends on a host of country-specific factors. Knowledge of the intentions of other Governments that are potential competitors for FDI is also important for another reason: Governments in different countries should avoid encouraging investments in the same lines of production, thereby lowering international prices. Something of this phenomenon is in evidence in such industries as garments and steel, which are favoured by new entrants into international markets for manufacturers.

This kind of industry-specific incentives merges with the incentives that would be appropriate to obtain certain kinds of behaviour from specific companies, for reasons of externalities. In both cases, the company and activity in question are usually identifiable. In most cases, the investors are international oligopolies that have proprietary technologies and products whose introduction into the domestic economy can have effects that go far beyond the benefits accruing to the factors of production directly engaged by the company. This is the case with most manufacturing products with complex technologies, but particularly those using information technologies. A special incentive for these companies may be entirely appropriate.

Industry- and activity-specific inducements to FDI can be usefully accompanied by performance requirements. For example, an incentive could be made conditional on the export of a certain proportion of output or on training programmes for domestic employees or managers.[8] In many cases, performance requirements can be implicit, since the foreign firm will have to apply for a special incentive not offered to all foreign investors and, in the process, it will have to disclose the nature of its operations in the country. This is a clear game-theoretic situation between dual monopolists, with the outcome determined by relative bargaining power. The more desirable the country as a location and the fewer the locational alternatives, the greater will be the possibility that the Government can shift oligopolistic rents from the company to the domestic economy and orient the foreign firm towards specific long-term development objectives.

Should performance requirements be used, in all or most cases, to steer TNCs to export markets? This issue has been amply researched recently in UNCTC-UNCTAD (1991). Export-performance requirements were more likely to be necessary when FDI was oriented mostly to domestic markets and when the inducement was mostly producing behind high trade barriers. In an era in which FDI is increasingly oriented towards global or regional markets and trade barriers in host countries are much lower, export-performance requirements are a less compelling policy tool. Moreover, performance requirements are a tool belonging to the proscriptive approach. Better results can be obtained by encouraging the establishment of firms that most likely will produce for foreign markets or introduce desired technologies.

An alternative is to blend performance requirements with specific incentives. In this option, there would be a general framework for FDI, with few limitations and requirements and no special incentives, and another one for companies with certain characteristics, which would be subjected to stiffer requirements but would also be rewarded with more generous incentives.

Another approach, which would skirt the problems of lengthy approvals, bureaucratic delays, case-by-case negotiations and having to apply different criteria to different investors (a process that lends itself to abuse) has already been mentioned: it is to adopt an automatic 'performance-based' corporate tax system favouring a few specific activities and which gives equal treatment to national and foreign firms.

CONCLUDING REMARKS

Clearly, the changing trade strategies of developing countries require a re-consideration not only of trade policy but also of investment policy, and particularly of policies towards FDI. If TNCs play an important role in the process of export expansion and diversification, it will not be sufficient to effect trade policy reforms while leaving FDI policy untouched. And in the area of services, trade and FDI policies merge. This is not to say that it is impossible to penetrate international markets without TNCs. But it will be certainly faster to use the medium of the TNC than deliberately to make do without them. Even arm's-length forms of relationship with TNCs such as subcontracting may require some investment.

Therefore, it will be useful for developing countries contemplating, or already implementing, a change in development strategy to consider the implications of the new strategy for FDI policies. In general terms, if the promotion of international competitiveness is the desired policy objective, then the more liberal and prescriptive FDI policies are, the better. And, as already noted, trade and macroeconomic policies become just as important as FDI policies themselves. In addition, a strategic trade policy can be usefully complemented by a strategic FDI policy encouraging investment in industries and activities that promote the acquisition of new comparative advantages.

NOTES

** The authors wish to thank an anonymous referee for helpful comments. An earlier version of this article was prepared for the UNCTAD Programme on Transnational Corporations.

1   The growing importance of transnational banks in the world economy is a special case of the more general phenomenon of the ascendancy of the TNC.

2   Mexico's trade with the United States accounts for over two-thirds of its total trade, and United States-based TNCs are Mexico's main foreign investors.

3   There were of course many other reasons, including deteriorating terms of trade for primary commodity exporters and the prevailing approaches to economic development and industrialization generally.

4   This does not mean that FDI for domestic markets has disappeared. The countries with large markets (Brazil and India, for example) can still expect to be attractive for market-seeking investment, if policies towards FDI are favourable and other conditions are met. In other cases, resource-seeking investment in developing countries could remain the most important kind.

5 Market regulation, for prudential and other reasons, is, of course, essential.
6 See Agosin and Ffrench-Davis (1993) for a contrast between the Asian experience with trade policy and the recent trade liberalization in Latin America.
7 It is often forgotten that the market can also make very wasteful mistakes.
8 An interesting example of this kind of behaviour is the agreement between the Government of Mexico and IBM whereby, in exchange for being allowed to set up an affiliate with 100 per cent ownership, IBM agreed, among other things, to set up facilities to train Mexican computer programmers (UNCTC, 1988, box IX.2).

REFERENCES

Agosin, M. R. and R. Ffrench-Davis (1993). Trade liberalization in Latin America. *CEPAL Review*, 50 (August), pp. 1–22.
Agosin, M. R. and D. Tussie (1993). Trade and growth: new dilemmas in trade policy – an overview. In *Trade and Growth: New Dilemmas in Trade Policy*, M. R. Agosin and D. Tussie, eds, London: Macmillan.
Bhagwati, J. (1982). Directly-unproductive, profit-seeking (DUP) activities. *Journal of Political Economy*, 90 (October), pp. 988–1002.
——— (1988). *Protectionism*. Cambridge, Massachusetts: The MIT Press.
Calderón, A. (1993). Tendencias recientes de la inversión extranjera directa en América Latina y el Caribe: elementos de politica y resultados. Paper prepared for a Seminar on Foreign Direct Investment in the Third World, Instituto de Relaciones Europeo-Latinoamericanas (IRELA), Madrid, 10–11 June 1993, mimeo.
Dunning, J. H. (1992). The global economy, domestic governance, strategies and transnational corporations: interactions and policy implications. *Transnational Corporations*, 1, 3 (December), pp. 7–45.
Krueger, A. O. (1974). The political economy of the rent-seeking society. *The American Economic Review*, 64 (June), pp. 291–303.
Krugman, P. R. (1987). Is free trade passé? *The Journal of Economic Perspectives*, 1 (Fall), pp. 131–144.
——— (1990). *Rethinking International Trade*. Cambridge, Massachusetts: The MIT Press.
Lahera, E. (1992). Convergencia de los esquemas de integración. ECLAC, LC/R. 1192, Santiago, October, mimeo.
Lawrence, R. Z. (1993). Futures for the world trading system and implications for developing countries. In *Trade and Growth: New Dilemmas in Trade Policy*, M. R. Agosin and D. Tussie, eds, London: Macmillan.
Ocampo, J. A. (1991). Las nuevas teorias del comercio internacional y los paises en vias de desarrollo. *Pensamiento Iberoamericano*, Madrid, No. 20 (July–December), pp. 193–214.
——— (1992). Developing countries and the GATT Uruguay Round: a (preliminary) assessment. In UNCTAD, *International Monetary and Financial Issues for the 1990s* (United Nations publication, UNCTAD/GID/G24/1), pp. 31–53.
Ozawa, T. (1992). Foreign direct investment and economic development. *Transnational Corporations*, 2, 1 (February), pp. 27–54.

Romer, P. M. (1990). Are nonconvexities important for understanding growth? *The American Economic Review*, 80 (May), pp. 97–103.
———— (1993). Two strategies for economic development, using ideas and producing ideas. In *Proceedings of The World Bank Annual Conference on Development Economics, 1992*, Washington, DC, pp. 62–91.
Tussie, D. (1993). The Uruguay Round and the trading system in the balance: dilemmas for developing countries. In *Trade and Growth: New Dilemmas in Trade Policy*, M. R. Agosin and D. Tussie, eds, London: Macmillan.
UNCTAD, Programme on Transnational Corporations (1993). *World Investment Report 1993: Transnational Corporations and Integrated International Production* Sales No. E.93.II.A.14.
UNCTC (1988). *Transnational Corporations in World Development: Trends and Prospects*. Sales No. E.88.II.A.7.
———— (1992). *The Determinants of Foreign Direct Investment: A Survey of the Evidence*. Sales No. E.92.II.A.2.
UNCTC-UNCTAD (1991). *The Impact of Trade-Related Investment Measures on Trade and Development: Theory, Evidence and Policy Implications*. Sales No. E.91.II.A.19.
UN-TCMD (1992). *World Investment Report 1992: Transnational Corporations as Engines of Growth*. Sales No. E.92.II.A.19.

12 International regulation of transnational business

Providing the missing leg of global investment standards*

*John M. Kline***

The regulatory framework for transnational corporations (TNCs) is changing as national laws become less restrictive and bilateral and multilateral negotiations attempt to coordinate legal standards and practices. The international system, however, still lacks an agreed set of investment principles to shape and guide this evolution. Proliferating partial agreements can result in a confusing regulatory kaleidoscope, leading to greater conflict between Governments and TNCs. Developing a broad framework for international investment would help stabilize the global economic system while giving direction and coherence to the regulatory environment facing transnational business.

Scholars have long recognized that the emergence of TNCs in the post-Second World War era posed unique challenges for national Governments. These enterprises were directly subject to each nation's authority where they operated, yet appeared fully controllable by no single political sovereign. Multinationally located and transnationally integrated operations yielded resources and options unavailable to soley national firms, giving TNCs more independence from a local government's policy direction. During the 1960s and particularly the 1970s, clashes arose between TNCs and national authorities, and between the 'host' and 'home' Governments of these enterprises, over a range of regulatory issues affecting TNC operations.

A multilateral resolution of investment controversies proved elusive without a firm international agreement on global investment principles. The 1948 Havana Charter and its proposed International Trade Organization foundered on a dispute over compensation for expropriated foreign properties. The post-war international economic order was therefore constructed around the International Monetary Fund and the International Bank for Reconstruction and Development

* Reprinted from *Transnational Corporations*, vol. 2, no. 1 (February 1993), pp. 153–64.

(The World Bank) to manage financial cooperation, and remnants from the International Trade Organization were gathered into the General Agreement on Tariffs and Trade to cover trade issues. This post-war structure can be represented as the two-legged stool depicted in Figure 12.1. The missing third leg, needed to achieve true system balance and stability, reflects the absence of international agreement on foreign-direct-investment (FDI) issues.

The 1980s radically altered the international economic scene, expanding the role and importance of FDI. Foreign direct investment grew faster than merchandise exports or average gross domestic product, with total FDI stock reaching $1.9 trillion by 1991. Investment decisions also increasingly influenced world trade flows. For example, 80 per cent of United States trade is undertaken by TNCs, while one-third occurs on an intra-firm basis, within the same TNC organization (UN-TCMD, 1992, p. 200).

Financial crises and global recession in the early 1980s left most developing countries struggling under an unpredented external debt burden, increasing their need but decreasing their attractiveness for FDI. Transnational corporations concentrated new investment in the 'triad' of Western Europe, North America and Japan, but FDI flows shifted from their traditional pattern. Japan's FDI outflows accelerated, while European TNCs alternated between investing abroad and turning inward to prepare for the European Community's internal market reforms. The United States attracted massive FDI inflows,

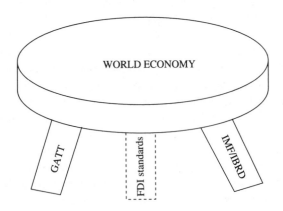

Figure 12.1 The post-war structure of international trade as a three-legged stool

becoming the world's largest host nation as well as remaining the largest home nation for TNCs. As the decade ended, communist regimes collapsed throughout Central and Eastern Europe, altering many nations' idealogical hostility to private foreign investment and injecting a new factor into the growing competition for FDI.

REGULATORY TRENDS OF THE 1990s

Three trends mark the present evolution of international investment regulations: less restrictive national laws; proliferating bilateral investment treaties (BITs); and expanding regional and multilateral negotiations on FDI issues.

The passage of less restrictive national laws governing FDI is the most obvious and widespread change in the regulatory climate for TNCs in the early 1990s. Countries throughout the world now actively compete for the productive growth opportunities that accompany private foreign investment. In particular, developing countries are dismantling restrictive measures that discourage or discriminate against foreign investors, creating a more open and facilitative investment climate. Formerly communist nations are similarly rushing to formulate modern FDI regimes to attract private capital previously excluded for ideological reasons from centrally planned and controlled economies. The shift in both these regions is from highly statist economies with protectionist, import-substitution development strategies to open, freer market policies that emphasize export-led growth. This change magnifies the potential benefits from foreign affiliates that can link up with the firm's globally integrated distribution and marketing system.

Some commentaries depict the United States as an ironic exception to this liberalization trend. The long-time champion of open FDI policy has struggled recently to adjust to political, economic and social strains resulting from its new role as a major FDI recipient. Despite vigorous public debate and numerous proposed restrictions on FDI, however, the only new measures actually adopted are national security review mechanisms that are not uncommon in most other countries for foreign mergers and acquisitions (Wallace and Kline, 1992, pp. 34–44).

A related but less discussed element of national FDI policy is the potential for home country Governments to place restrictions on capital outflows. Economic slow-downs and increased international competition multiply domestic pressures to keep capital, technology and employment at home. Although some Governments have created incentive programmes to encourage domestic-oriented research-and-production activities, few have resorted to overt distortions such as prohibiting or severely penalizing FDI.

The second significant regulatory change is the proliferation of bilateral investment treaties (BITs). These instruments are expanding in number and scope as a complement to less restrictive national laws. Initially negotiated in the 1960s between European nations and their former African colonies, these treaties more than doubled during the 1980s to over 400 (UNCTC and ICC, 1992). Most recent activity has involved Latin America, Central and Eastern Europe and the United States. United States BITs also introduced new commitments regarding entry and access conditions and proscriptions on trade performance requirements (UN-TCMD, 1992, pp. 77–78). Perceived as an important symbolic as well as substantive step in building an attractive FDI climate, bilateral treaties are likely to expand further. However, the different concerns, priorities and relative bargaining positions among treaty partners ensure that the resulting pattern of bilateral agreements lacks the overall coherence and consistency desirable for transnational business.

Third, FDI issues are also central to an expanding set of regional and multilateral negotiations. Regionally, the European Community's transformation from a common trade area into an internally integrated market involves forging common regulations on investment as well as trade and monetary issues. Although not intended as a fully integrated regional market, the United States–Canada Free Trade Agreement as well as the North American Free Trade Agreement both incorporate provisions addressing FDI standards and regulations.

Multilaterally, the Uruguay Round of Multilateral Trade Negotiations broached a number of investment issues for the first time. Trade performance requirements figure prominently among topics discussed as trade-related investment measures, while negotiations on trade in services and on intellectual property rights relate as much to FDI as to traditional trade debates (UN-TCMD, 1992, pp. 74–75). The outcome of these negotiations, including possible progress on investment-related topics, remains unclear in early 1993. Final results, however, will certainly not represent more than a first step in formulating a multilateral accord and expanding cooperation on these issues. Additionally, although GATT includes most of the world's trading nations, new agreements are increasingly limited in their coverage by the shift from traditional most-favoured-nation principles to conditional reciprocity as the basis for inclusion in an agreement.

The Organization for Economic Co-operation and Development (OCECD) has the most successful record in forging multilateral agreement on international investment issues. An initiative now under consideration envisions developing a broad new investment instrument that incorporates and builds on OECD's early capital-liberalization codes, as well as its 1976 Declaration on International Investment and Multinational Enterprises. These accords mix binding multilateral obligations with statements of policy goals and include a governmentally endorsed set of voluntary guidelines for TNC behaviour. Further progress by OECD is desirable.[1] Nevertheless, the relatively similar perspectives and objectives of that organization's industrialized country members, compared with those of the full global community, limit any likely accord's utility for addressing the complete range of TNC issues.

In 1992, the Development Committee of the World Bank undertook a new effort, studying existing legal instruments governing FDI at the national, bilateral and regional levels. The Committee then considered a draft set of 'Guidelines on the Treatment of Foreign Direct Investment'. These Guidelines focus on the legal treatment of FDI, with the objective of improving the investment climate and encouraging greater FDI flows. The Development Committee has called these guidelines to the attention of member Governments. The World Bank's Multilateral Investment Guarantee Agency (MIGA) and the International Center for Settlement of Investment Disputes (ICSID) also provide practical services useful in structuring the relationship between foreign investors and host Governments.

The United Nations addresses TNC issues, most generally through the work of its Commission on Transnational Corporations, but also in topical actions taken by organizations including the United Nations Conference on Trade and Development (UNCTAD), the International Labour Organization (ILO), the World Health Organization (WHO) and the United Nations General Assembly's consideration of issues such as consumer protection. The mandate of the Commission on Transnational Corporations included the most comprehensive international attempt to formulate a Code of Conduct that would address both government and corporate rights and responsibilities on FDI issues. Begun in the virulent atmosphere of the mid-1970s, this exercise was judged politically deadlocked in 1992, despite achieving substantive agreement on most elements of a possible code.

Failure to break the political impasse on the Code leaves the United Nations system and, indeed, the world community, without an umbrella set of FDI principles to connect and shape the diverse and still-growing array of particularistic accords emerging from bilateral, regional and multilateral settings. This lack of progress in the United Nations also tends to disenfranchise many (particularly developing) countries, leaving them isolated at the margins of discussions on FDI issues that will nevertheless importantly influence their future development potential. Equally troubling, the resulting international regulatory environment for transnational business threatens to become a morass of binding and non-binding partial instruments that overlap on some issues while leaving broad areas of FDI policy and transnational business activity uncovered by effective regulations or guidelines.

THE REGULATORY ENVIRONMENT FOR TRANSNATIONAL CORPORATIONS

The term 'regulation' generally implies the use of legally binding rules enforceable by governmental authority. Transnational business, however, operates in a regulatory environment populated by both 'hard' (binding) laws and regulations, and a variety of 'soft' (non-binding) standards and procedures.[2] As depicted in Figure 12.2, these measures can be arrayed along a horizontal dimension based on their scope of geographic coverage, beginning with unilateral national actions and running through bilateral and regional accords to truly global agreements.

On the vertical dimension, 'soft' and 'hard' approaches divide roughly along a middle axis. Binding instruments typically specify the detailed basis for actions ranging from dispute settlement to policy harmonization to full economic integration. Non-binding measures encompass a class of more general agreements. These instruments outline broad standards or processes to enhance cooperation and coordination among concerned parties, up through arrangements providing for dispute settlement procedures.

This concept is elaborated in Figure 12.3, which identifies selective agreements or groups of regulatory measures that populate the international business environment. For example, national laws are binding unilateral instruments that provide the basis for a country's economic integration. The European Community is the most advanced example of regional regulation that has moved from policy harmonization towards full economic integration, most recently through enactment of the 1992 internal market reforms.

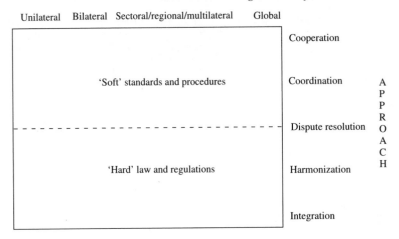

Figure 12.2 Regulatory environment: type of coverage

The United States–Canada Free Trade Agreement provides a constrasting example, restricted geographically to a bilateral instrument and focused on a more limited range of policy harmonization. In comparison, the North American Free Trade Agreement (NAFTA) is a regional accord that addresses a somewhat expanded issue agenda but still falls closer in approach to dispute resolution than to the European Community's example of economic integration. On the other hand, most BITs barely reach the dispute settlement line, dependent on a limited range of agreement on FDI policy principles. The United States–European Community antitrust accord aims to reach dispute settlement procedures on a multilateral scale, while ICSID and MIGA provide global mechanisms that help ameliorate or resolve investment disputes.

The 1976 OECD Declaration combines several agreements that build on earlier accords but is probably best described as advanced multilateral policy coordination rather than substantive policy harmonization. The OECD and Council of Europe's accords on privacy and the OECD agreement on the transport of hazardous substances are more limited, function-specific examples of procedural coordination on a multilateral scale. Regionally, recent framework agreements between the United States and Latin American nations suggest policy cooperation and coordination, but in reality constitute little more than a commitment to discuss policy issues and problems in an amicable manner.

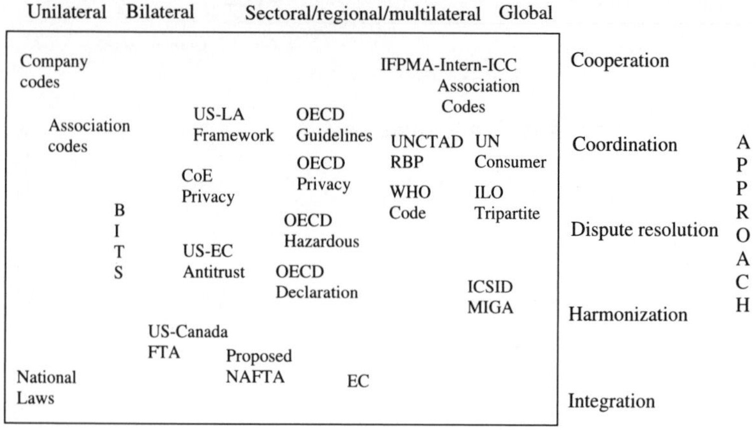

Unilateral   Bilateral   Sectoral/regional/multilateral   Global

Company codes			IFPMA-Intern-ICC Association Codes
Association codes	US-LA Framework	OECD Guidelines	
	CoE Privacy	OECD Privacy	UNCTAD RBP UN Consumer
B I T S	US-EC Antitrust	OECD Hazardous	WHO Code ILO Tripartite
		OECD Declaration	ICSID MIGA
	US-Canada FTA		
National Laws		Proposed NAFTA EC	

Cooperation

Coordination

Dispute resolution

Harmonization

Integration

A P P R O A C H

Figure 12.3 Regulatory environment: coverage by instruments

In addition to traditional international accords, a host of new soft law standards appeared beginning in the mid-1970s. Sparked by the rise of TNCs, these instruments often outlined voluntary standards for corporate good conduct as well as governmental policies towards TNCs. The OECD Guidelines for Multinational Enterprises, a part of the 1976 OECD Declaration, remain the most extensive of these instruments. Aimed at improving TNC policy coordination and cooperation among the industrialized countries, these multilateral Guidelines break with tradition by addressing themselves directly to TNC behaviour rather than dealing solely with national regulation of corporate activity. Although not meant to supersede national law, they do call for business conduct exceeding corporate legal obligations in areas where insufficient political consensus exists to support a binding multilateral accord. The Guidelines depend on voluntary adherence backed by public suasion to influence corporate behaviour.

A number of other multilateral and international agreements adopted a similar approach. Included among these instruments, which address specific areas of corporate conduct, are the UNCTAD Code on Restrictive Business Practices, the United Nations Consumer Protection Guidelines, the WHO Code on the Marketing of Breast-Milk Substitutes, and the ILO Tripartite Declaration on TNCs and social policy.

Along with governmentally endorsed voluntary standards, self-regulation plays an important role in framing the regulatory environment for international business. Several international business associations promote codes of conduct, including those adopted by the International Chamber of Commerce (ICC) and by sectoral associations such as the International Federation of Pharmaceutical Manufacturers Associations (IFPMA). National business and professional associations also formulate codes of conduct for their membership. Finally, individual company codes constitute the most applied form of unilateral, voluntary self-regulation by TNCs.

These selected instruments, arrayed around the regulatory environment depicted in Figure 12.3, illustrate the expanding maze of mandatory and voluntary mechanisms that confront contemporary transnational business. A single TNC's operations can be affected simultaneously by many, if not most, of these measures, as well as by numerous other regulations not specifically cited in this article. Both gaps and overlaps appear throughout this regulatory fabric because the various instruments lack consistency and coherence. No agreed global framework on FDI principles exists to help gather and channel these disparate elements into a supportive structure for transnational business policy.

ASSESSING AN EVOLVING REGULATORY PICTURE

Figure 12.3 usefully locates selected examples of regulatory instruments within the global environment, but it does not give an accurate reflection of their prevalence. The shading in Figure 12.4 depicts the relative frequency and scope of these instruments' use, with the darker areas representing the more numerous examples. National laws, of course, still comprise the bulk of business regulation. These measures are adopted unilaterally, aimed at controlling corporate actions within an integrated national economy. Although their numbers are increasing, regulatory instruments become more scarce as the spectrum shifts towards global coverage, concentrating in non-binding approaches as coverage becomes more general.

In Figure 12.4, the bottom right corner (binding regulations providing for global integration) will remain empty unless some form of successful world government arises. The opposite upper left corner contains at least several hundred individual corporate codes adopted by major TNCs during the late 1970s to early 1980s. Considering, however, that an estimated 35,000 TNCs now engage in international commerce, this instrument is still rather sparse in its coverage. The major interplay now seems to occur in the middle to the upper right

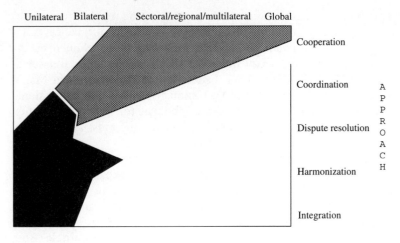

Unilateral   Bilateral   Sectoral/regional/multilateral   Global

Cooperation

Coordination   A
P
P
R
Dispute resolution   O
A
C
Harmonization   H

Integration

Figure 12.4 Regulatory environment coverage

corner, with the proliferation of devices from BITs through multi-lateral coordination mechanisms that address particular aspects of FDI-related policy.

Clearly no single regulatory approach will suffice for the foreseeable future. Policy harmonization can only proceed on a regional or multilateral scale as specific issues mature to the point where sufficient political consensus exists to reach a mutually agreeable outcome. As suggested by the slow pace of discussions on investment-related issues in the Uruguay Round negotiations, progress in this respect cannot be rushed. True policy harmonization requires substantive binding agreements on applied details. Until that point is reached, the world community must place renewed emphasis on practical mechanisms to reduce intergovernmental frictions and resolve disputes over particular policy differences.

Corporate self-regulation can play an important role in this effort. Currently, the momentum appears to have dissipated from the drive to establish and apply voluntary business codes, either individually or through collective associations. This development is understandable given current global competition for FDI and concomitant governmental efforts to attract TNCs. Unfortunately, this conducive environment for FDI contains the seeds for its own demise.

Larger, traditional TNCs that were associated with controversies in the 1970s now generally operate in a more open and publicly sensitive manner, consistent with their adopted corporate codes and a substantial, long-term commitment to the global economy. On the other hand, thousands of new, smaller TNCs have less accumulated stake in overseas locations and are under greater pressures to produce quick results. This scenario may lead enterprises to opt for short-term gains that can result from unresponsive or even abusive behaviour in relation to public policy goals and needs. Lacking an applicable set of transnational business standards, disappointment and frustration from unmet or misplaced expectations could again make national policy makers suspicious of TNC actions.

Extending effective corporate codes of conduct to cover these myriad of new players is a daunting but essential task for the international business community. The most practical way to accomplish this goal may be for the corporate community to work with governmental authorities to formulate a comprehensive voluntary code for transnational business. The OECD Guidelines could provide a good starting point for such a document, but a new exercise must be more inclusive, both in its geographic coverage and in the scope of issues considered. Many new TNCs come from non-OECD nations, and the countries most susceptible to potential controversies over TNC activity are developing nations and former central market economies that also lie outside OECD. Likewise, the range of issues relevant to contemporary transnational business demand a comprehensive approach and forum for their resolution, including matters such as environmental protection, product and worker safety, and the security of global financial markets.

The United Nations provides the most comprehensive, inclusive forum for reaching agreement on FDI principles and TNC operations. Unfortunately, the institution is burdened by the history of the politically deadlocked debate over the TNC Code of Conduct. Concern over 'ghosts from the past' prevents involved parties from focusing on the new shape of global TNC activities and the FDI issues associated with them (UNCTC, 1990).

Despite the currently conducive climate for FDI, a framework of global principles is needed to guide investment relationships and TNC activities into the next century. Both public and private sector participants will be better off if the missing leg of global investment standards can be added to stabilize the regulatory structure that supports the world economy. An inclusive framework accord on FDI principles and TNC conduct standards could help meet this need. Such a goal is worth a new look and a new effort.

NOTES

** This article is based on a presentation given by the author at the Scanticon III Seminar, organized by the Transnational Corporations and Management Division and the Friedrich Ebert Foundation for the United Nations Second Committee Delegates, in Princeton, New Jersey, on 18–20 June 1992.

1   See, Guertin and Kline (1989). See also OECD Secretariat Note, 'Feasibility study of a wider investment instrument', 19 November 1992.

2   See Adelman (1988), especially chapters 1, 2 and 10.

REFERENCES

Adelman, Carol C., ed. (1988). *International Regulation: New Rules in a Changing World Order. A Lehrman Institute Book*. San Francisco: ICS Press.

Guertin, Donald L. and John M. Kline (1989). *Building on International Investment Accord*. Occasional Paper. Washington, DC: The Atlantic Council of the United States.

OECD (1992). Committee on International Investment and Multinational Enterprises. Feasibility study of a wider investment instrument. Note by the Secretariat. Paris, 19 November.

United Nations Centre on Transnational Corporations (1990). UNCTC Current Studies, Series A, No. 16, *The New Code Environment*. Sales No. E.90.II.A.7.

————— and International Chamber of Commerce (1992). *Bilateral Investment Treaties 1959–1991*. Sales No. E.92.II.A.16.

United Nations, Transnational Corporations and Management Division, Department of Economic and Social Development (1992). *World Investment Report 1992: Transnational Corporations as Engines of Growth*. Sales No. E.92.II.A.19.

Wallace, Cynthia Day and John M. Kline (1992). *EC 92 and Changing Global Investment Patterns*. Washington, DC: Center for Strategic and International Studies.

13 The domestic domain

The new international policy arena*

*Sylvia Ostry***

By the end of the 1980s, 'globalization' had become the term for accelerating interdependence. This third wave of international linkage, after the expansion of trade and the internationalization of financial markets, is dominated by flows of investment and technology and by increased international corporate and research networking. The primary agent of globalization is the transnational corporation. The primary driving force is the revolution in information and communication technologies. Like each phase of tightening linkage, globalization enhances opportunities for growth but also increases risk and vulnerability. Growth is enhanced by improved efficiency, more rapid production and the adoption of new technology. Risk is heightened because globalization creates growing pressure for convergence of policies, a pressure which touches the sensitive issue of sovereignty. In a globalizing world, competition among transnational corporations in sophisticated products and services (an increasing proportion of world trade) is also competition among systems. A globalizing world has a low tolerance for system divergence – and that is the wellspring of new sources of international friction, system friction. A bilateral United States–Japanese approach to resolving system friction can be destabilizing and, while the European approach to harmonization is desirable, it is unobtainable. The solution lies in mounting an international initiative to promote the convergence of policies related to innovation and more balanced access to investment and technology flows. Most of the policies which will be the subject of this new international initiative are in the domestic domain: the new international policy arena.

* Reprinted from *Transnational Corporations*, vol. 1, no. 1 (February 1992), pp. 7–26.

As the world is preparing to move into the twenty-first century, the arena for international policy cooperation is moving beyond traditional arenas to domestic policies. The basic reason for that shift lies in changes in the extent and nature of the international linkages among countries which have produced a new type of friction that can be called *system friction*. The struggle over competitiveness in the Triad (Japan, the United States and the European Community), which has generated the policies targeted at so-called strategic industries, is a symptom of this far broader malady of system friction. Those developments are briefly described below and the policy options required to mitigate or contain the new discord are explored.

INTERNATIONAL LINKAGE

There have been three phases of growing international linkages among countries since the Second World War. The first, the golden age of the 1950s and 1960s, was driven by *trade*, launched by the dismantling of protectionist barriers in successive GATT rounds. Over the decade of the 1970s, three massive commodity and oil shocks initiated the second phase, which was characterized by *financial integration*, via the recycling of the OPEC surplus. The wave of financial integration accelerated in the 1980s, fed by the revolution of deregulation and privatization in the United Kingdom and the United States and the emergence of the Japanese current account surplus.

The world is now at the outset of a third phase called *globalization*, which is led by a surge in foreign direct investment (FDI) (UNCTC, 1991). After the Second World War, FDI was characterized by *le défi américain* in Western Europe. The present upsurge, which began in 1983 and has steadily picked up speed, is very different in both origin and destination. By 1983 the United States had become a net *recipient* of FDI (that is, large outflows were outweighed by still larger inflows). By 1985, Japan became the largest net direct investor (owing to large outflows and negligible inflows), followed by the United Kingdom and the Federal Republic of Germany. Both outward and inward FDI are dominated by the Group of Five — France, Germany, Japan, the United Kingdom and the United States.

Apart from the dynamic Asian economies, the developing countries have been largely excluded from this trend. FDI is much more concentrated than are trade flows: the Group of Five accounts for over 75 per cent of FDI, but just over 40 per cent of world trade. If present investment flows are extrapolated, a conservative estimate suggests that they will grow at twice the rate of trade flows in the 1990s.

The prime *agent* of this third phase is the transnational corporation (TNC). TNCs have a variety of objectives and rarely make decisions on the basis of only one consideration. One important factor driving globalization today, however, is the increase in research-and-development (R&D) costs produced by the race for the technological frontier in leading-edge sectors. That has stimulated not only a wave of international mergers and acquisitions (the major form of FDI), but has also spawned an array of new forms of international networking among TNCs, including R&D/technology alliances. This technology networking has become so prominent as to deserve a new term: *technoglobalism*. It is even more concentrated than investment: over 90 per cent of the technology agreements are made between companies with their home base in the Triad.

So the third phase of international linkage is centred on capital and technology flows. To a considerable degree, it has tended to exclude the non-OECD countries.

While it is convenient to delineate those three phases of international linkages chronologically, it is important to stress that they are not separate and independent of each other, but rather closely interrelated in a complex fashion. Particularly striking, for example, is the relationship between investment and trade. Thus a large and growing proportion of world trade involves intra-enterprise trade. For Japan and the United States, for example, trade related to FDI now accounts for over half of the total trade flows.

Further, another manifestation of growing international linkages has been the changing nature of trade itself: and increasing proportion of trade among industrialized countries is in technologically sophisticated manufactured products produced by large firms operating in imperfectly competitive markets. In the twenty years between 1966 and 1986, high-technology goods climbed from 14 per cent to 22 per cent of world manufacturing exports. And, finally, over the same period, powerful new players have entered the global arena, most importantly Japan.

Indeed, it has been the concern over the Japanese growth model and the role played by targeting so-called strategic sectors and technologies that have made competitiveness such a high-profile issue in the Triad. Early in the 1980s, the conflict with Japan centred on asymmetry of import access to the Japanese market. While that is still an issue, the targeting debate has widened to a concern about policies allegedly designed to create competitive advantage. While the debate about Japanese targeting is by no means settled, the most important new development during the 1980s has been the 'policy spillover' involving various kinds of support for strategic sectors in the other two Triad members. In addition to those new forms of government intervention, changes have also taken place in the discipline of economics – the climate of ideas – which have undermined the liberal orthodoxy concerning the role of markets versus Governments, in both trade and industrial policy, for leading-edge, high-technology industries.[1]

Thus, in sum, changes in a transformed and far more interdependent international economy have spawned the new international friction manifested in the struggle over leading-edge sectors and technologies, but reflecting also a much more pervasive phenomenon of system friction. The reason is that the battle for market share in leading-edge sectors involves not only competition among TNCs, but rivalry among the different market systems which influence the ability of an enterprise to compete.

SYSTEM FRICTION

Economists have long ignored cultural, historical or institutional differences as factors of significance in market analysis. While interest in international economies has greatly increased, international forecasting models, for example, are based on the assumption that there is only one market model and thus the different 'country blocks' all have identical structural properties.

More recently, however, some economists have urged that a better understanding of institutional (including regulatory) differences among countries may be significant, though it may be difficult to incorporate them into theoretical or econometric modelling. One reason for that changing view in the early 1980s was the markedly different reaction, within OECD, to the second OPEC oil shock (Ostry and Koromzay, 1982). A more important reason for the interest in different system properties, however, was the debate over competitiveness and the challenge of Japan, which stimulated a vast outpouring of analysis of the Japanese paradigm of successful innovation.[2] Indeed, in the analysis of the innovation process more generally, the importance of institutional factors has been increasingly highlighted (Dosi, 1988).[3]

It is clearly beyond the scope of the present article to describe in any detail the burgeoning literature on institutional differences within the Triad. A highly stylized depiction would distinguish three dominant models:

- The United States paradigm of a *pluralist market economy* with its aggressive financial markets is strongly consumer- and short-term oriented. Its strength is dynamism and flexibility. Its dominant ethos is private-sector competition and minimal government. But producer interest groups generate an *ad hoc* 'implicit' industrial policy response.
- The Continental European models are variants of the *social market economy* and involve more extensive government interaction with the 'social partners'. 'Social market' implies a recognition of market imperfections and a governmental responsibility to rectify them as well as to provide public goods. An elastic definition of 'public goods' may sometimes blur the line between the role of the market and the role of the State.
- The Japanese *corporatist market economy* is unique in its long view, in its producer orientation, in its strategic use of cooperation and competition and blending of macro and micro policies, in the close and continuing interface of the State with business and in its remarkable capacity to adapt to external shock.

In that context, it is useful to distinguish two aspects of those systems: the cultural and historical roots that influence behaviour, tastes and institutions on the one hand, and Government policies (which, of course, are also affected by the cultural legacy) on the other. The reason for this dinstinction is that the appropriate domain for international policy cooperation is Government policy, *not* tastes, preferences or behaviour, which should be accepted as 'given', although, of course, not immutable.

As many studies have shown, both cultural legacy and government policy affect the competitiveness of the firm. Fundamental to competitiveness is *innovation*: the search, development and adoption of new products and processes. Innovation stems from the interaction between capabilities *within* the firm and industry and its *external* environment, an omnibus term which comprises government policy (R&D, education, macro policy, trade policy, investment policy, competition policy, capital market regulation, etc.) and behavioural phenomena, such as the tastes and attitudes of consumers, workers, entrepreneurs, etc.[4]

One of the more important insights that is emerging from studies of the innovation process is that some national systems are more consonant (system friendly) with particular technological paradigms than others. An example is the United States leadership, which dates from the end of the nineteenth century and is based on the Fordist paradigm of mass production (Nelson, 1990); Japan is more system friendly to the more flexible manufacturing paradigm of electronics-based technology (Freeman, 1987, pp. 55–90). But systems can adapt and, indeed, the process of market competition is one major transmission mechanism of adaptation.

Moreover, expanded international linkages (especially through FDI) and the revolution in transport, information and communication technologies also create pressures for adaptation and a momentum to convergence that goes well beyond the organization and behaviour of the firm.

There are many who would argue that competition among firms and a gradual process of system convergence are both necessary and sufficient to sustain the health of the world economy as long as Governments refrain from self-defeating protectionist or interventionist policies. But, as pointed out above, the competitiveness of the firm depends not only on its *own* competive strength, but also on the *interaction* of its capabilities with the capabilities of the external environment in which it operates. Smart firms may have the potential to build superb mousetraps, but not to determine the key policy and institutional aspects of their external environments (Dosi, 1988, pp. 1, 121; Roobeek, 1990).

So competition among firms is also competition among systems; the slow 'natural' process of convergence will produce serious discord – system friction – along the way. A globalizing world has a low tolerance for system divergence. Continuing instability and growing pressure for new forms of managed trade are the likely outcomes. But a new approach to mitigating system friction is, in fact, to undertake an international policy process to promote the convergence of those Government policies which are most relevant to the process of innovation. Most of those policies are domestic: *the new international arena is within the borders of the nation-state.*

If a process of international policy cooperation is undertaken to promote convergence, it is important to ask: convergence to what? What is the regulatory model to be promoted? As suggested above, there is no single paradigm 'out there'. Of course, the overall objective must be to promote convergence towards policies that are compatible with market-oriented outcomes. But, as the following discussion will illustrate, in some policy areas no clear-cut guidelines emerge. In such cases, the regulatory standards themselves will be an output of the process of harmonization.

It is instructive to note that two processes of convergence are now in fact under way in the international economy. The most advanced – *locational competition* – is that emerging in Europe, catalysed by 'Europe 1992'. The choice laid out in the 1985 White Paper to base market completion on 'mutual recognition' and the free flow of mobile factors of production launched a process which has been described by one anlayst as follows (Giersch, 1988, p. 5):

> competition between different regulatory systems . . . which is free competition among different locations . . . for internationally mobile resources, such as capital and entrepreneurship and also labour with a high content of human capital.

The implicit answer to the question 'convergence to what?' given by locational competition, would be *that* regulatory system that best reflects the preferences of the mobile resources, especially capital and entrepreneurship. So locational competition is a market-like process by which convergence emerges *ex post*, a result of the invisible hand, so to speak. But even in the case of European locational competition, there will be the need for the visible hand of the Commission in instances of significant divergence of key regulatory instruments, such as competition policy, captial market regulation, social policy and taxation. This process of *ex ante* convergence is likely to prove contentious and difficult – although ultimately successful – because of the enhanced power of Brussels and the considerable political momentum generated by Europe 1992 and the events in Central and Eastern Europe.

The European locational competition process of convergence is attractive because it involves limited supranational intervention, thus minimizing political difficulties as well as the high risk of policy error in a period of rapid change and heightened uncertainty. But it could not be duplicated at a global – or even an OECD – level at the present time, not only because the basic conditions of mutual recognition and the free flow of factors do not exist there, but also, and more importantly, because the divergences in regulation are wider (as between Japan, for example, and the United States) and there is not yet the strong political will at the international level to yield sovereignty or share power that now exists in Europe.

The other very different process of policy convergence recently launched is the bilateral United States–Japan 'structural impediments initiative' (SII), which covers a vast range of subjets – macro and micro polices as well as corporate culture and consumer tastes – and is tied to demonstrable results in the bilateral trade balance. On the micro-policy front, a major issue is the divergence in competition policy between Japan and the United States. But so many other items (both regulatory and cultural) were included in the United States list of over 200 specific suggestions that it has elicited a perception from a number of quarters that the Japanese are different and therefore, special rules are required only for them. Behind that lies a quite unacceptable view of convergence of 'everything'[5] (to the Americal model?). Moreover, another serious danger in SII is that it is unlikely to produce the desired changes in the bilateral trade balance (which is influenced by many factors unrelated to the negotiations) and thus risks inflaming congressional animosity and increasing the pressure for managed trade arrangements. Finally, a process of convergence that is bilateral and non-transparent is hardly the most desirable or effective way of dealing with a fundamental systemic issue.

If the European approach is desirable but unattainable and the bilateral approach likely risky and potentially destabilizing, the only feasible alternative for initiating a process of harmonization is to place the issue in a multilateral forum, which has a representation of not merely the main players (namely, OECD members), but also of developing countries, which inevitably will be affected by any such harmonization. The establishment of a policy regime without their participation will leave a large scope for friction and discord. One option would be to set up, at OECD (along the lines of the ongoing 'dialogue with the dynamic Asian economies'), a special working group, which would include OECD countries and selected non-member countries. Another suggestion could be UNCTC, which has the secretariat expertise and the mandate to cover the broad range of policies relevant to the exercise.

PROMOTION OF CONVERGENCE: A POST-URUGUAY PROGRAMME

The idea behind the promotion of convergence is an extension of the multilateral rules-based system, originally designed for international trade, to include domestic rules which significantly affect enterprise performance (competitiveness) and market access not only for goods and services, but also for investment and technology flows. Since the new international arena has now expanded to domestic concerns, it would be fairer – and would be seen as fairer – if TNCs were to compete under the same set of domestic rules in different countries. Similarly, persistent marked asymmetry of access for investment and technology will generate serious friction because broad overall reciprocity is fundamental to sustaining political support for the multilateral system.

There are at least three questions that would have to be confronted if a 'post-Uruguay programme' were to be launched:

- What policies will be selected?
- How is convergence to be achieved?
- Will convergence lead to overall reciprocity?

Some answers to these questions are set forth below. But it should be recognized that what is being proposed is not only a major new thrust in international policy cooperation, but also an incursion into contentious analytic territory – broadly the determinants of innovation and thus of competitiveness – where there is considerable disagreement among economists and policy analysts. Thus the 'answers' should be regarded as proposals for discussion.

WHAT POLICIES?

The major criterion for policy selection is impact on the innovation process, because, for advanced countries, innovation is the primary determinant of competiveness at the level of the firm and of rising productivity at the national level. But in the case of some policies of undeniable importance in that context (education and training are the best examples), the international friction stems more from access or reciprocity issues than from divergence *per se* (see below). In others, for example fiscal policy, while the impact on innovation via savings, investment and the cost of capital is considerable, there are other forums, specifically Bretton–Woods institutions and the Group of Seven, where a policy coordination process is already under way. Finally, the Uruguay Round agenda includes a number of key items central to the innovation process, such as intellectual property, anti-dumping regulations and industrial and agricultural product standards. A successful outcome will lead to the reduction if not the elimination of policy divergence.

Taking all of this into account, it is proposed that an *initial* list of policies for multilateral coordination should include competition policy, R&D policies, foreign-direct-investment policy and financial market regulation as it affects corporate governance.

In the case of *competition policy*, several high-profile issues are already on the international agenda and provide a useful starting point. As mentioned above, a number of these were prominent in SII (vertical arrangements in the Japanese *keiretsu*, different enforcement procedures in the two countries, etc.). The differing treatment of research and production joint arrangements in the United States, as compared with both Japan and the European Community, has also generated a lively debate in the United States, with a number of experts in the innovation field arguing in favour of anti-trust reforms that go beyond the 1984 National Cooperative Research Act and others warning of the danger of cartel-like behaviour (Jorde and Teece, 1990; Brodley, 1990; Shapiro and Willig, 1990).[6] Thus, it would be useful to begin with an analysis of differences in both vertical and horizontal arrangements (including enforcement) among the Triad members and an assessment of the impact of those differences on performance.

In merger law, which is of increasing importance because of the large increase in transnational mergers and acquisitions (including newer modes, such as strategic alliances), there does not appear to be any difference in *substantive* law, the language is remarkably similar in most jurisdictions. The divergence – and conflict – arises in *application*, since the general prohibition against mergers which will (or are likely to) substantially lessen competition leaves ample scope for discretion on the part of the authorities. The situation is even more complicated in the United States, where all 50 States can exercise jurisdiction independently from the federal Government. For corporations planning transnational mergers, the degree of uncertainty created by differences in enforcement of merger law is a major impediment to rational decision-making.

In the area of R&D, a number of policy issues need probing. One of the most obvious is Government subsidies, including sectorally targeted tax incentives. The presence of large externalities (that is, benefits that spread beyond the firm to other firms or industries) has long provided a rationale for Government intervention in basic research, where private firms have little incentive to invest because the benefits cannot be fully captured (appropriated) in profits. (Another rationale is that pure science is a public good.) But the new debate about subsidies centres not on basic research, but on the middle ground between basic research and proprietary technology (so-called generic research), usually involving cooperative arrangements between firms organized and partly funded by Governments (thus raising, in addition to the subsidy question, the competition-policy issue mentioned above).

The difficulty of defining this 'middle ground' requires a good deal of analysis and discussion before proceeding to new international disciplines. As experts in innovation have emphasized, this is because there is no clear-cut boundary between basic research, generic technology and commercial application (the 'linear' model of innovation), but rather a complex nexus of interaction and feedback (the 'simultaneous' or network model of innovation) (Jorde and Teece, 1990, pp. 76–78; Ziman, 1990). The extent and nature of Government intervention which affects this more realistic model of innovation goes well beyond subsidies. Indeed, subsidies may be the least important factor, as the Japanese innovation paradigm with its unique 'blend of cooperation, competition, and shared information and objectives' (Ostry, 1990, p. 64) amply demonstrates. So progress on the subsidies front, while certainly important and desirable, should be seen as only one part of a much broader issue, which is the impact of Government policies on the innovation process.

Finally, there is the thorny question of membership in Government-sponsored R&D consortia. There has already been a dispute over the membership of foreign subsidiaries in the European consortium Jessi and the American Sematech (Ostry, 1990, pp. 66–75). The basic reason for the exclusion (seldom spelled out) rests on the concept of strategic industries or technologies. There is no settled definition of that concept and indeed the word 'strategic' has multiple meanings and its use is more confusing than enlightening. One definition of a strategic sector would be one for which an exploitable advantage for a foreign firm or another country could have serious, widespread and long-term consequences. The risks would be especially high if the foreign supplier were a monopoly or a cartel, and high sunk costs reduced the credible threat of entry (Flamm, 1990). In such industries, the major means of appropriating returns to product innovation comes from 'first mover' advantage, that is getting there first and building up continuing and cumulative product improvement (as in semi-conductors, computers, telecommunication, airframes and aircraft engines) (Levin *et al.*, 1990). Thus, the question of how to define 'strategic' and other questions (for example, what is a 'foreign' firm or, indeed, is there a need for a supranational competition authority?) will have to be confronted before disciplines or codes of behaviour on Government-sponsored consortia can be agreed.

In the *FDI policy* sphere, the Uruguay Round of GATT is dealing with a limited aspect of that issue in the trade-related investment measures (TRIMs) negotiations. Essentially, what is at issue is some form of discipline on trade-distorting measures, such as performance requirements of one kind or another. With the benefit of hindsight it is now clear that the push for TRIMs by the United States reflected the world of the 1970s and early 1980s, when there was widespread hostility in the developing countries to TNCs. The world of the 1990s will likely be dominated by a competitive bidding for investment as the countries of Central and Eastern Europe and the developing countries seek to supplement their shortage of domestic savings and technology.

Within the OECD area, the main problem is less likely to be overt investment inducements (tax holidays, subsidies, etc.) than direct and indirect measures to influence the content or quality of investment, such as local content regulation or rules of origin.[7] Another FDI issue, already evident in the United States, relates to the ownership of strategic assets (in a national security rather than a commercial sense). A large number of bills that would constrain FDI are currently pending in the Congress of the United States.

But the major source of system friction in the investment area relates to asymmetry of access, or overall reciprocity. Indeed, the United States has announced that it will raise the issue of its 'investment imbalance' with Japan in a new round of SII follow-up, citing the 1989 figures of $32.5 billion of Japanese investment in the United States versus $1.64 billion of United States investment in Japan. Within the European Community, the reciprocity question has surfaced in the differences in ease of take-overs (mergers), the chief mechanism of FDI, among different member countries, especially the United Kingdom versus Germany. This relates to the fourth policy issue: *financial market regulation* as it affects corporate governance.

A recent study prepared for the European Commission (Booz-Allen Acquisition Services, 1989) documents the marked differences in take-over activity in the European Community during the 1985–1988 period and examines the reasons for those differences, that is the obstacles to mergers. Those include a long list of structural differences (especially size and sophistication of equity markets and the role of banks in corporate ownership and control); and a variety of regulatory differences (for example, anti-trust, company law, labour law and stock market regulations governing take-overs). Much of this is also relevant to the Japanese system, which, in a number of respects, resembles that of Germany. In particular, in both countries, companies are more heavily owned by banks and other corporations.[8]

While some of those differences can be reduced by regulatory changes (and, indeed, the European Commission will be undertaking to implement a number of these), this study, and numerous others, have emphasized the structural differences between the United Kingdom and United States model, on the one hand, and the German and Japanese model on the other. The differences in composition of ownership, that is the respective role of shareholders versus banks (also a reflection of the cultural legacy of countries), will be much more resistant to change. This is very important because the composition of ownership has a significant influence on the way corporations are managed, although the popular image of a clear-cut dichotomy between the Anglo-Saxon short-term 'financially driven' versus the German-Japanese long-term 'industrial growth' model is too simplistic.[9]

In sum, this complex area of financial markets impacts both on corporate governance (and, therefore, on competitiveness) and on reciprocity of access for FDI. There is clearly some scope for regulatory harmonization, but the structural differences are more deep seated and will be difficult to change; as a consequence, the reciprocity issue is likely to be a continuing source of friction as it is in goods markets and as it will be in the technology area. Before turning to the reciprocity question, however, the second question needs to be addressed.

THE PROCESS OF HARMONIZATION

The objectives of the process of harmonization in a multilateral forum would be to:

- Analyse, for each policy, the differences among countries, perhaps starting with the Triad;
- Assess the main impact of those differences on industrial and trade performance;
- Draw up a mutually agreed set of policy *guidelines*, a *timetable* for reform, and a *means* of monitoring progress (surveillance).

Those are extremely complex problems and would require skilled staff assistance in providing objective analysis and information. There is a good reason to launch the process as quickly as possible. It would be desirable, in the analytic phase, to include business representatives and outside experts. The process of promoting policy convergence itself would require a special intergovernmental committee.

Because the subject matter covers a number of areas, the effective operation of the committee would involve a greater degree of coordination within national capitals than is customary. But greater coordination within national capitals is, of course, desirable in and of itself, however difficult to launch and maintain. In most national capitals and in the general public there is no real understanding that the new international arena is within the border. Separating trade policy from competition policy, R&D, financial market regulation and so forth only made sense when tariffs were the most important obstacle to international linkage.

Finally, it is important to emphasize again that, while policy convergence is a desirable objective to pursue in international co-operation, it will not miraculously dissolve all points of international friction. Different cultural legacies will affect consumer tastes and preferences and corporate behaviour. National infrastructures (especially education and training) are extremely important, as is macropolicy. And, finally, convergence may reduce but will not eliminate marked asymmetry of access in the areas of investment and technology.

RECIPROCITY[10]

The concept of reciprocity underlying GATT is that of a broad balance of benefits in market access for goods. For a variety of historical reasons, even after more than forty years of negotiations, there still exists today some examples of marked asymmetry of access to markets for goods. This has been a source of considerable political friction, eroding the commitment to a rules-based multilateral system.[11]

As noted before, in the case of FDI, there are significant differences even among countries in OECD in ease of access via mergers (the main vehicle of investment *flows*). In addition, there are large differences in the present *stock* of FDI, with the most marked asymmetry apparent in Japan.[12] There would be little purpose in focusing on the stock issue, however, which is largely the result of past policies, including overt investment barriers, now for the most part dismantled. The issue of *flows* relates less to overt barriers than to structural characteristics of financial markets and regulatory differences across a number of different policies. Thus policy harmonization will narrow the asymmetry over time and an ongoing, multilateral surveillance process should help contain the political friction stemming from the basic notion of 'unfairness', which is at the heart of the reciprocity debate. This would be facilitated by making the process as transparent as possible through publication of analytical studies and 'progress reports' at ministerial meetings, for example.

The question of reciprocity of access in technology is in some respects more complex. A firm secures the information necessary to solve technological problems from many sources. The relevant knowledge base varies according to the particular technology, and a distinction can be made between the degree of 'publicness' and universality versus 'tacitness' and specificity (Dosi, 1988; Nelson, 1990).[13] Scientific inputs are typically public and so is much generic technology, although to access such inputs requires a sophisticated base in research and development. But public knowledge is itself complementary to the more specific and tacit knowledge generated within the firm. And it is the firm-specific knowledge which results in new products and processes.

The crucial point in those distinctions in that, with the necessary investment in research and development, it is easier to access the *public* than the *tacit* part of the knowledge base. If, as in the case of the United States, the knowledge system is characterized by a much heavier weight of unversity-based research and technology than that of Europe and Japan, that system is *structurally* more accessible.

But there are also avenues of access to tacit, specific knowledge: hiring employees from innovating firms or buying new high-technology start-up firms are examples. Again, in systems where employee mobility is greater, small start-up firms more prevalent and take-overs easier, there will be a greater *structural* accessibility of the non-public knowledge base.

Thus, as in the case of investment, structural characteristics of different systems will generate asymmetry of access to technology. It will be essential to examine these issues in far greater depth and search for policies either to reduce or to compensate for differential access. Moreover, there is one relevant policy issue that could be tackled more quickly. This concerns the question of membership of foreign subsidiaries in Government-sponsored research consortia where specific reciprocity conditions could be spelled out as a first step in dealing with the broader issues raised earlier. The worst way of dealing with the problem of access asymmetry would be to attempt to stem the flow of knowledge across borders.

CONCLUSIONS

In the present article, a proposal has been put forward for promoting the convergence of a range of policies selected because of their direct or indirect impact on innovation and competitiveness. The list is suggestive, not exhaustive. Other candidates could include the taxation of TNCs; standards and testing procedures in selected leading-edge sectors; intellectual property norms; and standards and enforcement procedures to further the convergence process launched in GATT. The alternatives to promoting convergence are continuing friction, instability and aggressive bilateralism or an exclusionary form of managed trade.

Finally, such an initiative should be seen as a complement to the efforts of the Uruguay Round to strengthen GATT. If those efforts proved successful, and in particular if a World Trade Organization (WTO) is established, it would be important to ensure that strong informational links are forged between the chosen multilateral forum and the secretariat of WTO. In the early 1980s, much of the analytical work on trade and investment in services, intellectual property, investment and agriculture was carried out by OECD, the World Bank and UNCTC, and proved invaluable in helping launch and facilitate the Uruguay Round negotiations. Perhaps at the end of the new harmonization initiative proposed in this article, one could foresee a set of codes developed and then transferred to WTO for broader application. After all, the basic purpose of international policy cooperation is to further global integration by extending and adapting the multilateral rules-based system.

NOTES

** This article is based on a paper prepared by the author for a symposium organized by OECD in Paris on 30 October 1990.
1 For an account of policy developments and of the new international trade theory in this context, see Ostry (1990, chapter 3).
2 See Ostry (1990, chapter 3) for a select bibliography.
3 Many of the papers prepared for the OECD Conference on Technology and Economic Policy (TEP) focus on cultural, historical and institutional factors.
4 See Dosi (1988) for a literature survey and bibliography.
5 See Bhagwati (1989, pp. 45–46), who argues that 'if everything becomes a question of fair trade, the only outcome will be to remove altogether the possibility of ever agreeing to a rule-oriented trading system'.
6 See also Ostry (1990, chapter 3) for a discussion of NCRA as a response to the Japanese innovation paradigm.
7 See Ostry (1990, pp. 46–52) for a discussion of the European Community anti-dumping and rules-of-origin rules.
8 On the Japan – United States comparison, see Kester (1986).
9 For a discussion of the theoretical issues, see Williamson (1988) and Jensen and Meckling (1976).

10 For a discussion of the evolution of the concept and of the distinction between the basic commitment to symmetric rights and obligations in the contract and reciprocity as a negotiating modality, see Bhagwati (1988, pp. 35–37).
11 For a discussion about the reasons for Japan's alleged low import propensity, see Ostry (1990, pp. 9–10) and references cited therein. The issue of reducing or eliminating the 'special and differential' treatment for the more advanced developing countries has pervaded a number of negotiating groups in the Uruguay Round.
12 In 1989, the ratio of Japanese investment abroad to foreign investment in Japan was 23.6, up from 20.6 in 1984. See OECD (1987) and also Terry (1990).
13 See references cited in Dosi (1988).

REFERENCES

Bhagwati, Jagdish (1988). *Protectionism*. Cambridge, Massachusetts: The MIT Press.
——— (1989). U.S. trade policy today. Paper presented at Columbia University Conference on Trade Policy (8 September).
Booz-Allen Acquisition Services (1989). Studies on obstacles to take-over bids in the European Community: executive summary, prepared for the Commission of the European Communities, PGXV-B-2 (December).
Brodley, Joseph F. (1990). Antitrust law and innovation cooperation. *The Journal of Economic Perspectives*, 4, pp. 97–112.
Dosi, Giovanni (1988). Sources, procedures and microeconomic effects of innovation. *Journal of Economic Literature*, 26 (September), pp. 1120–1171.
Flamm, Ken (1990). Semiconductors. In *Europe 1992: An American Perspective*, Gary Clyde Hufbauer, ed., Washington, DC: Brookings Institution, pp. 225–292.
Freeman, Christopher (1987). *Technology Policy and Economic Performance: Lesson from Japan*. London: Pinto Press.
Giersch, Herbert (1988). Europe 1992 in an open world order. Paper presented at the Meeting of the European Council of Economists, Conference Board Session, Hamburg (20 October).
Jensen, Michael C., and William H. Meckling (1976). Theory of the firm: managerial behaviour, agency costs and ownership structure. *Journal of Financial Economics*, 3 (October), pp. 305–360.
Jorde, Thomas M., and David J. Teece (1990). Innovation and cooperation: implications for competition and antitrust. *The Journal of Economic Perspectives*, 4, pp. 75–96.
Kester, W. Carl (1986). Capital and ownership structure: a comparison of United States and Japanese manufacturing corporations. *Financial Management*, 15 (Spring), pp. 5–16.
Levin, Richard C., *et al.* (1987). Appropriating the returns from industrial research and development. *Brookings Papers on Economic Activity*, 3, pp. 783–832.

Nelson, Richard (1990). U.S. technological leadership: where did it come from and where did it go? *Research Policy*, 19, pp. 117–132.

OECD (1987). *International Investment and Multinational Enterprises.* Paris: OECD.

Ostry, Sylvia (1990). *Governments and Corporations in a Shrinking World: Trade and Innovation Policies in the United States, Europe and Japan.* New York: Council on Foreign Relations.

────── and Val Koromzay (1982). The United States and Europe: coping with change. *OECD Observer*, 16 (May), pp. 9–12.

Roobeek, Annemicke J. M. (1990). *Beyond the Technology Race: An Analysis of Technology Policy in Seven Industrial Countries.* Amsterdam: Elsevier Science Publishers.

Shapiro, Carl, and Robert D. Willig (1990). On the antitrust treatment of production joint ventures. *The Journal of Economic Perspectives*, 4, pp. 113–130.

Terry, Edith (1990). Looking in from the outside. *The Globe and Mail Report on Business* (26 September), pp. B1–2.

United Nations Centre on Transnational Corporations, *World Investment Report 1991: The Triad in Foreign Direct Investment.* Sales No. E.91.II.A.12.

Williamson, Oliver E. (1988). Corporate finance and corporate governance. *Journal of Finance*, (July), pp. 467–491.

Ziman, John (1990). Restructuring links: or darning a seamless web. London: Science Policy Support Group. OECD Conference on Technology and Competitiveness, Paris (24–27 June), (mimeo).

Select list of publications of the UNCTAD Division on Transnational Corporations and Investment

A. INDIVIDUAL STUDIES

Small and Medium-sized Transnational Corporations. Executive Summary and Report of the Osaka Conference. 60 pp. Free of charge.

World Investment Report 1994: Transnational Corporations, Employment and the Workplace. 482 pp. Sales No. E.94.II.A.14. $45.

World Investment Report 1994: Transnational Corporations, Employment and the Workplace. An Executive Summary. 34 pp. Free of charge.

Liberalizing International Transactions in Services: A Handbook. 182 pp. Sales No. E.94.II.A.11. $45. (Joint publication with the World Bank.)

World Investment Directory. Volume IV: Latin America and the Caribbean. 478 pp. Sales No. E.94.II.A.10. $65.

Conclusions on Accounting and Reporting by Transnational Corporations. 47 pp. Sales No. E.94.II.A.9. $25.

Accounting, Valuation and Privatization. 190 pp. Sales No. E.94.II.A.3. $25.

Environmental Management in Transnational Corporations: Report on the Benchmark Corporate Environment Survey. 278 pp. Sales No. E.94.II.A.2. $29.95.

Management Consulting: A Survey of the Industry and Its Largest Firms. 100 pp. Sales No. E.93.II.A.17. $25.

Transnational Corporations: A Selective Bibliography, 1991–1992. 736 pp. Sales No. E.93.II.A.16. $75. (English/French.)

Small and Medium-sized Transnational Corporations: Role, Impact and Policy Implications. 242 pp. Sales No. E.93.II.A.15. $35.

World Investment Report 1993: Transnational Corporations and Integrated International Production. 290 pp. Sales No. E.93.II.A.14. $45.

World Investment Report 1993: Transnational Corporations and Integrated International Production. An Executive Summary. 31 pp. ST/CTC/159. Free of charge.

Foreign Investment and Trade Linkages in Developing Countries. 108 pp. Sales No. E.93.II.A.12. $18.

World Investment Directory 1992. Volume III: Developed Countries. 532 pp. Sales No. E.93.II.A.9. $75.

Transnational Corporations from Developing Countries: Impact on Their Home Countries. 116 pp. Sales No. E.93.II.A.8. $15.

Debt-Equity Swaps and Development. 150 pp. Sales No. E.93.II.A.7. $35.

From the Common Market to EC 92: Regional Economic Integration in the European Community and Transnational Corporations. 134 pp. Sales No. E.93.II.A.2. $25.

World Investment Directory 1992. Volume II: Central and Eastern Europe. 432 pp. Sales No. E.93.II.A.1. $65. (Joint publication with ECE.)

World Investment Report 1992: Transnational Corporations as Engines of Growth: An Executive Summary. 30 pp. Sales No. E.92.II.A.24.

The East-West Business Directory 1991/1992. 570 pp. Sales No. E.92.II.A.20. $65.

World Investment Report 1992: Transnational Corporations as Engines of Growth. 356 pp. Sales No. E.92.II.A.19. $45.

World Investment Directory 1992. Volume I: Asia and the Pacific. 356. pp. Sales No. E.92.II.A.11. $65.

Climate Change and Transnational Corporations: Analysis and Trends. 110 pp. Sales No. E.92.II.A.7. $16.50.

Foreign Direct Investment and Transfer of Technology in India. 150 pp. Sales No. E.92.II.A.3. $20.

The Determinants of Foreign Direct Investment: A Survey of the Evidence. 84 pp. Sales No. E.92.II.A.2. $12.50.

The Impact of Trade-Related Investment Measures on Trade and Development: Theory, Evidence and Policy Implications. 108 pp. Sales No. E.91.II.A.19. $17.50. (Joint publication, UNCTC and UNCTAD.)

Transnational Corporations and Industrial Hazards Disclosure. 98 pp. Sales No. E.91.II.A.18. $17.50.

Transnational Business Information: A Manual of Needs and Sources. 216 pp. Sales No. E.91.II.A.13. $45.

World Investment Report 1991: The Triad in Foreign Direct Investment. 108 pp. Sales No. E.91.II.A.12. $25.

Transnational Corporations: A Selective Bibliography, 1988–1990. 618 pp. Sales No. E.91.II.A.10. $65. (English/French.)

Transnational Corporations in South Africa: A List of Companies with Investments and Disinvestments. 282 pp. Sales No. E.91.II.A.9. $50.00.

University Curriculum on Transnational Corporations*

    Vol. I   *Economic Development.* 188 pp. Sales No. E.91.II.A.5. $20.00.

    Vol. II   *International Business.* 156 pp. Sales No. E.91.II.A.6. $20.00.

    Vol. III *International Law.* 180 pp. Sales No. E.91.II.A.7. $20.00.

    * The Set: Sales No. E.91.II.A.8. $50.00.

Accountancy Development in Africa: Challenge of the 1990s. 206 pp. Sales No. E.91.II.A.2. $25. (Also available in French.)

Directory of the World's Largest Service Companies: Series I. 834 pp. ISSN 1014–8507. (Joint publication, UNCTC and Moody's Investors Service, Inc.) $99.

The Challenge of Free Economic Zones in Central and Eastern Europe. 444 pp. Sales No. E.90.II.A.27. $75.

Debt Equity Conversions: A Guide For Decision-Makers. 150 pp. Sales No. E.90.II.A.22. $27.50.

Transnational Corporations and Manufacturing Exports from Developing Countries. 124 pp. Sales No. E.90.II.A.21. $25.

Transnational Corporations in the Transfer of New and Emerging Technologies to Developing Countries. 141 pp. Sales No. E.90.II.A.20. $27.50.

Transnational Banks and the International Debt Crisis. 157 pp. Sales No. E.90.II.A.19. $22.50.

Transborder Data Flows and Mexico: A Technical Paper. 194 pp. Sales No. E.90.II.A.17. $27.50.

Transnational Corporations, Services and Uruguay Round. 252 pp. Sales No. E.90.II.A.11. $28.50.

The Uruguay Round: Services in the World Economy. 220 pp. ISBN 0-8213-1374-6. (Joint publication, UNCTC and World Bank.) $13.50.

Transnational Corporations in the Plastics Industry. 167 pp. Sales No. E.90.II.A.1. $20.

Objectives and Concepts Underlying Financial Statements. 32 pp. Sales No. E.89.II.A.18. $8.

Services and Development: The Role of Foreign Direct Investment and Trade. 187 pp. Sales No. E.89.II.A.17. $20.

Transnational Corporations in South Africa and Namibia: A Selective Bibliography. 98 pp. Sales No. E.89.II.A.13. $12.

Transnational Corporations in the Construction and Design Engineering Industry. 60 pp. Sales No. E.89.II.A.6. $9.

Foreign Direct Investment and Transnational Corporations in Services. 229 pp. Sales No. E.89.II.A.1. $26.

Data Goods and Data Services in the Socialist Countries of Eastern Europe. 103 pp. Sales No. E.88.II.A.20. $13.50.

Conclusions on Accounting and Reporting by Transnational Corporations: The Intergovernmental Working Group of Experts on International Standards of Accounting and Reporting. 58 pp. Sales No. E.88.II.A.18. $7.50. (Also available in Arabic, Chinese, French, Russian, Spanish.)

Executive Summary. Transnational Corporations in World Development: Trends and Prospects. 66 pp. Sales No. E.88.II.A.15. $3.

Joint Ventures as a Form of International Economic Co-operation: Background Documents of the High-Level Seminar Organized by the United Nations Centre on Transnational Corporations in Co-operation with the USSR State Foreign Economic Commission and the USSR State Committee on Science and Technology, 10 March 1988, Moscow. 210 pp. Sales No. E.88.II.A.12. $21.

Transnational Corporations: A Selective Bibliography, 1983–1987.
   Vol. I 441 pp. Sales No. E.88.II.A.9. $45.
   Vol. II 463 pp. Sales No. E.88.II.A.10. $49.

Transnational Corporations in World Development: Trends and Prospects 628 pp. Sales No. E.88.II.A.7. $56. (Also available in Arabic, Chinese, French, Russian, Spanish.)

International Income Taxation and Developing Countries. 108 pp. Sales No. E.88.II.A.6. $13.50.

Transnational Corporations in Biotechnology. 136 pp. Sales No. E.88.II.A.4. $17.

Foreign Direct Investment in the People's Republic of China: Report of the Round-Table Organized by the United Nations Centre on Transnational Corporations in Co-operation with the Ministry of Foreign Economic Relations and Trade, People's Republic of China, Beijing, 25 and 26 May 1987. 115 pp. Sales No. E.88.II.A.3. $15.50.

Bilateral Investment Treaties. 194 pp. Sales No. E.88.II.A.1. $20.

Consolidated List of Products Whose Consumption and/or Sale Have Been Banned, Withdrawn, Severely Restricted or Not Approved by Governments, Second Issue. (UNCTC in collaboration with FAO, WHO, ILO and other relevant intergovernmental organizations.) 655 pp. Sales No. E.87.IV.1. $60.

UNCTC Bibliography, 1974–1987. 83 pp. Sales No. 87.II.A.23. $12.

Licence Agreements in Developing Countries. 108 pp. Sales No. E.87.II.A.21. $13.50.

Transnational Corporations and Non-fuel Primary Commodities in Developing Countries. 89 pp. Sales No. E.87.II.A.17. $10.

Transnational Corporations in the Man-made Fibre, Textile and Clothing Industries. 154 pp. Sales No. E.87.II.A.11. $19.

Transnational Corporations and Technology Transfer: Effects and Policy Issues. 77 pp. Sales No. E.87.II.A.4. $11.

Analysis of Engineering and Technical Consultancy Contracts. 517 pp. Sales No. E.86.II.A.4. $45.

Transnational Corporations in the International Semiconductor Industry. 471 pp. Sales No. E.86.II.A.1. $41.

Trends and Issues in Foreign Direct Investment and Related Flows. 96 pp. Sales No. E.85.II.A.15. $11.

Environmental Aspects of the Activities of Transnational Corporations: A Survey. 114 pp. Sales No. E.85.II.A.11. $12.50.

Transnational Corporations and International Trade: Selected Issues. 93 pp. Sales No. E.85.II.A.4. $11.

B. SERIAL PUBLICATIONS

UNCTC Current Studies, Series A

No. 1. Patrick Robinson, *The Question of a Reference to International Law in the United Nations Code of Conduct on Transnational Corporations.* 22 pp. Sales No. E.86.II.A.5. $4.

No. 2. Detlev Vagts, *The Question of a Reference to International Obligations in the United Nations Code of Conduct on Transnational Corporations: A Different View.* 17 pp. Sales No. E.86.II.A.11. $4.

No. 3. *Foreign Direct Investment in Latin America: Recent Trends, Prospects and Policy Issues.* 28 pp. Sales No. E.86.II.A.14. $5.

No. 4. *The United Nations Code of Conduct on Transnational Corporations.* 80 pp. Sales No. E.86.II.A.15. $9.50. (Also published by Graham & Trotman, London/Dordrect/Boston. $31.50.)

No. 5. *Transnational Corporations and the Electronics Industries of ASEAN Economies.* 55 pp. Sales No. E.87.II.A.13. $7.50.

No. 6. *Technology Acquisition under Alternative Arrangements with Transnational Corporations: Selected Industrial Case Studies in Thailand.* 55 pp. Sales No. E.87.II.A.14. $7.50.

No. 7. *Foreign Direct Investment, the Service Sector and International Banking.* 71 pp. Sales No. E.87.II.A.15. $9. (Also published by Graham & Trotman, London/Dordrecht/Boston. $25.)

No. 8. *The Process of Transnationalization and Transnational Mergers.* 91 pp. Sales No. E.89.II.A.4. $12.

No. 9. *Transnational Corporations and the Growth of Services: Some Conceptual and Theoretical Issues.* 96 pp. Sales No. E.89.II.A.5. $12.

No. 10. *Transnational Service Corporations and Developing Countries: Impact and Policy Issues.* 50 pp. Sales No. E.89.II.A.14. $7.50.

No. 11. *Transnational Corporations and International Economic Relations: Recent Developments and Selected Issues.* 50 pp. Sales No. E.89.II.A.15. $7.50.

No. 12. *New Approaches to Best-practice Manufacturing: The Role of Transnational Corporations and Implications for Developing Countries.* 76 pp. Sales No. E.90.II.A.13. $12.50.

No. 13. *Key Concepts in International Investment Arrangements and Their Relevance to Negotiations on International Transactions in Services.* 66 pp. Sales No. E.90.II.A.3. $9.

No. 14. *The Role of Free Economic Zones in the USSR and Eastern Europe.* 84 pp. Sales No. E.90.II.A.5. $10.

No. 15. *Regional Economic Integration and Transnational Corporations in the 1990s: Europe 1992, North America and Developing Countries.* 52 pp. Sales No. E.90.II.A.14. $12.50.

No. 16. *The New Code Environment.* 54 pp. Sales No. E.90.II.A.7. $7.50.

No. 17. *Government Policies and Foreign Direct Investment.* 68 pp. Sales No. E.91.II.A.20. $12.50.

No. 18. *Foreign Direct Investment and Industrial Restructuring in Mexico.* 114 pp. Sales No. E.92.II.A.9. $12.

No. 19. *New Issues in the Uruguay Round of Multilateral Trade Negotiations.* 52 pp. Sales No. E.90.II.A.15. $12.50.

No. 20. *Foreign Direct Investment, Debt and Home Country Policies.* 50 pp. Sales No. E.90.II.A.16. $12.

No. 22. *Transnational Banks and the External Indebtedness of Developing Countries: Impact of Regulatory Changes.* 48 pp. Sales No. E.92.II.A.10. $12.

No. 23. *The Transnationalization of Service Industries: An Empirical Analysis of the Determinants of Foreign Direct Investment by Transnational Service Corporations.* 62 pp. Sales No. E.93.II.A.3. $15.00.

No. 24. *Intellectual Property Rights and Foreign Direct Investment.* 108 pp. Sales No. E.93.II.A.10. $20.

No. 25. *International Tradability in Insurance Services.* 54 pp. Sales No. E.93.II.A.11. $20.

No. 26. *Explaining and Forecasting Regional Flows of Foreign Direct Investment.* 58 pp. Sales No. E.94.II.A.5. $25.

UNCTC Advisory Studies, Series B

No. 1. *Natural Gas Clauses in Petroleum Arrangements.* 54 pp. Sales No. E.87.II.A.3. $8.

No. 2. *Arrangements Between Joint Venture Partners in Developing Countries.* 43 pp. Sales No. E.87.II.A.5. $6.

No. 3. *Financial and Fiscal Aspects of Petroleum Exploitation.* 43 pp. Sales No. E.87.II.A.10. $6.

No. 4. *International Debt Rescheduling: Substantive Issues and Techniques.* 91 pp. Sales No. E.89.II.A.10. $10.

No. 5. *Negotiating International Hotel Chain Management Agreements.* 60 pp. Sales No. E.90.II.A.8. $9.

No. 6. *Curricula for Accounting Education for East-West Joint Ventures in Centrally Planned Economies.* 86 pp. Sales No. E.90.II.A.2. $10.

No. 7. *Joint Venture Accounting in the USSR: Direction for Change.* 46 pp. Sales No. E.90.II.A.26. $12.

No. 10. *Formulation and Implementation of Foreign Investment Policies: Selected Key Issues.* 84 pp. Sales No. E.92.II.A.21. $12.

The United Nations Library on Transnational Corporations. (Published by Routledge on behalf of the United Nations.)

Set A (Boxed set of four volumes. ISBN 0–415–08554–3. £350):

Volume One: *The Theory of Transnational Corporations.* 464 pp.

Volume Two: *Transnational Corporations: A Historical Perspective.* 464 pp.

Volume Three: *Transnational Corporations and Economic Development.* 448 pp.

Volume Four: *Transnational Corporations and Business Strategy.* 416 pp.

Set B (Boxed set of four volumes. ISBN 0–415–08555–1. £350):

Volume Five: *International Financial Management.* 400 pp.

Volume Six: *Organization of Transnational Corporations.* 400 pp.

Volume Seven: *Governments and Transnational Corporations.* 352 pp.

Volume Eight: *Transnational Corporations and International Trade and Payments.* 320 pp.

Set C (Boxed set of four volumes. ISBN 0–415–08556–X. £350):

Volume Nine: *Transnational Corporations and Regional Economic Integration.* 331 pp.

Volume Ten: *Transnational Corporations and the Exploitation of Natural Resources.* 397 pp.

Volume Eleven: *Transnational Corporations and Industrialization.* 425 pp.

Volume Twelve: *Transnational Corporations in Services.* 437 pp.

Set D (Boxed set of four volumes. ISBN 0–415–08557–8. £350):

Volume Thirteen: *Cooperative Forms of Transnational Corporation Activity.* 419 pp.

Volume Fourteen: *Transnational Corporations: Transfer Pricing and Taxation.* 330 pp.

Volume Fifteen: *Transnational Corporations: Market Structure and Industrial Performance.* 383 pp.

Volume Sixteen: *Transnational Corporations and Human Resources.* 429 pp.

Box E (Boxed set of four volumes. ISBN 0–415–08558–6. £350):

Volume Seventeen: *Transnational Corporations and Innovatory Activities.* 447 pp.

Volume Eighteen: *Transnational Corporations and Technology Transfer to Developing Countries.* 486 pp.

Volume Nineteen: *Transnational Corporations and National Law.* 322 pp.
Volume Twenty: *Transnational Corporations: The International Legal Framework.* 545 pp.

International Accounting and Reporting Issues:
1984 Review. 122 pp. Sales No. E.85.II.A.2. $13.50.
1985 Review. 141 pp. Sales No. E.85.II.A.13. $15.
1986 Review. 158 pp. Sales No. E.86.II.A.16. $15.
1987 Review. 140 pp. Sales No. E.88.II.A.8. $17.
(Also published by Graham & Trotman, London/Dordrecht/Boston. $65.)
1988 Review. 95 pp. Sales No. E.88.II.A.3. $12.
1989 Review. 152 pp. Sales No. E.90.II.A.4. $12.
1990 Review. 254 pp. Sales No. E.91.II.A.3. $25.
1991 Review. 244 pp. Sales No. E.92.II.A.8. $25.
1992 Review. 328 pp. Sales No. E.93.II.A.6. $25.

National Legislation and Regulations Relating to Transnational Corporations:
Vol. I   (Part One) 302 pp. Sales No. E.78.II.A.3. $16.
Vol. I   (Part Two – Supplement) 114 pp. Sales No. E.80.II.A.5. $9.
Vol. II   338 pp. Sales No. E.83.II.A.7. $33.
Vol. III 345 pp. Sales No. E.83.II.A.15. $33.
Vol. IV 241 pp. Sales No. E.85.II.A.14. $23.
Vol. V   246 pp. Sales No. E.86.II.A.3. $23.
Vol. VI 322 pp. Sales No. E.87.II.A.6. $45.
Vol. VII 320 pp. Sales No. E.89.II.A.9. $36.

Transnational Corporations in South Africa and Namibia: United Nations Public Hearings:
Reports of the Panel of Eminent Persons and of the Secretary-General. 242 pp. Sales No. E.86.II.A.6. $65.
*Verbatim Records. 300 pp. Sales No. E.86.II.A.7.
Statements and Submissions. 518 pp. Sales No. E.86.II.A.8. $54.
Policy Instruments and Statements. 444 pp. Sales No. E.86.II.A.9.
Four-volume set – $200.
*May not be purchased separately.

Transnational Corporations in South Africa: Second United Nations Public Hearings, 1989:
Report of the Panel of Eminent Persons, Background Documentation. 162 pp. Sales No. E.90.II.A.6. $19.
Statements and Submission. 209 pp. Sales No. E.90.II.A.20. $21.

Transnational Corporations (formerly *The CTC Reporter*). Published three times a year. Annual subscription price: $35; individual issues $15.

Transnationals, a quarterly newsletter, is available free of charge.

United Nations publications may be obtained from bookstores and distributors throughout the world. Please consult your bookstore or write to:

United Nations Publications

Sales Section	OR	Sales Section
Room DC2-0853		United Nations Office at Geneva
United Nations Secretariat		Palais des Nations
New York, NY 10017		CH-1211 Geneva 10
USA		Switzerland
Tel: (1-212) 963-8302 or (800) 253-9646		Tel: (41-22) 917-1234
Fax: (1-212) 963-3489		Fax: (41-22) 917-0123

All prices are quoted in United States dollars.

For further information on the work of the Transnational Corporations and Investment Division, UNCTAD, please address enquiries to:

United Nations Conference on Trade and Development
Division on Transnational Corporations and Investment
Palais des Nations, Room E-8006
CH-1211 Geneva 10
Switzerland
Tel: (41-22) 907-5707
Fax: (41-22) 907-0194

Questionnaire

[TITLE]

In order to improve the quality and relevance of the work of the UNCTAD Division on Transnational Corporations and Investment, it would be useful to receive the views of readers on this and other similar publications. It would therefore be greatly appreciated if you could complete the following questionnaire and return to:

Readership Survey
UNCTAD Division on Transnational Corporations and Investment
United Nations Office in Geneva
Palais des Nations
Room E-8006
CH-1211 Geneva 10
Switzerland

1. Name and address of respondent (optional): _____
   _____
   _____

2. Which of the following best describes your area of work?
   Government   ○   Public enterprise   ○
   Private enterprise   ○   Academic or research
                                       institution   ○
   International organization   ○   Media   ○
   Not-profit organization   ○   Other (specify)   ○

3. In which country do you work? _____

4. What is your assessment of the contents of this publication?

Excellent	○	Adequate	○
Good	○	Poor	○

5. How useful is this publication to your work?

Very useful   ○   Of some use   ○   Irrelevant   ○

6. Please indicate the three things you liked best about this publication:

_____

_____

_____

7. Please indicate the three things you liked least about this publication:

_____

_____

_____

8. If you have read more than the present publication of the UNCTAD Division on Transnational Corporations and Investment, what is your overall assessment of them?

Consistently good	○	Usually good, but with some exceptions	○
Generally mediocre	○	Poor	○

9. On the average, how useful are these publications to you in your work?

Very useful   ○   Of some use   ○   Irrelevant   ○

10. Are you a regular recipient of *Transnational Corporations* (formerly *The CTC Reporter*), the Division's tri-annual publication which reports on the Division's and related work?

Yes   ○   No   ○

If not, please indicate here if you would like to receive a sample copy sent to the name and address you have given above.   ○

Index